DAVIDSON'S INTRODUCTORY

HEBREW GRAMMAR

SYNTAX

DAVIDSON'S INTRODUCTORY

HEBREW GRAMMAR

SYNTAX

4th Edition

J. C. L. Gibson

T&T CLARK
EDINBURGH

T&T CLARK LTD
59 GEORGE STREET
EDINBURGH EH2 2LQ
SCOTLAND

First Published 1994

ISBN 0 567 09713 7

British Library Cataloguing-in-Publication Data
A catalogue record for this book is available from the British Library

Typeset by C & C Ho, Edinburgh
Printed and bound in Great Britain by Bookcraft, Avon

TABLE OF CONTENTS

———•———

Preface   viii

Select Bibliography   ix

SYNTAX OF THE PRONOUN

Personal Pronouns   1

Demonstrative Pronouns   5

Interrogative and Indefinite Pronouns   7

The Relative Pronoun and Relative Clauses   9

Other Pronominal Expressions   13

SYNTAX OF THE NOUN AND NOMINAL CLAUSE

Gender   16

Number   18

Gender and Number Concord   20

A Note on Case   24

Definiteness and Indefiniteness. The Article   25

The Construct State   30

Nominal Coordination   36

Nominal Apposition   40

The Adjective. Comparison   43

The Numerals   46

Nominal Clauses and Subject Complements. Subject
Clauses   52

Quasi-Verbal Nominal Clauses   56

SYNTAX OF THE VERB AND ITS OBJECT

The Conjugations   60

The QATAL Conjugation   60

The YIQTOL Conjugation   70

The Moods. Imperative, Jussive and Cohortative   80

The *Vav* Consecutive Constructions   83

Vav Consecutive QATAL   85

Vav Consecutive YIQTOL   95

The Conjugations and Moods with Simple *Vav*   103
The Object of the Verb (Direct, Indirect, Complement).
    Object Clauses   107
Excursus: The Particles אֵת and לְ   115
Construction of the Passive   118
Two Verb Constructions   119

SYNTAX OF THE INFINITIVE AND PARTICIPLE
The Infinitive Absolute   122
The Infinitive Construct   127
The Participles   133

SYNTAX OF THE ADVERB AND ADVERBIAL PHRASES
   AND CLAUSES
Independent Adverbs   139
Nouns and Adjectives as Adverbs   143
Prepositional Phrases   145
Adverbial Clauses and Infinitive Phrases   151
    Conditional Clauses   152
    Temporal Clauses and Infinitive Phrases   157
    Causal Clauses and Infinitive Phrases   158
    Final or Purpose Clauses and Infinitive Phrases 159
    Result Clauses   160
    Comparative Clauses and Infinitive Phrases   161

SYNTAX OF THE SENTENCE
Simple, Complex, Compound and Incomplete Sentences   162
The Syntactic Role of Sentence Word-Order and of *Vav* 164
Circumstantial Clauses (Sentences)   166
Compound Sentences with *Vav*   169
    Conjunctive Sentences   170
    Chiastic Sentences   171
    Contrastive Sentences   172
    Antithetical Sentences   172
Compound Sentences with Other Conjunctions   174
    Inclusive Sentences   174
    Exclusive Sentences   175

Disjunctive Sentences   177
Compound Sentences with Apposition. Asyndeton   177
Sentences with Extraposition (*Casus Pendens*)   180
Questions   183
Wishes and Oaths   185
Exclamations   188

INDEX OF PASSAGES   189

INDEX OF SUBJECTS   225

PREFACE TO THE FOURTH EDITION

———◆———

This revision of Professor Davidson's *Hebrew Syntax* is based on the Third Edition of 1901. It follows broadly that edition's ordering of the topics, and not infrequently its treatment of individual constructions. But, as is only to be expected after so long an interval, a good number of modifications have had to be made to take account not only of subsequent research on points of detail but of modern trends in language study as a whole. Some of the modifications were adumbrated in Dr James Martin's companion volume on *Grammar*; others go beyond what he, understandably, considered appropriate for beginners. In my view the more advanced students for whom this textbook is intended should now be ready for these. I hope that the mixture of the old and the new which results fairly represents the best of current thinking in biblical Hebrew syntax in the last decade of the twentieth century.

I have profited from the reactions of my colleagues and research students at New College to explanations of this or that point of syntax which I have tried out on them; from discussion on matters of common interest which I have had with Dr Martin; and from advice and criticism received from Professor E. J. Revell of the University of Toronto during an extended leave spent in Edinburgh.

Special thanks are due to Craig Ho, Computing Officer at New College, and his wife Carmen who so skilfully word-processed the manuscript.

My last word has to be of A. B. Davidson, whose room at New College I now occupy, and whose portrait looks down on me as I pen this Preface. Even when changing it, I have learned more than I can say from his *Syntax*, and I dedicate this updating of it warmly to his memory.

New College, Edinburgh
June, 1994
J. C. L. Gibson

Select Bibliography

———•———

F. I. Andersen, *The Hebrew Verbless Clause in the Pentateuch*. Journal of Biblical Literature Monographs, 14. Nashville, Tennessee: Abingdon, 1970.

F. I. Andersen, *The Sentence in Biblical Hebrew*. Janua Linguarum, Series Practica, 231. The Hague: Mouton, 1974.

J. Barr, *Comparative Philology and the Text of the Old Testament*. Oxford: Clarendon, 1968.

C. Brockelmann, *Hebräische Syntax*. Neukirchener Verlag, 1956.

F. Brown, S. R. Driver, and C. A. Briggs, *A Hebrew and English Lexicon of the Old Testament*. Oxford: Clarendon, 1907 (for prepositions and conjunctions).

C. F. Burney, *Notes on the Hebrew Text of the Books of Kings*. Oxford: Clarendon, 1903.

G. B. Caird, *The Language and Imagery of the Bible*. London: Duckworth, 1980.

B. Comrie, *An Introduction to the Study of Verbal Aspect and Related Problems*. Cambridge University Press, 1976.

M. Dahood and T. Penar, "The Grammar of the Psalter" in M. Dahood, *Psalms*, III (The Anchor Bible), 361-456. Garden City, New York: Doubleday, 1970.

[A. B. Davidson -] J. Martin, *An Introductory Hebrew Grammar*. 27th ed. Edinburgh: T. & T. Clark, 1993.

G. R. Driver, *Problems of the Hebrew Verbal System*. Edinburgh: T. & T. Clark, 1936.

S. R. Driver, *A Treatise on the Use of Tenses in Hebrew*. 3rd ed. Oxford: Clarendon, 1892.

S. R. Driver, *Notes on the Hebrew Text and the Topography of the Books of Samuel*. 2nd ed. Oxford: Clarendon, 1913.

M. Eskhult, *Studies in Verbal Aspect and Narrative Technique in Biblical Hebrew Prose*. Studia Semitica Upsaliensia, 12. Stockholm: Almqvist and Wiksell, 1990.

H. Ewald, *Syntax of the Hebrew Language of the Old Testament*. Transl. from the 8th German ed. by J. Kennedy. Edinburgh: T. & T. Clark,

1879.

E. Jenni, *Die hebraischen Präpositionen*, vol. I, *Die Präposition Beth*. Stuttgart: Kohlhammer, 1992.

P. Joüon, *Grammaire de l'hébreu biblique*. 2nd ed. Rome: Pontifical Biblical Institute, 1923. Engl. transl. by T. Muraoka, 1991.

G. Khan, *Studies in Semitic Syntax*. London Oriental Series, 38. Oxford University Press, 1988.

E. König, "Syntactische Excurse zum Alten Testament", *Zeitschrift für die alttestamentliche Wissenschaft* 19 (1899), 259-287.

J. Kurylowicz, *Studies in Semitic Grammar and Metrics*. Warsaw: Prace Jezykoz-nawcze, 1972.

E. Y. Kutscher, *A History of the Hebrew Language*. Jerusalem: The Magnes Press/Leiden: Brill, 1982.

R. E. Longacre, *Joseph: A Study of Divine Providence: A Texttheoretical and Textlinguistic Analysis of Genesis 37 and 39-48*. Winona Lake, Indiana: Eisenbrauns, 1989.

J. Lyons, *Introduction to Theoretical Linguistics*. Cambridge University Press, 1968.

J. Macdonald, "Some Distinctive Characteristics of Israelite Spoken Hebrew", *Bibliotheca Orientalis* 32 (1975), 162-175.

L. McFall, *The Enigma of the Hebrew Verbal System: Solutions from Ewald to the Present Day*. Sheffield: The Almond Press, 1982.

D. Michel, *Tempora und Satzstellung in den Psalmen*. Bonn: Bouvier, 1960.

W. H. Mittins, *A Grammar of Modern English*. University Paperbacks, 211. London: Methuen, 1967.

T. Muraoka, *Emphatic Words and Structures in Biblical Hebrew*. Jerusalem: The Magnes Press/Leiden: Brill, 1985.

A. Niccacci, *The Syntax of the Verb in Classical Hebrew Prose*. Transl. by W. G. E. Watson. Journal for the Study of the Old Testament, Supplement Series, 86. Sheffield Academic Press, 1990.

D. Pardee, "The Preposition in Ugaritic", *Ugarit Forschungen* 7 (1975), 329-378; 8 (1976), 215-322, 483-493; 9 (1977), 205-231; 11 (1979), 685-692.

R. Polzin, *Late Biblical Hebrew: Towards an Historical Typology of Biblical Hebrew Prose*. Harvard Semitic Monographs, 12. Missoula, Montana: Scholars Press, 1976.

L. J. de Regt, *A Parametric Model for Syntactic Studies of a Textual*

Corpus, Demonstrated on the Hebrew of Deuteronomy 1-30. Studia Semitica Neerlandica, 24. Assen/ Maastricht: Van Gorum, 1988.

R. H. Robins, *A Short History of Linguistics* (esp. chs. 7, 8). London: Longmans, 1967.

J. F. A. Sawyer, *A Modern Introduction to Biblical Hebrew.* Stocksfield: Oriel, 1976.

W. Schneider, *Grammatik des biblischen Hebräisch.* Munich: Claudius, 1974.

M. S. Smith, *The Origins and Development of the Waw-Consecutive.* Harvard Semitic Studies, 39. Atlanta, Georgia: Scholars Press, 1991.

A. Sperber, *A Historical Grammar of Biblical Hebrew: A Presentation of Problems with Suggestions to their Solution.* Leiden: Brill, 1966.

E. Talstra, "Text Grammar and Hebrew Bible", *Bibliotheca Orientalis* 35 (1978), 169-174; 39 (1982), 26-38.

N. M. Waldman, *The Recent Study of Hebrew: A Survey of the Literature with Selected Bibliography.* Bibliographia Judaica, 10. Cincinnati: Hebrew Union College Press/Winona Lake, Indiana: Eisenbrauns, 1989.

B. K. Waltke and M. O'Connor, *An Introduction to Biblical Hebrew Syntax.* Winona Lake, Indiana: Eisenbrauns, 1990.

W. G. E. Watson, *Classical Hebrew Poetry: A Guide to its Techniques.* Journal for the Study of the Old Testament, Supplement Series, 26. Sheffield Academic Press, 1984.

J. Wash Watts, *A Survey of Syntax in the Hebrew Old Testament.* Grand Rapids, Michigan: Eerdmans, 1964.

R. J. Williams, *Hebrew Syntax: An Outline.* 2nd ed. University of Toronto Press, 1976.

Syntax of the Pronoun

————◆————

Personal Pronouns

§ 1. In their independent forms the Personal pronouns are normally employed only as subject. In other syntactic positions they are attached in the form of suffixes to other words.

(*a*) As a simple pron. standing for a person or thing already mentioned the independent form is most commonly found in nominal clauses. Like a subj.-noun it follows the patterns described in § 49. Thus in a simple declarative clause when the predicate is definite, the pron. precedes it, and the clause is one of identification. Ex. 6. 2 אֲנִי יהוה *I* am Yahweh, Is. 43. 11; 2 S. 12. 7 אַתָּה הָאִישׁ *you* are the man; Gen. 24. 65 הוּא אֲדֹנִי *he* is my master. And when it is indefinite, the pron. follows it, and the clause is one of classification. Ps. 119. 137 צַדִּיק אַתָּה *you* are *righteous;* Gen. 42. 11 כֵּנִים אֲנַחְנוּ we are *honest men.* The latter pattern may be overridden in a circumstantial clause where, following וְ *and,* the order subj.-pred. is obligatory; thus the classifying clause Gen. 18. 27 וְאָנֹכִי עָפָר וָאֵפֶר when I am (but) *dust and ashes.* There are also uncertainties in word order when the pred. of a nominal clause is a suffixed noun or a construct relation or a participle or a prepositional phrase; but these are often more apparent than real and by and large the principle that the placing of the subj. is dependent on the definiteness or indefiniteness of the pred. holds.

(*b*) Sometimes the subj. of a nominal clause is extraposed and is resumed with הוּא. Often there is no added meaning and the pron. functions as a mere copula, Gen. 36. 8 עֵשָׂו הוּא אֱדוֹם Esau *is* Edom. But in other cases there may be a contrast, explicit or implicit, with another person or a particular focus upon the subject. With a nominal subj., 1 K. 18. 39 יהוה הוּא הָאֱלֹהִים *Yahweh* (not Baal) is God, Deu. 4. 35, Nu. 16. 7. With a pronom. subj. of 1st pers., Is. 43. 25 אָנֹכִי אָנֹכִי הוּא מֹחֶה *I, yes I,* am blotting out (your transgressions); 51. 12; 52. 6. So 1 Chr.

1

21. 17 *it is I* (אֲשֶׁר) who have sinned. Of 2nd pers., 2 S. 7. 28 אַתָּה הוּא
הָאֱלֹהִים *you alone* are God, Is. 37. 16; 51. 9, 10, Jer. 14. 22, Ps. 44. 5,
Neh. 9. 6, 2 Chr. 20. 6.

(*c*) In verbal clauses the pron. is included or implied in the verbal
form and does not require to be expressed except where a subj. is
composite. Gen. 7. 1 בֹּא־אַתָּה וְכָל־בֵּיתְךָ go, *you and all your house*,
into the ark, Jud. 7. 10, 11; 11. 38, 1 K. 1. 21, Ru. 1. 6 etc. Or where it fills
a necessary slot in a circumstantial or other subj.-verb clause, Gen. 18. 13
וַאֲנִי זָקַנְתִּי seeing *I am old*. 42. 23.

In other contexts where it is used with a verbal form, the pron.
generally has more force. It may precede the verb or, less commonly,
follow it. Thus in various sent. types (§ 138ff.), pron. preceding: Gen 3. 15
הוּא יְשׁוּפְךָ רֹאשׁ וְאַתָּה תְּשׁוּפֶנּוּ עָקֵב *he* shall bruise your head, *while you*
shall bruise his heel; 33. 3; 42. 8, 19; 45. 8 לֹא־אַתֶּם שְׁלַחְתֶּם אֹתִי *it was
not you* who sent me here, *but* God, Deu. 3. 28, Hos. 2. 8, Am. 2. 9, 10.
Pron. following: Jud. 8. 23 לֹא־אֶמְשֹׁל אֲנִי *I* shall not rule over you ...; Y.
shall rule over you, Ex. 18. 19, 22; 20. 19, 2 S. 17. 15, 2 K. 10. 4, Jer. 17. 18.
Or to give prominence or focus, pron. preceding: Gen. 16. 5 *I* gave;
24. 60 be *you;* 43. 9, Jud. 5. 3, 1 K. 3. 6, Is. 41. 14; 43. 12. Espec. in
response to preceding statements or requests, as Gen. 21. 24 *I will swear;*
38. 17; 47. 30, Jud. 6. 18, 2 S. 3. 13, 1 K. 2. 18. And in the phrase
אַתָּה יָדַעְתָּ *you know*, used in arguments and appeals, Gen. 44. 27, Jos.
14. 6, 1 S. 28. 9, 2 S. 17. 8, 1 K. 2. 5, 15, 2 K. 4. 1. Pron. following: Jud.
8. 21 *rise yourself;* 11. 9, 1 S. 20. 8, 2 S. 12. 28, Is. 20. 6 and how shall *we*
escape?, Pr. 24. 32, then *I* saw. Espec. in Ecc., 1. 16; 2. 1, 11, 15 etc.

(*d*) An independent pron. may also follow a noun in any syntactic
position or a suff. to a noun or verb or prep. With גַּם: Gen. 4. 26 לְשֵׁת
גַּם־הוּא to Seth *also;* 4. 22; 10. 21; 27. 34 בָּרֲכֵנִי גַם־אָנִי bless *me too,* 1 S.
19. 23, 2 S. 17. 5, 1 K. 21. 19, Jer. 27. 7, Pr. 23. 15. Occasionally with אַף
also, Gen. 40. 16; *even,* Pr. 22. 19. Or pron. alone, with more force: Is.
7. 14 יִתֵּן אֲדֹנָי הוּא, the Lord *himself* will give a sign. Deu. 5. 3 כִּי אִתָּנוּ
אֲנַחְנוּ not with our fathers ... *but with us.* 1 S. 25. 24 בִּי־אֲנִי הֶעָוֺן *on me*
be the guilt. Nu. 14. 32; 18. 23, 1 S. 20. 42, 2 S. 19. 1, 1 K. 1. 26, Hag. 1. 4,
Ezr. 7. 21. Cf. suffixed אֵת following suff. to verb, Gen. 30. 20 זְבָדַנִי
אֱלֹהִים אֹתִי God has endowed *me* (with a good dowry).

Rem. 1. In nominal clauses where an extraposed pron. refers to God there is commonly an emphasis on his exclusiveness; many of the exx. come from Is. 40ff., where the peculiar phrase אֲנִי הוּא *I am he* is also found, 41. 4; 43. 10, 13; 46. 4; 48. 12, cf. Ps. 102. 28. In these הוּא seems to be pred. and expresses the divine self-consciousness. Cf. Ex. 3. 14.

Rem. 2. Occasionally indep. form occurs instead of suffix. 2 K. 9. 18 עַד־הֶם. Neh. 4. 17 אֵין אֲנִי, the pron. being co-ordinated with the following nouns. Nah. 2. 9 מִימֵי הִיא *all her days;* elsewhere מִימֶיהָ (1 S. 25. 28). In 1 Chr. 9. 22 הֵמָּה is properly obj. to verb as in Aramaic; Ezr. 5. 12. So Moabite Stone *l.* 18.

Rem. 3. In Pentateuch and occasionally (in some mss. frequently) elsewhere הוּא is common, and the gender is matter of pointing, Ex. 1. 16; no satisfactory explanation of this peculiarity has been found. A 3rd pers. pron. used *neuterly,* i.e. referring back to an action, circumstance etc. just spoken of, is normally attracted to the gender of a nominal complement, Deu. 4. 6 כִּי הִוא חָכְמַתְכֶם for *that* will be your wisdom. Outside Pent. there is often confusion, Ps. 73. 16 (הִיא) a wearisome task *it* (seemed) in my eyes, Job 31. 11 (הִיא, הוּא). Where however the reference is unspecific, the *fem.* is commoner, Jos. 10. 13, Jud. 14. 4, Job 9. 22, particularly if suff., Gen. 24. 14 וּבָהּ אֵדַע and *thereby* I shall know. Is. 47. 7 you did not consider אַחֲרִיתָהּ *the outcome of it.* Gen. 42. 36; 47. 26, Ex. 10. 11, Nu. 14. 1; 23. 19, 1 K. 11. 12. So זֹאת (§ 4, R. 1) and verbal forms, Jud. 11. 39 וַתְּהִי חֹק and *it became* a rule. Is. 7. 7; 14. 24, Am. 7. 6, Job 4. 5.

Rem. 4. There is a tendency, increasing in later Hebr., for *mas.* forms of 3rd pers. and, less frequently, 2nd pers. plur. suffixes to replace fem. Gen. 26. 15; 31. 9; 32. 16, Ex. 1. 21, Nu. 27. 7, 1 S. 6. 7, 10, Is. 3. 16, Job 1. 14, 15, Ru. 1. 8, 9, Dan. 1. 5; 8. 9, Ezr. 10. 3, Neh. 1. 9. In Ezekiel fem. forms are frequently replaced (e.g. 45. 23 ff.) and in Chr. they are absent (1 Chr. 23. 22, 2 Chr. 4. 7, 11 etc). Occasionally independent הֵמָּה stands for fem., Ru. 1. 22, Song 6. 8. See further § 18, R. 2.

§ 2. Suffixed forms of the Pers. pron. are attached to nouns, verbs and prepositions. (*a*) Suffixes to nouns are generally subjective. Gen. 4.1 אִשְׁתּוֹ *his* wife; 4. 10 אָחִיךָ *your* brother. But may be objective, directly: Gen. 16. 5 חֲמָסִי *my* wrong (that done to me), 4. 23; 18. 21, Lev. 10. 3 (those approaching *me*). Or indirectly: Ex. 2. 9: אֶתֵּן אֶת־שְׂכָרֵךְ I will give *your* hire, i.e. give *you* (your) wages, Jud. 4. 9 לֹא תִהְיֶה תִפְאַרְתְּךָ the glory shall not be *yours.* Gen. 39. 21 וַיִּתֵּן חִנּוֹ gave *him* favour. Ez. 27. 15 rendered *you* tribute. Cf. Hos. 2. 8 (a wall *against her*), Job 3. 10 (the womb *which carried me*).

(*b*) The verbal suff. usually expresses the direct *object,* Gen. 3. 13

הַנָּחָשׁ הִשִּׁיאַנִי the serpent beguiled *me;* 4.8 וַיַּהַרְגֵהוּ and slew *him.* So when אֵת is used, Gen. 40. 4 וַיְשָׁרֶת אֹתָם and served *them;* 41. 10. But often it represents an indirect object, Is. 27. 4 מִי יִתְּנֵנִי who will give *to me,* i.e. would that I had!, Zech. 7. 5 צַמְתֻּנִי אָנִי did you fast *for me?,* Job 31. 18 גְּדֵלַנִי כְאָב grew up *to me* as a father. This kind of construction (instead of prep.) is easier with suff., e.g. Job 6. 4 (are arrayed *against me*), Neh. 9. 28 (cried *to you*), Is. 44. 21 (forgotten *by me*), Gen. 37. 18 (conspired *against him*). Cf. Ps. 42. 5 (moved in procession *among them*).

§ 3. The relation of a noun to its material, quality and the like is often expressed by putting it in the construct state rather than by an adjective, הַר קֹדֶשׁ hill of holiness, *holy* hill. In such cases a suff. belongs to the whole expression, Ps. 2. 6 הַר קָדְשִׁי *my* holy hill, Is. 2. 20 אֱלִילֵי זְהָבוֹ *his* idols of gold; 13. 3; 30. 22, 23; 53. 5. Distinguish from constructions like Gen. 8. 9 כַּף־רַגְלָהּ the role of *its* foot or Lev. 6. 3 מַדּוֹ בַד *his* linen garment (§ 39, R. 1).

The noun with suff. normally (but not always, R. 1) forms a definite expression and a qualifying adj. has the Art. Gen. 43. 29 הֲזֶה אֲחִיכֶם הַקָּטֹן is this *your youngest brother?*

Rem. 1. In certain cases a suffixed noun may be indefinite, namely when it refers to a member or members of a generic class (§ 31); there may be but is not necessarily an implication that other members are in mind, but the expression is sufficiently unspecific to bring about the word order pred.-subj. in a nominal clause. Gen. 20. 5 אֲחֹתִי הוּא *she is a sister of mine,* Jud. 9. 3. Gen. 12. 13 אֲחֹתִי אָתְּ say that *you are my sister.* Lev. 18. 15 אֵשֶׁת בִּנְךָ הוּא *she is your son's wife.* Jos. 9. 11 עֲבָדֵיכֶם אֲנַחְנוּ *we are servants of yours.* So sometimes a full constr. phrase, § 29, R. 2.

Rem. 2. The quasi-verbal particles יֵשׁ (*there*) *is* and אֵין (*there*) *is not* always, and the demons. particle הִנֵּה *behold! here!* and the adv. עוֹד when functioning verbally (*is still, yet*) often take verbal suffixes. 1 S. 14. 39 כִּי אִם־יֶשְׁנוֹ though *it* (the guilt) *be* in Jon. my son. Ex. 5. 10 אֵינֶנִּי נֹתֵן *I am not* giving. Is. 65. 1 הִנֵּנִי here I am! Gen. 18. 22 עוֹדֶנּוּ עֹמֵד Abr. *was still* standing. But suff. of 3rd pers. is הַנּוֹ (once הִנֵּהוּ, Jer. 18. 3 *Ket.*) and of 1st pers. is בְּעוֹדִי in the sense *while I have being* (Ps. 104. 33; 146. 2) and מֵעוֹדִי *since I had being* (Gen. 48. 15, cf. Nu. 22. 30). Also עוֹדִי *I am still* with you (Ps. 139. 18). Cf. with interr. [אֵי] *where?* אַיֶּכָּה (Gen. 3. 9) but אַיּוֹ (Ex. 2. 20). § 52–4.

Rem. 3. Ellipsis of suffix. A suff. is often omitted where it can be supplied from the context, particularly after verbs of *giving, bringing, putting, telling* etc. Gen. 2. 19 וַיָּבֵא and brought *them,* 1 S. 17. 31 וַיַּגִּדוּ they told *them,*

1 S. 19. 13 וַתָּשֶׂם she put *them*. Gen. 12. 19; 18. 7; 27. 13, 14; 38. 18, Deu. 21. 12. In poetry *double-duty* suff. is common; this is the name given to a kind of ellipsis whereby a suff. present in one member of a parallelism serves also for a suff. missing in the other. Ps. 17. 8 כְּאִישׁוֹן בַּת־עָיִן like the apple of *your* eye; 107. 20 וִימַלֵּט delivered *them*, Job 23. 4 מִשְׁפָּט *my* case. Ps. 17. 14 *their* children; 18. 5 *his* lightnings; 51. 14 *your* generous spirit; 71. 9 *my* old age; 85. 10 *his* glory; 101. 1 *your* love and justice, Job 9. 11 see *him*; 38. 20 show *it*; 40. 24 *his* nose, Pr. 14. 24 *their* folly; 27. 23 *your* herds.

DEMONSTRATIVE PRONOUNS

§ 4. The near Demons. is זֶה, used both as a pron. and as an adj. There is no independent far Demons., though the Pers. pron. הוּא may be used adjectivally for *that*.

The person or entity pointed out by זֶה may already have been mentioned. Ru. 1. 19 הֲזֹאת נָעֳמִי is *this* Naomi? Gen. 9. 17 זֹאת אוֹת־הַבְּרִית *this* is the sign of the covenant, Deu. 34. 4, Is. 14. 26, Ez. 5. 5. Sometimes in the weakened sense of *such*. Ps. 24. 6 זֶה דּוֹר דֹּרְשָׁו *such* is the generation of those who seek him; 73. 12. Or be about to be mentioned. Gen. 20. 13 זֶה חַסְדֵּךְ *this* is the kindness which you must do to me; 40. 12, Nu. 30. 2, Deu. 12. 1, Jud. 4. 14.

The Demons. may occur in any syntactic position, though it is commonest (see exx. above) as subj. of a nominal identifying clause. Less commonly in a classifying clause, Ex. 2. 6 מִיַּלְדֵי הָעִבְרִים זֶה is this *one of the Hebrews' children?* Otherwise, with slightly more emphasis, as subj. of a verb. Gen. 5. 29 זֶה יְנַחֲמֵנוּ *this one* shall bring us relief, 1 S. 21. 16. As obj., 2 S. 13. 17 שִׁלְחוּ־נָא אֶת־זֹאת send *this* woman away, Gen. 29. 33, Is. 29. 11. Following a prep. or noun in constr., Gen. 2. 23 לְזֹאת יִקָּרֵא *this* (she) shall be called, 1 K. 22. 17. Gen. 29. 27 שְׁבֻעַ זֹאת the week of *this one*, Deu. 25. 16 כָּל־עֹשֵׂה אֵלֶּה all who do *such things*.

Rem. 1. When used neuterly זֹאת is commoner than *mas.* Gen. 42. 18 זֹאת עֲשׂוּ וִחְיוּ do *this* and you shall live. 42. 15 בְּזֹאת *by this* you shall be tested, 1 S. 11. 2 *on this condition.* Is. 5. 25 בְּכָל־זֹאת *for all this*, 9. 11, Hos. 7. 10. Am. 7. 3 עַל־זֹאת *concerning this.* But *mas.* is found, Gen. 6. 15; 24. 9, 2 K. 4. 43.

§ 5. When זֶה is repeated it represents both near and far Demons. and is equivalent to *this .... that, the one .... the other.* Is. 6. 3 וְקָרָא זֶה

אֶל־זֶה ... וְזֹאת אֹמֶרֶת and *one* was calling to *the other*. 1 K. 3. 23 זֹאת אֹמֶרֶת *this woman* says ... *and the other* says. Jos. 8. 22 אֵלֶּה מִזֶּה וְאֵלֶּה מִזֶּה *some* on *this* side *and some* on *that* side. Ex. 14. 20, 2 S. 2. 13, 1 K. 20. 29; 22. 20, Ps. 20. 8; 75. 8, Job 1. 16, Dan. 12. 2.

§ 6. The demons. adjectives הוּא, זֶה *this, that* have the same concord as other adj. But (1) they necessarily make their noun def., הָאִישׁ הַזֶּה *this man*, הַיָּמִים הָהֵם *those days,* and have themselves the Art. (2) In the case of nouns determined by pronom. suff., however, they are in appos. without the Art., Jos. 2. 14 דְּבָרֵנוּ זֶה *this business of ours,* Ex. 10. 1 אֹתֹתַי אֵלֶּה *these signs of mine.* Gen. 24. 8, Ex. 11. 8, Deu. 5. 29; 11. 18, Jud. 6. 14, 1 K. 8. 59; 10. 8; 22. 23, Jer. 31. 21, 2 Chr. 24. 18. Exceptionally Jos. 2. 17. (3) With another adj. or several they stand last, 1 K. 3. 6 הַחֶסֶד הַגָּדֹול הַזֶּה *this great* goodness (cf. *vs.* 9), Deu. 1. 19 וְהַנֹּורָא הַהוּא הַמִּדְבָּר הַגָּדֹול *that great and terrible* wilderness, Gen. 41. 35 הַשָּׁנִים הַטֹּבֹות הַבָּאֹת הָאֵלֶּה *those good coming* years. Exceptionally 2 Chr. 1. 10.

> *Rem. 1.* In some cases זֶה stands in appos. without the Art. before a noun. Gen. 2. 23 זֹאת הַפַּעַם *this* time, Is. 23. 13, Ezr. 3. 12, Song 7. 8. Before proper name, Ex. 32. 1 זֶה מֹשֶׁה; Jud. 5. 5, Ps. 68. 9 זֶה סִינַי, though this may mean *He of Sinai.* Before noun with suff., Jos. 9. 12, 13, Song 7. 8. So in later Hebr. הוּא before a proper name with the meaning *the same,* Ezr. 7. 6, 1 Chr. 26. 26.
>
> *Rem. 2.* In expressing time הַיֹּום הַזֶּה is used adverbially of present time, Ex. 13. 3, Jos. 3. 7. Less often with בְּ referring to the past, Gen. 7. 11. Cf. more commonly הַיֹּום *today,* Deu. 30. 15 etc. On the other hand בַּיֹּום הַהוּא refers either to past or to future time. Past, Gen. 15. 18; 33. 16. Future, Deu. 31. 17, 1 S. 3. 12 and frequently in prophetic speech, Is. 2. 11, 17, 20, Am. 8. 3, 9 etc. Cf. בַּיָּמִים הָהֵם of past, Gen. 6. 4, Jud. 21. 25; of future, Deu. 17. 9. Note anomalously בַּלַּיְלָה הוּא, Gen. 19. 33; 30. 16; 32. 23, 1 S. 19. 10. Cf. Moab. St. *l.* 3 הבמת זאת *this high place.*
>
> *Rem. 3.* The Demons. זֶה is used with interrogatives to add emphasis to the question, Gen. 27. 21 הַאַתָּה זֶה בְּנִי *are you really* my son Esau? § 7c. In the same way force is added to הִנֵּה and עַתָּה, 1 K. 19. 5 וְהִנֵּה־זֶה מַלְאָךְ and *suddenly* an angel. 1 K. 17. 24 עַתָּה זֶה יָדַעְתִּי *now indeed* I know. 2 K. 5. 22 have *just* come to me. And with זֶה preceding, to expressions of time with numerals, Gen. 27. 36 זֶה פַעֲמַיִם *now twice,* 31. 38 זֶה עֶשְׂרִים שָׁנָה *twenty years now,* 31. 41; 43. 10; 45. 6, Nu. 22. 28, Deu. 8. 2, Jos. 14. 10, Jud. 16. 15, 1 S. 29. 3, 2 S. 14. 2, Job 19. 3.

Rem. 4. The form זֶה is often a *relative* in poetry. Like אֲשֶׁר it suffers no change for gend. and number. Job 19. 19 וְזֶה אָהַבְתִּי נֶהְפְּכוּ־בִי and *they-whom* I loved are turned against me. Ps. 74. 2; 78. 54; 104. 8, Pr. 23. 22, Job 15. 17. Rarely in prose, Ex. 13. 8. The form זוּ (Ps. 132. 12 זוֹ) is also used. Ex. 15. 13 עַם־זוּ גָּאָלְתָּ the people *whom* you have redeemed.

Rem. 5. Rarer forms are זֹה and זוֹ for זֹאת; אֵל for אֵלֶּה; and הַלָּז, הַלָּזֶה and הַלֵּזוּ for הַזֶּה or הַזֹּאת. See Lex. An anomalous usage is Ps. 80. 15 גֶּפֶן זֹאת *this vine.* Cf. 2 K. 1. 2; 8. 8, 9. For adv. uses with בְּ, כְּ, מִן see Lex., § 15, R. 1e.

INTERROGATIVE AND INDEFINITE PRONOUNS

§ 7. The pron. מִי *who?* is used of persons, mas. and fem.; and מָה *what?* of things. Both are invariable for gend. and number.

(a) The pron. מִי may be used in all syntactic positions. Gen. 3. 11 מִי הִגִּיד לְךָ *who* told you? 24. 65; 33.5, Ex. 3. 11; 15. 11, Is. 6. 8. Gen. 24. 23 בַּת־מִי אַתְּ *whose* daughter are you? 32. 18 לְמִי אַתָּה *to whom* do you belong? 1 S. 12. 3; 24. 15, Ps. 27. 1. Is. 6. 8 אֶת־מִי אֶשְׁלַח *whom* shall I send? 1 S. 12. 3; 28. 11, 2 K. 19. 22. As obj. מִי is always preceded by אֶת. Partitively: 1 S. 22. 14 מִי בְכָל־עֲבָדֶיךָ *who among* all your servants? Is. 36. 20; 42. 23; 43. 9, Hag. 2. 3. With מִן, Jud. 21. 8, Is. 50. 11. Repeated for emphasis, Ex. 10. 8 מִי וָמִי הַהֹלְכִים *who exactly* are to go?

Exclamatory and rhetorical uses are common. In wishes, § 156b. Of modesty, Ex. 3. 11 מִי אָנֹכִי *who am I* that I should go?; 5. 2, 1 S. 18. 18. Of insult, 1 S. 25. 10 מִי דָוִד *who is David?*; 17. 26, Job 26. 4. Of surprise, Is. 49. 21 מִי יָלַד־לִי *who has borne me* these? And in general implying a strong negative, Ex. 15. 11 מִי־כָמֹכָה *who is like you* among the gods? Is. 40. 18, 25, Ps. 89. 7; 113. 5. 1 S. 4. 8 מִי יַצִּילֵנוּ *who can deliver us?* Deu. 9. 2, Is. 40. 12; 50. 8, 9, Mal. 3. 2, Ps. 130. 3, Job 9. 12; 13. 19, Pr. 20. 6; 31. 10. Expressing uncertainty, Pr. 24. 22 מִי יוֹדֵעַ *who knows?* 2 S. 12. 22, Est. 4. 14.

(b) The neut. מָה is also used in all positions. Gen. 31. 36 מַה־פִּשְׁעִי *what is* my offence? 32. 28, 2 K. 9. 18. Gen. 15. 8 בַּמָּה אֵדַע *by what* shall I know? Rarely after a noun, Jer. 8. 9 wisdom *of what* (what sort of w.)?; Nu. 23. 3. Gen. 4. 10 מֶה עָשִׂיתָ *what* have you done?; 15. 2. The אֶת is not used before *what.* Sometimes מָה may be translated *why?* Ex. 14. 15, 2 K. 7. 3.

With adj. and verbs מָה often has the sense of *how?, how!* Gen. 28. 17

מַה־נּוֹרָא *how* terrible! 2 K. 4. 43 מָה אֶתֵּן זֶה לִפְנֵי מֵאָה אִישׁ *how* shall I set such a thing before a hundred people? Ex. 10. 26, Ps. 133. 1, Job 9. 2; 31. 1. Other rhetorical uses are similar to those with מִי: Gen. 23. 15; 44. 15, Jud. 8. 1, 2, 1 K. 12. 16, 2 K. 8. 13, Ps. 8. 5, Job 22. 13, Lam. 2. 13.

(c) The interrog. prons. strengthen themselves by זֶה in questions. 1 S. 17. 56 בֶּן־מִי־זֶה הַנַּעַר *whose* son (I wonder) is the lad? 1 S. 10. 11 מַה־זֶּה הָיָה לְבֶן־קִישׁ *what in the world* has come over the son of Kish? Gen. 3. 13; 27. 20, Jud. 2. 2; 18. 24, 2 S. 12. 23, 1 K. 21. 5, Ps. 24. 8. § 6, R. 3.

§ 8. In indirect questions the Interrog. remains without change. Gen. 21. 26 לֹא יָדַעְתִּי מִי עָשָׂה I do not know *who did it;* 43. 22, Deu. 21. 1, Jos. 24. 15, 1 S. 17. 56. Mic. 6. 8 הִגִּיד לְךָ אָדָם מַה־טּוֹב he has shown you, O man, *what is good,* Gen. 2. 19; 37. 20, Ex. 2. 4, 1 S. 2. 5. The Interrogs. are also used as indef. pron., *whoever, whatever.* Jud. 7. 3 מִי־יָרֵא ... יָשֹׁב *whoever is afraid* ... let him return. Ex. 32. 26 מִי לַיהוה אֵלָי *whoever is for* Y., to me! 2 S. 18. 12 שִׁמְרוּ מִי have a care, *whoever you be!* Ex. 24. 14, Is. 54. 15. 1 S. 19. 3 וְרָאִיתִי מָה וְהִגַּדְתִּי לָךְ and if I see *anything* I will tell you. 2 S. 18. 23 וִיהִי־מָה אָרוּץ *come what may,* I will run. Nu. 23. 3, Job 13. 13; 26. 7, Pr. 9. 13. In some clauses of this form, however, the strict interrog. sense is probably still to be retained, Deu. 20. 5, Jud. 10. 18; 21. 5, Is. 50. 8. The form מִי אֲשֶׁר is also used, Ex. 32. 33, 2 S. 20.11, cf. מַה־שֶּׁ, Ecc. 1. 9.

Rem. 1. The neut. מָה may be used of persons if their circumstances are being enquired of, as 1 S. 29. 3 *what* are these Hebrews (doing here)? On the other hand, מִי is used of things when the idea of a person is involved, Jud. 13. 17 *what* is your name? Gen. 32. 28; 33. 8, Deu. 4. 7, Mic. 1. 5. Cf. Am. 7. 2, 5 *how* can Jacob stand?

Rem. 2. In phrases like מַה־בֶּצַע *what profit?* (Gen. 37. 26), the noun is used adverbially (more accurately, adnominally). Ps. 30. 10, Is. 40. 18, Mal. 3. 14, Ps. 89. 48, Job 26. 14. The construction is clearer when the words are separated, Jer. 2. 5 מַה־מָּצְאוּ ... עָוֶל *what* (with respect to) *evil* did your fathers find in me? 1 S. 20. 10; 26. 18, 2 S. 19. 29; 24. 13, 1 K. 12. 16.

Rem. 3. These uses of מָה are to be noted. Jud. 1. 14 מַה־לָּךְ *what to you?*, i.e. *what troubles you, is the matter with you, do you mean?* Gen. 21. 17, 1 S. 11. 5, Jon. 1. 6. And expecting a negative answer, Jud. 11. 12 מַה־לִּי וָלָךְ *what have I to do with you?* 2 S. 16. 10; 19. 23. 2 K. 9. 18, 19 מַה־לְּךָ וּלְשָׁלוֹם. Cf. Jer. 2. 18, Ps. 50. 16.

Rem. 4. For other interrogs. see §§ 152ff.

THE RELATIVE PRONOUN AND RELATIVE CLAUSES

§ 9. The pron. אֲשֶׁר is indeclinable. Its usage differs according as it is preceded by or as it contains an antecedent.

When the antecedent is expressed אֲשֶׁר serves merely to connect the antecedent to the relative clause. The kind of connection is specified by a pron. referring back to the antecedent and agreeing with it in gend., numb., and person. A resumptive adv. of place may replace the pron. This pron. or adv. is often understood. The antecedent is usually definite, less commonly indef. The relative clause may be either nominal or verbal.

(a) When the resumptive pron. is subj. it is expressed in a nominal clause which contains an adj. or a suffixed noun. Gen. 7. 2 the animal אֲשֶׁר לֹא טְהֹרָה הוּא *which is not clean*, Nu. 9. 13, Gen. 9. 3. Deu. 17. 15 a foreigner אֲשֶׁר לֹא־אָחִיךָ הוּא *who is not your brother*. But not often otherwise, Gen. 3. 3 הָעֵץ אֲשֶׁר בְּתוֹךְ הַגָּן the tree *which is in the middle of the garden*. In a verbal clause the pron. is represented by the verbal inflexion, as 15. 7 אֲנִי י׳ אֲשֶׁר הוֹצֵאתִיךָ I am Y., *who brought you out*, unless expressed in terms of § 1c.

(b) When the pron. is obj. (in a verbal clause) it is often expressed, Gen. 45. 4 אֲנִי יוֹסֵף אֲשֶׁר מְכַרְתֶּם אֹתִי I am Jos. *whom you sold*, Ps. 1. 4 כַּמֹּץ אֲשֶׁר תִּדְּפֶנּוּ רוּחַ like the chaff *which the wind drives*. Gen. 21. 2, Ex. 6. 5, 2 K. 19. 4, Jer. 28. 9; 44. 3. But oftener omitted, Deu. 13. 7 אֱלֹהִים אֲשֶׁר לֹא יָדַעְתָּ gods *whom you have not known*. Gen. 2. 8; 6. 7; 12. 1, Jud. 11. 39; 16. 30, 1 S. 7. 14; 10. 2, 2 S. 15. 7.

(c) When the resumptive pron. is suffix to a noun or prep., Deu. 28. 49 גּוֹי אֲשֶׁר לֹא־תִשְׁמַע לְשֹׁנוֹ a nation *whose tongue you do not understand*. Gen. 24. 3 the Canaanites אֲשֶׁר אָנֹכִי יוֹשֵׁב בְּקִרְבָּם *among whom I dwell*. 28. 3 הָאָרֶץ אֲשֶׁר אַתָּה שֹׁכֵב עָלֶיהָ the land *on which you lie*. Gen. 1. 11; 38. 25, Ex. 4. 17, Nu. 22. 30, Deu. 1. 22, Ru. 2. 12. In these cases the pron. requires to be expressed.

After words of time the prep. and suff. is however frequently omitted, so that אֲשֶׁר is equivalent to *when*, Gen. 45. 6, Jud. 4. 14, 2 S. 19. 25 עַד־הַיּוֹם אֲשֶׁר בָּא until the day *when* (in which) he came in peace, 1 K. 22. 25, cf. Gen. 6. 4 בַּיָּמִים הָהֵם וְגַם אַחֲרֵי־כֵן אֲשֶׁר in those days and also afterwards *when*. 40. 13.

(d) With adv. of place, Gen. 13. 3 הַמָּקוֹם אֲשֶׁר הָיָה שָׁם אָהֳלֹה the place *where* his tent was. 20. 13 כָּל־הַמָּקוֹם אֲשֶׁר נָבוֹא שַׁמָּה every place *whither* (to which) we shall come. 3. 23 הָאֲדָמָה אֲשֶׁר לֻקַּח מִשָּׁם the ground *whence* (from which) he was taken. Gen. 19. 27; 31. 13; 35. 15, Ex. 20. 21. Ex. 21. 13, Nu. 14. 24, Deu. 30. 3. Gen. 24. 5. The adv. may be omitted, esp. when the antecedent noun has prep., Gen. 35. 13, Nu. 13. 27, Ps. 84. 6.

§ 10. The word אֲשֶׁר often includes a pronom. antecedent, i.e. it is equivalent to *he-who, that-which, they-who, whom* or, indefinitely, *one-who* etc. In this case it admits prep. and אֵת. It occurs in any syntactic position. Gen. 7. 23 וַיִּשָּׁאֶר אַךְ־נֹחַ וַאֲשֶׁר אִתּוֹ בַתֵּבָה and only N. was left and *they-who* were with him in the ark. 43. 16 and he said לַאֲשֶׁר עַל־בֵּיתוֹ to *him-who* was over his house, 44. 1. 32. 24 he sent across אֵת־אֲשֶׁר־לוֹ *what* he possessed. 31. 1 וּמֵאֲשֶׁר לְאָבִינוּ of *that-which* is our father's. 9. 24 וַיֵּדַע אֵת אֲשֶׁר־עָשָׂה לוֹ בְּנוֹ he knew *what* his son had done to him. 2 K. 6. 16 רַבִּים אֲשֶׁר אִתָּנוּ מֵאֲשֶׁר אוֹתָם more are *they-who* are with us than *they-who* are with them (for אִתָּם). Jud. 16. 20 the dead whom he slew in death רַבִּים מֵאֲשֶׁר הֵמִית בְּחַיָּיו were more than *those-whom* he slew in his life.

> *Rem. 1.* The resumptive pron. is not usually omitted when suff. is involved, cf. Lev. 5. 24; 27. 24, Ru. 2. 2, Is. 8. 23; but sometimes even then, Is. 8. 12; 31. 6, Hos. 2. 14; 13. 10.
>
> *Rem. 2.* The adv. *there, thither* etc. is omitted after the compounds מֵאֲשֶׁר, עַל אֲשֶׁר, אֶל אֲשֶׁר, בְּכֹל אֲשֶׁר, בַּאֲשֶׁר, in designations of *place*, Ex. 5. 11; 32. 34, Jos. 1. 16, Jud. 5. 27, 1 S. 14. 47; 23. 13, 2 S. 7. 9; 8. 6; 15. 20, 1 K. 18. 12, 2 K. 8. 1. In Gen. 21. 17 *there* is expressed in a nominal clause.

§ 11. In both constructions in §§ 9, 10 אֲשֶׁר need not be used and the relative clause is in appos. to the antecedent (§ 9) or is a noun-equivalent (§ 10). The omission of אֲשֶׁר is typical of poetry but is sometimes found in prose. It is commoner with indef. antecedent.

When there is an antecedent, אֲשֶׁר may be omitted.

(*a*) When the resumptive pron. is subj., and whether this pron. is expressed (implied in the verb) or not. Deu. 32. 15 וַיִּטֹּשׁ אֱלוֹהַּ עָשָׂהוּ he forsook God *who made him*; *vs.* 17 new gods *which* had lately come. Jer. 13. 20; 31. 25, Is. 10. 3; 30. 5; 40. 20; 55. 13; 56. 2, Mic. 2. 10, Zeph. 3. 17, Job 31. 12. Particularly in comparisons, Jer. 14. 8 וּכְאֹרֵחַ נָטָה לָלוּן like a traveller *who turns aside* for a (single) night's lodging, *vs.* 9; 23. 29; 31. 18, Hos. 11. 10, Ps. 38. 14; 42. 2; 49. 13; 83. 15; 125. 1, Job 7. 2; 11. 16, Lam. 3. 1, Hab. 2. 14. So in nominal clauses, Jer. 5. 15 גּוֹי אֵיתָן הוּא a nation *which is ancient*. Gen. 15. 13 בְּאֶרֶץ לֹא לָהֶם in a land *which is not theirs*. Gen. 39. 4, *cf. vs.* 5, Hab. 1. 6, Ps. 85. 5, Pr. 26. 17.

(*b*) When the resumptive pron. is obj., whether it is expressed or not. Deu. 32. 17 אֱלֹהִים לֹא יְדָעוּם gods *whom* they knew not, cf. Jer. 44. 3. Is. 42. 16 בִּדְרֶךְ לֹא יָדָעוּ in a way *which* they do not know. Is. 6. 6; 15. 7; 55. 5, Ps. 9. 16; 18. 44; 118. 22, Job 21. 27. In comparisons, Nu. 24. 6 כַּאֲהָלִים נָטַע י' like aloes *which* Y. has planted. Jer. 23. 9, Ps. 109. 19, Job 13. 28.

(*c*) When the resumptive pron. is attached to noun or prep. Jer. 5. 15 גּוֹי לֹא־תֵדַע לְשׁוֹנוֹ a people *whose* speech you shall not understand. 2. 6. בְּאֶרֶץ לֹא עָבַר בָּהּ אִישׁ *through which* no one passes. Deu. 32. 37, Ex. 18. 20, Ps. 32. 2 (cf. Jer. 17. 7), Job 3. 15. With omission of pron., Is. 51. 1 הַצּוּר חֻצַּבְתֶּם the rock *out of which* you were hewn, Job 38. 26.

§ 12. Omission of אֲשֶׁר *he-who* etc. Is. 41. 24 תּוֹעֵבָה יִבְחַר בָּכֶם an abomination is *he-who* chooses you, Jer. 8. 13, Ps. 144. 2, Song 8. 5. Nu. 23. 8 מָה אֶקֹּב לֹא קַבֹּה אֵל how can I curse *him-whom* God has not cursed! (next clause without pron.). Ps. 12. 6 אָשִׁית בְּיֵשַׁע יָפִיחַ לוֹ I will set in safety *him-whom* they snort at, Is. 41. 2, 25, Job 24. 19. After prep. etc., Jer. 2. 8 אַחֲרֵי לֹא יוֹעִילוּ הָלָכוּ *after things-that* do not profit they have gone, cf. *vs.* 11. Ex. 4. 13 שְׁלַח בְּיַד תִּשְׁלָח send *through him-whom* you (care to) send. Is. 65. 1 נִדְרַשְׁתִּי לְלוֹא שָׁאָלוּ I was (ready to be) sought *by those-who* did not ask. Lam. 1. 14 בִּידֵי לֹא אוּכַל קוּם *into the hands of those-whom* I cannot withstand. Jer. 2. 11, Ps. 65. 5, Job 34. 32, 1 Chr. 15. 12, 2 Chr. 1. 4; 16. 9.

Rem. *1.* Such cases as 1 S. 10. 11 מַה־זֶּה הָיָה, 1 K. 13. 12 אֵי־זֶה הַדֶּרֶךְ הָלַךְ are probably to be construed: what is this *that* has happened? which is the way *that* he went? Gen. 3. 13, Jud. 8. 1, 2 K. 3. 8. Similarly after מִי הוּא, 1 S. 26. 14, Is. 50. 9, Job 4. 7; 13. 19.

Rem. *2.* In naming אֲשֶׁר is not used. The usual construction is a circumstantial clause, 1 S. 1. 1 וּשְׁמוֹ אֶלְקָנָה *whose* name was E., 9. 1, 2; 17. 12, 2 S. 3. 7 etc. Less frequently by a relative clause without אֲשֶׁר, Job 1. 1 אִיּוֹב שְׁמוֹ, 1 S. 17. 4, 23, 2 S. 20. 21, Zech. 6. 12. In naming God there are exceptions, perhaps due to liturgical usage, Ex. 15. 3, Is. 57. 15, Am. 5. 27, Jer.

46. 18. In naming two persons a construction with *the one ... the other* or similar is used, Gen. 4. 19; 10. 25; 11. 29, Ex. 18. 3, 1 S. 1. 2; 14. 49, Ru. 1. 4 etc. In identifying places parenthesis is usual, Gen. 14. 2 בֶּלַע הִיא־צֹעַר *Bela, i.e. Zoar*, cf. *vss*. 3, 17.

Rem. 3. In poetic parallelism אֲשֶׁר is sometimes omitted with *and* and a verb. Mal. 2. 16 וְכִסָּה *and* (I hate) *him-who* covers. Is. 57. 3 וַתִּזְנֶה (seed of an adulterer) and of *her-who* is a harlot. Am. 6. 1 וּבָאוּ *and* (woe to) *those-to-whom* the house of Israel comes!

Rem. 4. Some instances of omission of אֲשֶׁר in late prose are: Ezr. 1. 5, Neh. 8. 10, 1 Chr. 15. 12; 29. 3, 2 Chr. 1. 4; 16. 9; 20. 22; 30. 19.

§ 13. In some exx. where the antecedent is expressed, whether or not אֲשֶׁר is present, the antecedent is in the constr. state before the relative clause. Particularly in designations of time and place, Gen. 40. 3 מְקוֹם אֲשֶׁר יוֹסֵף אָסוּר שָׁם *the place where* Jos. was confined. Is. 29. 1 קִרְיַת חָנָה דָוִד *the city where* D. encamped. 1 S. 25. 15 כָּל־יְמֵי הִתְהַלַּכְנוּ אִתָּם *all the days* we went with them. Ex. 6. 28 בְּיוֹם דִּבֶּר יְ *on the day* Y. spoke. Gen. 39. 20, Lev. 13. 46; 14. 46, Nu. 3. 1; 9. 18, Deu. 32. 35, 2 S. 15. 21, 1 K. 21. 19, Jer. 22. 12; 36. 2, Hos. 1. 2; 2. 1, Ps. 4. 8; 18. 1; 56. 4, 10; 59. 17; 90. 15; 102. 3; 104. 8 (זֶה); 138. 3, Job 6. 17, 2 Chr. 29. 27. Probably therefore יוֹם in Deu. 32. 35 (cf. לְעֵת), Job 3. 3 (contrast הַלַּיְלָה) etc.; and possibly Gen. 1. 1 בְּרֵאשִׁית בָּרָא in the beginning *when* God created, cf. Hos. 1. 2. Also occasionally with other words? Gen. 49. 9 Benj. is זְאֵב יִטְרָף a wolf *which* ravins (a ravining w.). Ps. 81. 6 שְׂפַת לֹא יָדַעְתִּי a voice (lip) *which* I did not know. Jer. 48. 36.

Rem. 1. It is possible that some exx. cited earlier of antecedents like אִישׁ, דֶּרֶךְ etc. are constr., but equally that some cited in § 13 are not if they occur in poetry, which dispenses often with the Art.

Rem. 2. On זֶה, זוּ as relatives, § 6, R. 4. Also used as relative is שֶׁ, joined to the following word; it is regular in Song, Ecc., but it is not restricted to late passages. Following antecedent, Jud. 7. 12, Jon. 4. 10, Ps. 122. 3; 124. 8, Song 8. 8, Lam. 2. 15. *He who* etc., Ps. 137. 8, 9, Song 1. 7; 3. 1, Ecc. 1. 9, 1 Chr. 27. 27. Resumptive element omitted, Ps. 122. 4, Ecc. 1. 7 (constr.); 12. 3.

OTHER PRONOMINAL EXPRESSIONS

§ 14. The want of a reflexive pron. is supplied in various ways. (*a*) By the use of reflexive forms of the verb (Niph:, Hith.). Gen. 3. 10

וָאֵחָבֵא *and I hid myself.* 45. 1 לֹא יָכֹל לְהִתְאַפֵּק he was unable *to control himself.* 3. 8; 42. 7, 1 S. 18. 4; 28. 8, 1 K. 14. 2; 20. 38; 22. 30.

(*b*) By the ordinary personal pron., simple or suff.. Is. 7. 14 יִתֵּן אֲדֹנָי הוּא *the Lord himself* will give, § 1c. Jud. 3. 16 וַיַּעַשׂ לוֹ Ehud made *for himself.* Ex. 32. 13 to whom you swore בָּךְ *by yourself.* Jer. 7. 19 הַאֹתִי הֵם מַכְעִיסִים הֲלֹא אֹתָם do they provoke *me?* is it not *themselves* etc? Gen. 3. 7; 33. 17, Ex. 5. 7, 19, Is. 3. 9; 49. 26; 63. 10, Hos. 4. 14, Pr. 1. 18, Job 1. 12.

(*c*) By a separate word, esp. נֶפֶשׁ. Am. 6. 8 Y. has sworn בְּנַפְשׁוֹ *by himself.* 1 S. 18. 1, 3. Plur., Jer. 37. 9. So קֶרֶב, לֵבָב, לֵב heart. Gen. 8. 21 וַיֹּאמֶר אֶל־לִבּוֹ י' and Y. *thought with himself.* 18. 12 Sarah laughed בְּקִרְבָּהּ *within herself.* Gen. 24. 45, 1 S. 1. 13; 27. 1, Hos. 7. 2. Deu. 7. 17; 9. 4, 1 K. 12. 26, Is. 47. 8, Jer. 5. 24, Ecc. 2. 1 and *passim.* Also פָּנִים *face, presence, self.* 2 S. 17. 11 וּפָנֶיךָ הֹלְכִים בַּקְרָב *you yourself* going into battle. Ez. 6. 9 וְנָקֹטוּ בִּפְנֵיהֶם they shall loathe *themselves.* Ex. 33. 14, Deu. 4. 37, Ez. 20. 43; 36. 31, Job 23. 17. In ref. to *things,* עֶצֶם *bone, self-same, very.* Gen. 7. 13, Ex. 24. 10, Ez. 24. 2.

§ 15. The *indefinite,* unnamed pronom. subj. (Engl. *they, one*) is expressed in various ways. (*a*) By 3rd pers. sing. of verb, e.g. in naming, Gen. 11. 9 עַל־כֵּן קָרָא שְׁמָהּ ב' therefore *one called* its name Babel (its name *was called*). Gen. 16. 14; 21. 31, Ex. 15. 23. (3rd plur. in 1 S. 23. 28, 1 Chr. 11. 7; 14. 11.) Otherwise, Is. 7. 24 בַּחִצִּים וּבַקֶּשֶׁת יָבֹא שָׁמָּה with bow and arrows *one, men will come* there; Ex. 10. 5 וְלֹא יוּכַל לִרְאֹת הָאָרֶץ so that *no one shall be able* to see the earth. Gen. 38. 28; 48. 1, 1 S. 23. 22; 26. 20, 2 S. 15. 31; 16. 23, 1 K. 18. 26, Is. 6. 10; 8. 4; 14. 32; 40. 6 (and (*another*) *cried,* § 72, R. 3), Am. 6. 12, Mic. 2. 4. So by 3rd fem. of verb יֻלַּד, 1 K. 1. 6, and *he was born* next after Abs., Nu. 26. 59. Sometimes the cognate ptcp. is used as subj., Is. 28. 4 אֲשֶׁר יִרְאֶה הָרֹאֶה אֹתָהּ which *one, a man* (the seer) *sees;* vs. 24. Nu. 6. 9, Deu. 22. 8, 2 S. 17. 9, Is. 16. 10, Jer. 31. 5, Ez. 33. 4, Mic. 5. 2 (fem.).

(*b*) By 3rd plur. Gen. 29. 2 for from that well יַשְׁקוּ *they watered* the flocks (the flocks *were watered*); 1 S. 27. 5 יִתְּנוּ־לִי מָקוֹם *let* a place *be given* me. Gen. 41. 14; 49. 31, 1 S. 1. 25, 1 K. 7. 2; 15. 8, Jer. 8. 4; 16. 6 (sing. and plur.), Job 6. 2; 7. 3, Pr. 9. 11, 2 Chr. 25. 16.

(*c*) By ptcp., usually in plur. Gen. 39. 22 אֵת כָּל־אֲשֶׁר עֹשִׂים שָׁם הוּא הָיָה עֹשֶׂה whatever *was done* there, he was the doer of it. Is. 32. 12,

Jer. 38. 23, Neh. 6. 10, 2 Chr. 9. 28. More rarely sing., Is. 21. 11 אֵלַי קֹרֵא *one is calling* me from Seir

(*d*) Rarely by 2nd pers. (indef. *you*), except in the phrase עַד־בֹּאֲךָ *till you come* = as far as, Gen. 10. 19, 30; 13. 10, 1 K. 18. 46. Apparently Is. 7. 25 לֹא תָבוֹא שָׁמָּה *no one will come* there. In Prov. the sing. *you* is the pupil of the wise man, but cf. Pr. 19. 25; 26. 12; 30. 28, where the reference seems more general.

Rem. 1. Some other quasi-pronominal expressions are these: (*a*) *Some, several* may be expressed by plur. Gen. 24. 55 יָמִים *some* days; 40. 4 (cf. 27. 44; 29. 20 יָמִים אֲחָדִים *a few* days). Ez. 38. 17. By prep. מִן with noun. Gen. 30. 14 give me מִדּוּדָאֵי בְנֵךְ *some of* your son's mandrakes. Jer. 19. 1 מִזִּקְנֵי הָעָם *some of* the elders. Ex. 17. 5, Ps. 137. 3.

(*b*) *Any, every* by כֹּל. Deu. 16. 21 as an Ashera כָּל־עֵץ *any* (kind of) tree. Nu. 35. 22. Followed by plur., Gen. 3. 1; 4. 14, Lev. 4. 2. With neg., *none, nothing*, Deu. 28. 14, Jud. 13. 4, Ps. 143. 2. *Any one, one* by אִישׁ. Gen. 13. 16 אִם יוּכַל אִישׁ *if one* were able. *Anything*, דָּבָר Gen. 18. 14. *No, none* by אִישׁ ... לֹא; *nothing* לֹא ... דָּבָר. Gen. 45. 1 לֹא עָמַד אִישׁ *none* stood. Hos. 2. 12 אִישׁ לֹא יַצִּילֶנָּה *none* shall deliver her. 2 K. 10. 25 אִישׁ אַל־יֵצֵא let *no one* go out. Ex. 16. 19. Deu. 2. 7 לֹא חָסַרְתָּ דָּבָר you lacked *nothing*, 22. 26, 2 S. 17. 19, 1 K. 18. 21. Sometimes strengthened by כֹּל, 2 S. 18. 13. The phrase לֹא ... מְאוּמָה *nothing*, 1 S. 12. 4, cf. Gen. 22. 12. Indefinite uses of verbal subj., *one, they*, § 15 above.

(*c*) *This ... that, the one ... the other*, by זֶה ... זֶה, § 5, or אֶחָד ... אֶחָד, Ex. 17. 12, 1 K. 3. 25. *One another* by אִישׁ ... אָחִיו or אִישׁ ... רֵעֵהוּ, Gen. 13. 11; 11. 3, Ex. 16. 15; 32. 27, Is. 3. 5; *fem.* Ex. 26. 3, 5, Ez. 1. 23, Is. 34. 16.

(*d*) *Each* distributively by אִישׁ, Jud. 9. 55 וַיֵּלְכוּ אִישׁ לִמְקֹמוֹ; 7. 7, 1 S. 8. 22; 10. 25, 2 S. 6. 19, the noun usually sing., but usually plur. with *tents*, Jud. 7. 8 the men of Israel he dismissed אִישׁ לְאֹהָלָיו *every one to his tents*. 1 S. 13. 2. — Also by אֶחָד Is. 6. 2, Jud. 8. 18. With אִישׁ extraposed (*casus pendens*), Gen. 42. 35 הִנֵּה־אִישׁ צְרוֹר־כַּסְפּוֹ *every man's* bundle of money; 15. 10; 41. 12; 42. 25, Nu. 17. 17. So peculiarly Gen. 9. 5 מִיַּד אִישׁ אָחִיו at the hand of *every man's* brother, Zech. 7. 10; cf. 8. 17.

(*e*) *Such* is expressed by weakened זֶה (§ 4) or by כְּ with זֶה or suff., Gen. 44. 7 כַּדָּבָר הַזֶּה *such a thing*, plur. Gen. 39. 19. 41. 38 כָּזֶה *such a one*, Jer. 5. 9 *such a nation*. Jud. 19. 30 כָּזֹאת *such a thing*. Gen. 44. 15 אִישׁ אֲשֶׁר כָּמֹנִי *such as I*, 2 S. 9. 8. — 2 S. 17. 15 כָּזֹאת וְכָזֹאת *such and such*. Jos. 7. 20, 2 K. 5. 4; 9. 12. For *so and so* (person) Ru. 4. 1. Cf. 1 S. 21. 3; 2 K. 6. 8.

(*f*) Hebr. lacks possessive pron. and *mine, ours, yours, theirs* etc. are expressed by prep. and suff. Is. 43. 1 לִי אַתָּה you are *mine*, Gen. 48. 5. Gen. 26. 20 לָנוּ הַמַּיִם the water is *ours*. Jer. 44. 28 they shall know דְּבַר מִי יָקוּם

מִמֶּנִּי וּמֵהֶם whose word shall stand, *mine or theirs*. Also by אֲשֶׁר לִי, Gen. 39. 5 or שֶׁלִּי, Song 1. 6.

Syntax of the Noun and Nominal Clause

——•——

Gender

§ 16. Hebrew has only two genders, conventionally called *mas.* and *fem.*, though distinguishing between male and female animate beings is only one of their functions. Nouns are classified as mas. or fem. by using different uninflected forms or by using the uninflected form for mas. and a form with the ending הָ (and variants) for fem. Gender is extended from the noun to adj. and verbs with which it is linked (concord).

In the case of animate beings, distinction of gender is indicated —

(*a*) By the fem. termination, as אַיָּל *a hart*, fem. אַיֶּלֶת *a hind;* עֶלֶם *a youth*, fem. עַלְמָה *a maid;* עֵגֶל *a calf*, fem. עֶגְלָה.

(*b*) By different words, whether uninflected or inflected, as אָב *father*, אֵם *mother;* אִישׁ *man, husband*, אִשָּׁה *woman, wife;* עֶבֶד *servant*, אָמָה *maid;* חֲמוֹר *he-ass*, אָתוֹן *she-ass;* אַיִל *ram*, רָחֵל *ewe*.

(*c*) Or the same word may be used for both genders (epicene). The noun may be gramm. mas., as אֲלָפִים *cattle* (only plur.), בָּקָר *large cattle* (coll.; plur. *head of cattle*), דֹּב *bear*, זְאֵב *wolf*, כֶּלֶב *dog*, פֶּרֶא *wild ass;* or fem., as אַרְנֶבֶת *hare*, חֲסִידָה *stork*, יוֹנָה *dove*, נְמָלָה *ant*, צֹאן *small cattle, sheep, goats* (coll.). Occasionally gramm. concord is *ad sensum*, Gen. 32. 16 גְּמַלִּים מֵינִיקוֹת *milch camels*, 2 K. 2. 24 שְׁתַּיִם דֻּבִּים *two she-bears;* but not normally, Gen. 24. 63 גְּמַלִּים בָּאִים *camels were coming*, Hos. 13. 8 דֹּב שַׁכּוּל *a bear robbed of her cubs.* In Jer. 2. 24 פֶּרֶא mas. is oddly construed as both mas. and fem. In Deut. נַעַר is both *boy* and *girl*, but with the expected concord. Hebr. has no word for *goddess*, and אֱלֹהִים has to be used, 1 K. 11. 5.

§ 17. Of inanimate things the following classes of unmarked nouns are usually fem. —

(*a*) Proper names of countries and cities, as בָּבֶל *Babylon*, צִידוֹן *Sidon.* Words like מוֹאָב *Moab* etc. when used as name of people are usually mas., but fem. when the name of a country. Perhaps therefore a head noun like אֶרֶץ *land of* and עִיר *city of*, both fem., or עַם *people of*, mas., is to be understood. Thus place names with בֵּית, mas., are mas., as בֵּית לֶחֶם *Bethlehem*, בֵּיתְאֵל *Bethel*, as are (with נָהָר mas. understood) names of rivers, as פְּרָת *Euphrates*, הַיַּרְדֵּן *Jordan*, even if fem. in form, as אֲמָנָה, 2 K. 5. 12 (*Qere*). However, גַּן־עֵדֶן is fem., though גַּן *garden* is mas., Gen. 2. 15. Naturally fem. is בַּת צִיּוֹן (Is. 1. 8), בַּת־צֹר (Ps. 45. 8) etc. of inhabitants or people; the plur. בָּנוֹת refers to female inhabitants.

(*b*) Common names of definite places, as districts, quarters of the earth etc., as עִיר *city*, תֵּבֵל *the world*, כִּכָּר the *circle* (of the Jordan), שְׁאוֹל *Hades* (mas. as personified, Is. 14. 9), תֵּימָן the *south*, צָפוֹן *north*, Is. 43. 6. But there are exceptions. אֶרֶץ is occasionally mas., תְּהוֹם *deep* is both mas. and fem., שָׁמַיִם plur. *heavens* is always mas., as is יָם *sea*, נָהָר *river*.

(*c*) The names of instruments, utensils used by man, and members of the body, particularly such as are double, as חֶרֶב *sword*, כּוֹס *cup*, נַעַל *shoe;* עַיִן *eye*, אֹזֶן *ear*, רֶגֶל *foot*, etc. So of animals, קֶרֶן *horn*. Again there are exceptions, as mas. אַף *nose, nostrils*, עֹרֶף *neck*, פֶּה *mouth*.

(*d*) The names of the elements, natural powers and unseen forces, as אֵשׁ *fire*, נֶפֶשׁ *soul*, רוּחַ *wind, spirit* (usually), שֶׁמֶשׁ the *sun* (usually), but יָרֵחַ *moon* is mas.

§ **18.** In addition to its role in indicating female animate beings, the fem. ending is used for these classes of nouns. — (*a*) It is preferred for abstract nouns, as אֱמֶת *truth*, גְּבוּרָה *strength*, though some abstracts are mas., as חַיִל *strength*, כָּבוֹד *glory*, or plur., § 20*b*. There are also a number of mas./fem. pairs, as עֵזֶר and עֶזְרָה *help*, צֶדֶק and צְדָקָה *righteousness;* attempts to distinguish between the two forms semantically have not been successful. Cf. Is. 3. 1 (hendiadys). Many of the abstracts are adj. and ptcp. used nominally, as רָעָה *evil*, Hos. 5. 9; נֶאֱמָנָה *a sure thing*, Am. 3. 10; נְכֹחָה what is *straightforward*, cf. Mic. 3. 9. Esp. in plur., Gen. 42. 7 קָשׁוֹת *harsh things, harshly*, Is. 32. 4, 8 צָחוֹת *clear things, plainly*, נְדִיבוֹת *liberal things*. Cf. Nu. 22. 18; 24. 13, Jos. 2. 23; 3. 5, 2 S. 2. 26, 2 K. 8. 4; 25. 28, Is. 26. 10; 28. 22; 30. 10; 42. 9; 43. 18; 48. 6; 58. 11; 59. 9; 64. 2, Zeph. 3. 4. The mas. plur. is sometimes used in poetry, Ps. 16. 6, 11, Pr. 8. 6 נְגִידִים. Cf. also Gen. 2. 9 טוֹב וָרָע.

(*b*) Collectives, which are often *fem.* of ptcp., as אֹרְחָה *a caravan* (from אֹרֵחַ *a traveller*), גּוֹלָה *captivity* (גּוֹלֶה *captive, exile*), יֹשֶׁבֶת

inhabitants, Is. 12. 6 אֹיֶבֶת *enemy* (of a people), דַּלָּה *the lower classes*, 2 K. 24. 14, Jer. 40. 7, plur. Jer. 52. 15, 16. Cf. Mic. 4. 6, Zeph. 3. 19, Ez. 34. 4.

(c) The *fem.*, however, sometimes is used as *nomen unitatis* when the mas. is coll., as אֳנִי *fleet*, 1 K. 9. 26, אֳנִיָּה *a ship*, Jon. 1. 3, 4; שֵׂעָר *the hair*, 2 S. 14. 26, שַׂעֲרָה *a hair*, Jud. 20. 16, 1 K. 1. 52 and prob. Job 9. 17 (*for a hair*), but coll. 4. 15; שִׁירָה *a song*, Is. 5. 1, mas. generally coll. 1 K. 5. 12, though also singular, e.g. Is. 26. 1. So מֶרְכָּבָה *a chariot*, Gen. 41. 43 with מֶרְכָּב, 1 K. 5. 6. Perhaps פִּשְׁתָּה *wick*, Is. 42. 3; 43. 17, cf. Hos. 2. 7, 11, *flax*.

> *Rem. 1.* Sometimes the fem. of a mas. noun is used with a figurative sense, as יָרֵךְ *thigh*, *loins* (sing. and plur.), יַרְכָּתַיִם du. *sides* (of locality); מֵצַח *forehead*, *front*, מִצְחָה *shin-front*, *greave*; יוֹנֵק *suckling child*, יוֹנֶקֶת *sucker*, *shoot*.
>
> *Rem. 2.* As in other lang. with only two gend., mas. is the prior. In the case of suff., § 1, R. 4; adj. § 42, R. 3. In the case of verbs, the mas. is apt to be used for the 3 plur. fem. YIQTOL, 1 K. 11. 3, Song 6. 9, even in cases like Gen. 20. 17. For plur. imper., Is. 32. 11, Zech. 6. 7. For 2 sing. fem. YIQTOL, Is. 57. 8, Jer. 3. 5. These tendencies should not be cited to underscore the andocentric nature of OT religion, which is based on a single male deity. This belief, however, has a few surprising gramm. corollaries, e.g. the epicene noun אֱלֹהִים *God* and *goddess*, and the mas. verb in Deu. 32. 8 צוּר יְלָדְךָ *the rock which bore you*, cf. Jer. 30. 6.
>
> *Rem. 3.* The fem. is preferred to express the neuter, § 1, R. 3.

NUMBER

§ 19. Like gender, number is a category of the noun extended from it to other parts of speech. Number distinguishes between the sing. and plur. (and in some surviving cases, dual) of countable persons, animals and things; but it also has other functions.

§ 20. Many nouns are used only in plur. — (a) Such words as express the idea of something composed of parts, e.g. of several features, as פָּנִים *face*, צַוְּארִים *neck* (also sing.), or of tracts of space or time, שָׁמַיִם *heavens*, מַיִם *water*, עֲבָרִים *region on the other side*, Is. 7. 20; חַיִּים *life*, עוֹלָמִים *eternity*, Is. 45. 17, נְצָחִים *id.*, נְעוּרִים *time of youth*, זְקֻנִים *time of old age*, etc.. Cf. מַרְגְּלוֹת *area around feet*, Ru. 3. 4, סְפָרִים *a letter* (also sing.), 2 K. 20. 12, Jer. 29. 25.

(b) Some abstract nouns, as סַנְוֵרִים *blindness*, בְּתוּלִים *virginity*,

מֵישָׁרִים *uprightness,* כִּפֻּרִים *atonement,* זְנוּנִים *whoredom,* שִׁלֻּמִים *requital,* תַּהְפֻּכוֹת *perversity,* etc. The plur. may express a combination of the elements or characteristics composing the thing, or of the acts realising it, or simply intensification (c). See also § 21, R. 2, 3.

(c) The plur. may also express an *intensification* of the sing. (the so-called plur. of eminence or majesty). So אֱלֹהִים *God,* and analogically קְדוֹשִׁים *Holy One,* Hos. 12. 1, Pr. 30. 3, עֶלְיוֹנִים *Most High,* Dan. 7. 18, and ptcp. used nominally of God: of עֹשָׂה, Is. 54. 5, Ps. 149. 2, Job 35. 18, cf. Is. 22. 11; of עֹזֵר, Ps. 118. 2; of נֹטֶה, Is. 42. 5. Ptcp. as pred., Jos. 24. 19. This is not a survival of polytheism, though the idea of God in council may be gramm. exploited, Gen. 1. 26; 2. 22. See also § 26, R. 3. Similar words are אֲדֹנִים *lord, master,* of God, Deu. 10. 17, Ps. 8. 2; 136. 3, of human, 1 K. 1. 43 and בְּעָלִים *owner, master,* only of human, Ex. 21. 29, Is. 1. 3, Job 31. 39, Ecc. 7. 12. Plur. ptcp. of humans, Jud. 11. 35 *a sore trouble to us,* Is. 10. 15 *him who wields it.* Plur. of mythological creature: Ps. 74. 13 תַּנִּינִים *the monster,* Job 40. 15 *Behemoth (the* beast). So apparently תְּרָפִים *teraphim,* even of one image.

§ 21. Many nouns in sing. have a *collective* meaning. Collectives which do exclusive or regular duty for the plur. are אָדָם *humankind,* אֱנוֹשׁ *id.,* טַף *children;* בָּקָר *cattle,* בְּהֵמָה *id.,* (domestic) *beasts,* חַיָּה (wild) *beasts,* צֹאן *sheep, goats,* רִמָּה *worms,* רֶמֶשׂ *creeping things,* עוֹף *birds;* דֶּשֶׁא *grass, vegetation,* זֶרַע *seed,* חָצִיר *grass, herbage,* עֵשֶׂב *plants, herbage,* פְּרִי *fruit;* דִּמְעָה *tears,* רֶכֶב *chariots.* But many other words may on occasion be used in the sing. as coll., as אִישׁ *men,* נֶפֶשׁ *persons,* אַרְבֶּה *locusts,* שׁוֹר *oxen,* Gen. 49. 6, עֵץ *trees,* Gen. 3. 8, אֶבֶן *stones,* עִיר *cities.* 1 K. 22. 47 הַקָּדֵשׁ *hierodouli,* 2 K. 11. 10 הַחֲנִית *spears* (beside a plur.), 2 K. 25. 1. 1 K. 16. 11 רֵעֵהוּ *his comrades* (beside a plur.), 1 Chr. 20. 8. Frequently in enumerations, e.g. נַעֲרָה בְתוּלָה חָלָל *slain,* 2 S. 23. 8; *young virgins,* Jud. 21. 12; מֶלֶךְ *kings,* 1 K. 20. 1 (more usual Jud. 1. 7); גֶּפֶן *vines,* Is. 7. 23; מָשָׁל *proverbs,* 1 K. 5. 12; and expressions like עֹשֵׂה מִלְחָמָה *warriors,* 2 Chr. 26. 13; רֹעֵה צֹאן, Gen. 47. 3, cf. 2 K. 24. 14; הַסַּבָּל *the burden bearers,* Neh. 4. 4. In these occasional usages the nouns are equivalent to *class* nouns, which often prefer the sing. (§ 31). See also Numerals, § 47, R. 1.

Rem. 1. Apart from the Num. שְׁנַיִם *two,* מָאתַיִם, *two hundred,* אַלְפַּיִם *two thousand,* the dual only occurs with some human or animal bodily members, אָזְנַיִם *ears*, כְּנָפַיִם *wings*, and with some units of measurement and time, אַמָּתַיִם *two cubits*, יוֹמַיִם *two days*. In the first case the dual often serves as plur. after numerals and כֹּל, e.g. Is. 13. 7 כָּל־יָדַיִם; and where there is a plur. form, it may have a figurative sense, קַרְנַיִם *horns* (of animal), קְרָנוֹת *horns* (of altar). Several nouns with apparently dual endings are not duals but plur. (מַיִם *water*, שָׁמַיִם *heavens*) or unexplained (צָהֳרַיִם *noon*, מִצְרַיִם *Egypt*, unless this refers to Upper and Lower Egypt).

Rem. 2. When sing. is coll., the plur. may break it into its units or elements, as עֵצִים *timber* (pieces of wood); חִטִּים *wheat* in grain, 2 S. 17. 28 (חִטָּה *wheat* in crop, Ex. 9. 32); דָּמִים spilt *blood*, Gen. 4. 10.

Rem. 3. Some abstract nouns have both sing. and plur. forms, the latter perhaps intensifying the idea of the sing., 1 S. 2. 3 דֵּעוֹת *knowledge*, Jud. 11. 36 *vengeance*, Is. 40. 14 *understanding*, Ps. 16. 11 *joy*, Ps. 88. 9 *abomination*. Cf. § 20c. So probably in the case of other words where both sing. and plur. are used with sing. meaning, esp. in poetry: Gen. 49. 4 *bed* (both sing. and plur.), Ps. 63. 7; 2 K. 22. 20 *grave*, Job 17. 1; Zech. 9. 9 *ass;* Ps. 46. 5 *habitation*, 132. 5.

Rem. 4. The plur. is sometimes used to express uncertainty or choice, Deu. 17. 5 *to* (one of) *your gates*, Jud. 12. 7 *in* (one of) *the cities* of Gilead, Neh. 6. 2.

Rem. 5. The ending in the divine title אֲדֹנָי is probably not a 1st pers. sing. suff. with an intensive plur., but an otherwise unattested יִ, with honorific function; cf. Ez. 29. 16 (God speaking), Dan. 9. 9 (A. our God) but also Ps. 35. 23.

Rem. 6. Plur. of compound expressions are variously formed. Nu. 1. 2 בֵּית אָבוֹת *father's houses, clans*, 1 S. 31. 9 בֵּית עֲצַבֵּיהֶם *their idol temples*. — Jos. 1. 14 גִּבּוֹרֵי חַיִל *men of valour, wealth*, Jer. 8. 14 עָרֵי הַמִּבְצָר *fenced cities*. — 1 Chr. 7. 5 גִּבּוֹרֵי חֲיָלִים; Gen. 42. 35 צְרֹרוֹת כַּסְפֵּיהֶם *their bundles of money*, 1 K. 13. 32 בָּתֵּי הַבָּמוֹת *the houses of the high places*.

GENDER AND NUMBER CONCORD

§ 22. On concord with adjectives see §§ 41, 42: with numerals §§ 46ff. The transfer of gender and esp. number from nouns to the verbal predicate is particularly complicated. Three general tendencies are to be noted —

1. When the verb, as ideally it does, stands first, there is a tendency for it to be put in its most basic form, the 3 *mas.* sing.

2. There is a tendency to construe according to *the sense* rather than the grammar, hence gramm. singulars, such as collectives, are often

joined with plur. verbs, esp. when they refer to persons.

3. On the other hand, there is a tendency for plur. nouns, esp. when they refer to animals or are abstract plur., to be construed with a 3rd pers. *fem. sing.* verb (a use connected with other non-sexual uses of the gender, § 18).

§ 23. Agreement of simple subj. — (*a*) When subj. precedes the pred. (as e.g. in a circumstantial clause), there is general agreement in gend. and numb., whether the subj. be person or thing. Gen. 15. 12 וְתַרְדֵּמָה נָפְלָה *a deep sleep fell;* vs. 17 וַיְהִי הַשֶּׁמֶשׁ בָּאָה when *the sun was gone down;* 16. 1. But exceptions occur, Mal. 2. 6 וְעַוְלָה לֹא־נִמְצָא *evil was not found.* Gen. 15. 17 וַעֲלָטָה הָיָה *and it was dark.* Ex. 12. 49, Jer. 50. 46, Zech. 6. 14, cf. *vs.* 7, Job 20. 26.

(*b*) When verb precedes, while agreement in gend. and numb. is usual, esp. when subj. is personal, the verb is often in 3 sing. mas., even though the subj. be plur. or fem. This is common with הָיָה *to be.* Gen. 1. 14 יְהִי מְאֹרֹת וְהָיוּ *let there be* lights, and *let them be* signs. Is. 17. 6 חָזַק מִמֶּנּוּ הַמִּלְחָמָה וְנִשְׁאַר־בּוֹ עֹלֵלוֹת *gleanings shall be left;* 2 K. 3. 26 *the battle was too strong* for him, cf. *vs.* 18. Deu. 32. 35, Is. 13. 22; 24. 12, Jer. 36. 32. Nu. 9. 6 וַיְהִי אֲנָשִׁים אֲשֶׁר הָיוּ, 1 K. 11. 3 וַיְהִי־לוֹ נָשִׁים שָׂרוֹת *he had* seven hundred *wives, princesses.*

(*c*) Subjects in dual are necessarily joined with plur. pred., verb or ptcp. Gen. 48. 10 וְעֵינֵי יִשְׂ׳ כָּבְדוּ מִזֹּקֶן the eyes of Israel *were dim* from age. 2 K. 21. 22; 22. 20. Contrast 1 S. 4. 15, Mic. 4. 11 (§ 25). Ptcp., 1 S. 1. 13, 2 S. 24. 3, Is. 30. 20, Hos. 9. 14, 2 Chr. 16. 9.

§ 24. Agreement of composite subj. When the subj. consists of several elements joined by *and.* — (*a*) When subj. is first the verb is usually plur. 2 S. 16. 15 וְאַבְשָׁלוֹם וְכָל־הָעָם בָּאוּ Abs. and all the people *came,* Gen. 8. 22; 18. 11. But sometimes the verb is sing., agreeing either with the word next it or with the chief element of the composite subj., or the several parts of subj. all forming one conception. 2 S. 20. 10 Joab and Abishai his brother רָדַף *pursued.* Hos. 4. 11 whoredom and wine and new wine יִקַּח־לֵב *take away* the understanding. Hos. 9. 2, Deu. 8. 13. Neh. 5. 14 אֲנִי וְאַחַי לֹא אָכַלְתִּי neither I nor my brothers *ate.* 2 S. 3. 22, Est. 4. 16. If parts of the subj. be of different gend. pred. is usually mas., Gen. 18. 11, but cf. Jer. 44. 25.

(*b*) When the verb is first it perhaps oftenest agrees in gend. and

numb. with the element of the subj. which is next it; but it may be in
plur. When the subj. has once been mentioned following verbs are in
plur. Gen. 31. 14 וַתַּעַן רָחֵל וְלֵאָה וַתֹּאמַרְנָה R. and L. *answered and said;*
Nu. 12. 1 וַיְדַבֵּר מִרְיָם וְאַהֲרֹן ... וַיֹּ֖אמְרוּ Mir. and Aaron *spoke and said;*
Gen. 3. 8 וַיִּתְחַבֵּא הָאָדָם וְאִשְׁתּוֹ *hid themselves.* Gen. 7. 7; 9. 23; 21. 32;
24. 50, 55; 37. 7; 44. 14, Jud. 5. 1; 8. 21, 1 S. 11. 15; 18. 3; 27. 8, 1 K. 1. 34,
41. — Plur., Gen. 40. 1, Ex. 5. 1; 7. 20, Nu. 20. 10; 31. 13. Or it may be
mas. sing. (§ 23*b*), Joel 1. 13.

(*c*) When the subj. is a pron. and noun, the pron. must be expressed
whether verb be sing. or plur., § 1*c*. Plur. verb, Gen. 24. 54. Even when
two nouns are subj. a pron. referring to the first must be expressed if any
words separate it from the second, Gen. 13. 1; 35. 6; 38. 12; 50. 14, 22, Jud.
9. 48, Neh. 2. 12, cf. Jos. 22. 32. When composite subj. is of different
persons 1st pers. precedes 2nd and 2nd the 3rd. 1 K. 1. 21 *I and my son.*
1 S. 14. 40; 20. 23, Nu. 20. 8, Gen. 43. 8.

§ 25. Agreement of collectives. With sing. nouns having a coll.
meaning the verb is often construed in the plur. according to sense:
particularly when the coll. term refers to persons, but sometimes also
when it refers to animals or things. Gramm. agreement in sing. is also
common, and the two constructions often interchange. When the pred.
is first it may be in sing. while following verbs are in plur. Hos. 4. 6 נִדְמוּ
עַמִּי my people *are destroyed,* cf. Is. 5. 13 גָּלָה עַמִּי *is gone into exile;* Is. 9. 8
וְיָדְעוּ הָעָם כֻּלּוֹ the people *shall know,* the whole of *it.* 1 K. 18. 39 וַיַּרְא
כָּל־הָעָם וַיִּפְּלוּ when all the people *saw* it, *they fell* on their faces. Ex.
1. 20; 4. 31, Jud. 2. 10. Gen. 41. 57 וְכָל־הָאָרֶץ בָּאוּ all the world *came;*
1 S. 14. 25; 17. 46, 2 S. 15. 23. Nu. 14. 35 הָעֵדָה הַזֹּאת הַנּוֹעָדִים this
congregation *that are met together.* With creatures: Gen. 30. 38 תָּבֹאןָ
הַצֹּאן the flock *used to come,* Ps. 144. 13. So fem. pl. with בָּקָר Job 1. 14;
mas. pl. 1 Chr. 27. 29, cf. 1 K. 8. 5. With things: Jer. 48. 36 יִתְרַת
עָשָׂה אָבָדוּ the gain he has made *is lost.* Is. 15. 4, Hos. 9. 6, Hag. 2. 7, Ps.
119. 103. Comp. 1 S. 2. 33 *increase* in a personal ref. — Ex. 15. 4, Jud.
9. 36, 37 *people* sing. and plur., so 1 S. 13. 6, cf. *vss.* 15, 16. Jud. 1. 22; 9. 55,
2 K. 25. 5, Am. 1. 5, Hos. 10. 5; 11. 7, Is. 16. 4; 19. 13. Gen. 34. 24. Nu.
20. 11; 21. 7, Job 8. 19.

§ 26. On the other hand, plur. of inanimate objects that may be
grouped under one conception, of animals, and abstract plur. are

frequently construed with fem. sing. of verb. Either subj. or pred. may come first. 1 S. 4. 15 וְעֵינָיו קָמָה *and his eyes* (dual) *were set*, Mic. 4. 11. Joel 1. 20 בַּהֲמוֹת שָׂדֶה תַּעֲרוֹג אֵלֶיךָ *the beasts* of the field *pant* towards you. Ps. 103. 5 תִּתְחַדֵּשׁ כַּנֶּשֶׁר נְעוּרָיְכִי *your youth is renewed* like the eagle. Gen. 49. 22, Is. 34. 13; 59. 12, Jer. 4. 14; 12. 4, Mic. 1. 9, Ps. 18. 35; 37. 31, Neh. 13. 10, Job 12. 7; 14. 19; 20. 11. Cf. 2 S. 24. 13. There is no need for *Qere* in Deu. 21. 7, Ps. 73. 2, שפכה. Occasionally such plur. nouns are followed by a 3 *mas.* sing. verb (cf. § 23*b*), Gen. 47. 24, Ecc. 2. 7. Cf. Is. 16. 8, Hab. 3. 17.

Rem. 1. Attraction of gender. The verb may agree with the second member of a subj. constr. phrase. 1 K. 17. 16 וְצַפַּחַת שֶׁמֶן לֹא חָסֵר *the cruse of oil did not fail.* Is. 2. 11, 1 S. 2. 4, Lev. 13. 9, Job 21. 21; 29. 10; 38. 21. In nominal clauses with resumptive pron., the pron. may agree with pred. Jer. 10. 3 חֻקּוֹת הָעַמִּים הֶבֶל הוּא *the customs of the nations are* false, Lev. 25. 33. So the verb *to be* when it is used in similar clauses, Gen. 31. 8, Pr. 14. 35. The pred. usually agrees with noun after כֹּל *all*, Hos. 9. 4, Gen. 5. 5, Ex. 15. 20, but not universally, Hos. 10. 14, Is. 64. 10.

Rem. 2. General plur. are sometimes construed with sing. verb from a tendency to individualise or distribute. Ex. 31. 14 מְחַלְלֶיהָ מוֹת יוּמָת *any who profane it* (sabbath) *shall be put to death.* Lev. 17. 14; 19. 8, Zech. 11. 5, Pr. 14. 9; 27. 16; 28. 1. So sing. ptcp. in nominal clause: Gen. 27. 29 אֹרְרֶיךָ אָרוּר *any that curse you shall be cursed*, Nu. 24. 9, Pr. 3. 18. In particular a sing. suff. frequently refers back to plur. verb. Is. 2. 20 אֲשֶׁר עָשׂוּ־לוֹ *which they made* each *for himself.* 2. 8; 30. 22, Hos. 4. 8. Cf. Ex. 28. 3, Ps. 141. 10. So sing. suff. referring back to plur. noun, Deu. 4. 37; 7. 3; 21. 10, Jos. 2. 4, Is. 5. 23; 56. 5, Zech. 14. 12.

Rem. 3. The plur. in § 20 are variously construed. Many nouns which occur only in plur. like מַיִם, שָׁמַיִם, פָּנִים take plur. verbs (and adj.), though twice פָּנִים takes 3 fem. sing., 2 S. 10. 9, Job 16. 16 *Ket.* Nouns expressing an extension in time like זְקוּנִים, חַיִּים and most abstract plur. are usually construed as sing. Intensive plur. such as בְּעָלִים, אֲדֹנִים, אֱלֹהִים are usually in concord with sing. verb (and adj.). When אֱלֹהִים means *gods* it takes a plur., and in a few cases even when it is *God*, Gen. 20. 13 (or in an address to foreigner is *the gods* meant?); 35. 7, Ex. 22. 8 (in both of which a polytheistic background may be detected or be being exploited, cf. Gen. 28. 12).

Rem. 4. Names of nations are construed in three ways: (*a*) with mas. sing., the name being thought of as that of a personal ancestor (but cf. § 17*a*), Ex. 17. 11, Is. 19. 16, Am. 1. 11, 1 Chr. 18. 5; 19. 15, 16, 18, 19. (*b*) Or *ad sensum* with plur., 2. S. 10. 17, 1 K. 20. 20, 2 K. 6. 9, 1 Chr. 18. 2, 13. (*c*) Or with fem.

sing., when the ref. is to the country or when the population is treated as a coll., often personified, 2 S. 8. 2, 5, 6; 10. 11; 24. 9, Is. 7. 2, Jer. 13. 19, 1 Chr. 19. 12, Job 1. 15. The constructions *a, b, c* may interchange in the same passage, Jer. 48. 15, Am. 2. 2, 3, Hos. 14. 1, Mal. 2. 11.

Rem. 5. When there are several predicates one may be in agreement and the other left uninflected, Is. 33. 9, Mic. 1. 9, Zech. 5. 11; cf. on adj. § 42, R. 3. But irregularity in gend. and numb. is, in fact, not uncommon, Jer. 31. 9, Zech. 6. 7; Ez. 20. 38, Lam. 5. 10.

A Note on Case

§ 27. The noun in Hebr. fulfils its various gramm. functions by syntactical means as in English, not through a system of cases as in Latin or Greek or some other Semitic languages. Though traditionally Hebr. Grammars have used terms like accusative and genitive to describe functions which, e.g. in Arabic, are identified by acc. and gen. case endings, this is neither necessary nor (because of the danger of inaccuracy) wise. The discovery from Ugaritic that the locative ending הָ as in הַבַּיְתָה, Gen. 19. 10, does not derive from an old accusative ending but had originally a consonantal sound, is a warning of the kind of error that may arise.

Rem. 1. The oblique plur. and dual case endings survive formally in plur. יִם, dual יִם. Due to the presence of a weak third radical a similar ending survives in אָבִיךָ *your father*, etc. It is strangely an original dual oblique which survives in the plur. constr. ending יְ. An occasional nominative plur. survives in names, e.g. the place name פְּנוּאֵל (alongside פְּנִיאֵל). The so-called *Vav* and *Hireq compaginis* (of connection), found intermittently with the first member of a constr. relation in poetry and in a few bound phrases in prose, may be lengthened forms of old sing. nominative *u* and genitive *i*, but this is doubtful; they now serve only a decorative purpose, Gen. 1. 24 חַיְתוֹ־אֶרֶץ *beast(s)* of the earth; 49. 11 בְּנִי אֲתֹנוֹ *his ass's colt.* Is. 22. 16, Ps. 110. 4, Lam. 1. 1.

Rem. 2. **Enclitic *Mem*,** though not a case form, is a similar rare survival in poetry. It is found (vocalisation unknown and with no obvious function) frequently in the Ugar. poetic tablets added to nouns (even in constr.), prep. and verbs. Its presence in Hebr. was not recognised by the Massoretes who accommodated it in various awkward ways into the text, e.g. in Ps. 29. 6 as a mas. plur. suff. (וַיַּרְקִידֵם) which destroys the parallelism (cf. AV, RSV) and in Ps. 18. 16 by transferring it to the beginning of the next word (cf. the parallel text 2 S. 22. 16). It is perhaps also to be recognised in the peculiar אֱלֹהִים צְבָאוֹת, Ps. 59. 6; 80. 5, 8, 15, 20 (over against אֱלֹהֵי צְבָאוֹת, Am. 5. 14, 15, 16, etc.). On the equally peculiar יהוה צְבָאוֹת see § 35, R. 6. The poetic forms of the prep. בְּמוֹ, כְּמוֹ, לְמוֹ are probably connected, but not the adverbial ־ם found in חִנָּם, יוֹמָם, שִׁלְשׁוֹם; this *Mem* is also known from Ugar., e.g. *shpshm, with the sun.*

DEFINITENESS AND INDEFINITENESS. THE ARTICLE

§ 28. Pronouns always have a definite reference, to the speaker or hearer, or to some third person or thing. Some nouns, e.g. proper names, are also definite in reference. Other nouns (including adj. and ptcp. used as nouns) are made definite by prefixing the Article, though not always in ways that accord with Engl. usage. Hebr. has no indefinite article. It should also be noted that poetry very often lacks the Art. where prose would use it. A noun without the Art. may therefore in prose be definite in itself or indefinite, whereas in poetry it may additionally be definite from its context.

> *Rem. 1.* The num. אֶחָד *one* is sometimes used to make up the lack of an indef. art. Ex. 16. 33, 1 S. 7. 9, 12, 1 K. 19. 4; 22. 9, 2 K. 7. 8; 8. 6. Or it has the more specific sense of *a certain,* Jud. 9. 53; 13. 2, 1 S. 1. 1, 1 K. 13. 11, 2 K. 4. 1. The words אִישׁ *man,* אִשָּׁה *woman* prefixed to another term also express specific indefiniteness, Jud. 6. 8 אִישׁ נָבִיא *a prophet;* 4. 4, 2 S. 14. 5; 15. 6, 1 K. 3. 16; 7. 14; 17. 9.

§ 29. Nouns which are definite in themselves and do not require Art. are — (*a*) Proper names of persons, countries, cities, rivers etc., as יהוה (presumably) *Yahweh,* מֹשֶׁה *Moses,* מוֹאָב *Moab,* צֹר *Tyre,* פְּרָת *Euphrates.* (*b*) Certain appellatives with unique reference which approximate to proper names, as שְׁאוֹל *Sheol,* תֵּבֵל *the World,* תְּהוֹם *the Deep.* So generally the divine titles עֶלְיוֹן *the Most High,* שַׁדַּי (meaning unknown) and often אֵל (originally the deity *El*) and אֱלֹהִים (§ 20c) *God;* and perhaps some of the cases cited in § 31, R. 2, e.g. אֹהֶל מוֹעֵד *the Tent of Meeting,* שַׂר־צָבָא *the Commander-in-chief.*

The Constr. is definite if it precedes a *definite* noun or a pronom. suffix, though it does not itself have the Art.; but there are exceptions (R. 2).

Rem. 1. Some unique appellatives used as place names retain the Art., as הַלְּבָנוֹן Lebanon (*the white* mountain), הַיַּרְדֵּן Jordan (?), הַגִּבְעָה Gibeah (*the* hill), הָעַי Ai (*the* mound). Usage fluctuates, thus both אֱלֹהִים and הָאֱלֹהִים, both שַׂר־צָבָא (2 S. 2. 8) and שַׂר הַצָּבָא (1 S. 17. 55). In poetry some appellative-like nouns always occur without the Art., notably צַלְמָוֶת *Shadow of Death;* but in poetry there is always uncertainty. This word is dubiously derived from the root צלם *to be dark* (otherwise unattested in Hebr.); it is almost always σκιὰ θανάτου in Sept.

Rem. 2. A definite second member normally makes the whole constr. relationship definite. But sometimes, as in the case of suffixed nouns (§ 3, R. 1), such a constr. remains indef. Thus in a classifying nominal clause it may precede the pred., Gen. 24. 34 עֶבֶד אַבְרָהָם אָנֹכִי I am *a slave of Abraham.* Contrast the identifying clause in *vs.* 65 הוּא אֲדֹנִי he is *my master.* In most of the exx. the first noun is (or may be regarded as) a class noun and the second a proper name. 23. 6 *a prince* of God; 29. 12 *a son* of Reb., Deu. 7. 25 *an abomination* to Y., Jud. 6. 22 *an angel* of Y. (def. in *vs.* 20), Mal. 2. 7 *a messenger* of Y. of hosts. But cf. Lev. 4. 21 *a sin-offering* for the assembly. Elsewhere the context indicates that the phrase is indef., 1 S. 4. 12 אִישׁ בִּנְיָמִן *a man* of B., Lev. 14. 34 *a house,* Gen. 9. 20, Deu. 22. 19, Jud. 10. 1. So also sometimes when the second noun has the generic Art. (§ 31). Gen. 41. 42 רְבִד הַזָּהָב *a chain of gold.* Cf. 1 S. 25. 36 *a king's banquet.* Jud. 8. 18. In poetry the generic Art. may, like the Art. in general (§ 31, R. 3), be omitted, Song 1. 11 הַכֶּסֶף but זָהָב.

Rem. 3. In compound prop. names the Art., if used, maintains its usual place. 1 S. 5. 1 אֶבֶן הָעֵזֶר *Ebenezer.* And so with gentilics, Jud. 6. 11, 24 אֲבִי הָעֶזְרִי *the* Abiezrite, 1 S. 17. 58 בֵּית הַלַּחְמִי *the* Bethlehemite. 6. 14.

Rem. 4. A number of cases occur of Art. with constr. or with suffixed noun. In some cases the text may be faulty. Thus in Gen. 24. 67 *Sarah his mother* may be a gloss taken in from the margin, and in Gen. 31. 13 the phrase *that appeared to you* may have dropped out (Sept.). But other cases are paralleled and should not be questioned. In Lev. 27. 23 הָעֶרְכְּךָ is a technical phrase, cf. Jos. 8. 33. הַבַּת יְרוּשָׁלַם in Lam. 2. 13, cf. 1 S. 26. 22 (*Ket.*), 2 K. 7. 13 (*Ket.*), Jer. 48. 32. בְּתוֹךְ הַדָּבְרוֹ in Mic. 2. 12, cf. Jos. 7. 21, 2 K. 15. 16.

§ 30. Determination by Art. — With individual persons or things the Art. is used when they are *known,* and definite to the mind for any reason, e.g.

(*a*) From having been already mentioned. Gen. 18. 7 וַיִּקַּח בֶּן־בָּקָר he took *a calf; vs.* 8 he took בֶּן־הַבָּקָר אֲשֶׁר עָשָׂה *the calf* which he had got ready. Or otherwise well known to the audience, Am. 1. 1 לִפְנֵי הָרָעַשׁ before *the earthquake.*

(*b*) Or from being the only one of their kind, as הַשֶּׁמֶשׁ *the sun*, הַיָּרֵחַ *the moon; the* earth, *the* high priest, *the* king etc.

(*c*) Or, though not the only one of the class, when usage has given prominence to a particular individual of the class, as הַנָּהָר *the river* (Euphrates). הַבַּעַל *the lord* (Baal), הַשָּׂטָן *the adversary* (Satan), Job 1. 6, Zech. 3. 1, הַיְאֹר *the stream* (Nile, cf. Am. 8. 8 *the stream* of Egypt), הַכִּכָּר *the circle* (of Jordan), הַבַּיִת *the house* (Temple), Mic. 3. 12, Ps. 30. 1, הָאֱלֹהִים *the* (only) God.

(*d*) Or when the person or thing is an *understood* element or feature in the situation or circumstances. Gen. 24. 20 she emptied her pail אֶל־הַשֹּׁקֶת into *the trough*. 35. 17 וַתֹּאמֶר הַמְיַלֶּדֶת and *the midwife* said, 38. 28. So 18. 7 *the boy*; 22. 6 *the fire* and *the knife*; 26. 8 *the window*, Ex. 2. 15 *the well*, Jud. 3. 25 *the key*, 1 S. 19. 13, 2 S. 18. 24, Pr. 7. 19. Engl. also uses the def. Art. in such cases; at other times it employs an unemphatic pronom. suffix, but not Hebr., Gen. 24. 64 she lighted מֵעַל הַגָּמָל from *her camel*; vs. 65 she took הַצָּעִיף *her veil*; 47. 31 *his bed*. Jud. 3. 20, 2 S. 19. 27, 1 K. 13. 13, 27, 2 K. 5. 21.

(*e*) It is a peculiar extension of this usage when, in narratives particularly, persons or things are treated as definite, the person simply from the part he is playing, and the thing from the use being made of it. In this case Engl. uses the indef. Art. 2 S. 17. 17 וְהָלְכָה הַשִּׁפְחָה וְהִגִּידָה *a maid* used to go and tell them. 1 S. 9. 9 כֹּה אָמַר הָאִישׁ *a man* used to say this. Jos. 2. 15 וַתּוֹרִדֵם בַּחֶבֶל she let them down with *a rope*. Ex. 17. 14 write this בַּסֵּפֶר in *a book;* 1 S. 10. 25, Jer. 32. 10, Job 19. 23. — Deu. 15. 17, Ex. 21. 20 with *a rod*, Nu. 22. 27, Jos. 8. 29 on *a tree*, Jud. 4. 18 *a rug*, vs. 21 *a tent peg*, vs. 19 *a milk bottle*, 6. 38 *a cupful*, 9. 48; 16. 21; 3. 31. So probably Is. 7. 14 *a young woman*. Gen. 9. 23 *a garment* (less naturally *his*, i.e. Noah's). Deu. 22. 17, Jud. 8. 25, 1 S. 21. 10 (some passages may belong to *d*). So with rel. clause, Ps. 1. 1, Jer. 49. 36. With creatures, Gen. 8. 7 הָעֹרֵב *a raven*, vs. 8 *a dove* (unless these are generic usage, § 31*c*).

Rem. 1. The so-called vocative often has the Art. 1 K. 18. 26 הַבַּעַל עֲנֵנוּ *O Baal*, hear us! 2 K. 9. 5 אֵלֶיךָ הַשַּׂר unto you, *Captain?* Jud. 6. 12 עִמְּךָ י' Y. is with you, *O man of valour*. Jud. 3. 19, 1 S. 17. 58, 2 S. 14. 4, Hos. 5. 1, Jer. 2. 31, Is. 42. 18, Joel 1. 2, Zech. 3. 8. The noun with Art. may be regarded as in appos. to *you* understood. Cf. Job 19. 21, Mal. 3. 9,

Mic. I. 2. — 2 K. 9. 31, Is. 22. 16; 47. 8; 54. I, 11, Zeph. 2. 12.

Rem. 2. In such cases as הַיּוֹם *to-day*, הַלַּיְלָה *to-night*, הַפַּעַם *this time*, Gen. 2. 23, הַשָּׁנָה *this year*, Jer. 28. 16, Art. has a noticeably demons. function. Jud. 13. 10 בָּא בַיּוֹם came *the other day, that day* is defined by the circumstance that occurred on it.

Rem. 3. To *e* belongs the phrase וַיְהִי הַיּוֹם, I S. 1. 4; 14. I, 2 K. 4. 8, 11, 18, Job 1. 6, 13; 2. 1. Less natural is *the day was.* Gen. 28. 11 *a place;* hardly *the sanctuary.*

§ 31. In addition to these unique or particular usages the Art. also denotes *classes* of persons, creatures or things. This generic use is very common, particularly in *sing.,* either to describe the whole class or an individual person etc. as representative of it.

(*a*) The sing. of gentilic nouns is so used, as Gen. 13. 7 הַכְּנַעֲנִי *the Canaanite,* 15. 21. The plur. also with Art., rarely without, though פְּלִשְׁתִּים *Philistines,* is more common; cf. 2 S. 21. 12.

(*b*) So adjectives, as הַצַּדִּיק *the righteous,* הָרָשָׁע *the wicked.* The Art. is frequently omitted in poetry; see the Wisdom writings, *passim.* Here also plur. is not uncommon, Ps. I. 4-6.

(*c*) The various classes of creatures, as Gen. 18. 7 *the* cattle, herd. Esp. in comparisons. Jud. 14. 6 כְּשַׁסַּע הַגְּדִי as one rends *a kid.* 2 S. 17. 10 כְּלֵב הָאַרְיֵה like the heart of *a lion.* Ps. 33. 17 שֶׁקֶר הַסּוּס *a horse* is vain for deliverance. So Ecc. 7. 26 הָאִשָּׁה *a woman* (i.e. women). I S. 26. 20 *a partridge,* Jud. 7. 5 as *a dog* laps, I S. 17. 34, Am. 3. 12; 5. 19. 2 K. 8. 13 מָה עַבְדְּךָ הַכֶּלֶב what is your servant, *a dog* (your dog of a s.)?

(*d*) So other well known objects, such as precious metals and stones and, in general, any common article, though usage fluctuates here; Gen. 2. 11 אֲשֶׁר־שָׁם הַזָּהָב where there is *gold.* Am. 2. 6, Gen. 13. 2, 2 Chr. 2. 13, 14. Gen. 11. 3 *bricks, bitumen, mortar.* I K. 10. 27, Is. 28. 7.

(*e*) And, in general, in comparisons. Is. 1. 18 אִם־יִהְיוּ חֲטָאֵיכֶם כַשָּׁנִים כַּשֶּׁלֶג יַלְבִּינוּ though your sins be *like crimson,* they shall be white *as snow.* 10. 14 וַתִּמְצָא כַּקֵּן יָדִי and my hand has found *like a nest* the wealth of the nations. Nu. 11. 12, Jud. 16. 9, I K. 14. 15, 2 S. 17. 3, Hos. 6. 4, Deu. 1. 44, Is. 34. 3; 51. 8; 53. 6, 7, Mic. 4. 12. In poetry the Art. may be missing, Is. 13. 14; 29. 5; 41. 2, Hos. 2. 5.

Rem. 1. Any object or thing well known may receive the generic Art., e.g. affections or diseases, Gen. 19. 11 *blindness,* Zech. 12. 4 *madness,* Lev.

13. 12 *leprosy*. So plagues, calamities, as *blasting, mildew* etc., Am. 4. 9, Hag. 2. 17, Deu. 28. 21, 22, Ex. 5. 3, 2 K. 6. 18. So moral qualities as *faithfulness*, Is. 11. 5, etc. Also physical elements as *fire* in the frequent *burn* בָּאֵשׁ, Deu. 7. 5 etc.; *darkness*, Is. 9. 1. In all these cases, however, usage fluctuates, the Art. being most frequent with prefixed prep. (and therefore in poetry possibly due to the Massoretes).

Rem. 2. Poetry very often lacks Art. where prose would use it, Ps. 2. 2, 8 מַלְכֵי־אָרֶץ *the* kings of the earth; 72. 17 לִפְנֵי־שֶׁמֶשׁ before *the* sun, etc., etc. The incidence is increased (see R. 1) if many nouns with בְּ, כְּ, לְ pointed as def. are regarded as Massoretic interference. In general the Art. is less used in earlier than in later poetry.

There are indications that a similar situation had once obtained in prose. The Art. is sometimes missing from archaising phrases chiefly known from poetry, as *earth and heaven*, Gen. 2. 4, Ps. 148. 13, Gen. 14. 19; *beast*(s) *of the earth*, Gen. 1. 24, cf. Ps. 50. 10; 104. 11, 20, Is. 56. 9. Also from some familiar expressions, Ex. 27. 21 אֹהֶל מוֹעֵד *tent of meeting* (as we say "to church", cf. John 6. 59 ἐν συναγωγῇ); 1 K. 16. 16 שַׂר צָבָא *commander in chief*. But see § 29*b*. So from *king*, 1 K. 21. 10, 13 curse God *and king*, cf. 1 K. 16. 18, Am. 7. 13. Gen. 24. 11 לְעֵת עֶרֶב *at evening time*, Deu. 11. 12 *to year's end*, 4. 47. And from semi-technical terms like *gate, court* (§ 42, R. 2). More generally, as in poetry, from some familiar nouns, as *head* (Is. 37. 22), *hand* (Neh. 13. 21, Mic. 7. 16), *face* (Gen. 32. 31), *mouth* (Nu. 12. 8), etc. The nouns *heart, soul, eyes* etc., when following a constr. adj., usually want the Art. in poetry, as Ps. 7. 11 (upright *of heart*), sometimes in prose, as Jud. 18. 25 (bitter *in soul*). Particularly when, as essentially coll., they follow כֹּל, Is. 1. 5 (*the whole head*), 2 K. 23. 3 (*with all heart, soul*). So Gen. 3. 20 (*all living*), 6. 12 (*all flesh*), 7. 14 (*every bird of every sort* (wing)) but *ibid.* with Art. *every wild animal*, vs. 21 וְכֹל־הָאָדָם *all humans* (contrast כָּל־אָדָם, Ps. 39. 6). In prose plur. nouns after כֹּל usually take Art.

Rem. 3. In later writings particularly, but not exclusively, the Art. is used like a relative pron., as subj. or obj. to a verb and with prep., Jos. 10. 24, Jud. 13. 8, 1 S. 9. 24 (*what is upon it*), Ez. 26. 17, 1 Chr. 26. 28; 29. 8, 17, 2 Chr. 1. 4 (older usage Jud. 5. 27, Ru. 1. 16), 29, 36, Ezr. 8. 25; 10. 14, 17.

A number of cases accented after Art. as QATAL of ע״ע verbs may be *fem. ptcp.*, e.g. Gen. 18. 21 their cry הַבָּאָה *which is come*; 46. 27, Is. 51. 10, Ru. 1. 22; 4. 3. Gen. 21. 3 הַנּוֹלַד־לוֹ and the mas. ע״ע forms in 1 K. 11. 9, Is. 56. 3 broaden the evidence, however, and prompt caution. So does Jos. 10. 24 with a plur. mas. verb, though the spelling is anomalous.

The Construct State

§ 32. A noun in the construct *state* before anther noun is reduced phonetically wherever possible, making the whole expression as near as may be a single accentual unity. The semantic relation between the two nouns is also very close, covering all the nuances of Engl. *of* and several which are in Engl. expressed by other prep. or by an adj. The term genitive should not be used to denote the second noun (§ 27). Here the noun in the constr. state is called A, and the second noun B.

The constr. (A) may be a noun or an adj., or a ptcp. or infin. used nominally. The second noun (B) may be replaced by a pronom. suff. or, on occasion, a clause. According as B is def. or indef., so is the whole phrase, but this is not simply a matter, esp. in poetry but also in prose (§ 29, § 31, R. 2), of the presence or absence of the Art. On other structural features see § 36.

In meaning the relationship of B to A may, broadly speaking, be subjective (§ 33) or objective (§ 34) or adjectival (§ 35).

§ 33. In the *subjective* usages a personal B "possesses" A or it is the agent (or, if impersonal, the instrument) of the action expressed or implied by A.

(*a*) By "possesses" (in its gramm. sense) is meant that B owns A, or is a relative of A, or has A as a bodily part or a condition or a quality, etc. Is. 1. 22 כַּסְפֵּךְ *your* silver, Jer. 7. 4 י׳ הֵיכַל the temple *of Y.*, Gen. 40. 1 מַשְׁקֵה מֶלֶךְ מִצְרַיִם the butler *of the king of E.*, cf. 31. 18. Gen. 3.6 אִישָׁהּ *her* husband, cf. 36. 6. Gen. 24. 30 יְדֵי אֲחֹתוֹ the hands *of his sister*, Is. 6. 10 לֵב־הָעָם הַזֶּה the heart *of this people*, cf. Gen. 4. 10, Song 7. 1ff., Gen. 23. 1 חַיֵּי שָׂרָה the life *of S.*; so נֶפֶשׁ *soul* in all its meanings. 1 K. 5. 10 חָכְמַת שְׁלֹמֹה the wisdom *of S.*, Is. 2. 17 גַּבְהוּת אָדָם the highness (haughtiness) *of men*, 38. 9 חָלְיוֹ *his* sickness, Ps. 19. 1 כְּבוֹד־אֵל the glory *of God*, 103. 17 חֶסֶד י׳ the loving kindness *of Y.*

(*b*) By agency is meant that B is the subj. of the verbal idea contained in A. Many A nouns which are in Engl. thought of as abstract nouns or as qualities possessed by someone are more appropriately classified here than under *a* because of their verbal derivation and their concrete usage. 1 S. 15. 10 וַיְהִי דְבַר י׳ the word *of Y.* came (was) to

Samuel, cf. Jer. 1. 1, Am. 1. 1. Ex. 14. 13 רְאוּ אֶת־יְשׁוּעַת י׳ see the salvation *of Y.* Pr. 11. 6 צִדְקַת יְשָׁרִים the righteous behaviour *of the upright* delivers them, cf. Gen. 30. 33 (*my* honest dealing), Jud. 5. 11 (plur. triumphs). Ps. 72. 1 give the king מִשְׁפָּטֶיךָ *your* (skill in making) judgements. Is. 55. 8 לֹא מַחְשְׁבוֹתַי *my* thoughts are not *your* thoughts. 2 S. 16. 23 עֲצַת אֲחִיתֹפֶל the counsel *of A.* which he counselled. 1 K. 10. 9 בְּאַהֲבַת י׳ אֶת־יִשְׂרָאֵל because of *Y.'s* love for Israel. Is. 9. 6 קִנְאַת־י׳ the zeal *of Y.* will do this. Often in constr. chains the agency is carried by a suff.: Ps. 25. 7 חַטֹּאות נְעוּרַי the sins *of my* youth, 8. 3. Ps. 60. 10 סִיר רַחְצִי *my* wash basin, 107. 30 (*my desired* haven), Is. 10. 6 (*who incur my* wrath).

Commonly A is passive ptcp., Is. 53. 4 מֻכֵּה אֱלֹהִים smitten *of* (by) *God*, Job 14. 1. So (or similar) when B is *instrument*, Is. 22. 2 לֹא חַלְלֵי חֶרֶב וְלֹא מֵתֵי מִלְחָמָה not slain *by the sword* nor dead *through war*, Gen. 41. 6, Is. 1. 7.

§ 34. When, on the other hand, B is used *objectively* it is the recipient of or otherwise affected by the action expressed or implied by A. Frequently A is active ptcp., Gen. 3. 5 יֹדְעֵי טוֹב וָרָע knowing *good and evil*, Is. 5. 18 מֹשְׁכֵי הֶעָוֹן dragging *on iniquity*, cf. vs. 23, Ps. 19. 8. Is. 40. 8 מְבַשֶּׂרֶת צִיּוֹן is probably not (note fem. verb, *get you up*) O thou that tellest good tidings *to Zion* (AV) but (§ 35*a*) O Zion *that bringest good tidings* (RV). Indirectly of motion to and from, Is. 38. 18 יֹרְדֵי־בוֹר those going down *to the Pit*, Gen. 23. 10 (cf. Jud. 1. 24 מְבוֹא הָעִיר), Gen. 9. 10 יֹצְאֵי הַתֵּבָה those leaving *the ark*, Is. 59. 20 שָׁבֵי פֶשַׁע those turning *from transgression*. Of presence in, Ps. 88. 6 שֹׁכְבֵי קֶבֶר those lying *in the grave*, Gen. 4. 20; 19. 25. Otherwise, Ex. 3. 8 אֶרֶץ זָבַת חָלָב וּדְבַשׁ a land flowing *with milk and honey*.

When A is a noun the ways in which it affects B are very varied. Gen. 16. 7 דֶּרֶךְ שׁוּר *the way to Sh.*, 3. 24, Jer. 21. 8, Ps. 139. 24. Gen. 18. 2 זַעֲקַת סְדֹם *the outcry against* S. and G. 42. 19 שֶׁבֶר רַעֲבוֹן בָּתֵּיכֶם *corn* (needful) *for the famine in your houses.* 2 S. 8. 10 אִישׁ מִלְחֲמוֹת תֹּעִי engaged in *wars with T.* Is. 11. 2 רוּחַ חָכְמָה וּבִינָה a spirit *of* (inducing) wisdom and understanding, 19. 14, Hos. 4. 12. Is. 32. 2 סֵתֶר זֶרֶם a covert *from* the rain. 53. 5 מוּסַר שְׁלוֹמֵנוּ *the chastisement that* brought healing to us. Jer. 16. 7 כּוֹס תַּנְחוּמִים *the cup of* (bringing) consolation. Jer. 50. 28 נִקְמַת הֵיכָלוֹ *vengeance on behalf of* his temple. Am. 8. 10 כְּאֵבֶל יָחִיד

like *the mourning for* an only son, Gen. 27. 41. Obad. 10 חֲמַס אָחִיךָ *the violence done to* your brother, Gen. 16. 5, Hab. 2. 17. Pr. 1. 7 יִרְאַת י' *the fear of* Y., 2. 19 אָרְחוֹת חַיִּים *the paths to* life (cf. *vs.* 18). When B is suff., § 2*b*.

§ 35. Hebr. has a relatively meagre stock of adj., and B is very frequently used *adjectivally*, i.e. explicative in various ways of A.

(*a*) *Class* definitions belong here. B may identify a member of the class indicated by A. Gen. 6. 14 עֲצֵי גֹפֶר *gopher-wood*, Ex. 25. 7 *onyx* stones, Jer. 24. 2 *first-ripe* grapes. Esp. in naming, Gen. 2. 15 גַּן־עֵדֶן the garden of *Eden*, 15. 8 נְהַר־פְּרָת the river *Euphrates*, Is. 41. 14 תּוֹלַעַת יַעֲקֹב you worm *Jacob*, 40. 9 *O Zion,* herald(ess) of good news (see § 34). Note בַּת יְרוּשָׁלַם (Is. 37. 22 etc.) daughter (who is) *Jerusalem*. Or, alternatively, A is adjectival and identifies the member of the class indicated by B, Gen. 8. 9 כַּף־רַגְלָהּ *the sole of* its foot, Is. 9. 5 פֶּלֶא יוֹעֵץ *wonderful* (wonder of a) counsellor, Gen. 16. 12 פֶּרֶא אָדָם *a wild ass* among men, Nu. 23. 19 בֶּן־אָדָם *son of* (who represents) mankind (frequently in Ez., 2. 1 etc.; so Aram. in Dan. 7. 13); so (in effect) בְּנֵי יִשְׂרָאֵל, Ex. 1. 17 etc., and similar constructs used ethnically, בְּנֵי הַנְּבִיאִים, 1 K. 20. 35 etc., used of a professional group, בְּנֵי הָאֱלֹהִים, Gen. 6. 2 etc., divine *beings;* Is. 1. 4 זֶרַע מְרֵעִים *a race of* evildoers. 1 K. 10. 15, Is. 29. 19, Ez. 36. 38, Ps. 1. 1, Pr. 15. 20, 2 Chr. 2. 7.

(*b*) B may indicate the material of which A is made, Gen. 24. 22 נֶזֶם זָהָב a *golden* ring, Ex. 20. 24 מִזְבַּח אֲדָמָה an *earthen* altar. Gen. 3. 21, Jud. 7. 13, 1 K. 6. 36, Is. 2. 20, Ps. 2. 9. Or the commodity of which A is a unit of measure or receptacle, Jud. 6. 19 אֵיפַת־קֶמַח an ephah *of meal*, Gen. 21. 14, 1 S. 16. 20; 17. 17, 1 K. 18. 12, 14. Or in numerical statements simply what is being counted, Gen. 40. 12 שְׁלֹשֶׁת יָמִים three *days*, 8. 9 כָּל־הָאָרֶץ all *the earth*, Ps. 51. 3 כְּרֹב רַחֲמֶיךָ according to *your* many mercies, Gen. 18. 4 מְעַט מַיִם a little *water*. A special usage (§ 44, R. 4) expresses the superlative, e.g. Ex. 26. 33 קֹדֶשׁ הַקֳּדָשִׁים the holy of (among) *holy places*.

Apposition (§ 39) is a frequent alternative for many of the usages of the constr. relation in *a* and *b*. See also Numerals, §§ 46ff.

(*c*) B may describe an attribute or quality of A, 1 K. 20. 31 מַלְכֵי חֶסֶד *clement* kings, Jud. 11. 1 גִּבּוֹר חַיִל a *valiant* hero, Lev. 19. 36 מֹאזְנֵי צֶדֶק *right* balances, Is. 43. 28 שָׂרֵי קֹדֶשׁ *holy* princes. More generally, Is.

51. שִׂמְחַת עוֹלָם *everlasting* joy, Ex. 3. 8 (cf. § 34) a land *flowing* with milk and honey, Zech. 11. 4 צֹאן הַהֲרֵגָה the flock (destined) *for slaughter*, Is. 13. 3 עַלִּיזֵי גַאֲוָתִי (Zeph. 3. 11). Is. 13. 8; 22. 2; 28. 4; 32. 2, Ex. 29. 29, Ps. 5. 7; 23. 2, Pr. 1. 9; 5. 19, Zeph. 3. 4. Jer. 20. 17 *with child always*. — The equivalence of this constr. relation to the adj. appears from the loose constructions, Deu. 25. 15 אֶבֶן שְׁלֵמָה וָצֶדֶק a *full* and *right* weight; 1 S. 30. 22 כָּל־אִישׁ רָע וּבְלִיַּעַל every *bad* and *worthless* man.

(d) The opposite relationship is found when A is adj. or ptcp. and B specifies the extent or point of its application. Is. 6. 5 אִישׁ טְמֵא־שְׂפָתַיִם a man *unclean of lips*, Ex. 32. 9 עַם־קְשֵׁה־עֹרֶף הוּא they are *a stiffnecked people*, Gen. 24. 16 וְהַנַּעַר טֹבַת מַרְאֶה מְאֹד and the girl was very *pretty*, 2 S. 9. 13 פִּסֵּחַ שְׁתֵּי רַגְלָיו *lame in* his *two feet*, 1 S. 25. 3 הָאִשָּׁה טוֹבַת שֶׂכֶל וִיפַת תֹּאַר וְהָאִישׁ רַע מַעֲלָלִים the woman was *of great discretion and beautiful in form*, but the man was *evil in* (his) *doings*. Gen. 12. 11; 26. 7; 29. 17; 39. 6; 41. 2-6, Ex. 4. 10; 6. 12, Deu. 9. 6, 13, Jud. 3. 15; 18. 25, 1 S. 2. 5; 22. 2, 2 S. 4. 4, Is. 1. 4, 30; 3. 3; 19. 10; 29. 24; 54. 6, Am. 2. 16, Ps. 24. 4, Job 3. 20; 9. 4, Lam. 1. 1, Song 5. 8.

Rem. 1. Some kind of subjective relationships do not fit the definitions given in § 33; e.g. after יוֹם the verbal ideal is expressed by B, Is. 34. 8 יוֹם נָקָם a day *of* (Y.'s) *vengeance*, 22. 5; 58. 5; 37. 3 יוֹם צָרָה a day *of* (on which I suffer) *distress*, cf. Gen. 35. 3, Jud. 13. 7 יוֹם מוֹתוֹ; Jer. 12. 3 יוֹם הֲרֵגָה a day *of* (their) *slaughter*. In 2 S. 4. 4 שְׁמֻעַת שָׁאוּל *the news about* S. and J., A is verbal but B describes neither possessor or agent but simply the subject matter, Gen. 29. 13, Is. 23. 5. Many other constr. relations may be loosely classified as subjective, e.g. B contains A, Ex. 34. 28 דִּבְרֵי הַבְּרִית *the words of the covenant;* is contained in A, 24. 7 סֵפֶר הַבְּרִית *the book of the covenant*, Nu. 10. 33 אֲרוֹן בְּרִית יי *the ark of Y's covenant*.

Rem. 2. When B denotes an attribute, it forms along with A a single conception, and hence takes any suff., Ps. 2. 6 הַר קָדְשִׁי *my holy hill*, Deu. 1. 41, Is. 2. 20; 9. 3; 30. 22; 31. 7; 64. 9, 10, Zeph. 3. 11, Job 18. 7. Cf. § 3.

Rem. 3. B of attribute or quality is esp. common with certain nouns, אִישׁ, אִשָּׁה *man, woman*, בֵּן, בַּת *son, daughter*, בַּעַל [בַּעֲלָה] *owner, possessor*. Ex. 4. 10 אִישׁ דְּבָרִים a *good speaker*, Job 11. 2 א' שְׂפָתַיִם *glib-tongued* (of lips), 2 S. 16. 7 א' דָּמִים *murderer*, Pr. 25. 24 אֵשֶׁת מִדְיָנִים a *scolding woman*, 31. 10 אֵשֶׁת חַיִל a *virtuous wife*. 1 S. 14. 52 בֶּן־חַיִל *mighty man*, 26. 16 בְּנֵי מָוֶת *deserving death*, 1. 16 בַּת בְּלִיַּעַל *shameless woman*. In stating age, 1 S. 4. 15 בֶּן־תִּשְׁעִים וּשְׁמֹנֶה שָׁנָה *ninety-eight years old*, etc. Gen. 37. 19 בַּעַל הַחֲלֹמוֹת this *dreamer*, 2. K. 1. 8 ב' שֵׂעָר *hairy*, Pr. 23. 2 ב' נֶפֶשׁ *of large appetite*, Is. 50. 8

בַּעַל מִשְׁפָּטִי my *accuser*, 1 S. 28. 7 אֵשֶׁת בַּעֲלַת־אוֹב a woman who is a *medium* (see also § 36, R. 4).

Rem. 4. Adverbs may play a nominal role and stand in position B, 1 K. 2. 31 דְּמֵי חִנָּם *causeless* bloodshed, Nu. 29. 6 עֹלַת הַתָּמִיד *the continual* burnt-offering, Ex. 39. 14 אַנְשֵׁי תָמִיד men (who) *continually* pass through (עֹבְרִים) the land, Deu. 26. 5 מְתֵי מְעָט *few* men. 2 S. 24. 24, Hab. 2. 19, Ez. 30. 16.

Rem. 5. The construction in § 35*d* is the usual one in Hebr. of the type *integer vitae;* a noun used "adverbially" (adnominally would be more accurate) after adj. and ptcp. is uncommon, e.g. Is. 40. 20 (poor *in oblation*), Job 15. 10 (older *in days*). Contrast 30. 1 (younger לְיָמִים *in days*). The prep. בְּ is generally used of members of the body when constr. is not employed, Am. 2. 15, Pr. 17. 20.

Rem. 6. Place names may be put in constr., as Ur of the Chaldees, Gen. 11. 31, Aram of the two rivers, 24. 10, Mizpeh of Gilead, Jud. 11. 29. So divine names before a place, Nu. 25. 3 בַּעַל פְּעוֹר *Baal of Peor*, cf. in an inscr. from Kuntillet Ajrud יהוה שמרן *Y. of Samaria*. Unique are גִּבְעַת שָׁאוּל *Gibeah of Saul* (1 S. 11. 4), *Zion of the Holy One* of Israel (Is. 60. 14) and the frequent title יהוה צְבָאוֹת *Y. of hosts* (cf. 1 S. 17. 45 where it is in appos. to אֱלֹהֵי מַעַרְכוֹת יִשְׂרָאֵל *the God of the armies of Israel*). Attempts to explain the latter phrase as appositional, *Y.* (who is, belongs among) *the hosts* (sc. of heaven) or as deriving from an old liturgical formula *He who creates the hosts* (of heaven) (Hiph. from הוה = היה) are not convincing; nor, as the *lectio difficilior*, should it be regarded as breviloquence for the gramm. regular י' אֱלֹהֵי צ' *Y., the God of hosts*, 2 S. 5. 10 etc. Finally, it should be noted that no proper names, place, divine or personal, take a suff. in Hebr.; this suggests that in the above inscr. from Kuntillet Ajrud אשרתה cannot mean *his* (Y.'s) *Ashera*, i.e. his consort, but *his* (or better, *its*, i.e. Samaria's) *sacred place, pole*, cf. Is. 10. 11, Am. 8. 14.

§ 36. Some other matters of structure. — (*a*) B may occasionally be replaced by a relative clause, § 13. Or by a prep. phrase when the prep. normally goes with an active ptcp. in A, Is. 9. 1 יֹשְׁבֵי בְּאֶרֶץ צַלְמָוֶת those *dwelling in*, Ps. 2. 12 כָּל־חוֹסֵי בוֹ all *taking refuge in* him. Jud. 5. 10, Is. 5. 11; 14. 19; 30. 18; 64. 3, Jer. 8. 16, Ez. 38. 11, Ps. 84. 7, Job 24. 5. Otherwise: Is. 28. 9 גְּמוּלֵי מֵחָלָב *weaned from* milk, 56. 10 אֹהֲבֵי לָנוּם *loving to* slumber. Peculiarly Jer. 33. 22 מְשָׁרְתֵי אֹתִי *ministering to me*. More loosely, Is. 9. 2 שִׂמְחַת בַּקָּצִיר *joy* (as) *in harvest*, Ez. 13. 2.

(*b*) The constr. relation may also be split by the ה of direction (e.g. Gen. 44. 14 בֵּיתָה יוֹסֵף), by Enclitic Mem (§ 27, R. 2) and, in some phrases, by *Vav* and *Hireq compaginis*. But normally nothing is permitted to come between A and B. An adj. qualifying either must therefore stand outside the expression, Joel 3. 4 יוֹם י׳ הַגָּדוֹל the *great* day of Y., Gen. 27. 15 בִּגְדֵי עֵשָׂו בְּנָהּ הַגָּדֹל הַחֲמֻדוֹת the *best* garments of her *elder* son Esau. Is. 36. 9.

(*c*) For the same reason two coordinated constr. may not govern B. Commonly a suff. is used with the second (and any further) noun. Thus Gen. 41. 8 he called all the magicians of Eg. וְאֶת־כָּל־חֲכָמֶיהָ *and all its wise men* (= all the mag. and w. m. of Eg.). Or the suff. on B may be omitted, Gen. 40. 1 the butler of the king of Eg. וְהָאֹפֶה *and the baker*, Ps. 64. 7. Or *periphrasis* by prep. לְ may be used, Gen. 40. 5 הַמַּשְׁקֶה וְהָאֹפֶה אֲשֶׁר לְמֶלֶךְ מִ׳. Periphrasis is had recourse to when the first member of the relationship is to be preserved indef., the second being def., 1 S. 16. 18 בֶּן לְיִשַׁי *a* son of Jesse, cf. 20. 27 בֶּן־יִשַׁי *the* son of J. (David). And in some other instances, R. 3. But periphrasis is not obligatory if the context is unambiguous, allowing a def. constr. phrase to be treated as indef. (§ 29, R. 2); and it may, of course, be used simply for variety, Gen. 40. 5 above, 1 S. 14. 16, Jer. 12. 12.

> *Rem. 1.* Sometimes an adj. is used nominally and brought within the chain of constructs. Is. 28. 16 a corner-stone יְקְרַת *of preciousness* of a foundation; perhaps *vss.* 1, 4 flower נֹבֵל of *a faded-thing* (faded flower) of its proud glory, Jer. 4. 11 *wind of dryness*. In some cases a non-constr. appears in such a chain, Is. 28. 1 גֵּיא־שְׁמָנִים הֲלוּמֵי יָיִן *the fat valley* of those overcome by wine, Ps. 68. 22, Pr. 21. 6. This is difficult to explain as either appos. or an "adverbial" usage (with respect to).
>
> *Rem. 2.* Rare instances of two constr. before B are Ez. 31. 16, Dan. 1. 4, perhaps stereotyped phrases. Occasionally the first word seems to stand loosely in abs., Is. 55. 4. On the other hand, when one constr. governs two following nouns, it may be repeated before each, Gen. 24. 3 *God* of heaven *and God* of earth, 11. 29; 14. 13, Jos. 24. 2. But often not, Gen. 14. 22; 28. 5, Ex. 3. 6, 16 (contrast 4. 5), 1 K. 18. 36. There is nothing unusual in several nouns after one constr., Deu. 8. 8; 32. 19, Jud. 1. 7, 9, Is. 1. 11, 28; 37. 3; 64. 10, Ps. 5. 7, Pr. 3. 4.
>
> *Rem. 3.* The periphrastic construction is used: (1) When it is wished to preserve the indefiniteness of A, 1 S. 16. 18 (above); 17. 8, 1 K. 2. 39, Gen. 41. 12, Nu. 25. 14, Song 8. 1. Similarly the so-called לְ of authorship, Hab. 3. 1 and traditionally the common לְדָוִד (psalm) *of, by David*, unless this means *for* the davidic king, *authorised by* or the like, as in Ps. 42. 1 לַמְנַצֵּחַ *for* the choirmaster, לִבְנֵי־קֹרַח *belonging to* (the collection of) the sons of K.

(2) When it is desired to retain for A the somewhat greater distinctiveness given by the Art., Gen. 25. 6; 29. 9; 47. 4, Jud. 6. 25, 1 S. 21. 8, 1 K. 4. 2, 2 K. 5. 9, Ps. 116. 15; 118. 20. (3) When it is necessary to retain a def. designation or expression in its completeness. 1 K. 15. 23 סֵפֶר דִּבְרֵי הַיָּמִים לְמַלְכֵי יה׳ the book of *The Chronicles of the Kings of Judah,* 2 K. 11. 4 *the centurions of,* Ru. 2. 3 *the field-portion of* Boaz (but cf. 2 K. 9. 25), Nu. 27. 16; 30. 2, Gen. 41. 43, Jos. 19. 51, 2 S. 2. 8, 2 Chr. 8. 10. (4) For the same reason periphrasis is usual in dates and with numerals. Gen. 7. 11 in the 600th year לְחַיֵּי נֹחַ *of the life* of N., 1. K. 3. 18 בַּיּוֹם הַשְּׁלִישִׁי לְלִדְתִּי *on the third day after I gave birth,* Gen. 16. 3, 1 K. 14. 25, etc. Cf. on dates, § 48c. (5) The suff. may be circumscribed, perhaps with some emphasis. 1 K. 1. 33 הַפִּרְדָּה אֲשֶׁר־לִי *my* mule; cf. *vs.* 38, Ru. 2. 21, Lam. 1. 10, cf. 3. 44. So the curious אִשָּׁה לִי *my* wife (a. w. of mine) 2 Chr. 8. 11. After already suffixed noun, Song 1. 6 כַּרְמִי שֶׁלִּי *my own* vineyard, Ps. 27. 2.

Rem. 4. A noun in appos. with a constr. phrase may be attracted into the constr., 1 S. 28. 7 אֵשֶׁת בַּעֲלַת אוֹב *a woman* possessing an Ob., Deu. 21. 11, Is. 23. 12; 37. 22, Jer. 14. 17. And sometimes a noun in constr. is suspended by being repeated, or by the interposition of a synonym in appos., Gen. 14. 10 *pits,* pits of bitumen, Nu. 3. 47, Jud. 5. 22, 2 S. 20. 19 *the peaceable* (and) *the faithful* in Israel, 2 K. 10. 6, Jer. 46. 9, Ps. 78. 9, Job 20. 17, Dan. 11. 14.

Nominal Coordination

§ 37. Coordination between nouns (or their equivalents) is, as between verbs, nearly always achieved through *Vav.* Hebr. possesses very few other coordinators (§ 38), and sometimes even their functions are usurped by *Vav* - or, to put it more accurately, their functions may be sufficiently fulfilled by the context and it left to *Vav* to provide a non-committal coordinator. When *Vav* joins a number of nouns or phrases, it is usually repeated before each, Gen. 20. 14 צֹאן וּבָקָר וַעֲבָדִים וּשְׁפָחֹת sheep *and* cattle *and* male *and* female slaves; 24. 35, Deu. 12. 18; 14. 5, Hos. 2. 21 (prep. phrases), 24, Jer. 42. 1. But sometimes it is used only before the last, as in Engl., Gen. 5. 32; or the last two or more, Deu. 18. 10, 11; or only before the second, Ps. 45. 9; or the words are disposed in pairs, Hos. 2. 7. These occurrences are hardly enough to establish patterns.

The form וָ is often used when the first syllable of the following word is stressed, Gen. 19. 19 וָמַתִּי *and* I die; but particularly when such a word is the second of a related pair, Ex. 2. 12 כֹּה וָכֹה *this way and* that; 10. 8

מִי וָמִי *who* (among them)?, Deu. 25. 13 אֶבֶן וָאֶבֶן *two different weights;*
32. 7 דּוֹר וָדוֹר *many generations* (Ps. 10. 6; 100. 5), Gen. 1. 2 (waste *and*
void); 2. 19 (good *and* evil); 14. 19 (heaven *and* earth); 31. 44 (I *and* you),
1 K. 21. 13 (God *and* king).

In some cases *Vav* has *explanatory* rather than coordinating force,
with a certain emphasis on the word it explains, Ps. 74. 11 your hand *and*
(*even*) *your right hand;* 85. 9 to his people *and to his saints*, Zech. 9. 9 *and*
(*namely*) *on a colt.* Often with the specifying sense *and that*, Am. 3. 11 a
foe *and that* round about; 4. 10 *and that* into your nostrils. Is. 57. 11, Jer.
15. 13, 1 Chr. 9. 27. Cf. 2 S. 13. 20 וְשֹׁמֵמָה (*and that*) desolate, Ps. 68. 10
וְנִלְאָה (*and it*) languishing, Lam. 3. 26 וְדוּמָם *and that* (in) silence.

For the various ways in which *Vav* coordinates verbs (clauses) see
§ 84ff. and references there.

§ 38. For specific purposes other conjunctions are used, notably to
express inclusion, exclusion and disjunction.

(*a*) The chief *inclusive* conjunction is גַּם. It may be used with the
second of two or the last in a series of nouns (or equivalent), Gen. 6. 4 in
these days וְגַם אַחֲרֵי־כֵן and *also* afterwards; 7. 3 take with you ... גַּם
מֵעוֹף הַשָּׁמַיִם שִׁבְעָה שִׁבְעָה *also* of the birds of the air seven pairs. Or
more often attached to each, Gen. 24. 25 גַּם־תֶּבֶן גַּם־מִסְפּוֹא *both* straw
and provender; 43. 8. Jud. 8. 2, 1 S. 2. 26 גַּם עִם־י' וְגַם עִם־אֲנָשִׁים *both*
with Y. *and* with men. Other exx. of גַּם ... גַּם: Gen. 44. 16; 47. 3, 19, Nu.
18. 3, Zeph. 2. 14. The use of two coordinators, גַּם ... וְגַם or וְגַם, is less
usual and strictly speaking redundant, unless two clauses are being linked
(see below). The combination וְ ... וְ is used in the same sense but, though
translated *both ... and* in Engl., it is simply conjunctive in Hebr., Ps.
76. 7 וְרֶכֶב וָסוּס *both* chariot and *horse.* Nu. 9. 14, Jer. 32. 20, Job 34. 29.
When influenced by a *negative*, this *both ... and* becomes *neither ... nor*,
but again any disjunctive sense is carried in the phrase as a whole, not by
גַּם. 1 S. 21. 9 גַּם־חַרְבִּי וְגַם כֵּלַי *neither* my sword *nor* my weapons;
20. 27, 1 K. 3. 26.

Sometimes the parts of an inclusive phrase are distributed over two
clauses. Gen. 4. 4 Cain brought ... וְהֶבֶל הֵבִיא גַם־הוּא and Abel *also*
brought; Gen. 32. 20 he commanded the first ... and he commanded גַּם
אֶת־הַשֵּׁנִי *also* the second. In these two exx. גַּם coordinates the subj. or

obj. and *Vav* separately coordinates the clauses. Ps. 84. 4. But in other
cases the inclusive meaning extends to the verb, Gen. 24. 44 גַּם־אַתָּה
you *yourself* drink וְגַם לִגְמַלֶּיךָ and I will *also* draw for your camels; 3. 6;
29. 27; 32. 21. This usage is strictly speaking interclausal, as it is when
occasionally גַּם precedes a verb, Is. 44. 12. See further on inclusive
coordination of clauses § 43.

The conjunction אַף may also precede nouns and phrases or verbs,
but it does not link nouns in an inclusive series, nor is אַף ... אַף found
in the sense of *both ... and*. It mostly (as either אַף or וְאַף) occurs in the
second of two clauses and behaves similarly to גַּם or וְגַם. Gen. 40. 16
אַף־אֲנִי בַּחֲלוֹמִי I *also* (had a dream and) in my dream. Deu. 15. 17, Jud.
5. 29. אַף is commoner before verbs than גַּם.

Neither גַּם nor אַף may be used with suff. but only with the full
pron. (§ 1*d*). Gen. 26. 21 וַיָּרִיבוּ גַּם־עָלֶיהָ and they *also* quarrelled over
it; 27. 34. Deu. 2. 20 אַף־הוּא it *also* is considered. Sometimes גַּם may be
translated *I for my part, in my turn* rather than *also*, though it is the
context not the conjunction that supplies the idea of correspondence
with a previous statement, Hos. 4. 6 because you have forgotten ... *I for
my part* (גַּם־אֲנִי) will forget. Ez. 5. 8, 11, Pr. 1. 26. So גַּם and אַף when
they seem to add emphasis (*even, indeed*) to the second of two
statements. Before noun etc., Hos. 7. 9 (גַּם), Lev. 26. 39 (אַף). Or more
commonly verb, Is. 47. 3 (גַּם); 41. 10 (אַף). In a number of cases where
there is no obvious connection with anything said previously גַּם and אַף
are properly regarded not as conjunctions but as adverbs or (before a
noun) adnominal qualifiers. Gen. 27. 33, 2 S. 17. 10, Is. 44. 12, Ps. 16. 6,
Job 14. 3.

(*b*) The chief *exclusive* coordinating conjunctions are רַק and אַךְ.
These exclude at phrase (nominal) level, Gen. 47. 22 the land became
Pharaoh's ... רַק אַדְמַת הַכֹּהֲנִים *only* the land of the priests he did not
buy; 14. 24. Gen. 20. 12 she is the daughter of my father אַךְ לֹא *but* not
the d. of my mother. In Gen. 7. 23 the exclusive phrase is spread over
two clauses: they were blotted out from the earth וַיִּשָּׁאֶר אַךְ־נֹחַ and *only*
N. was left. Or they exclude at clause level, Gen. 19. 8 (רַק), Ex. 12. 16
(אַךְ). There is sometimes ambiguity; in Deu. 12. 16 רַק הַדָּם לֹא תֹאכֵלוּ
may mean *only* the blood you shall not eat, or *only* you must not eat the
blood. See further on exclusive clauses § 144.

When there is nothing mentioned previously from which exclusion may be made, רַק and אַךְ have a limiting or restrictive effect and are adnominal qualifiers or adverbs rather than conjunctions. Exx. of רַק with noun or similar: Gen. 6. 5 רַק רַע *only, nothing but* evil; 26. 29 רַק־טוֹב; 41. 40 רַק הַכִּסֵּא *only* in respect of the throne will I be greater (or better, *only* I, the throne); 20. 11 (*surely*), 1 K. 8. 9 (with neg., *except*). Exx. of אַךְ: Gen. 18. 32 אַךְ־הַפַּעַם *just* this once; 34. 15 אַךְ־בְּזֹאת *only* on this condition, Ex. 12. 15 (on the *very* first day), Nu. 12. 2 (by Moses *alone*), Deu. 16. 15 (*altogether* joyous), Is. 19. 11 (*utterly* foolish); 36. 5 (*mere* words).

After a *negative* or anything, as a question, implying a neg. the adversative כִּי אִם (cf. Engl. *but*) or the negative בִּלְתִּי are preferred for indicating exclusion, either coordinating clauses or, less frequently, as adnominal qualifiers. As the latter, כִּי אִם Gen. 28. 17 (*nothing other than*), Nu. 26. 35 (*except*), Is. 42. 19 (*but*). בִּלְתִּי: Gen. 21. 26 (*except today*), Ex. 22. 19 (*except* to Y.), 1 S. 2. 2 (*besides you*). The negative בִּלְעֲדֵי is only and the exclusive זוּלָתִי nearly always used with a noun or equivalent: Gen. 41. 44 (*apart from*); Deu. 1. 36 (*with the exception of*). The forms לְבַד מִן ,לְבַד and מִלְּבַד are properly prepositions: Gen. 2. 18 (*alone, by himself*); Ex. 12. 37 (*besides*); Gen. 46. 26 (*not including*).

(c) *Disjunctive* coordination. *Or* is expressed in Hebr. by אוֹ. Linking nouns or phrases, Gen. 24. 49 עַל־יָמִין אוֹ עַל־שְׂמֹאל to the right *or* to the left; 24. 50 רַע אוֹ טוֹב bad *or* good; 44. 8 כֶּסֶף אוֹ זָהָב silver *or* gold. Gen. 44. 19, Ex. 5. 3; 21. 18, 32, 37, Deu. 13. 2, Jud. 21. 22, 1 S. 2. 14. When repeated, אוֹ ... אוֹ is *whether ... or*, Ex. 21. 31 אוֹ־בֶן יִגַּח אוֹ־בַת יִגַּח *whether* it gore a boy *or* a girl, Lev. 5. 2. In the same sense the conditional אִם ... אִם may be used, Ex. 19. 13 אִם בְּהֵמָה אִם אִישׁ לֹא יִחְיֶה *whether* beast *or* man, it shall not live. Deu. 18. 3, 2 S. 15. 21. So אִם ... וְאִם, Jer. 42. 6, Pr. 20. 11. On disjunctive clauses see § 45.

Negative disjunction is expressed by conjunctive *Vav* preceded by a neg., Nu. 23. 19 לֹא אִישׁ אֵל ... וּבֶן־אָדָם God is not a man ... *nor* is he a human being. Gen. 45. 6, Deu. 5. 14, Jud. 6. 4. Or more strongly with inclusive גַם added, 1 S. 16. 8, 9. Clearly the neg. carries the disjunctive weight. Similarly the inclusive גַם ... גַם or the conjunctive וְ ... וְ become disjunctive *neither ... nor* when influenced by neg. (above *a*).

NOMINAL APPOSITION

§ 39. Apposition relates nouns more closely than coordination. It places together two nouns which agree for definiteness or indefiniteness and are identical or overlapping in reference. The second noun is in apposition to the first and specifies the common or shared relationship. This is usually a relationship of class or material or even quality of the kind alternatively expressed by a constr. phrase (§ 35). For clauses in appos., cf. § 146ff.

Nominal apposition is used more extensively than in Engl., and brings together two nouns as follows —

(*a*) The person or thing and its name. 2 S. 3. 31 הַמֶּלֶךְ דָּוִד (the) *king David;* Nu. 34. 2 הָאָרֶץ כְּנַעַן *the land* (of) *Canaan;* 1 Chr. 5. 9 הַנָּהָר פְּרָת *the river Euphrates,* Gen. 14. 6 בְּהַרֲרָם שֵׂעִיר in *their mountain Seir.* Gen. 24. 4, 1 S. 3. 1, 1 K. 4. 1; 16. 21, 24, Ezr. 8. 21; 9. 1. The order *David the king* also occurs, 2 K. 8. 29, 1 S. 30. 7, Is. 39. 3 as, with *land, river,* etc. does a constr., Nu. 34. 2 אֶרֶץ כְּנַעַן, Gen. 15. 18 נְהַר־פְּרָת.

If the personal name be second the object marker אֵת, if used with the appellative, has to be repeated. Gen. 4. 2 אֶת־אָחִיו אֶת־הֶבֶל *his brother Abel;* 48. 13, Deu. 26. 15. So commonly a prep., Gen. 24. 4 לִבְנִי לְיִצְחָק *to my son Is.;* 21. 10, though exceptions occur, Gen. 24. 12 עִם אֲדֹנִי אַבְרָהָם, 1 S. 25. 19, espec. in the phrase *my, your people Israel,* Deu. 21. 8, etc. On the other hand, there is no repetition of אֵת or prep. with appell. when second. Gen. 16. 3 אֶת־הָגָר שִׁפְחָתָהּ *H. her maid;* 11. 31; 12. 5; 24. 59. Gen. 4. 8 rose up אֶל־הֶבֶל אָחִיו *against A. his brother;* 11. 28.

(*b*) The person or thing and its *class.* 1 K. 7. 14 אִשָּׁה אַלְמָנָה *a widow woman;* 2 K. 9. 4 הַנַּעַר הַנָּבִיא the *young* (man who was the) *prophet* (in question, *vs.* 1); Ex. 24. 5 זְבָחִים שְׁלָמִים *sacrifices* (of) *peace-offerings* (constr. זִבְחֵי שׁ, 29. 28). Deu. 22. 23, 1 S. 2. 13, 2 S. 10. 7. Gen. 21. 20 a *shooter,* a *bowman* may be a case of appos. or, like the indef. מַיִם following הַמַּבּוּל in Gen. 6. 17, of a common noun glossing a rarer one.

(*c*) The thing and its *material.* 2 K. 16. 17 הַבָּקָר הַנְּחֹשֶׁת the *brazen oxen;* Deu. 16. 21 אֲשֵׁרָה כָּל־עֵץ an *Ashera* (of) *any wood;* Ex. 39. 17

הָעֲבֹתֹת הַזָּהָב the *cords* (of) *gold;* Ex. 28. 17 four טוּרִים אֶבֶן *rows* (of) *stones* (constr. 39. 10); 2 Chr. 4. 13 two *rows pomegranates*, Ez. 22. 18, 1 Chr. 15. 19, Zech. 4. 10.

(*d*) The measure or weight, often with a number, and the thing measured or weighed. In certain exx. the phrase containing the measure or weight seems to be made def. by Art. or suffix, but is clearly regarded as sufficiently indef. to admit an indef. noun in appos. to it. 2 K. 7. 1, 16, 18 סְאָה סֹלֶת וְסָאתַיִם שְׂעֹרִים a *seah* (of) *flour* and *two seahs* (of) *barley*, Gen. 18. 6 שְׁלֹשׁ סְאִים קֶמַח סֹלֶת *three seahs* (of) (flour, viz.) *fine flour* (also in appos.), Ru. 2. 17 כְּאֵיפָה שְׂעֹרִים about an *ephah* (of) *barley*. Ex. 29. 40 רְבִעִית הַהִין יַיִן the (a) *fourth of a hin* (of) *wine; ib.* a *tenth* (of an ephah of) *fine flour*, Nu. 15. 4; Ex. 9. 8 מְלֹא חָפְנֵיכֶם פִּיחַ כִּבְשָׁן *handfuls* (lit. fill of the hollow of *your* hands) (of) *ashes from the kiln* (constr.); 16. 33 the (an) *omer* (-full) (of) *manna*, Nu. 22. 18, 1 K. 18. 32, Lev. 6. 13. — Gen. 41. 1 שְׁנָתַיִם יָמִים *two years* (of) *time*, 2 S. 13. 23. 2 S. 24. 13 שֶׁבַע שָׁנִים רָעָב *seven years* (of) *famine; ib. three days* (of) *pestilence*. Gen. 45. 11, 1 Chr. 21. 12. Gen. 29. 14 חֹדֶשׁ יָמִים a *whole month*, Nu. 11. 20, Deu. 21. 13, 2 K. 15. 13. 2 K. 3. 4 100,000 *rams, wool* (fleeces), 1 S. 16. 20 an *ass-load* (of) *bread* (alternatively an *ass laden with b.*). — 1 K. 16. 24 בְּכִכְּרִים כֶּסֶף for *two talents* (of) *silver*, 2 K. 5. 23, cf. *vs.* 17; 1 S. 17. 5.

With different order, Neh. 2. 12 אֲנָשִׁים מְעַט a *few men*, Is. 10. 7; Nu. 9. 20 יָמִים מִסְפָּר *days, a number* (many), 2 S. 8. 8; 24. 24, 1 K. 5. 9. Ex. 27. 16 a *curtain* (of) *twenty cubits.*

(*e*) Even the person or thing and its quality or character. 1 K. 22. 27 לֶחֶם לַחַץ וּמַיִם לַחַץ *bread and water* (of) *affliction*, cf. Is. 30. 20; Ps. 60. 5 יַיִן תַּרְעֵלָה *wine* (of, i.e. causing) *reeling*; Pr. 22. 21 אֲמָרִים אֱמֶת *truthful words* (constr. earlier), Zech. 1. 13, Is. 3. 24 *work* (of) *crisping*, Dan. 8. 13. Ez. 18. 6 אִשָּׁה נִדָּה a *woman* (in her time of) *impurity*. 1 K. 6. 7.

Rem. 1. In cases where a noun without Art. follows a noun which (unlike the exx. in § 39*d*) is patently def. in reference, it is probably used "adverbially" (*in respect of*), e.g. 1 Chr. 28. 18 הַכְּרוּבִים זָהָב *the gold cherubim*, Lev. 6. 3 מִדּוֹ בַד *his linen garment*, Ps. 71. 7 מַחֲסִי עֹז *my strong refuge*, 2 S. 22. 23, Ez. 16. 27, Hab. 3. 8. So Lev. 26. 42 בְּרִיתִי יַעֲקֹב *my covenant with J.*, cf. Is. 28. 18. Distinguish from cases like Ps. 38. 20 שֹׂנְאַי שֶׁקֶר *those wrongfully hating me*; 35. 19; 69. 5; 119. 86, Ez. 13. 22 involving ptcp. or infin., which are properly adverbial.

Rem. 2. The word כֹּל *all* with suff. is often placed in appos., 2 S. 2. 9 יִשְׂרָאֵל כֻּלֹּה Israel *all of it*, 1 K. 22. 28, Is. 9. 8; 14. 29, 31, Jer. 13. 19, Ez. 11. 15; 14. 5; 20. 40, Mic. 2. 12. The archaic form of suff. is common, Is. 15. 3; 16. 7, Jer. 2. 21; 8. 6, 10; 20. 7. — In such phrases as 1 S. 4. 10 וַיָּנֻסוּ אִישׁ לְאֹהָלָיו *each* is in appos. to the verbal subj.; sometimes אִישׁ precedes, Is. 13. 8, 14. For pron. in appos. cf. § 1*c*; § 6, R. 1.

Rem. 3. An anticipative pron. sometimes precedes the subj. or obj., which then stands in appos. to the pron., Ex. 2. 6 וַתִּרְאֵהוּ אֶת־הַיֶּלֶד *and she saw him, the child,* Ez. 10. 3 בְּבֹאוֹ הָאִישׁ *when he came, the man.* Ex. 7. 11; 35. 5, Lev. 13. 57, Josh. 1. 2, 1 K. 21. 13, 2 K. 16. 15, Jer. 31. 1, Ez. 3. 21; 42. 14; 44. 7, Ps. 83. 12, Pr. 5. 22, Song 3. 7, 1 Chr. 5. 26; 9. 22, Ezr. 3. 12; 9. 1, Dan. 11. 11, 27. This usage is common in Aram., and increases with time, but it is not restricted to late passages. See § 150, R. 4.

Rem. 4. When the same word is repeated in appos. *intensity* of various kinds is expressed, e.g. the superl. of adj., 1 S. 2. 3 *very proudly,* Is. 6. 3 *most holy,* Ecc. 7. 24 *very deep.* With nouns Gen. 14. 10, Ex. 8. 10, 2 K. 3. 16, Jud. 5. 22, Joel 4. 14. — With words of time the idea of *continuity,* Deu. 14. 22 שָׁנָה שָׁנָה *year* (by) *year,* though the usage with בְּ is commoner, Deu. 15. 20 שָׁנָה בְשָׁנָה, 1 S. 1. 7, Nu. 24. 1, Jud. 16. 20, 2 K. 17. 4. Cf. Deu. 2. 27 *always* (only) *by the road,* 16. 20 *always justice.* Ex. 23. 30, Deu. 28. 43.

With Numerals the idea of *distribution,* Gen. 7. 2 *seven pairs* (vs. 9 *two* (by) *two*), Jos. 3. 12, Is. 6. 2 (sometimes with *and,* 2 S. 21. 20, 1 Chr. 20. 6). Gen. 32. 17 each flock separately, 2 K. 17. 29.

(When the same word is repeated with *and* the idea of variety is expressed, Deu. 25. 13, 14 *stone and stone* (different weights), Ps. 12. 3, 1 Chr. 12. 34, Pr. 20. 10. The usage is common in later style to express *respective, various, several,* 1 Chr. 28. 14 the *respective services,* vs. 16 the *various tables.* 1 Chr. 26. 13, 2 Chr. 8. 14; 11. 12; 19. 5, etc., Ezr. 10. 14, Neh. 13. 24, Est. 1. 8, 22, and often. With כֹּל prefixed, Est. 2. 11 *every day,* 2 Chr. 11. 12.)

§ 40.

Characteristic of Hebr. is the extension of the appositional construction to nominal clauses. Gen. 11. 1 all the earth had (lit. *was*) שָׂפָה אֶחָת וּדְבָרִים אֲחָדִים *one language and few* (or, the same) *words;* 14. 10 the valley *was pits, pits* (full of pits), Is. 5. 12 whose feasts *are* (replete with) *harp and lyre,* etc., Ps. 45. 9 all your robes *are* (fragrant with) *myrrh,* etc., Ezr. 10. 13 the season *was rains* (rainy). Gen. 13. 10, 2 S. 17. 3, 1 K. 10. 6, Is. 7. 24; 65. 4, Jer. 24. 2; 48. 38, Mic. 5. 4, Ez. 2. 8; 27. 36, Zech. 8. 13, Ps. 10. 5; 19. 10; 25. 10; 55. 22; 92. 9; 109. 4; 110. 3; 111. 7; 120. 7, Pr. 3. 17; 8. 30, Job 3. 4; 5. 24; 8. 9, 2 Chr. 9. 5 (cf. 10. 11).

The Adjective. Comparison

§ 41. The adj. differs from a noun in appos. in describing a state or quality of its accompanying noun which is (broadly speaking) incidental rather than integral to it. But like a noun in appos. or indeed the second member of a constr. relation it follows the noun whose meaning it modifies. Like them it agrees with its accompanying noun for definiteness or indefiniteness but unlike them it also agrees with it in gender and number. Gen. 21. 8 מִשְׁתֶּה גָדוֹל *a great feast;* 20. 9 חֲטָאָה גְדֹלָה *a great sin;* Is. 5. 9 בָּתִּים רַבִּים *many houses;* Deu. 9. 1 עָרִים גְּדֹלֹת *great cities.* Is. 14. 3 הָעֲבֹדָה הַקָּשָׁה *the hard service;* 1 S. 12. 22 שְׁמוֹ הַגָּדוֹל *his great name;* Gen. 41. 7 הַשִּׁבֳּלִים הַדַּקּוֹת *the thin ears of corn;* Is. 8. 7 מֵי הַנָּהָר הָעֲצוּמִים *the mighty waters* of the River. If there be several adj. the concord of all is the same, Is. 27. 1 בְּחַרְבּוֹ הַקָּשָׁה וְהַגְּדוֹלָה וְהַחֲזָקָה with his *sore* and *great* and *strong sword.*

The concord of the adj. when *pred.* is the same as when it is qualificative, except that it is indef. with a def. subject. It usually precedes, most clauses of this type being classifying, 1 K. 2. 38 טוֹב הַדָּבָר *the word is good,* Hos. 9. 7, Jer. 12. 1 צַדִּיק אַתָּה *you are righteous.* But this order is overridden in e.g. a circumst. or adversative clause in which the subj. comes first, Nu. 13. 28 וְהֶעָרִים בְּצֻרוֹת גְּדֹלֹת מְאֹד *now* (or *but*) *the cities are fortified* (and) *very large.* See further Nomin. Cl., § 49.

§ 42. The adj. having no dual is used in *plur.* with dual nouns, Is. 35. 3 בִּרְכַּיִם כֹּשְׁלוֹת *failing knees;* 42. 7 עֵינַיִם עִוְרוֹת *blind eyes,* Ex. 17. 12 וִידֵי מֹשֶׁה כְּבֵדִים *now the hands* of M. were *heavy* (*hand* mas. only here, cf. Ez. 2. 9). Gen. 29. 17, 1 S. 3. 2, Ps. 18. 28; 130. 2, Pr. 6. 17, 18.

With collectives agreement may be grammatical in the *sing.,* or *ad sensum* in the *plur.,* 1 S. 13. 15 הָעָם הַנִּמְצְאִים עִמּוֹ *that people that were present* with him; but in *vs.* 16 הָעָם הַנִּמְצָא. § 25.

With intensive plur. the adj. is usually sing., Is. 19. 4 אֲדֹנִים קָשֶׁה *a harsh master,* Ps. 7. 10 אֱלֹהִים צַדִּיק *O righteous God;* but sometimes plur., Josh. 24. 19 אֱלֹהִים קְדֹשִׁים *a holy God* (cf. plur. verb Gen. 20. 13; 35. 7). So 1 S. 17. 26 א׳ חַיִּים *the living God,* Deu. 5. 23, Jer. 23. 36, but also חַי א׳ 2 K. 19. 4, 16. Cf. *Teraphim* of single image, 1 S. 19. 13, 16; but in Gen. 31. 34 Ter. is treated as plur. § 26, R. 3.

On concord of demons. adj. הוא, זֶה cf. § 6.

Rem. 1 Occasionally the adj. seems to precede the noun, particularly רַב in plur. (sing. Is. 21. 7; 63. 7, Ps. 31. 20; 145. 7) Jer. 16. 16, Ps. 32. 10; 89. 51, Pr. 7. 26; 31. 29, Neh. 9. 28, 1 Chr. 28. 5, probably on the analogy of a numeral. Other cases may be explained as pred., Is. 28. 21 *strange is* his work, or as an element in an appositional construction, Is. 23. 12 *O violated one*, virgin etc.; 53. 11, Jer. 3. 7, 10 *Treacherous*, her sister.

Rem. 2. Sometimes the noun is defined and adj. without the Art. (1) Counting adj. like אֶחָד *one*, אַחֵר *another*, רַבִּים *many* may, on the analogy of numerals, dispense with the Art:, Gen. 42. 19 (Art. *vs.* 33), 1 S. 13. 17, 2 K. 25. 16, Jer. 24. 2, Ez. 10. 9; Gen. 43. 14, Jer. 22. 26; Ez. 39. 27. (2) In some cases an adj. is apparently used "adverbially", specifying a particular condition of the noun, Gen. 37. 2, Nu. 14. 37, 1 S. 2. 23 (Sep. wants), Is. 57. 20, Ez. 4. 13; 34. 12, Hag. 1. 4, Ps. 18. 18; 92. 12. (3) In 2 S. 6. 3 *new cart* may express a single idea (cf. Mic. 2. 7) to which Art. is prefixed. Cf. the formulas אֱלֹהִים חַיִּים, חַי 'א the *living God*.

In other cases the adj. is defined and noun without Art. (1) Phrases with a num. or כֹּל followed by a noun and adj. may be made def. by prefixing Art. to adj. only. Gen. 21. 29; 41. 26, Nu. 11. 25, cf. 2 S. 20. 3, Gen. 1. 21; 9. 10. (2) Certain half-technical terms (§ 31, R. 2) which do not take Art. have Art. on a qualifying adj.; so adj. following *court* (1 K. 7. 12, 2 K. 20. 4 *Qere*, Ez. 40. 28, 31), *gate* (Ez. 9. 2, Zech. 14. 10), *entrance* (Jer. 38. 14). Also following *way* (1 S. 12. 23, Jer. 6. 16, cf. Jud. 21. 19), *day*, particularly ordinals (Gen. 1. 31, Ex. 12. 15; 20. 10, Deu. 5. 14, Lev. 19. 6; 22. 27, cf. Is. 43. 13. (3) Other exx. 1 S. 6. 18; 16. 23, 2 S. 12. 4, 2 K. 20. 13 (Jer. 6. 20, Song 7. 10), Jer. 17. 2 (Ps. 104. 18); 32. 14, Zech. 4. 7, Ps. 62. 4, Neh. 9. 35. (4) With ptcp. Jud. 21. 19, Jer. 27. 3; 46. 16 (Zech. 11. 2).

Rem. 3. When two adj. qualify a *fem.* noun the second is sometimes left in *mas.* (uninflected). 1 K. 19. 11 רוּחַ גְּדוֹלָה וְחָזָק a *great* and *strong* wind, Jer. 20. 9 (1 S. 15. 9). So in nominal clauses a pred. adj. when first may remain uninflected, Ps. 119. 137 יָשָׁר מִשְׁפָּטֶיךָ *upright* are your judgements, cf. *vs.* 155, espec. if it is טוֹב, Jud. 8. 2, Gen. 49. 15, 1 S. 19. 4, 2 K. 5. 12, Ps. 73. 28; 119. 72; 147. 1, Pr. 17. 1; 20. 23.

Rem. 4. The adj. is sometimes used nominally after noun in constr., 2 K. 18. 17 חַיִל כָּבֵד a *great force*, Is. 22. 24 כָּל־כְּלֵי הַקָּטָן all the *smallest vessels*, Song 7. 10 יֵין הַטּוֹב wine *of the best*. Deu. 19. 13; 27. 25, Jer. 22. 17 (cf. 2 K. 24. 4), Nu. 5. 18, 2 K. 25. 9 (Am. 6. 2 ?), Zech. 14. 4, Ps. 73. 10; 74. 15 (cf. Ex. 14. 27); 78. 49; 109. 2, 2 Chr. 4. 10, Ecc. 1. 13; 8. 10. — Other exx. of adj. used nominally, Gen. 30. 35, 37 (exposing *the white*), Deu. 28. 48 (and *nakedness*), Jos. 3. 4 (*a distance*), Jud. 9. 16; 14. 14 (*sweetness*), Jos. 24. 14, 2 K. 10. 15, Jer. 2. 25; 15. 15; 30. 12, Is. 28. 4 (§ 36, R. 1), *vs.* 16, Ps. 111. 8, Job 33. 27. — Conversely the noun may follow a constr. adj. used nominally, often with superlative meaning, Jud. 5. 29 (the *wisest*), Is. 19. 11; 35. 9, Ez. 7. 24; 28. 7.

Ex. 15. 16, 1 S. 16. 7; 17. 40, Jer. 15. 15, Ps. 46. 5; 65. 5.

Rem. 5. The adj. when it expresses the characteristic attribute of a noun is sometimes used instead of it, Is. 24. 23 הַלְּבָנָה the *moon* (*the white*), הַחַמָּה the *sun* (*the hot*); 30. 16 קַל *horse* (*swift*), Jer. 8. 16, Mal. 3. 11 הָאֹכֵל *the eater* (*locust*). Mostly in poetry.

§ 43. *Comparison.* The language possessing no special form, comparison is made (*a*) by the simple form of the adj., followed by prep. מִן, Gen. 3. 1 עָרוּם מִכֹּל חַיַּת הַשָּׂדֶה *more cunning than* all the wild animals; Deu. 11. 23 גּוֹיִם גְּדֹלִים מִכֶּם *nations greater than* you; Hos. 2. 9 כִּי טוֹב לִי אָז מֵעַתָּה *it was better* for me then *than* now; 1 S. 9. 2 גָּבֹהַּ מִכָּל־הָעָם *taller than* any of the people. Jud. 14. 18, 1 S. 24. 18, 2 S. 19. 8. With *better* the subj. is often an infin., Gen. 29. 19, Ps. 118. 8, 9, Pr. 21. 3, 9 (§ 51).

(*b*) By a stative verb and מִן, Gen. 41. 40 אֶגְדַּל מִמֶּךָּ *I will be greater than* you; 29. 30 וַיֶּאֱהַב אֶת־רָחֵל מִלֵּאָה *he loved* R. *more than* L., 2 S. 1. 23 מִנְּשָׁרִים קַלּוּ מֵאֲרָיוֹת גָּבֵרוּ *they were swifter than* eagles and *stronger than* lions. With active verbs, Gen. 19. 9 עַתָּה נָרַע לְךָ מֵהֶם now *will we treat you worse than* them. Gen. 37. 4; 48. 19, Deu. 7. 7, Jud. 2. 19, 1 S. 18. 30, 2 S. 6. 22; 18. 8; 20. 5, 6, 1 K. 5. 10, 11; 10. 23; 14. 9.

§ 44. The *superlative* is expressed by the simple adj. with Art., or in constr. before a noun or pron., 1 S. 17. 14 וְדָוִד הוּא הַקָּטָן and David was *the youngest;* 18. 17 בִּתִּי הַגְּדוֹלָה *my eldest* (*elder*) daughter, Deu. 21. 3. — 2 K. 10. 6 גְּדֹלֵי הָעִיר *the great(est) men* of the city; Jer. 6. 13 מִקְּטַנָּם וְעַד־גְּדוֹלָם from *the least* to *the greatest* of them. Gen. 9. 24; 10. 21; 29. 16; 42. 13; 43. 29, Jud. 6. 15; 15. 2, 1 S. 9. 21, Mic. 7. 4, Jon. 3. 5, 2 Chr. 21. 17, Ps. 45. 13. See also § 42, R. 4. Absolute superlativeness is expressed by מְאֹד *very,* Jud. 3. 17 בָּרִיא מְאֹד *very fat,* Gen. 12. 14; 41. 31, which may be intensified by prep. עַד, 1 K. 1. 4 וְהַנַּעֲרָה יָפָה עַד־מְאֹד (now) the girl was *extremely pretty,* 2 S. 2. 17, Gen. 27. 33; or בִּמְאֹד מְאֹד Ez. 9. 9; or מ' is repeated without prep., Nu. 14. 7.

Rem. 1. The adj. or verb with מִן may often be rendered by *too* or *rather than.* Gen. 18. 14 הֲיִפָּלֵא מֵי' דָּבָר is anything *too hard for* Y.? (Deu. 17. 8, Jer. 32. 17, 27), Jud. 7. 2 רַב מִתָּתִּי *too many for me to give,* 1 K. 8. 64 קָטֹן מֵהָכִיל *too small to contain,* Gen. 4. 13 גָּדוֹל מִנְּשׂוֹא *too great to bear* (or *to forgive*), Is. 49. 6 *too light to be,* Ex. 18. 18, 1 K. 19. 7, Gen. 26. 16; 36. 7, Ru. 1. 12, Hab. 1. 13, Ps. 139. 12 *too dark for you.* So with מְעַט, Is. 7. 13 is wearying men *too little* for you? Nu. 16. 9. — Hos. 6. 6 knowledge of God *rather than burnt offerings;* Ps. 52. 5 evil *rather than good,* Hab. 2. 16, Job 7. 15.

Rem. 2. That an adj. is being used comparatively may have to be deduced from the context, Jud. 9. 2 which is *better* for you? 1 K. 18. 27 cry *more loudly,* cf. *vs.* 26. And sometimes an adj. before מִן is omitted and has to be understood, Is. 10. 10 (greater or more) *than* (those of) *Jerusalem,* Job 11. 17 (clearer) *than noon,* Is. 40. 17; 41. 24, Ps. 62. 10.

Rem. 3. A superl. sense is expressed by joining a noun with its own plur., Gen. 9. 25 a *slave of slaves* (lowest slave), Ex. 26. 33 *holy of holies* (most holy place), Is. 34. 10 *for all eternity,* Ecc. 1. 2 *vanity of vanities,* Jer. 3. 19; 6. 28, Song 1. 1, cf. Deu. 10. 17, 1 K. 8. 27.

Rem. 4. Like the simple adj. the abstract noun in constr. may convey superl. meaning, as טוֹב *the best* (Gen. 45. 18, Is. 1. 19), מֵיטָב *the best* (1 S. 15. 9, 15), מִבְחָר *the choicest* (Ex. 15. 4, Deu. 12. 11), רֵאשִׁית, רֹאשׁ *the chiefest* (Nu. 24. 20, Am. 6. 1, 6).

Rem. 5. A kind of superl. sense is given to a word by connecting it with the divine name (אֵל, אֱלֹהִים, יהוה). Probably the idea was that God originated the thing, or that it belonged to him, and was therefore extraordinary, even godlike; but sometimes the meaning appears to be "in God's estimation", cf. Gen. 10. 9, Acts 7. 20. Gen. 23. 6 נְשִׂיא אֱלֹהִים *a mighty prince,* Ps. 36. 7 כְּהַרְרֵי אֵל *like the great mountains,* Song 8. 6 שַׁלְהֶבֶתְיָה *a most vehement flame,* Jon. 3. 3 עִיר גְּדוֹלָה לֵאלֹהִים *an exceeding great city.* Gen. 30. 8 (*mighty wrestlings*), 1 S. 14. 15 (*a very great panic*), Ps. 68. 16 (*a lofty hill*); 80. 11 (*the mighty cedars*). Not so likely Gen. 1. 2 (NEB *a mighty wind*).

The Numerals

§ 45. The Numeral *one* is mostly an adj., having the usual place and concord (§ 41). 1 S. 2. 34 בְּיוֹם אֶחָד *in one* (a single) *day,* 1 K. 18. 23 הַפָּר הָאֶחָד *the one* ox, Gen. 11. 6 שָׂפָה אַחַת *one speech;* 32. 9 הַמַּחֲנֶה הָאַחַת *the one* company. Occasionally the Art. is lacking in a defin. phrase, § 42, R. 2.

But it may be construed nominally — (*a*) in constr. before plur. noun, Gen. 22. 2 אַחַד הֶהָרִים *one* of the mountains, 2 S. 2. 1, Job 2. 10; (*b*) in constr., but followed by מִן, Gen. 3. 22 אַחַד מִמֶּנּוּ *one* of us; 2. 21, Lev. 13. 2, Nu. 16. 15, 1 S. 9. 3, 1 K. 19. 2; 22. 13, 2 K. 6. 12; 9. 1; less commonly in absol., 1 S. 16. 18 אֶחָד מֵהַנְּעָרִים *one* of the young men; 26. 22, 2 S. 2. 21; (*c*) itself preceded by a sing. noun in constr. (§ 42, R. 4), Lev. 24. 22 מִשְׁפַּט אֶחָד *one* judgement, 2 K. 12. 10, Is. 36. 9.

Rem. 1. On adj. אֶחָד as substitute for indef. Art. see § 28, R. 1. On Deu. 6. 4 see § 49, R. 3. Plur. אֲחָדִים means *few, a few*, Gen. 11. 1; 29. 20.

§ 46. The Cardinals 2 - 10 are nouns, construed with the counted noun either in a constr. or an appositional phrase. Concord in the case of *two* is normal, but the Num. 3 - 10 have the opposite gender to the counted noun; no satisfactory explanation of this peculiarity has yet been given. The counted noun is plur. (very exceptionally sing. coll., 2 K. 22. 1).

(*a*) With *indef.* nouns *two* is more commonly in constr. than in appos. 2 K. 5. 22 שְׁנֵי נְעָרִים *two young men*, Gen. 19. 8; 41. 50, Ex. 25. 12, Deu. 4. 13, Jud. 3. 16, 1 S. 1. 2. 1 K. 3. 16 שְׁתַּיִם נָשִׁים *two women*, Deu. 17. 6, 1 K. 10. 19; 17. 12; 18. 23, 2 K. 2. 24. In the case of 3 - 10 Appos. is the dominant pattern. Gen. 29. 34 שְׁלֹשָׁה בָנִים *three sons.* Deu. 19. 2 שָׁלֹשׁ עָרִים *three cities.* 31. 10 שֶׁבַע שָׁנִים *seven years.* Gen. 30. 20; 45. 23; 47. 2, Deu. 3. 11; 16. 9, 16, Jos. 6. 4; Jud. 9. 34; 16. 8, 1 S. 1. 8; 17. 12, 2 S. 21. 6, 1 K. 7. 4, 30, Job 1. 2. Exceptionally 1 K. 11. 16 שֵׁשֶׁת חֳדָשִׁים *six months.* There are also two general exceptions — (1) With יָמִים *days* the constr. is usual. Jud. 19. 4 שְׁלֹשֶׁת יָמִים *three days*, Gen. 17. 12, Deu. 5. 13; 16. 4, 8, 13, Jos. 1. 11; 6. 3; but cf. 2 K. 2. 17 שְׁלֹשָׁה יָמִים. (2) So before *other* Num., 1 S. 25. 2 שְׁלֹשֶׁת אֲלָפִים *three thousand.* 1 K. 5. 30 שְׁלֹשׁ מֵאוֹת *three hundred.* Jos. 7. 3; 8. 12, Jud. 3. 29; 4. 6, 13; 15. 11, 1 S. 26. 2.

(*b*) With *def.* nouns the Num. is mostly in constr. before the counted noun. Gen. 1. 16 אֶת־שְׁנֵי הַמְּאֹרֹת הַגְּדֹלִים *the two great lights.* 19. 16 שְׁתֵּי בְנֹתָיו *his two daughters.* Deu. 10. 4 עֲשֶׂרֶת הַדְּבָרִים *the ten words.* Jos. 10. 16 חֲמֵשֶׁת הַמְּלָכִים *the five kings.* Jud. 3. 3 חֲמֵשֶׁת סַרְנֵי *the five lords* of the Ph. 1 S. 16. 10 שִׁבְעַת בָּנָיו *his seven sons.* Gen. 40. 12, 18, Nu. 23. 4, Jud. 14. 12; 18. 7, 1 S. 17. 13, 2 S. 21. 22; 23. 16, 1 K. 21. 13, 2 K. 25. 18, Zech. 6. 5. But appos. is found, the Num. lacking Art. (R. 2). 1 S. 17. 14 שְׁלֹשָׁה הַגְּדֹלִים *the three eldest*, Jos. 6. 8, 23; 15. 14, 1 K. 11. 3. Cases like Am. 1. 3, 6, 9 etc. are according to § 29, R. 2. See also § 42, R. 2.

(*c*) The Num. may follow the noun is appos., mostly but not exclusively in late passages. 1 Chr. 12. 39 יָמִים שְׁלוֹשָׁה *three days.* Gen. 32. 15, 16, Nu. 29. 26, 2 K. 25. 16, 1 Chr. 22. 14; 25. 5, 2 Chr. 3. 12; 4. 8, Ezr. 8. 15, Neh. 2. 11, Dan. 1. 5, 12, 15, cf. Jos. 21 *passim. Def.*, 1 K. 7. 27 אֶת־הַמְּכֹנוֹת עֶשֶׂר נְחֹשֶׁת *the ten stands* of bronze (§ 39, R. 1).

Rem. 1. The *gend.* of 3 - 10 is sometimes inexact, in some cases corrected by *Qere*, Gen. 7. 13, Ex. 26. 26, Ez. 7. 2; 45. 3, Job 1. 4, 1 Chr. 3. 20.

Rem. 2. Numerals, whether 2 - 10 or larger, are regarded as sufficiently def. to be able in appos. phrases to dispense with the Art. Cases like Nu. 16. 35, Jos. 4. 4 are quite exceptional. Num. as independent nouns, however, may take Art. 2 S. 23. 23 *the three, the thirty;* Gen. 18. 29 *the forty;* 2 K. 1. 13 *the third fifty; vs.* 14 *the former* (pl.) *fifties;* with suff. *vs.* 9. Gen. 14. 9, Nu. 3. 46, Deu. 19. 9. They may also take suff., especially the units, as שְׁנֵינוּ *we two,* שְׁלָשְׁתָּם *the three of them,* etc. Nu. 12. 4, 1 S. 25. 43, 2 S. 21. 9, Ez. 1. 8, Dan. 1. 17. Cf. 1 K. 3. 18 שְׁתַּיִם אֲנַחְנוּ *we two,* 1 S. 20. 42. Num. followed by אֵלֶּה with Art. Deu. 19. 9; by אֵלֶּה without Art. Gen. 9. 19; 22. 23; in constr. before אֵלֶּה Ex. 21. 11, 2 S. 21. 22, Is. 47. 9.

Rem. 3. The order counted noun - Num. (whether 2 - 10 or larger) increases in later passages, but never completely replaces the order Num. - noun. It should not therefore be taken as a firm feature of Late Hebr. Other factors, e.g. the use of Num. in official lists and documents (and in citations from these) may be involved. The same is probably true of other usages of Num. whose incidence increases in such passages.

Rem. 4. As a rhetorical device in *numerical sayings* a Num. may be joined, with וֹ or more commonly without, to the one above to express an indeterminate number, Engl. *two or three,* etc. Thus with *one* first Deu. 32. 30, Jer. 3. 14, Ps. 62. 12, Job 33. 14; 40. 5; with *two* first 2 K. 9. 32, Is. 17. 6, Hos. 6. 2, Am. 4. 8; with *three* first Jer. 36. 23; Am. 1. 3-15; 2. 1-6; with *four* first Is. 17. 6; with *seven* first Mic. 5. 4, Ecc. 11. 2. Where the saying is more precise and instances are given, these may accord with the smaller Num. (*six ... seven* Job 5. 19-22) or with the larger (*three ... four* Pr. 30. 15-16, 18-19, 21-31; *six ... seven* Pr. 6. 16-19).

§ 47. Cardinals above the units have the counted noun in *plur.* (except collectives, words of time, measure and weight, and certain class nouns, Rem. 1). They stand in appos. and mainly precede their noun - but may follow, espec. in later passages (see § 46, R. 3). When they follow, the counted noun is plur., even though otherwise employed in sing.

(*a*) The *teens* 11 - 19. In these the units *one* and *two* and (against the usage when it is independent) *ten* agree in gend. with the counted noun, whereas 3 - 9 (as when they are independent) take the opposite gender. Gen. 37. 9 אַחַד עָשָׂר כּוֹכָבִים *eleven stars.* 2 S. 9. 10 חֲמִשָּׁה עָשָׂר בָּנִים *fifteen sons.* Jos. 4. 8 שְׁתֵּי־עֶשְׂרֵה אֲבָנִים *twelve stones* (fem.). 2 Chr. 13. 21 שֵׁשׁ עֶשְׂרֵה בָנוֹת *sixteen daughters.* Gen. 32. 23; 42. 13, Ex. 15. 27; 24. 4;

27. 15, Nu. 17. 14; 29. 14, 15, Deu. 1. 23, Jos. 15. 41, Jud. 3. 14, 2 S. 2. 30; 19. 18, 1 K. 18. 31, 2 K. 14. 21.

(b) The *tens* 20 - 90. These are *mas.* plur. forms and are not marked for gender. Jud. 12. 14 אַרְבָּעִים בָּנִים *forty sons.* Gen. 18. 24 חֲמִשִּׁים צַדִּיקִם *fifty righteous.* 32. 16 אֲתֹנֹת עֶשְׂרִים *twenty she-asses.* Gen. 18. 26, 28, Ex. 15. 27; 21. 32, Jud. 1. 7; 8. 30; 10. 4; 12. 14; 14. 11-13, 2 S. 3. 20; 9. 10, 2 K. 2. 16; 10. 1; 13. 7; 15. 20, Ez. 42. 2; 45. 12.

(c) Numbers composed of tens and units are treated as a single number, e.g. *twenty-and-three*, and as they stand in appos. both elements remain in the abs. (cases like 2 K. 2. 24 are exceptional). The gend. of the unit changes in the normal way. Jud. 10. 2 עֶשְׂרִים וְשָׁלֹשׁ שָׁנָה *twenty-three years* (Rem. 1). Espec. but not only in later style the order *three-and-twenty* occurs, as does a tendency, in either order, to repeat the counted noun with each element of the Num. § 46, R. 3.

Jud. 7. 3 עֶשְׂרִים וּשְׁנַיִם אָלֶף *twenty-two thousand* (cf. Rem. 1). Nu. 7. 88 ע׳ וְאַרְבָּעָה פָּרִים *twenty-four oxen.* Dominant order: Nu. 35. 6, Jos. 12. 24; 19. 30; 21. 39, Jud. 10. 3; 20. 15, 35, 46, 2 K. 10. 14, Ez. 11. 1, 1 Chr. 2. 22; 12. 28. Unit first: Gen. 11. 24, Ex. 38. 24, Nu. 3. 39, 43; 26. 22; 31. 38, Jud. 20. 21. Repetition of *year, years*: Gen. 5. 15; 12. 4; 23. 1; 25. 7. Cf. Gen. 5 *passim*, Gen. 11. 13-25. Lev. 12. 4, 5 (repet. of *day, days*), Nu. 31. 32ff. (of *thousand, thousands*)

(d) The usage is the same with מֵאָה *hundred*, מָאתַיִם, מֵאוֹת (all in abs.; constr. מְאַת occasional, Gen. 11. 10); with אֶלֶף *thousand*, אֲלָפַיִם, אֲלָפִים (constr. אַלְפֵי occasional, Ex. 32. 28, Job 1. 3). 1 K. 18. 4 מֵאָה נְבִיאִים *a hundred prophets.* Jud. 15. 4 שְׁלֹשׁ־מֵאוֹת שׁוּעָלִים *three-hundred foxes.* 1 K. 3. 4 אֶלֶף עֹלוֹת *a thousand burnt-offerings.* 2 K. 3. 4 מֵאָה אֶלֶף אֵילִים *a hundred thousand rams.* 2 K. 18. 23 אַלְפַּיִם סוּסִים *two thousand horses.* Exx. of *hundred*: Jud. 7. 22, 1 S. 17. 7; 18. 25; 25. 18; 30. 21, 2 S. 3. 14; 8. 4; 14. 26; 16. 1, 1 K. 7. 20; 10. 17; 11. 3, Jos. 7. 21. Exx. of *thousand*: 1 S. 13. 5; 17. 5, 1 K. 5. 6, Job 42. 12.

Also found is רְבָבָה and (late) רִבּוֹ, רִבּוֹא (fem.) *ten thousand, myriad*: Gen. 24. 60, Jon. 4. 11, Ezr. 2. 64, 1 Chr. 29. 7.

(e) When the expression is def. the Art. usually goes with the counted noun, and the Num. is def. in itself. Jud. 7. 7 שְׁלֹשׁ מֵאוֹת הָאִישׁ *the three hundred men* (Rem. 1). 17. 3 אֶת־אֶלֶף וּמֵאָה הַכֶּסֶף *the eleven hundred* (shekels of) *silver* (Rem. 2). 1 S. 30. 21 מָאתַיִם הָאֲנָשִׁים *the two hundred men.* Cf. § 46, R. 2. Gen. 18. 28, Ex. 26. 19; 36. 24, Jos. 4. 20, Jud. 7. 22; 18. 17, 1 K. 7. 44, 2 Chr. 25. 9.

Rem. 1. Apart from the regular collectives (בָּקָר *cattle*, צֹאן *sheep*, רֶכֶב cavalry, גּוֹלָה *captives*, etc.) many other nouns may be used collectively (or is the usage "adverbial"?) after Num., exceptionally after the units (Ex. 16. 22, 2 K. 8. 17; 22. 1; 25. 17 *Ket.*), much more frequently after the teens, tens and above. See § 21. Among the commonest so used are אֶלֶף *thousand* when preceded by another Num., and words of time, measure and weight: יוֹם *day*, לַיְלָה *night* (as in Gen. 7. 4), חֹדֶשׁ *month* (often plur.), אַמָּה *cubit* (often plur.), the measures כֹּר and בַּת, כִּכָּר *talent* (also plur.), גֵּרָה, שֶׁקֶל (oftenest plur.), etc. Other nouns frequently so used are אִישׁ *man*, נֶפֶשׁ *person*, שֵׁבֶט *tribe.* Rarer exx.: Gen. 33. 19 (unit of money), Ex. 24. 4 (*pillar*), Nu. 35. 6 (*city*), Deu. 7. 9 (*generation*), Jud. 21. 12 (*virgin*), 1 K. 5. 12 (*proverb*); 20. 1, 16 (*king*), Est. 1. 1 (*province*). Usage fluctuates considerably; comp. 1 K. 10. 16 with 17 (*shield, shields*) and 2 K. 2. 16 with 17 (*man, men*). — Adj. and words in appos. attached to such phrases may agree gramm. in sing. (1 S. 22. 18, 1 K. 20. 16) or *ad sensum* in plur. (Jud. 18. 16, 1 K. 1. 5). § 25.

Rem. 2. Words readily understood in expression of weight or measure, as *shekel, ephah*, may be omitted. Gen. 24. 22 עֲשָׂרָה זָהָב *ten* (shekels) *gold.* Gen. 20. 16 אֶלֶף כֶּסֶף *a thousand* (pieces of) *silver.* Ru. 3. 15 שֵׁשׁ שְׂעֹרִים *six* (ephahs) *barley.* Gen. 45. 22, Jud. 17. 10, 1 S. 17. 17 (*loaves*); 21. 4, 1 K. 10. 16 (*talents*).

§ 48. The Ordinals. — (*a*) The ordinals *first - tenth* are adj. and used regularly. Jud. 19. 5 בַּיּוֹם הָרְבִיעִי *on the fourth day.* 2 K. 18. 9 בַּשָּׁנָה הָרְבִיעִית. So always in stating the number of the *month* (cf. *c*), 1 Chr. 27. 2-13.

(*b*) From *eleventh* upwards the Card. numbers do duty for ordinals, and Art. is not generally used with the noun. Deu. 1. 3 בְּאַרְבָּעִים שָׁנָה *in the fortieth year.* 2 K. 25. 27 בִּשְׁנֵים עָשָׂר חֹדֶשׁ *in the twelfth month.* Ex. 16. 1, Deu. 1. 2, 3, 2 K. 25. 27, Jer. 25. 3, 1 Chr. 24. 12-18; 25. 18-31.

(*c*) In stating dates there are some peculiarities. 1. The phrase "of the month" is circumscribed by prep., לַחֹדֶשׁ, and *day* is often omitted. Ex. 16. 1 בַּחֲמִשָּׁה עָשָׂר יוֹם לַחֹדֶשׁ *on the fifteenth day of the month.* 2 K. 25. 27 בְּעֶשְׂרִים וְשִׁבְעָה לַחֹדֶשׁ *on the twenty-seventh of the month.* Even the Card. 1 - 10 are greatly used in this case, mostly with om. of *day.* 2 K. 25. 8 בְּשִׁבְעָה לַחֹדֶשׁ *on the seventh.* Deu. 1. 3 בְּאֶחָד לַחֹדֶשׁ *on the first.* Gen. 8. 5, Lev. 23. 32, Ez. 1. 1, Zech. 7. 1, cf. 2 Chr. 29. 17, Ezr. 3. 6.

2. The word *year* is very often put in the constr. before the whole

phrase, Num. and year. 2 K. 8. 25 בִּשְׁנַת שְׁתֵּים עֶשְׂרֵה שָׁנָה *in the year of twelve years* (the twelfth year), 1 K. 16. 8, 15, 29, 2 K. 8. 25; 14. 23; 15. 13, 17, 23, 27; 25. 8. And with *year* understood: 1 K. 15. 25, 28 בִּשְׁנַת שְׁתַּיִם *in the year of two* (years), 1 K. 16. 10; 22. 41, 2 K. 3. 1; 15. 30, 32; 18. 10; 24. 12, Zech. 7. 7, Ezr. 5. 13, Neh. 1. 1, Dan. 1. 21; 2. 1. Less commonly *year* is in constr. before the def. Ord. (1 - 10). 2 K. 17. 6 בִּשְׁנַת הַתְּשִׁיעִית *in the year of the ninth* (year), 2 K. 25. 1, Jer. 32. 1, Ezr. 7. 8, Neh. 2. 1; 5. 14.

Rem. 1. The Art. seems used with the Num. in cases where the whole expression is def., as Lev. 25. 10, 11, *the fiftieth year* (of jubilee), Deu. 15. 9, 1 K. 19. 19; but occasionally also in other cases falling under *b - c* above: Ex. 12. 18, Nu. 33. 38, 1 K. 6. 38, 1 Chr. 24. 16; 25. 19; 27. 15. Its place varies, cp. 1 K. 19. 19 שְׁנַיִם עָשָׂר with 1 Chr. 25. 19 הַשְּׁנֵים עָשָׂר.

Rem. 2. Distributives. — (*a*) These may be expressed by Card., with לְ *to*: 1 K. 10. 22 אַחַת לְשָׁלֹשׁ שָׁנִים *once to = every three years.* Ex. 16. 22, 1 K. 5. 2, Ez. 1. 6. (*b*) By repeating the Num., Gen. 7. 2, 3, 9, 15, Ex. 17. 12, 1 K. 8. 13, Ez. 40. 10. § 39, R. 4. Very often the whole phrase is repeated, Is. 6. 2 *six wings, six wings to each*, Jos. 3. 12, Nu. 13. 2; 34. 18, Ex. 36. 30.

Rem. 3. Multiplicatives are expressed variously. — Thus: *as much as* you, they, etc., by כָּכֶם, כָּהֶם, 2 S. 24. 3, Jer. 36. 32, Deut. 1. 11. — *Double* by מִשְׁנֶה, used in Appos. either before or after the noun, Gen. 43. 12 (after), *vs.* 15 (before), Ex. 16. 5, 22. Also by שְׁנַיִם, Ex. 22. 3, 6, 8, *twofold.* — By the *du. fem.* of Num., as 2 S. 12. 6 אַרְבַּעְתָּיִם *fourfold.* Gen. 4. 15 שִׁבְעָתַיִם *sevenfold.* Is. 30. 26, Ps. 12. 7. Or by the simple Card., Lev. 26. 21, 24, cf. Gen. 4. 24 — By יָדוֹת (hands), Gen. 43. 34 *fivefold*, Dan. 1. 20 *tenfold.* Cf. Gen. 26. 12 מֵאָה שְׁעָרִים *a hundredfold.*

Times is expressed by פַּעַם (foot). Gen. 2. 23 הַפַּעַם *this time.* Jos. 6. 3 פ' אַחַת *one time.* Neh. 13. 20 וּשְׁתַּיִם פ' *once or twice.* Gen. 27. 36; 43. 10 פַּעֲמַיִם *two times*, Ex. 23. 17 שָׁלֹשׁ פְּעָמִים *three times.* Gen. 33. 3, Nu. 14. 22, Deu. 1. 11, 2 S. 24. 3, 1 K. 22. 16, 2 K. 13. 19, Job 19. 3, Neh. 4. 6. With פַּעַם omitted, 2 K. 6. 10 שְׁתַּיִם, אַחַת *once, twice.* 1 K. 10. 22, Job 40. 5. Also בְּאַחַת, בִּשְׁתַּיִם, 1 S. 18. 21, Job 33. 14, Nu. 10. 4. With similar omission, שֵׁנִית *a second time* (Gen. 41. 5, Is. 11. 11), בַּשְּׁלִישִׁת *a third time* (1 S. 3. 8), בַּשְּׁבִעִית *a seventh time* (1 K. 18. 44). — Other words for *times* are רְגָלִים, מֹנִים; see Lexx.

Rem. 4. Fractions. — Apart from חֲצִי *half*(1 K. 16. 21) fractions are formed: (*a*) by separate words, as רֹבַע (also רֶבַע) *a fourth*, חֹמֶשׁ *a fifth*, עִשָּׂרוֹן *a tenth.* (*b*) By the *fem.* of Ordin. as שְׁלִשִׁית *a third.* Above *tenth* the Card. must be used, Neh. 5. 11. The noun of measure, weight, etc., usually has the Art. after the fraction, § 39*d*.

Nominal Clauses and Subject Complements. Subject Clauses.

§ 49. Nominal clauses in Hebr. link together two nouns or noun-equivalents as subj. and predicate without a copula verb like Engl. *is, was, will be* (the time of the clause is supplied by the context). The term "verbless" is sometimes preferred, but it obscures the fact that such clauses, like phrases linking together two nouns in the constr. relation or by apposition or a noun and adj., belong to the syntax of the noun. There are discernible patterns for the sequence of subj. and pred. in these clauses (Andersen), but they may be countermanded by other patterns, and exceptions are not uncommon.

(*a*) When both subj. and pred. are definite, the subj. precedes the pred. and the clause is one of identification. Gen. 6. 9 אֵלֶּה תּוֹלְדֹת נֹחַ *these* are the generations of N. 27. 22 הַקֹּל קוֹל יַעֲקֹב *the voice* is J.'s voice. Ex. 3. 6 אָנֹכִי אֱלֹהֵי אָבִיךָ *I* am the God of your father. Ps. 74. 12 וֵאלֹהִים מַלְכִּי yet *God* is my king. Pr. 10. 1 וּבֵן כְּסִיל תּוּגַת אִמּוֹ and *a (the) foolish son* is a sorrow to (the sorrow of) his mother. 18. 11 הוֹן עָשִׁיר קִרְיַת עֻזּוֹ *the rich man's wealth* is his strong city. Gen. 26. 29; 28. 17; 31. 43; 39. 9, Ex. 4. 22; 6. 7, Nu. 11. 16, Deu. 4. 6; 10. 17; 19. 4, 1 S. 16. 12, Is. 7. 9, Mic. 7. 6, Ps. 16. 5; 23. 1; 27. 1; 121. 5, Pr. 10. 5; 12. 5; 14. 24; 18. 11, Job 40. 18, etc. With subj. extraposed and resumed by הוּא etc., Gen. 2. 14 וְהַנָּהָר הָרְבִיעִי הוּא פְרָת and *the fourth river* is the Euphrates, Deu. 10.9 י' הוּא נַחֲלָתוֹ *Y.* is his inheritance. Other exx. § 1*b*.

(*b*) When the subj. is def. and the pred. indef., the pred. precedes the subj. and the clause is one of classification. Gen. 7. 2 and of the animals אֲשֶׁר לֹא טְהֹרָה הִוא which are *not clean*. 43. 12 אוּלַי מִשְׁגֶּה הוּא perhaps it was *a mistake*. Lev. 16. 4 בִּגְדֵי־קֹדֶשׁ הֵם they are *holy garments*. Deu. 32. 4 צַדִּיק וְיָשָׁר הוּא he is *just and right*. Jud. 12. 5 הַאֶפְרָתִי אַתָּה are you *an Ephraimite*? Is. 40. 7 אָכֵן חָצִיר הָעָם surely the people are *grass*. Pr. 28. 11 חָכָם בְּעֵינָיו אִישׁ עָשִׁיר a (the) *rich man* is *wise* in his own eyes. Ecc. 7. 3 טוֹב כַּעַס מִשְּׂחֹק sorrow is *better than laughter*. Gen. 2. 18; 42. 11; 47. 13; 49. 9, Ex. 34. 14, Lev. 2. 6; 3. 12, Nu. 13. 19, Deu. 1. 14; 4. 6, 21, Is. 6. 5; 40. 28, Jer. 2. 12, Zeph. 1. 14, Ps. 11. 7; 25. 8, 16; 103. 8; 119. 105, 129, 137, etc. With extraposition and resumption, Nu. 1. 4 אִישׁ רֹאשׁ לְבֵית־אֲבֹתָיו הוּא each (shall be) *head* of his fathers' house, Deu.

32. 4 הַצּוּר תָּמִים פָּעֳלוֹ the Rock, his work is *perfect*. Gen. 34. 21; 49. 20, Lev. 15. 2, 20, Nu. 14. 7, Deu. 4. 24, Jer. 10. 3.

An indef. pred. may include some suffixed nouns and structurally def. constr. phrases, notably where a class or generic noun is involved. Lev. 4. 21 חַטַּאת הַקָּהָל הוּא it is *a sin-offering of the assembly*. Jud. 9. 3 בֶּן־חֲכָמִים אֲנִי בֶּן־מַלְכֵי־ he is *a brother of ours*. Is. 19. 11 אָחִינוּ הוּא I am *a son of wise men, a son of ancient kings*. Ps. 2. 7 בְּנִי אַתָּה קֶדֶם you are *my son* (a son to me). Other exx. § 3, R. 1; § 29, R. 2. Gen. 29. 12, Deu. 23. 8.

(c) There are a number of syntactic structures which override these patterns. Thus a nominal circumstantial clause like all circumstantial clauses has the subj. first, leading to an order contrary to *b* when it is classifying. Gen. 13. 2 וְאַבְרָם כָּבֵד מְאֹד now A. was *very rich*. 14. 18 וְהוּא כֹהֵן לְאֵל עֶלְיוֹן and he was *a priest* of El Elyon. 29. 17 וְעֵינֵי לֵאָה רַכּוֹת now L.'s eyes were *weak*. Gen. 2. 12; 29. 31, Ex. 14. 22; 17. 12, etc. So in the case of a well-formed conjunctive or contrastive sent. in which the subj. comes first in both clauses; this kind of sent. is common in poetry. Ps. 19. 8-10 תּוֹרַת י׳ תְּמִימָה the law of Y. is *perfect*, etc. Pr. 15. 8 זֶבַח רְשָׁעִים תּוֹעֲבַת י׳ וּתְפִלַּת יְשָׁרִים רְצוֹנוֹ the sacrifice of the wicked is *an abomination to Y.*, while (but) the prayer of the righteous is *his delight*. Ex. 15. 6, Is. 1. 23; 5. 28, Jer. 5. 16, Pr. 15. 19, Job 3. 19, etc.

In the second half of a chiastic sent. either the pattern in *a* or that in *b* may be overridden. Job 4. 6 (Qere) הֲלֹא יִרְאָתְךָ כִּסְלָתֶךָ וְתִקְוָתְךָ תֹם דְּרָכֶיךָ is not *your fear* (of God) your confidence, and *the integrity of your ways* your hope? Pr. 20. 23 *an abomination to Y.* are diverse weights וּמֹאזְנֵי מִרְמָה לֹא־טוֹב and false scales are *not good*. 1 S. 17. 33, Is. 5. 7; 48. 4; 55. 8, Nah. 1. 3, Pr. 3. 18; 6. 23; 9. 10; 20. 23.

(d) Pattern *b* is also suspended when the subj. contains כֹּל *all, every*; this nearly always comes first, in classifying as in identifying clauses. Gen. 6. 5 וְכָל־יֵצֶר מַחְשְׁבֹת לִבּוֹ רַק רַע כָּל־הַיּוֹם and (that) every inclination of the thoughts of his heart was only *evil* continually (contrast the previous clause). Is. 40. 6 כָּל־הַבָּשָׂר חָצִיר all flesh is *grass* (contrast vs. 7). Ex. 27. 17, Is. 1. 5, Ps. 96. 5; 119. 86, 151, Pr. 16. 2; 21. 2, Ecc. 1. 8; 2. 17. However, when the phrase with כֹּל is extraposed, normal order obtains with the resumptive pron., Gen. 42. 11.

Pattern *b* seems to be further disrupted when the pred. is a participle with verbal force; this generally follows its subj. Clearly its ability to take an obj. marks it off from, e.g. an adjective, and for that reason it may have been judged unsuitable to take part in the distinction between identifying and classifying. For exx. see § 113*b*. However, a ptcp. may have nominal force and as such occur in normal initial position as pred. of a classifying clause. Gen. 42. 9 מְרַגְּלִים אַתֶּם you are *spies; vs.* 34. Jud. 15. 11 כִּי־מֹשְׁלִים בָּנוּ פְּלִשְׁתִּים that the Ph. are *rulers* over us. Possibly 1 S. 3. 13 (*blasphemers*), though the text is suspicious. In constr. phrase, Gen. 22. 12, Pr. 14. 2 (*fearer of God, Y.*).

(*e*) No preferred sequence is evident when pred. is a numeral or adverb (properly "adnominal") or prep. phrase. Compare Ex. 27. 12 with Gen. 6. 15; 1 S. 19. 3 with Gen. 2. 12; Nu. 2. 17 with 16. 3. However, partitive phrases with מִן always precede the subj., Ex. 2. 6 מִיַּלְדֵי הָעִבְרִים זֶה this is *one of the Hebrews' children.*

> *Rem. 1.* Mediaeval Arab grammarians distinguished as verbal, clauses beginning with a verb and as nominal, those which, whether or not they contained a verb, began with a noun; and some scholars interested in syntax above the sentence have adopted this distinction in their treatment of Hebr. usage. There is much to be said for it. A verbal clause emphasizes what is being done, a "nominal" clause of either kind who or what is involved in the action; and such clauses may have different roles in an extended text, as most clearly in prose narrative (see § 58*b*) where clauses beginning with *Vav* cons. YIQTOL carry the story line and clauses beginning with a noun introduce a new participant, draw attention to a circumstance affecting a person, place, object, etc. But at the level of the clause itself the distinction is not so useful; there relationships between noun and noun and noun and verb have to be analysed, and "nominal" clauses with a verb have perforce to be treated separately from those which, as in this sect., lack a verb.
>
> *Rem. 2.* Interr. and precative nominal clauses have their own peculiarities. In interr. nominal clauses מִי and מָה are pred., as is made clear where a reply is given; yet they always occupy initial position, though in the answering clauses the corresponding pred. has the position proper to an identifying or classifying clause. For question with identifying answer cf. Gen. 27. 32, Zech. 2. 2 and for question with classifying answer cf. Gen. 47. 3; 48. 8-9. (After interr. הֲ normal word order is maintained, cf. Jud. 12. 5 in *b* above).
>
> In prec. clauses the sequence is the opposite of the sequence in corresponding declarative clauses. Thus in the verbal kind with a ptcp., the ptcp. as pred. comes first (cf. בָּרוּךְ *blessed be* in Gen. 14. 19, Deu. 28. 3; אָרוּר

cursed be in Gen. 3. 14; 9. 25), while in a prec. nominal clause proper, which is usually classifying, it is the subj. noun which comes first (cf. Deu. 33. 22 in contrast with Gen. 49. 9; the former context is of blessing, the latter of prophecy).

Rem. 3. In a number of cases a proper name seems to be pred., as in an identifying clause with subj. containing שֵׁם *name;* the name is in effect the information supplied. Gen. 11. 29 שֵׁם אֵשֶׁת־אַבְרָם שָׂרָי the name of A.'s wife was *S.* 2. 11, 13, 14, 1 S. 1. 1-2, Ru. 1. 2-4, etc. So in a classifying clause in a contrastive sentence, Ex. 9. 27 הַצַּדִּיק י׳ the one in the right is *Y.* (cf. the next clause).

Probably יהוה is pred. in Deu. 6. 4, Is. 33. 22 (our God, judge, etc. is *Y.*), though the sequence is the opposite of what is expected in an identifying clause. The second part of Deu. 6. 4 may be a classifying clause (Y. is *one*); if it is, the sequence is acceptable, אֶחָד being a numeral, but as in the first part the sequence may be abnormal if Gen. 41. 25 is taken as a parallel. Other more certain cases of abnormal order involving יהוה are Ex. 15. 3 (first clause; Y. is *a man of war*) and Nu. 14. 18, Nah. 1. 3 (Y. is *slow to anger*) (contrast Ex. 34. 6, Ps. 103. 8, etc.); and, with שְׁמְךָ *your name* in second place, Ex. 15. 3 (second clause), Am. 4. 13; 9. 6, etc. It is significant that all of these utterances either reflect or may be assumed to derive from liturgical usage, and this may be the reason for the changed word order. A fuller syntactical examination of liturgical language is clearly called for.

However it is interpreted, Deu. 6. 4 poses difficulties. The traditional rendering *The Lord our God is one Lord* is put into question if it is translated more literally, *Y. our God is one Y* (unless it is Y. who dwells in the Temple over against, e.g. *Y. of Samaria* in the Kuntillet el-Ajrud inscrs.). The second part, taken (see above) as an independent clause, may be thought to show too theoretical an interest in monotheism for early OT times. My own preference is for taking it as an appos. phrase, with אֶחָד having an "adnominal" function similar to לְבַדּוֹ *only, alone* elsewhere (2 K. 19. 15, Is. 37. 16, Neh. 9. 6; cf. Matt. 4. 10, citing Deu. 6. 13). This is an unparalleled usage, but it at least emphasizes Y.'s exclusive right to Israel's allegiance, a matter more relevant to OT thought than his oneness: *Our God is Y., Y. alone.*

Rem. 4. The normal negative in nomin. clauses is לֹא, placed first in the clause, Ex. 4. 10 לֹא אִישׁ דְּבָרִים אָנֹכִי I am *not* an eloquent man. Gen. 37. 13, Ex. 14. 12, Deu. 22. 2, 1 S. 2. 24.

§ 50. *Subject Complements.* When the verb הָיָה is used the nominal part of the pred. may be called the subj. complement. Thus when הָיָה is used statively, Gen. 42. 11 לֹא־הָיוּ עֲבָדֶיךָ מְרַגְּלִים your servants are not *spies.* In past narrative, 3. 1 וְהַנָּחָשׁ הָיָה עָרוּם now the serpent was *cunning.* As an indicative future, 9. 25 עֶבֶד עֲבָדִים יִהְיֶה *a slave of slaves* shall he be. As a juss., I. 3 יְהִי אוֹר let there be *light*.

In other verbal clauses what would in a nominal clause be the pred. may serve as a complement qualifying either the subj. or the obj. For this "adnominal" usage along with an obj. (e.g. Gen. 3. 8) see § 92. Exx. of subject complement, Gen. 15. 2 וְאָנֹכִי הוֹלֵךְ עֲרִירִי seeing I go *childless;* 38. 11 שְׁבִי אַלְמָנָה remain *a widow;* Ru. 1. 21 אֲנִי מְלֵאָה הָלַכְתִּי I went (away) *full* (note obj. complement in next clause). Gen. 25. 8, 25; 37. 35, Deu. 3. 18, Jos. 1. 14, 1 S. 19. 20, 1 K. 22. 10, 2 K. 18. 37, Am. 2. 14, Jer. 31. 8, Job 1. 21; 24. 5, 10; 27. 19, Ps. 109. 7. Possibly Job 19. 25 stand (as) *last*. Obj. complements become subj. complements when the verb is passive. Deu. 4. 27 וְנִשְׁאַרְתֶּם מְתֵי מִסְפָּר and you shall be left *few in number*. 24. 7 כִּי יִמָּצֵא אִישׁ גֹּנֵב if a man is found *stealing*. Pr. 17. 28 even a fool who keeps silent חָכָם יֵחָשֵׁב is considered *wise*. Gen. 31. 15, Ex. 22. 3, Deu. 21. 1; 22. 22, Jer. 33. 11, Pr. 27. 14, Est. 6. 2, Dan. 1. 15, Ezr. 9. 15.

§ 51. *Subject clauses.* Clauses may replace nouns. Relative clauses (with or without אֲשֶׁר) are strictly speaking in appos. to their antecedent; or they may form with it a constr. relation; or they may contain the antecedent (*he who, that which*, etc.) and be themselves the subj. or obj. of another clause or follow a prep. See further § 9-13. Clauses beginning with כִּי or אֲשֶׁר *that* are similarly nominal in function. They are common as the obj. of verbs of saying, seeing, remembering, etc. (see § 90), less common as the subj. of a nominal clause. With pred. *good, better*, Lam. 3. 27 טוֹב לַגֶּבֶר כִּי יִשָּׂא עֹל בִּנְעוּרָיו it is good for a man *that he bear the yoke in his youth*, 2 S. 18. 3, Ecc. 5. 4. As pred., Gen. 6. 15 זֶה אֲשֶׁר תַּעֲשֶׂה אֹתָהּ this is *how you are to make it*. As subj. of passive verb, 1 S. 23. 13. So, with ellipsis, in cases like אַף כִּי, *furthermore* (it is a fact) *that, so much the more* (*less*), etc.; see § 116c and under Inclusive Clauses.

Quasi-Verbal Nominal Clauses

§ 52. Clauses with the construct nouns יֵשׁ, אַיִן and עוֹד and with the demons. particle הִנֵּה are basically nominal in their structure, but show some features which may almost be described as verbal.

יֵשׁ and אַיִן form a constr. relation with a following noun and are used either, as in a straightforward nomin. clause, as subj. to a non-verbal or participial pred. or absolutely in the sense *there is, is not*. When a suffix is attached, however, it takes the form used with verbs as though regarded almost as an obj. (see § 3, R. 2); and both words may be separated from their nouns and so become equivalent almost to a verb. The time reference, as in normal nomin. clauses, is taken from the context. Clauses with יֵשׁ or אֵין differ from these in being concerned not so much to identify or classify the subj. as to assert or deny its existence, presence, relevance, etc.

Thus with pred. following, Gen. 28. 16 אָכֵן יֵשׁ י' בַּמָּקוֹם הַזֶּה *surely Y. is in this place*. 43. 4; 44. 26. Gen. 20. 11 רַק אֵין־יִרְאַת א' בַּמָּקוֹם הַזֶּה only *there is no fear of God in this place*. 37. 29 אֵין־יוֹסֵף בַּבּוֹר Jos. *was not in the pit*. 39. 11; 41. 8, Nu. 14. 42, Jud. 21. 25. When a pers. pron. is subj., it appears as suffix; a following verb is usually ptcp., Gen. 24. 42 אִם־יֶשְׁךָ־נָּא מַצְלִיחַ דַּרְכִּי if now *you will* prosper my way; Jud. 6. 36. Ex. 5. 10 אֵינֶנִּי נֹתֵן לָכֶם תֶּבֶן *I will not give you straw*; 2 K. 17. 26 יֹדְעִים אֵינָם *they do not know*. Gen. 20. 7; 31. 2; 39. 9, Jud. 3. 25, Jer. 14. 12.

Used absolutely, Gen. 18. 24 אוּלַי יֵשׁ חֲמִשִּׁים צַדִּיקִם *perhaps there are fifty righteous people*. 42. 1, 2 S. 9. 1, 1 K. 8. 10, Is. 44. 8, Ru. 3. 12. Common in aphorisms, Ecc. 6. 1 יֵשׁ רָעָה *there is* an evil which I have seen. Pr. 11. 24; 12. 18; 13. 7, 23; 14. 12, Ecc. 2. 21; 4. 8; 7. 15. יֵשׁ לְ *to have*, Gen. 33. 9, 1 S. 17. 46, Job 14. 7. Ex. 2. 12 and he saw that אֵין אִישׁ *there was no-one*; Gen. 2. 5 וְאָדָם אַיִן and *there was no one* to till (in appos.). Gen. 42. 13, Nu. 21. 5, 1 K. 20. 40, 2 K. 19. 3. אֵין לְ, Gen. 11. 30, Nu. 27. 9, Deu. 22. 27, Lam. 1. 2.

Detached, in any position in the clause. Gen. 43. 7 הֲיֵשׁ לָכֶם אָח *do you have* a brother?; 1 S. 21. 5 כִּי־אִם־לֶחֶם קֹדֶשׁ יֵשׁ but *there is* holy bread. 20. 8. Gen. 40. 8 וּפֹתֵר אֵין אֹתוֹ and *there is no* interpreter of it. 37. 24; 47. 13, Jer. 8. 22; 30. 13, Mic. 7. 2 וְיָשָׁר בָּאָדָם אָיִן and one upright among men *there is not*.

Rem. 1. On the use of יֵשׁ and אֵין as gerundives followed by לְ with infin., *is (not) to be, must (not) be done*, see § 108. On בְּאֵין *for want of, without*, מֵאֵין *from lack of, without* see Lex.

§ 53. עוֹד is, like יֵשׁ and אֵין, properly a noun in the constr. state, though it is in Engl. usually translated adverbially. It can be used to qualify a nominal phrase, or be attached to the subj. of a nomin. clause, or operate independently along with a verb as in effect an adverb. It usually, but not always, takes verbal suffixes. It expresses variously the ideas of continuance (*still*), of addition (*yet, more*), of repetition (*again*), even of exclusion (*besides*).

Continuance: Gen. 18. 22 וְאַבְרָהָם עוֹדֶנּוּ עֹמֵד and Abr. was *still* standing. 29. 7; 43. 7; 44. 14, Ex. 4.18, Nu. 9. 13, Jud. 8. 20, 1 S. 13. 7, 1 K. 22. 46, Is. 5. 25. Addition: Gen. 7. 4 לְיָמִים עוֹד שִׁבְעָה after *yet* seven days; Ex. 2. 3 וְלֹא־יָכְלָה עוֹד הַצְּפִינוֹ and (when) she could *no longer* hide him; 17. 46 עוֹד מְעַט *yet a little while*. Gen. 8. 22, Is. 10. 25; 49. 20, Jer. 10. 20, Ps. 42. 6, Ru. 1. 14. Repetition: Gen. 4. 25 וַיֵּדַע אָדָם עוֹד and Adam *again* knew his wife. 18. 29; 24. 20, Ex. 3. 15, Deu. 13. 17, Jer. 32. 15. Exclusion: Deu. 4. 39 אֵין עוֹד there is none *besides*. 1 S. 16. 11, 2 K. 4. 6, Is. 45. 5; 47. 8, Ecc. 12. 9.

> *Rem. 1.* עוֹד may take the prepp. בְּ and מִן. Gen. 25. 6 בְּעוֹדֶנּוּ חַי *while* he was *yet* alive; 40. 13 בְּעוֹד שְׁלֹשֶׁת יָמִים *within* three days. With nomin. suff., Ps. 104. 33 בְּעוֹדִי *as long as* I live; Gen. 48. 15 מֵעוֹדִי *ever since I was*, i.e. all my life. § 3, R. 2.

§ 54. הִנֵּה (shortened form הֵן) has both demonstr. and exclamatory force. Its quasi-imper. function is recognised by the Engl. transl. *behold* (and this may explain its partial use of verbal suffixes); but properly it is not inviting someone to look so much as drawing attention to the presence of a person or object. With only a suff. attached it is used as in effect an exclamation; thus הִנֵּנִי (Gen. 22. 1) means *here I am!* and not *look at me*; Rem. 1. It is also an exclamation when on its own it introduces a clause beginning with a verb, calling attention to a whole situation rather than a single person or thing; Rem. 2. But its most characteristic use is, with following noun or suffix, to focus attention on the subj. of a nominal or participial clause as he or it has been or is or is about to become involved in some situation or action. In all its usages there is a strong nuance of immediacy or surprise or at any rate of importance or significance.

Thus in pres. contexts, Gen. 20. 3 הִנְּךָ מֵת *behold, you* are a dead man; 27. 11 הֵן עֵשָׂו אָחִי אִישׁ שָׂעִיר *behold, my brother E.* is a hairy man. Deu. 1. 10, Ps. 139. 8, Job 2. 6. Sometimes the indep. pron. is used, Gen. 24. 13 הִנֵּה אָנֹכִי נִצָּב *behold, I* am standing. Ru. 3. 2. And sometimes הִנֵּה

is used on its own, the pron. being understood, Gen. 18. 9 הִנֵּה בָאֹהֶל *behold* (she) is in the tent.

In past contexts, Ex. 2. 6 וְהִנֵּה־נַעַר בֹּכֶה and *behold, the child* was weeping. Gen. 15. 12; 18. 2, Deu. 9. 13, Jud. 9. 43. In dream reports, Gen. 40. 9; 41. 3, Jer. 18. 3. A subj. suff. is often understood, Gen. 24. 30; 37. 15, 1 K. 19. 5.

In fut. contexts, Is. 7. 14 הִנֵּה הָעַלְמָה הָרָה וְיֹלֶדֶת *behold, a young woman* shall conceive and bear a son; Am. 4. 2 הִנֵּה יָמִים בָּאִים *behold, days* are coming. Ex. 4. 23; 32. 34, Is. 13. 17; 43. 19, Jer. 11. 22.

> *Rem. 1.* Exx. of exclamatory phrases: Gen. 12. 19; 27. 1, Ex. 24. 8, Nu. 14. 40, 1 S. 3. 4, 2 S. 15. 26, Job 38. 35. הֵן is not used with suffixes:
>
> *Rem. 2.* הִנֵּה and הֵן often introduce a circumstance or action in past or present, on which a request, proposal, intention, course of action, conclusion etc. is founded. Before a noun or suff. they are still focussing attention on a person or thing and therefore functioning nominally. Is. 6. 8 הִנְנִי שְׁלָחֵנִי *here am I*, send me; Ex. 6. 30 הֵן אֲנִי עֲרַל שְׂפָתַיִם *behold, I* am of uncirumcised lips; how then, etc.? Gen. 11. 6; 29. 11, Ex. 1. 9, Nu. 23. 9, 24, 1 K. 22. 13, Is. 50. 11, Job 25. 5. Presumably this is also the case when the subj. comes first in a verbal clause, Gen. 3. 22 הֵן הָאָדָם הָיָה *behold, the man* has become like one of us, and now, lest, etc. Ex. 6. 12, Is. 40. 15. But when הִנֵּה or הֵן precede a verb (or an adverbial phrase followed by a verb), they emphasize the whole clause and are simply exclamatory. 2 K. 5. 20 הִנֵּה חָשַׂךְ אֲדֹנִי *see, my master* has spared this N. the Syrian ... I will run after him. Gen. 15. 3; 19. 34, Nu. 17. 27, Is. 42. 9; 50. 1, Job 9. 11-12 (YIQTOL). (On other occasions, of course, הִנֵּה or הֵן with a verb simply introduce an announcement; with performative QATAL, Gen. 1. 29; 17. 20; with YIQTOL, Is. 41. 11; 50. 2, Ps. 68. 34).
>
> *Rem. 3.* On הִנֵּה as a syntactic marker in extended discourse or narrative see § 72, R. 4, § 80.

Syntax of the Verb and its Object

——•——

The Conjugations

§ 55. The two verbal conjugations of Hebr., traditionally called perfect and imperfect but in this volume identified simply by QATAL and YIQTOL, mark distinctions of *aspect*, not of tense. They do not locate a situation or event *in* time, but view it in its relation *to* time. Thus QATAL (the perf.) identifies a situation or event as static or at rest, YIQTOL (the impf.) as fluid or in motion. It is left to the context to indicate by various means, e.g. an adverb of time, whether the situation or event is past, present or future. The expression of mood as distinct from aspect comes within the sphere of YIQTOL, sometimes involving modified forms (cohortative, jussive, imperative). There is also in each conjugation a special form used with *Vav* to express a succession of situations or events *over* time (the so-called conversive or consecutive constructions).

> *Rem. 1.* The distinction being advanced here is in essence one between states and actions. This is a broader distinction than that between perfect and imperfect or, as linguists prefer to say nowadays, perfective and imperfective. It also cuts across that distinction, since sometimes states may be imperfective and actions perfective. Patently, therefore, the terms perfect and imperfect ought to be abandoned as misleading.
>
> *Rem. 2.* The Engl. verbal system is very different from the Hebr. and it is always necessary to remember that translations are only approximations. Thus Engl. possesses, like Hebr., aspect and mood but, unlike Hebr., it also possesses tense (*come, came*); and indeed it cannot express aspect and mood without bringing in tense as well (*have, had come; is, was coming; may, might come*, etc.). In all translations into Engl. there are therefore bound to be indications of tense present which do not belong to the Hebr. verbal forms but are taken over by the translator from their context.

The QATAL Conjugation

§ 56. QATAL denotes states, whether natural or arising from some action; and it denotes actions which are in effect treated as states since they occur in contexts that are static and independent (non-contingent).

§ 57. In the present time frame characteristic of prose discourse and poetry QATAL is used -

(*a*) As a stative category in the strict sense to describe a physical or mental condition, as *to be, be like, be clothed with, be full of, be high, great, small, deep, clean, be young, old, be many,* etc.; *to know, remember, refuse, trust, rejoice, hate, love, desire, hope, be angry, just, good,* etc. As in other languages, some stative verbs may take an object, direct or otherwise.

Exx., Gen. 4. 6 לָמָּה חָרָה לָךְ why *are you angry* (lit. *is it hot* to you)? 27. 2 זָקַנְתִּי לֹא יָדַעְתִּי יוֹם מוֹתִי *I am old, I do not know* the day of my death. Jud. 14. 16 רַק שְׂנֵאתַנִי וְלֹא אֲהַבְתָּנִי *you only hate me, and do not love me.* Ps. 3. 2 מָה־רַבּוּ צָרָי how many are my foes! 104.1 גָּדַלְתָּ מְאֹד *you are* very *great.* Is. 1. 15 יְדֵיכֶם דָּמִים מָלֵאוּ your hands *are full of* blood. Rem. 1.

(*b*) Chiefly in the 1st pers., to describe the formal execution or performance of a number of actions involving blessing, swearing, worshipping, promising, bargaining or the like; the speaker is in effect viewed as in the state of doing the action. Deu. 26. 3 הִגַּדְתִּי הַיּוֹם *I profess* this day; 2 S. 17. 11 כִּי יָעַצְתִּי but *my counsel is.* 19. 8 בַּיהוה נִשְׁבַּעְתִּי *I swear* by the Lord. 24. 23 הַכֹּל נָתַן אֲרַוְנָה all (this) A. *gives* to the king. 2 K. 9. 3 מְשַׁחְתִּיךָ לְמֶלֶךְ *I anoint you* king. Is. 42. 1 נָתַתִּי רוּחִי עָלָיו *I (will) put* my spirit upon him. Ps. 2. 7 הַיּוֹם יְלִדְתִּיךָ this day *I beget you.* 129. 8 בֵּרַכְנוּ אֶתְכֶם *we bless you.* Gen. 9. 13; 14. 22; 15. 18; 22. 16; 23. 11, 13, Nu. 14. 20, Deu. 4. 26; 30. 15, 18, 19, 1 S. 17. 10, 2 S. 16. 4; 19. 30, 1 K. 2. 42; 3. 13, Is. 43. 3, Jer. 22. 5; 42. 19, Ez. 36. 7, Ps. 130. 1, Job 7. 16, Song 2. 7.

In a report, Ru. 4. 3 מָכְרָה נָעֳמִי N. *is selling* (it). In a letter ("epistolary perf."), 1 K. 15. 19 הִנֵּה שָׁלַחְתִּי לָךְ see, *I am sending* you. 2 K. 5. 6, 2 Chr. 2. 2.

(*c*) Largely in poetry, to describe a number of actions which are tantamount to states in that they occur in non-specific, i.e. typical or recurrent situations. Such QATALs often accompany stative QATALs (*a*

above), and are often interspersed among YIQTOLs and ptcps. which
also in the context express present meaning. Ps. 1. 1, 2 blessed is the man
who *does not walk* (לֹא הָלַךְ) ... *does not stand* (לֹא עָמַד) ... *does not sit*
(לֹא יָשָׁב), but ... on his law *he meditates* (יֶהְגֶּה) day and night. 2. 1 why
do the nations *rage* (רָגְשׁוּ) and the peoples *plot* (יֶהְגּוּ) in vain? 84. 4
גַּם־צִפּוֹר מָצְאָה even the sparrow *finds* a house. Jer. 8. 7 even the stork
in the heavens *knows* (יָדְעָה) her times, and the turtledove etc. *keep*
(שָׁמְרוּ) the time of their coming. Job 7. 9 כָּלָה עָנָן (as) the cloud *fades*.
Ps. 10. 3, 13, 14; 14. 2-3; 33. 10; 37. 14; 40. 5; 46. 7; 65. 10, 12; 90. 5-9;
97. 6-9; 103. 10-13; 111. 4-5, Pr. 1. 7; 3. 13; 14. 19; 30. 15-16, 20; 31. 13ff., Job
3. 17-18; 6. 19-21; 14. 11-12; 24. 10; 28. 3-11, Is. 40. 7-8; 57. 1, Jer. 14. 2-6.

(*d*) Very commonly in a role similar to that of the Engl. present
perf., to express the idea of a person having previously done some action
or, to put it more broadly, to denote a present state flowing from a past
action. Sometimes Engl. prefers to translate with a past tense,
emphasizing the pastness of the action rather than its effect; but this is
not a Hebr. usage. Gen. 3. 11 מִי הִגִּיד לְךָ *who* (*has*) *told* you? 4. 6
לָמָה נָפְלוּ פָנֶיךָ why *has* (*is*) your face *fallen*? 18. 15 לֹא צָחַקְתִּי *I did not
laugh*. Is. 1. 4 עָזְבוּ אֶת־יי *they have forsaken* Y. 40. 21 ... הֲלֹא הֻגַּד
הֲבִינוֹתֶם *has it not been told ... have you not understood*? Job 1. 20 naked *I
came forth* (יָצָתִי) ... Y. *gave* (נָתַן) and Y. *has taken away* (לָקָח). Gen.
4. 10; 12. 18; 26. 22; 46. 31, Ex. 5. 14, Nu. 22. 34, Jud. 10. 10; 11. 7, 1 S.
12. 3; 14. 29, Is. 14. 5; 23. 8-9; 49. 14, Jer. 12. 7; 20. 7. In subord. clauses,
Gen. 3. 12 הָאִשָּׁה אֲשֶׁר נָתַתָּה the woman whom *you gave*. 3. 14 כִּי עָשִׂיתָ
זֹאת because *you have done* this. 22. 12 וְלֹא חָשַׂכְתָּ seeing *you have not
withheld* your son. 1 S. 12. 5 Y. is witness ... כִּי לֹא מְצָאתֶם that *you have
not found* anything in my hand. Is. 14. 24 וְכַאֲשֶׁר יָעַצְתִּי and (that) as *I
have counselled*, it shall stand. Gen. 6. 7; 37. 6; 45. 4; 48. 9, Is. 8. 5; 31. 6;
44. 1, Jer. 9. 21; 20. 17, Dan. 10. 12, Neh. 5. 19. Impersonal use, Jud.
19. 30 לֹא־נִהְיְתָה וְלֹא־נִרְאָתָה such a thing *has never happened* or *been
seen*. Ecc. 1. 9.

In some passages in poetry Engl. may translate this QATAL with a
present tense, implying that the state-cum-action is still going on. This is
in fact a common enough implication of the usage as a whole, cf. above
Is. 1. 4; 40. 21, etc. In the passages we are concerned with the implication
is given expression in Engl. because the QATAL (like that in *c*) often

dovetails with stative QATALs and with present YIQTOLs. Cf. Ps. 102 where a series of such QATALs in *vss.* 9-10 is preceded in *vss.* 6-8 by a series of statives; and note particularly כָּל־הַיּוֹם (*vs.* 9). Ps. 22. 13 many bulls *surround me* (סְבָבוּנִי) ... *encircle me* (כִּתְּרוּנִי). 26. 4-5 *I do not sit* (יָשַׁבְתִּי) ... *I do not go* (אָבוֹא) ... *I hate* (שָׂנֵאתִי) ... *I do not dwell* (אֵשֵׁב). 17. 10-11; 40. 5; 74. 1; 88. 17-19; 109. 2-3; 139. 1-6, Job 3. 25-26; 9. 25-26.

Rem. 1. Exx.of stative QATAL. אבה *be willing*, Deu. 25. 7; אבל *mourn*, Is. 33. 9, Joel 1. 19; אהב *love*, Gen. 22. 2; 27. 4, 9; בטח *trust*, 2 K. 18. 19, 20, Ps. 13. 6; 25. 2; 31. 7; גבה *be high*, Is. 3. 16; 55. 9, Job 25. 5; גדל *be great*, Gen. 19. 13, Ps. 92. 6; 104. 1; דמה *be like*, Is. 1. 19, Ez. 31. 2, 18, Ps. 102. 7; 144. 4, Song 7. 8; היה *be*, Gen. 26. 28; 42. 11, 31; 46. 32, 34, Nu. 19. 18; זקן *be old*, Gen 18. 13; 27. 2, Ru. 1. 12; חסה *take refuge*, Ps. 7. 2; 11. 1; 16. 1; 31. 2; חפץ *be pleased, wish*, Deu. 25. 8, Is. 1. 11, Ps. 40. 9; חרה ל *be angry*, Gen. 4. 6, Jon. 4. 4, 9; טוב *be good*, Nu. 24. 5; טהר *be clean*, Pr. 20. 9; יגע *be tired*, Ps. 6. 7; ידע *know, passim*; יפה *be fair*, Song 7. 2; יחל Hiph. *hope*, Ps. 130. 5; לבש *be clothed with*, Ps. 104. 1; מאן Pi. *refuse*, Ex. 7. 14, Nu. 22. 13, Deu. 25. 7; מאס *despise*, Am. 5. 21, Job 7. 16; מלא *be full of*, Gen. 29. 21, Is. 1. 15; 2. 6, Ps. 104. 24, Pr. 12. 21, Mic. 3. 8; מלך *be king, reign*, 1 S. 12. 14, 1 K. 1. 13, 18, Ps. 47. 9; נאוה *be beautiful*, Is. 52. 7; נקה Niph. *be blameless*, Jud. 15. 3; עלץ *exult*, 1 S. 2. 1; עמק *be deep*, Ps. 92. 6; עצם *be strong, numerous*, Gen. 26. 16, Jer. 5. 6; קוה Pi. *hope*, Gen. 49. 18, Ps. 130. 5; קטן *be small*, Gen. 32. 10; קלל *be light, unimportant, swift*, Jer. 4. 13, Job 7. 6; 40. 4, Niph. 2. K. 20. 10, Is. 49. 6; רבב *be great, many*, Gen. 18. 26, 1 S. 25. 10, Jer. 5. 6, Ps. 3. 2; 104. 4; רום *be high*, 1 S. 2. 1; שבע *be sated with*, Is. 1. 11; שמח *rejoice*, 1 S. 2. 1, Ps. 16. 9; 122. 1, Is. 9. 2; שנא *hate*, Gen. 26. 27, Am. 5. 21, Ps. 5. 6; 31. 7; תאב *long for*, Ps. 119. 40.

Rem. 2. In past contexts, narrative as well as spoken, a stative QATAL tends to adopt the nuance of entering upon the state, Gen. 3. 22 the man *has become* like one of us; 24. 1 Abr. *had become old*; 34. 19 because he *had found delight*, 2 K. 8. 25 Ahaziah *became king*. So in form of VAYYIQTOL, Gen. 21. 8 and the child *grew* (*became great*). In the YIQTOL conjugation the stative verbs naturally take on the various meanings of that conjugation. The stative usages of the verbs in *b* and *c* are of course occasional and do not occur outside the contexts indicated.

Rem. 3. The common phrase כֹּה אָמַר י׳ (Jer. 7. 3, Ez. 2. 4, etc.), though usually translated by Engl. present tense, is prob. not a present stative usage as in *b, c*, but reflects the prophetic consciousness of having received a message from Y.; it belongs under *d*, thus Y. *has said*. In the alternative יֹאמַר י׳ (Is. 1. 11, etc.), which always occurs in parenthesis, the emphasis is on the content of the message as it is being delivered. On the other hand, the phrase מָלַךְ י' (Ps. 93. 1; 96. 10, etc.) is most naturally taken as a stative usage, *Y. is king;* it is dubiously rendered *Y. has become king* (sc. as of now in the liturgy). This use of the Engl. present perf. to describe an action that has *just* taken place is peculiar, and ought not to be transferred to the Hebr. QATAL. The usage belongs to *a* above, as Ps. 2. 7 (RSV wrongly, today *I have begotten* you) belongs to *b*.

Rem. 4. In those passages where QATALs and YIQTOLs or ptcps. seem in Engl. translation to be interchangeable, it should be remembered that it is the context not the verbal form that leads to the use of an Engl. present tense; the verbal forms in Hebr. are not interchangeable but have different aspectual nuances. The QATAL identifies different kinds of states, the YIQTOL and ptcp. different kinds of continuing action. It is even more confusing when Engl. translates some of the exx. under *d* by a past tense; by so doing it removes the QATAL in *d* from the present time frame which in Hebr. it shares with the QATALs in *a-c* and quite obscures, in a way that a rendering by an Engl. present tense does not, its essentially stative function. Incidentally, there is in poetry an overlap between the QATALs in *c* and those in *d*, and some usages in both paragraphs could be reassigned; it depends on how one judges what is general and what is specific.

§ 58. QATAL is used to denote states and actions regarded as states which are set by the context in the past.

(*a*) In non-narrative discourse and poetry this QATAL is variously represented in Engl. The priority of one state of having done to another may be rendered by a pluperf., the Engl. form which has that precise function; but just as often a present perf. is used, relating both states to the present, or a past tense, signifying the past action and ignoring the ensuing state. Thus Is. 53. 6 all we like sheep תָּעִינוּ *have* (or *had*) gone astray; Job 42. 5 שָׁמַעְתִּי I *had* (or *have*) heard of you by the hearing of the ear, but now my eye רָאָתְךָ *has seen* (or *sees*) you; Gen. 3. 11 who *told* (or *has told,* הִגִּיד) you ... *have you eaten* (אָכַלְתָּ) of the tree which I *commanded* you (or *had commanded* you, צִוִּיתִיךָ) not to eat? None of these distinctions is of course carried by the Hebr. form and (where they are there) have to be picked up by the translator from the wider context.

(*b*) In formal prose narrative the past time frame comes with the genre. The stative character of QATAL is represented in Engl. by the pluperf. when the context has it describing an event or situation prior to the time of the narrative. But when it denotes an event or situation contemporary with the time of the narrative, Engl. does not distinguish its similarly stative role from the very different role played by VAYYIQTOL, translating both by a simple past tense. QATAL is not in fact a true narrative form. It is not, as the oft quoted rule implies, an alternative to VAYYIQTOL used when due to the vagaries of word order another word or phrase happens to come between *Vav* and the verb. Rather, VAYYIQTOL carries forward the sequence of events while QATAL marks a pause in that sequence to enable a different kind of statement to be made; and the changed word order is an integral element of that different kind of statement.

The pause in the sequence of events may be small, as when a negative precedes QATAL, Gen. 31. 33 וְלֹא מָצָא but *he did not find* (them). Or much more significant as in the use of circumst. clauses (§ 135) which begin with the subj., usually with, sometimes without *Vav;* by their nature these clauses supply tangential or background information and thus enhance the stative role of QATAL, Gen. 20. 4 וַאֲבִימֶלֶךְ לֹא קָרַב אֵלֶיהָ now Abim. *had not approached* her; Job 1. 1 אִישׁ הָיָה *there was* a man. Gen. 3. 1; 26. 15; 31. 19, 34; 39. 1, 1 S. 9. 15; 25. 21, etc. Circumstantial clauses may also be employed to round off a story or episode, 2 S. 18. 17 וְכָל־יִשְׂרָאֵל נָסוּ and all Israel *fled.* Jud. 4. 3. Or to reidentify a participant after an absence, 2 K. 9. 1 וֶאֱלִישָׁע הַנָּבִיא קָרָא then E. *summoned.* In each case a pause is felt, in the first following, in the second preceding the statement. But see § 137, R. 1. Other clauses beginning with the subj. or the obj. occur in constructions which have as their purpose the expression of non-sequential situations, either simultaneous or contrastive. Gen. 13. 12 אַבְרָם יָשַׁב ... וְלוֹט יָשַׁב A. *dwelt* in the land of Canaan, while (but) Lot *dwelt* among the cities of the valley. With chiasmus, 4. 4-5 וַיִּשַׁע י' אֶל־הֶבֶל ... וְאֶל־קַיִן ... לֹא שָׁעָה Y. had regard to Abel ... but to Cain ... *he had no regard.* 40. 21-22. See further § 138ff.

QATAL occasionally occurs first in a clause, but only if the clause is linked appositionally to the previous clause. Since apposition is a device of restatement or amplification (§ 146) there is normally no advance in the narrative. Gen. 21. 14 וַיִּתֵּן אֶל־הָגָר שָׂם עַל־שִׁכְמָהּ and he gave (it) to H., *he put* (*putting*) it upon her shoulder; 44. 4, 12; 48. 14, etc. With QATAL later in the clause 7. 20; 8. 19, etc.

Finally, QATAL is used in subord. clauses which have by nature the function of qualifying or giving a reason for a previous statement; the narrative is again perceptibly halted. Gen. 2. 8 and he put there the man אֲשֶׁר יָצָר whom *he had formed;* 6. 6 and Y. saw כִּי רַבָּה רָעַת הָאָדָם that the evil of men *was great;* 28. 11 כִּי־בָא הַשֶּׁמֶשׁ for the sun *had gone down.* 18. 8, 33; 19. 28, Nu. 22. 2, 1 S. 6. 19; 28. 20, 1 K. 11. 9, etc.

(*c*) Narrative stretches occur quite often within prose discourse and poetry; but these are reports or reminiscences rather than formal narrative, and do not always follow the conventions in *b*.

In discourse narrative passages are recognised by the use of VAYYIQTOL and they may as in formal narrative preface the sequence of VAYYIQTOLs with a statement of circumstance, Gen. 41. 9-10 אֶת־חֲטָאַי אֲנִי מַזְכִּיר הַיּוֹם פַּרְעֹה קָצַף ...וַיִּתֵּן אֹתִי I remember my faults today; Ph. *was angry* with his servants, and he put me in prison, etc. Deu. 1. 6. But just as often they begin abruptly with the story itself, and with QATAL in initial position. This is not a construction that is permitted in formal narrative but (see § 57*d*) it is found frequently enough in non-narrative contexts in discourse. The initial QATAL in narrative discourse is, it seems, still being related to the present of speaker and audience and still identifies a state of having done. Gen. 42. 30 דִּבֶּר הָאִישׁ ... אֹתָנוּ קְשׁוֹת וַיִּתֵּן the man ... *spoke* roughly to us, and gave us out to be spies. Jud. 11. 15, 2 S. 3. 23; 6. 12; 12. 27, etc. There is little obvious difference when the subject is highlighted and comes first, Gen. 44. 19 אֲדֹנִי שָׁאַל my lord *asked* his servants 42. 10; 47. 1, 2 K. 3. 7. § 137, R. 1.

(*d*) Narratives or episodes within them may in poetry also begin with QATAL, Ps. 107. 4 תָּעוּ בַמִּדְבָּר *they* (*some*) *wandered* in the desert, cf. *vs.* 10; 106. 6. But there it is chiefly conformity to poetic parallelism that is required. The VAYYIQTOL so common in prose narrative is on the whole frugally used; usually the story has to proceed through a succession of discrete verses with within each verse an event described twice. QATALs can occur at the start of a verse, simply omitting *Vav* cons. (asyndeton), almost as though it were introducing a new episode, Ps. 68. 19 עָלִיתָ לַמָּרוֹם *you ascended* on high; 78. 13 בָּקַע יָם *he divided* the sea. Or they can occur at the start of a clause, being therefore in apposition with a previous clause and repeating or amplifying its meaning, Ps. 68. 19 שָׁבִיתָ שֶּׁבִי לָקַחְתָּ מַתָּנוֹת *you led* captives, *you took* gifts. Or they can occur anywhere within a clause and therefore be regarded as contributing to what is, by the nature of parallelism, a static situation, Ps. 68. 19 (לְקַחְתָּ); 78. 25 לֶחֶם אַבִּרִים אָכַל the bread of angels each *ate*, cf. שָׁלַח; *vs.* 24 נָתַן. In other words, nothing in the use of QATAL in poetic narrative removes from it its essentially stative character. If difficulties arise from its collocation in such passages with the (short) YIQTOL with past meaning (§ 62; it is the same YIQTOL that appears in the *Vav* cons. construction), these are difficulties for the Engl. translator rather than the Hebr. audience. Engl. is forced to use a past tense for both and so obscures the aspectual patterning which a Hebr. ear would appreciate. The QATAL catches well the episodic and staccato feel of poetic narrative while, in the (relative) absence of a *Vav* cons. form, the (short) YIQTOL serves to supply it with movement. This patterning, differing from poem to poem, may be studied in Pss. 68, 78, 105, 106, 107 *passim*, etc.

> *Rem. 1.* Asyndeton (simply dispensing with *Vav*) and apposition (properly repeating or amplifying the meaning) are not always easy to distinguish. See the discussion in §§ 146-8.

§ 59. QATAL is used to denote states and actions viewed as states, which the context sets in the future; these usages are naturally, like the present usages in §57, restricted to non-narrative discourse and poetry.

(*a*) In the sense of the Engl. future perf. (which Engl. in fact rarely uses) QATAL indicates that a situation or event, though fut., is prior to another fut. situation or event. Gen. 24. 19 I will draw for your camels also עַד אִם־כִּלּוּ לִשְׁתֹּת until *they* (*shall*) *have done* drinking. 2 S. 5. 24 כִּי אָז יָצָא י׳ for then Y. *has* (*will have*) *gone out* before you. Gen. 28. 15; 48. 6, 1 S. 1. 28, 2 K. 7. 3, Is. 4. 4; 6. 11; 16. 12, Jer. 8. 3, Mic. 5. 2, Ru. 2. 21.

(*b*) More directly related to the speaker's or poet's present, QATAL represents a fut. action not as an action but as a state of doing or having done.

This QATAL may occur in the protasis of a real condition, 2 S. 15. 33 אִם עָבַרְתָּ אִתִּי וְהָיִתָ עָלַי לְמַשָּׂא *if you go on with me*, you shall be a burden to me. Exx. § 121*b*. Or in questions expressing astonishment, incredulity on the like. Gen. 18. 12 after I have grown old הָיְתָה־לִּי עֶדְנָה *shall I have* pleasure? Jud. 9. 9 הֶחֳדַלְתִּי אֶת־דִּשְׁנִי *shall I abandon* my fatness? cf. vss. 11, 13. Gen. 21. 7, Nu. 23. 10, 23, 1 S. 26. 9, 2 K. 20. 9, Jer. 30. 21, Ez. 18. 19, Hab. 2. 18, Ps. 10. 13; 11. 3; 39. 8; 80. 5, Job 12. 9.

It is also found in straight prediction, occasionally in prose discourse but more frequently in poetry, notably prophetic poetry. This "prophetic perf." (as it is traditionally called) preserves its stative nature by being found on its own, or following כִּי or לָכֵן, or being suddenly interjected among fut. YIQTOLs and *Vav* cons. QATALs. Only a few passages are of any length. It may be regarded as injecting a note of permanency into the prediction. Gen. 30. 13 כִּי אִשְּׁרוּנִי בָּנוֹת for the women *will call me happy*. Is. 5. 13 לָכֵן גָּלָה עַמִּי therefore my people *will go into exile*. 9. 1 the people that walk in darkness *will see* (רָאוּ) a great light ... on them *will* the light *shine* (נָגַהּ). *Vs.* 5 כִּי־יֶלֶד יֻלַּד־לָנוּ בֵּן נִתַּן־לָנוּ for a boy *will be born* to us, a son *will be given* to us. Nu. 24. 17, Jud. 15. 3, 2 K. 20. 9, Is. 2. 11; 5. 14; 9. 1-6; 11. 8, 9; 13. 9, 10; 14. 24; 28. 2; 35. 2, 6; 43. 14; 46. 13; 47. 9; 52. 15; 60. 4, Jer. 4. 29; 31. 5, 6, Hos. 4. 6; 5. 5; 10. 7, Ps. 6. 9, 10; 20. 7, 9; 22. 30; 37. 38; 85. 11, 12, Job 5. 20, 23.

> *Rem. 1.* The term "prophetic perf." is simply descriptive, but not the terms "perf. of certainty" or "confidence". These terms presuppose the older view of QATAL as denoting completed action which is then due to the will or imagination of the speaker or poet exceptionally transferred to the future; but it is an ordinary QATAL and it is transferred to the fut. by the context in which it occurs. That the usage is considered unusual, however, is shown by the variations in the cons. forms which follow it in those passages where there is a continuation. It may either be followed by *Vav* cons. YIQTOL (Is. 5. 15; 9. 5, Ps. 22. 30) or *ad sensum* by *Vav* cons. QATAL (Is. 2. 11; 5. 14, Ps. 20. 9). See further § 74, R. 2.

§ 60. QATAL is by its stative character (being in a state of doing or having done) unsuitable for expressing mood or contingency, but it sometimes attracts such nuances from its context.

(*a*) So in the case of כִּי with QATAL following a question or a negative, 1 S. 17. 26 who is this uncircumcised Philistine כִּי חֵרֵף *that he should defy?* Gen. 40. 15 I have done nothing כִּי־שָׂמוּ אֹתִי *that they should put* me in a dungeon. Jud. 8. 6; 9. 28; 18. 23, etc. (In other passages there is not this nuance, Gen. 20. 9; 31. 36, etc.)

(*b*) So in condit. sent. where QATAL may occur in either protasis or (as *Vav* cons.) apodosis, it is the particles אִם and לוּ which impart

respectively real and unreal (irreal) mood. 2 K. 7. 4 ... אִם־אָמַרְנוּ נָבוֹא
וָמַתְנוּ וְאִם־יָשַׁבְנוּ פֹה וָמָתְנוּ if *we say*, Let us go into the city ... *we shall
die*, but if *we stay* here ... *we shall* (also) *die*. Jud. 13. 23 לוּ חָפֵץ לַהֲמִיתֵנוּ
לֹא־לָקַח ... עֹלָה if *he had meant* to kill us *he would not have accepted* a
burnt offering. Cf. also cases like Gen. 26. 10 כִּמְעַט שָׁכַב אַחַד הָעָם one
of the people *might* easily *have lain* with your wife. 2 K. 13. 19. See
further § 122, R. 1.

(c) So also in hypothetical wishes with לוּ, whether directed at past
or future. Nu. 14. 2 לוּ־מַתְנוּ בְּאֶרֶץ מ׳ *would we had died* in the land of
Eg.! Is. 63. 19 לוּא קָרַעְתָּ שָׁמַיִם *o that you would rend* the heavens! And
so presumably in the case of the so-called "precative perf.", which is
restricted to poetry and occurs in passages where a translation as though
it were a juss. or an imper. is either demanded or makes better sense. It is
not uncommon in prayers and appeals in Pss., Lam., very rare elsewhere.
In 3rd pers., Ps. 67. 7 אֶרֶץ נָתְנָה יְבוּלָהּ *let* the earth *yield* its increase, cf.
vss. 6, 8; 10. 16; 67. 6; 107. 42; 109. 28; 129. 4, Lam. 1. 21. Elsewhere, Is.
43. 9 and possibly Job 21. 16; 22. 18. In 2nd pers., Ps. 4. 2 when I am in
distress הִרְחַבְתָּ לִּי *do you give me room*, cf. previous line. If the QATAL
in Lam. 3. 55 (קָרָאתִי) is performative (see § 57b, and cf. Ps. 17. 6; 130. 1)
I call on your name, then שָׁמַעְתָּ in vs. 56 is prec., *do listen to* my voice,
and אַל־תַּעְלֵם *do not close* your ear, follows naturally, as do the prec.
QATALs in vss. 57-61 (*come near*, etc.; note the imper. שָׁפְטָה *judge* my
cause, vs. 59). Ps. 3. 8; 7. 7; 25. 11; 31. 6; 56. 9; 60. 6; 61. 6 (with emphatic
כִּי); 85. 2-4 (?); 119. 21; 140. 8. A unique example in prose is probably
Gen. 40. 14 כִּי אִם־זְכַרְתַּנִי only *do you remember* me.

Rem. 1. The great majority of the above exx. of prec. QATAL are linked
appositionally to an imper. or juss. or to another prec. QATAL. Only in four
cases are they followed by *Vav* with a verb, in Ps. 109. 28 by *Vav* cons.
YIQTOL, in Is. 43. 9 and Lam. 1. 21 by ordinary *Vav* with YIQTOL (juss.),
and in Gen. 40. 14 by *Vav* cons. QATAL (exceptionally with enclitic נָא־).
There is a similar uncertainty about what follows in the case of the proph.
QATAL (§ 59, R. 1).

Some of the exx. cited are not as convincing as others; Ps. 85. 2-4 may
have past reference; in Ps. 10. 16 the QATAL may be proph. as apparently in
vs. 17 or, alternatively, the three QATALs in vs. 17 may be prec.; in Ps. 25. 11
the QATAL is itself preceded by *Vav* and may be an unusual instance of *Vav*
cons. QATAL, though in its context it still has volitive force. The latter

remark is important and is worth stressing; neither the prec. QATAL nor the *Vav* cons. QATAL nor for that matter the proph. QATAL carries future or volitive meaning within itself but derives such meaning from the verbs with which it collocates or from other markers in the context.

The YIQTOL Conjugation

§ 61. The YIQTOL (traditionally, imperfect) conjugation denotes actions and processes as opposed to states and is the appropriate conjugation for expressing various kinds of mood and contingency. There is evidence in some verbal paradigms of two discrete forms, a shorter expressing (1) simple action and (2) the "jussive" mood, and a longer expressing (1) extended action or process and (2) the "future" and associated moods. In most paradigms, however, these two forms have merged, and even in the paradigms which retain them the long form commonly replaces the short. This can often make it difficult in passages which lack a surviving short form or a helpful context to be sure whether a merged YIQTOL form has a nuance properly carried by the short form or one properly carried by the long.

> *Rem. 1.* On the unsuitability of the term "imperfect" see § 55, R. 1. The YIQTOLs which have shortened forms occur in the Hiph. of "regular" verbs, in verbs medially and finally "weak" (קוּם ,שׂים; גלה), and in geminate verbs (סבב).

§ 62. The (short) YIQTOL denotes simple action, i.e. action which is not viewed as iterative or progressive. It is widespread (as *Vav* cons. YIQTOL) in past narrative contexts, but is also found in poetry in the other two time settings.

(*a*) In prose narrative this YIQTOL is (with a few possible exceptions, Rem. 1) restricted to the position immediately following *Vav* (i.e. VAYYIQTOL). In narrative poetry, however, the parallelistic structure does not favour the use of cons. forms and the (short) YIQTOL is found on its own in any position in a verse or line. QATAL too (§ 58*d*) is used more freely in poetic than in prose narrative. Both QATAL and (short) YIQTOL are usually translated by an Engl. past tense but are *not* simple alternatives, but have different aspectual nuances; the QATAL marks the episodic nature of poetic narrative, while the (short) YIQTOL sustains as it can (as, when it is used, does the *Vav* cons. YIQTOL) its forward movement.

That the narrative YIQTOL in poetry goes back to an original short YIQTOL is shown by the frequent use of shortened forms where these exist; and most clearly by some chance variations in the narrative portions in the two versions of the same poem in 2 S. 22 and Ps. 18. Thus *vs.* 12 in 2 S. 22 וַיָּשֶׁת and in Ps. 18 יָשֶׁת (*and*) *he made* darkness his covering; *vs.* 14 in 2 S. 22 יַרְעֵם and in Ps. 18 וַיִּרְעֵם (*and*) *he thundered*. Cf. *vs.* 7 in 2 S. 22 וַיִּשְׁמַע and in Ps. 18 יִשְׁמַע. In this particular poem there are about the same number of *Vav* cons. and free standing YIQTOL forms, and about half that number of QATALs. There are similar series of (short) YIQTOLs interspersed in varying measures among *Vav* cons. YIQTOLs and QATALs in Ex. 15. 4-10 (note *vs.* 5 יְכַסְיֻמוּ the deeps *covered them*, *vs.* 10 כִּסָּמוֹ the sea *covered them*); Deu. 32. 8-20 (note *vs.* 8 יַצֵּב *he fixed*, *vs.* 18 the rock which bore you תֶּשִׁי *you forgot*); Ps. 44. 10-15; 68. 8-15 (note *vs.* 15 תַּשְׁלֵג *it snowed* on Zalmon); 74. 3-8, 12-15; 78 *passim* (note *vs.* 26 יַסַּע, *vs.* 52 וַיַּסַּע (*and*) *he led out*); 104. 6-9; 107 *passim* (note *vs.* 29 יָקֵם *he turned* storm into silence).

Some of the unshortened YIQTOLs in these poems may be frequentatives, and this has often been argued; but it is not enough to do this on semantic grounds. Thus a good candidate would be Ps. 78. 14 which speaks of leading the people in daytime by cloud and at night by fire; but the verb is *Vav* cons. YIQTOL, וַיַּנְחֵם. There is in fact no reason to doubt that the actions described are narrative actions and that the time they last is not in these contexts relevant; nor for that matter is it possible to see them as other than perfective in aspect. We should presumably regard in the same light the YIQTOLs in other narrative passages, e.g. Ps. 80. 9-13; 116. 3-4; Hab. 3. 3ff.; Job 4. 12-16, etc. And indeed in other past contexts, e.g. Job 3. 3 cursed be the day אִוָּלֶד בּוֹ *on which I was born*; 15. 7, 8, Is. 51. 2, etc. There is a whole area here which has scarcely begun to be investigated.

A rare surviving example in prose seems to be provided by Jud. 2. 1 אַעֲלֶה אֶתְכֶם *I brought you up* from Eg.; the form is long YIQTOL, but it is followed by *Vav* cons. YIQTOL. Cf. (with simple *Vav*) Dan. 8. 12 וַתַּשְׁלֵךְ *and it cast* truth to the ground.

(*b*) There are a number of short YIQTOLs from the relevant

paradigms in poetic passages set in present and in future time, about which it is not so easy to be sure. Perhaps they hint at a wider distinction in present contexts in general between simple action and extended action forms, and in future contexts between an indicative (short) YIQTOL (i.e. with non-jussive meaning) and an indicative (long) YIQTOL. But unlike the usage in *a*, which is parallelled in prose by the *Vav* cons. YIQTOL, these usages are not represented in prose, where the field is dominated by the (long) YIQTOL. This matter too requires further investigation. Rem. 2.

Rem. 1. The conjunct. אָז *then, at that time*, often and the adv. טֶרֶם *not yet* and the conjuncts. בְּטֶרֶם, טֶרֶם *before* nearly always take YIQTOL.

אָז with YIQTOL is restricted to prose narrative, but it does not indicate sequence; rather it points to something taking place at the time of the narrative. It may also be followed by QATAL, but this usage is found in poetry as well as prose and often has a sequential role. Otherwise there seems little difference between the two usages other than the expected aspectual nuance. It has been argued that the YIQTOL is iterative (*used to*) or ingressive (*began to*); but though either of these senses may be possible in some instances (e.g. Ex. 15. 1 אָז יָשִׁיר *at that time* Moses *used to, began to sing*) they are both excluded in many others (e.g. Deu. 4. 41 אָז יַבְדִּיל *at that time* Moses *set apart* three cities; Jos. 8. 30 אָז יִבְנֶה *at that time* Joshua *built* an altar); and in any case an ingressive sense is only definitely attested for the YIQTOL of stative verbs, § 57, R. 2. It would seem most reasonable to conclude, in spite of the long forms just quoted, that the usage is perfective, as it is in the case of the QATAL, and that the form is properly the (short) YIQTOL - as indeed it is in one instance, 1 K. 8. 1 אָז יַקְהֵל *at that time* Solomon *assembled* (2 Chr. 5. 2 אָז יַקְהֵיל). Other exx. of YIQTOL, Nu. 21. 17, Jos. 10. 12; 22. 1; 1 K. 3. 16; 9. 11; 11. 7 (יִבְנֶה); 16. 21; 2 K. 8. 22 (2 Chr. 21. 10). Exx. of QATAL, Gen. 4. 26 אָז הוּחַל *at that time it was begun* (*men began*), Jud. 8. 3 אָז רָפְתָה *then* their anger *was abated*, Ex. 4. 26, Jos. 10. 33. In narrative poetry, Gen. 49. 4, Ex. 15. 15, Jud. 5. 11, 19. In non-narrative contexts, Jos. 22. 31, Ps. 119. 92, Ecc. 2. 15.

On the other hand, as conjuncts. with YIQTOL, טֶרֶם once and בְּטֶרֶם frequently occur in a present - fut. context, in poetry as well as prose, Is. 65. 24 וְהָיָה טֶרֶם יִקְרָאוּ and *before they cry*, I shall answer, Gen. 45. 28 that I may see him בְּטֶרֶם אָמוּת *before I die*. Gen. 27. 4, Ex. 1. 19, Deu. 31. 21, 1 S. 9. 13, Is. 7. 16; 8. 4, etc. It is therefore probably a conditioned usage when this is transferred to a past context, Ex. 12. 34 the people took their dough טֶרֶם יֶחְמָץ *before it was leavened*, Jer. 1. 5 וּבְטֶרֶם תֵּצֵא *and before you came out* of the womb. Gen. 24. 45, Ex. 12. 34, Jos. 2. 8; 3. 1, Ps. 119. 67. Gen. 27. 33; 37. 18; 41. 50, Jud. 14. 18, 1 S. 2. 15, Is. 48. 5; 66. 7. This suggests that the adv. טֶרֶם *not yet*, which is only found in narrative prose, should be regarded in a similar light, Gen. 2. 5 וְכָל־שִׂיחַ ... טֶרֶם יִהְיֶה ... טֶרֶם יִצְמָח when *no plant ... was yet* in the earth and *no herb ... had yet sprung up;* 19. 4, Nu. 11. 35, 1 S. 3. 3. The YIQTOL in other words is a normal long YIQTOL as in § 63a.

Rem. 2. Exx. of short YIQTOL in present time, Ps. 90. 3 תָּשֵׁב *you turn* men *back* to destruction, Job 18. 9 a snare יַחֲזֵק *seizes hold* on him. Ps. 11. 6 (יַמְטֵר); 25. 9 (יַדְרֵךְ); 58. 5 (יַאְטֵם); 72. 13 (יָחֹס), Job 17. 2 (תָּלַן); 20. 26 (יְרַע), vs. 28 (יִגֶל); 27. 8 (יֵשֶׁל); 36. 14 (תָּמֹת); 37. 4, 5 (יַרְעֵם); 38. 24 (יָפֵץ); 40. 8 (תָּפֵר), vs. 9 (תַּרְעֵם), Pr. 12. 26 (יָתֵר).

Exx. of short YIQTOL in future time, Gen. 49. 17 יְהִי־דָן נָחָשׁ Dan *shall be* a serpent in the way, Is. 27. 6 in days to come יַשְׁרֵשׁ יַעֲקֹב Jacob *shall take root.* 1 S. 2. 10 (יַרְעֵם), Is. 61. 10 (תָּגֵל), Nah. 3. 11 (תְּהִי), Zech. 9. 5 (תֵּרֶא); 10. 7 (יָגֵל). The exx. in Deu. 28 with its lists of blessings and curses are probably jussives, though rendered by an Engl. fut. tense, vs. 8 (יְצַו), vs. 21 (יַדְבֵּק), vs. 36 (יוֹלֵךְ).

It should also be noted that there are not a few cases in poetry of simple *Vav* followed by either a short or a long YIQTOL; these occur in all three time settings and seem on the whole to have a coordinating rather than a consecutive function. § 79.

§ 63. The (long) YIQTOL expresses actions which are iterative (frequentative), customary or habitual, distributive or, in some cases simply proceeding at a particular point in time. It is found in narrative prose in past contexts and in both prose and poetry in discourses which are set by their context in present time. In both these genres, as in its other usages (§ 64), it resists the initial position in a clause or that immediately following *Vav*, though rather more consistently in prose than in poetry.

(*a*) Of actions iterative, customary, etc. in the past. Gen. 2. 6 וְאֵד עַל־פְּי י' יַעֲלֶה and a mist *used to, would* go up, Nu. 9. 18 יִסְעוּ בְּנֵי יִשְׂרָאֵל וְעַל־פְּי י' יַחֲנוּ at Y.'s command the Israelites *set out* and at Y.'s command *they encamped* (cf. next clause); 1 S. 2. 19 וּמְעִיל קָטֹן תַּעֲשֶׂה־לוֹ אִמּוֹ and a little robe his mother *used to make* for him; Job 1. 5 כָּכָה יַעֲשֶׂה אִיּוֹב כָּל־הַיָּמִים so Job *used to do* regularly; 2 Chr. 9. 21 once every three years תָּבוֹאנָה אֳנִיּוֹת תַּרְשִׁישׁ the ships of T. *came* (home). Gen. 6. 4; 29. 2; 31. 29, Nu. 11. 5, 9, Deu. 2. 11, 20, Jud. 6. 4, 5; 17. 6, 1 S. 1. 5, 7, 2 S. 12. 3, 31; 17. 17; 20. 18, 1 K. 5. 25, 28; 10. 5; 18. 10, 2 K. 4. 8; 13. 20,

1 Chr. 20. 3. With distributive nuance, Gen. 2. 19 וְכֹל אֲשֶׁר יִקְרָא־לוֹ
הָאָדָם and *whatever he called it;* 1 S. 18. 5 בְּכֹל אֲשֶׁר יִשְׁלָחֶנּוּ שָׁאוּל יַשְׂכִּיל
wherever S. sent him he was successful; 13. 17-18; 14. 47, 2 K. 3. 25, Jer.
36. 18. Of an action going on at or around the same time as another
action, 1 S. 1. 10 וַתִּתְפַּלֵּל עַל־י׳ וּבָכֹה תִבְכֶּה and *she prayed to Y.,*
weeping bitterly; Is. 6. 4 and the foundation of the threshold shook
וְהַבַּיִת יִמָּלֵא עָשָׁן ... while the temple *filled up* with smoke. Ex. 8. 20;
21. 36, 2 S. 15. 37; 23. 10, Jer. 52. 7, Ezr. 9. 4, 1 Chr. 11. 8. With negative
verb, Gen. 2. 25 וְלֹא יִתְבּשָׁשׁוּ and *they were not ashamed;* 1 S. 13. 19
וְחָרָשׁ לֹא יִמָּצֵא now a smith *was not (to be) found.* 1 S. 1. 13, 2 S. 2. 28,
1 K. 8. 8, 2 K. 23. 9.

In prose narrative these usages are recognised by the intrusion of a
long YIQTOL form which is not intrinsic to the genre and in the longer
passages by its collocation with *Vav* cons. QATAL; like plain QATAL
they halt the progress of the story. In poetic narrative they are more
difficult to detect because of the frequent presence of other (properly
short) YIQTOLs which are in fact narrative forms (§ 62*a*), but cf. Ps.
42. 5 these things I remember ... כִּי אֶעֱבֹר בַּסָּךְ how *I used to pass along*
in the throng. Jud. 5. 8, 2 S. 1. 22, Ps. 55. 15.

(*b*) Of an even wider range of actions in the present. Thus in
comparisons with כֵּן *so,* כַּאֲשֶׁר *as,* and similar words. Gen. 29. 26 לֹא־
יֵעָשֶׂה כֵן בִּמְקוֹמֵנוּ *it is not so done* in our country; Jud. 7. 5 כַּאֲשֶׁר
יָלֹק הַכֶּלֶב *as a dog laps.* Gen. 50. 3, Ex. 33. 11, Deu. 1. 31, 44; 2. 11, 20;
28. 29, 1 S. 5. 5; 19. 24, 2 S. 5. 8, Am. 3. 7, 12, Ps. 103. 13, Job 7. 2. In
proverbial sayings and general truths, Ex. 23. 8 כִּי הַשֹּׁחַד יְעַוֵּר פִּקְחִים
for a bribe *blinds* the clear-sighted; Pr. 10. 4 וְיַד חָרוּצִים תַּעֲשִׁיר but the
hand of the diligent *brings riches.* Deu. 16. 19, 1 S. 16. 7; 24. 24, 2 S.
11. 25, 1 K. 8. 46, Ps. 1. 3-6; 103. 15-16, Pr. 1. 20-21; 10. 1-3; 12. 2; 13. 5;
15. 1; 26. 20, etc. Of a characteristic or habit, 2 K. 9. 20 כִּי בְשִׁגָּעוֹן יִנְהָג
for *he drives* furiously. Gen. 44. 5, Deu. 10. 17, 1 S. 23. 22, Is. 13. 17, 18.
Here belong many poetic passages describing typical divine, human or
animal conduct; the QATAL in § 57*c* often has a similar meaning and
often occurs in the same passages. Ps. 37. 30 the mouth of the righteous
יֶהְגֶּה חָכְמָה *utters* wisdom, and his tongue תְּדַבֵּר מִשְׁפָּט *speaks* justice;
65. 12 עִטַּרְתָּ (QATAL) *you crown* the year with your bounty וּמַעְגָּלֶיךָ
יִרְעֲפוּן and your chariot tracks *drip* fatness; Job 21. 12 יִשְׂאוּ *they* (the

wicked) *lift up* tambourine and lyre וְיִשְׂמְחוּ and *rejoice* to the sound of the flute; Pr. 6. 8 תָּכִין *she* (the ant) *prepares* her food in summer, אָגְרָה *she stores* her supplies in harvest. Is. 43. 17, Ps. 10 *passim*; 29. 8-9; 73. 5-9; 90. 3-6; 92. 13-15; 103. 15-16; 104. 10-13, Job 8. 11-19; 14. 18-22; 18. 5-20. But also of actions repeated or general over a limited period, 1 K. 22. 8 כִּי לֹא־יִתְנַבֵּא עָלַי טוֹב for he *does not* (never) *prophesy*(ies) good concerning me. Ex. 13. 15; 18. 15-16, 1 S. 9. 6, 2 K. 6. 12.

In poetry, YIQTOL also frequently denotes actions repeated or continued over a longer or shorter period, but these are as often specific as they are general. These usages equate not only with QATALs as in § 57c but with QATALs as in § 57d; it is among them that we should look for surviving instances of the (short) YIQTOL in present fut. time (see § 62b and R. 2). Exx. from prophetic denunciations: Is. 1. 23 the orphan לֹא יִשְׁפֹּטוּ *they do not treat with justice*, and the widow's grievance לֹא־יָבוֹא אֲלֵיהֶם *does not reach* them; Jer. 6. 23 bow and spear יַחֲזִיקוּ *they grasp* ... וְלֹא יְרַחֵמוּ and *they show no mercy*, the sound of them כַּיָּם יֶהֱמֶה is like the *roaring* sea and on horses יִרְכָּבוּ *they ride*. Is. 5. 11-12; 9. 17; 14. 8; 41. 5-7, Jer. 5. 21-22, Hos. 4. 8, 13; 7. 1-3, 14-16, Mic. 3. 11, Nah. 2. 5-6. From descriptions of personal experience: Ps. 16. 10 כִּי לֹא־תַעֲזֹב for *you do not give up* my life to Sheol, לֹא־תִתֵּן *you do not let* your faithful one (*Qere*) see the pit; 138. 7 though I walk in the midst of trouble, תְּחַיֵּנִי *you preserve my life*, against the wrath of my enemies תִּשְׁלַח *you stretch out* your hand וְתוֹשִׁיעֵנִי (§ 85) and your right hand *saves me*. 22. 8, 18-19; 35. 11-12; 50. 19-20; 55. 4-6; 56. 4-7; 83. 3-6; 102. 12, Job 30. 16-22. Also notworthy are addresses to God, as Ps. 28. 1 אֵלֶיךָ יְ' אֶקְרָא to you, O Y., *I cry*; 22. 3; 25. 1; 61. 3; 102. 3; 142. 2-8 (contrast the QATAL in 130. 1; 141. 1, etc.). In other cases (26. 6; 77. 2) it is more likely that the verb is a substitute for cohort.

> *Rem. 1.* Connected with the distributive use of YIQTOL is its use (1) in describing a boundary line and naming its *successive* points, Jos. 16. 8, interchanging sometimes with *Vav* cons. QATAL, 15. 3. Cf. 1 K. 6. 8. (2) In describing the course of an ornamentation, 1 K. 7. 15, 23 *ran round*, 2 Chr. 4. 2. (3) In stating the amount of metal that went to *each* of a class of articles, 1 K. 10. 16, 2 Chr. 9. 15. (4) In describing the quantity which a vessel, etc., contained, 1 K. 7. 26. So the details of collecting and disbursing moneys, 2 K. 12. 12-17. - In 2 K. 8. 29 (9. 15) the preceding plur. *wounds* perhaps distributes the verb *wounded* (QATAL in 2 Chr. 22. 6).

Rem. 2. Allied to *b* above is the use of YIQTOL in poetry to form attributive clauses, descriptive of the subj. or obj. of the clause. § 13. Gen. 49. 27 Benjamin is זְאֵב יִטְרָף *a ravening wolf;* Is. 40. 20 chooses עֵץ לֹא־יִרְקַב *a tree that does (will) not rot;* Hos. 4. 14 עָם לֹא־יָבִין *an undiscerning people* shall come to ruin; Is. 51. 12 man *that dies (mortal* man); Zeph. 3. 17 *a victorious warrior.* Particularly in comparisons, Job 9. 26 כְּנֶשֶׁר יָטוּשׂ *as an eagle swooping;* 7. 2 as a servant *longing.* Deu. 32. 11, Is. 62. 1, Jer. 23. 29. Used adverbially, Is. 30. 14 *unsparingly,* Ps. 26. 1 *without wavering.*

Rem. 3. In questions with *why?* YIQTOL is commonly used of an action that has already occurred, Ex. 2. 13 לָמָּה תַכֶּה רֵעֶךָ why *do you (did you) strike* your fellow? Gen. 32. 30; 44. 7, Ex. 3. 3, 1 S. 1. 8; 17. 8; 28. 16. Engl. knows the same idiom. In questions with *whence? from where?* this is, however, not the the case, though it has been claimed to be. YIQTOL is properly used when the questioner either knows or supposes that the journey is still in progress, and a QATAL when he knows that it is concluded. Thus with QATAL in the question, Gen. 16. 8; 42. 7. With YIQTOL in the question and a ptcp. or similar in the answer, Jud. 17. 9; 19. 17, Job 1. 7. With YIQTOL in the question and, correcting a wrong impression, QATAL in the answer, Jos. 9. 8, 2 S. 1. 3, 2 K. 20. 14.

§ 64. In future time settings YIQTOL expresses both indicative actions and actions which depend on a previous action (contingent) or on the intention or other feelings of the speaker (modal). There is some evidence in poetry of a surviving short YIQTOL with indicative force in such settings (§ 62*b*), but in prose and in most poetry the contrast between simple and extended action seems to be neutralised, with only the long YIQTOL being used indicatively. In non-indicative contexts the aspectual distinction between two kinds of action is not relevant, and the short YIQTOL has a volitive function (jussive), as do the other two special moods formed on YIQTOL base (imper., cohort.); on these see next sect. The long YIQTOL also has some volitive functions but is chiefly used to express, in the appropriate context, the modal and contingent functions not carried by the special moods. As noted in § 63, it differs from these, however, in one important respect, resisting in prose (though not always in poetry) the initial position in a clause which these usually occupy or the position following *Vav* which they share with the *Vav* cons. QATAL.

(*a*) In indicative contexts the (long) YIQTOL expresses the simple future (denoted in Engl. by the auxiliary verbs *will, shall*). The standpoint is mostly that of the speaker's present. Thus after a negative, Ex. 4. 1 וְהֵן לֹא יַאֲמִינוּ לִי but see, *they will not believe* me. Or an infin. absol., Gen. 3. 16 הַרְבָּה אַרְבֶּה עִצְּבוֹנֵךְ *I will greatly increase* your pain. Or a statement of time, Is. 24. 21 וְהָיָה בַּיּוֹם הַהוּא יִפְקֹד י' on that day Y. *will punish*. Gen. 15. 14; 40. 13, Is. 49. 20. After כִּי *for*, כֵּן *so, thus*, לָכֵן *therefore*: Ex. 6. 1, Nu. 14. 28, Is. 10. 16; 20. 4, Jer. 30. 11. Or a prep. phrase: Gen. 3. 14, Is. 11. 3, Mic. 4. 2. After a fronted subj., Nu. 14. 32 וּפִגְרֵיכֶם אַתֶּם יִפְּלוּ but as for you, your dead bodies *shall fall*, Gen. 3. 15; 46. 3-4, Jer. 30. 16. See also § 1c (pron.). Or obj., Gen. 3. 15 וְאֵיבָה אָשִׁית and emnity *I will put*. Or subj. or obj. in chiasmus, Is. 11. 6 the wolf shall dwell with the lamb, וְנָמֵר עִם־גְּדִי יִרְבָּץ and the leopard *shall lie down* with the kid. Gen. 12. 12 they will slay me וְאֹתָךְ יְחַיּוּ but you *they will spare*. Commonly beginning the main clause following a subord. clause; for exx. see Condit., Temporal clauses.

In subord. clauses YIQTOL is used in all three time frames. As a fut. in present, Deu. 4. 26 to witness כִּי־אָבֹד תֹּאבֵדוּן מַהֵר that *you will soon utterly perish*, 2 K. 8. 12. In narrative, as a fut. in past, 1 K. 7. 7 he made the Hall of the Throne אֲשֶׁר יִשְׁפָּט־שָׁם where he *was to, would dispense* justice, Gen. 43. 25, Nu. 14. 31, 2 K. 13. 14, Ps. 78. 6. As a fut. in fut., with almost the fut. perf. sense usually expressed by QATAL (§ 59a), Deu. 12. 29 כִּי יַכְרִית י' when Y. *cuts* (*shall have cut*) *off*. Gen. 29. 8 עַד אֲשֶׁר יֵאָסְפוּ until all the flocks *are gathered together*. Nu. 20. 17, Is. 4. 4; 6. 11. On the similar use of בְּטֶרֶם *before* with YIQTOL in both past and fut. time see § 62, R. 1.

In extended prose discourse the role of YIQTOL vis-à-vis VeQATAL is similar to that of QATAL vis-à-vis VAYYIQTOL in past narrrative (§ 58b); but there are differences. After the introductory phrase, clause or paragr. (circumstantial, temporal, conditional, causal, etc.) the *Vav* cons. QATAL carries forward the sequence of the discourse; and there is usually (see exx. above) a detectable reason for its non-use, be it simply to make a negative statement or, more significantly, to mark a movement in time, to indicate that two actions take place simultaneously rather than consecutively, to introduce a contrast, to highlight the subj. or obj. of a clause, etc. All of these consns. necessitate another word after the *Vav*, and the normal future YIQTOL is therefore used. On occasion, however, a subj. or obj. is placed first in a clause and followed by YIQTOL in what seem to be a natural sequence, i.e. where a *Vav* cons. QATAL would be expected; e.g. subj. in Ex. 7. 18, obj. in Deu. 7. 20, 25; this does not happen with non-circumst. QATAL consns. in prose narrative. Apposition is also commoner than in prose narrative, the only context in which (long) YIQTOL is allowed to come first (e.g. Gen. 15. 15; Deu. 7. 5, 10, 21) while, on the other hand, circumst. clauses with subj. followed by YIQTOL (e.g. Ex. 4. 15) are much less common than their counterparts with QATAL in prose narrative. Moreover, fut. discourse is frequently shot through with backward references which use QATAL; or with instructional or precative passages where (short) YIQTOL as a jussive normally comes first and not infrequently follows *Vav;* or with passages using the more strictly modal nuances of the (long) YIQTOL, as in *c* and *d* below, to ask questions, indicate doubts and possibilities, express purposes, and so on. Two corollaries follow: on the one hand, the relationship between the "on line" *Vav* cons. QATAL and the "off line" YIQTOL is in fut. discourse considerably closer than that between the "on line" *Vav* cons. YIQTOL and the "off line" QATAL in past narrative and, on the other hand, fut. discourse is very much more varied and less homogeneous than is past narrative. Illumine from Gen. 28. 13-15; 41. 26-36; 44. 18-34; almost any discourse in Deu.; 2 S. 17. 1-3, 7-13, etc.

(*b*) In poetic discourse as in poetic narrative there are some additional features which have to do with the parallelistic structure and its avoidance of coordination. Thus appos. or asyndetous clauses beginning with YIQTOL are found in prose discourse (see *a* above) but are much more common in poetry, Ps. 64. 9 and he will bring them to ruin ..., יִתְנוֹדְדוּ כָּל־רֹאֵה בָם all who see them *will shake their heads;* 12. 6; 68. 23, Is. 3. 5; 13. 12, 16; 41. 16, etc. In poetry also YIQTOL may occasionally begin a discourse, Is. 35. 1 יְשֻׂשׂוּם מִדְבָּר וְצִיָּה the wilderness and dry land *shall be glad* (note enclitic *Mem*, § 26, R. 2). Or much more frequently a verse or line, in effect taking the place of *Vav* cons. QATAL, Is. 18. 6 יֵעָזְבוּ יַחְדָּו *they will be left* all together; 13. 12, 16; 42. 15, 16, Hos. 9. 17, Ps. 2. 9; 52. 7, etc.

(*c*) In non-indicative contents the (long) YIQTOL expresses the speaker's desire, intention, doubt, incredulity, etc. concerning some ensuing action. The shades of meaning of YIQTOL in such usages are manifold, corresponding (according to the context) to Engl. *will* (of volition), *shall* (of command), *may* (of possibility or permission), *can* (of capability), *am to*, *must* (of obligation), *should* (of deliberation), etc. in the present; and to *would, should, might, could, was to*, etc. in the past or indirect speech. Particularly in emphatic commands, in wishes, questions, denials, conditions, after certain particles like אוּלַי *perhaps*, etc. Gen. 2. 19 לִרְאוֹת מַה־יִּקְרָא לוֹ to see what *he would call* it; 3. 2 מִפְּרִי עֵץ־הַגָּן נֹאכֵל from the fruit of the trees in the garden *we may eat*; 3. 3 לֹא תֹאכְלוּ מִמֶּנּוּ *you shall* (*must*) *not eat* of it; 18. 25 הֲשֹׁפֵט כָּל־ הָאָרֶץ לֹא יַעֲשֶׂה מִשְׁפָּט *shall* (*should*) *not* the judge of all the earth *do* right? 20. 9 deeds אֲשֶׁר לֹא־יֵעָשׂוּ that *ought not to be done*; 27. 45 לָמָה אֶשְׁכַּל שְׁנֵיכֶם why *should I be bereaved of* you both? 32. 13 the sand of the sea הֲיָדוֹעַ נֵדַע כִּי יֹאמַר אֲשֶׁר לֹא־יִסָּפֵר which *cannot be counted*; 43. 7 *were we* in any way *to know* that *he would say?* Deu. 5. 13 שֵׁשֶׁת יָמִים תַּעֲבֹד six days *shall you labour*; Jud. 9. 28 who is Ab. כִּי נַעַבְדֶנּוּ that *we should serve* him? 16. 15 אֵיךְ תֹּאמַר how *can you say?* 17. 8 to live בַּאֲשֶׁר יִמְצָא wherever *he might find* a place; Jer. 3. 19 I thought (said) אָבִי תִקְרְאִי־לִי how *I would set* you among my sons ... אֵיךְ אֲשִׁיתֵךְ (that) *you would call* me My Father; Am. 3. 3 הֲיֵלְכוּ שְׁנַיִם יַחְדָּו *can* two *walk* together? Ps. 5. 5 לֹא יְגֻרְךָ רָע evil *may not lodge with* you; Job 7. 16 לֹא לְעֹלָם אֶחְיֶה *I would not live* for ever; 9. 15 לִמְשֹׁפְטִי אֶתְחַנָּן *I must appeal for mercy* to my accuser; *vs.* 20 אָנֹכִי אֶרְשָׁע *I am to be condemned*. Gen. 2. 17; 44. 8, 9, 15, 34; 47. 15, Ex. 2. 4; 3. 11, 14 (?), Deu. 5. 7-18, Jud. 8. 6, 1 S. 18. 18; 20. 2, 5; 23. 13, 2 S. 2. 22; 3. 33; 6. 9; 14. 14, 2 K. 18. 13, Am. 3. 8, Ps. 8. 5; 11. 1; 13. 2, 3, Job 4. 17; 6. 3, 11; 7. 12, 17; 9. 16; 11. 7, etc. After אוּלַי *perhaps, it may be, supposing*: Gen. 16. 2; 18. 29; 24. 5, Nu. 23. 27, 1 S. 6. 5, 1 K. 18. 5, 2 K. 19. 4, Am. 5. 15. After לוּ *what if?*, Gen. 50. 15; *oh that!*, Gen. 17. 18, Job 6. 6. Frequently in the protasis of conditional sent. (q.v. for exx.); also in apodosis, Gen. 13. 16, Job 9. 20.

(d) In many of the exx. in *a-c* the YIQTOL, as well as having indic. or modal meaning, expresses the contingency of one action upon another, especially in the apodosis of condit. sent. or the main clause of a temporal or causal sent. This is its basic function following telic conjunctions, as לְמַעַן *in order that*, אֲשֶׁר *that*, לְבִלְתִּי *that not*, פֶּן *lest*. Ex. 4. 5 לְמַעַן יַאֲמִינוּ that *they may believe*; Deu. 4. 40 אֲשֶׁר יִיטַב לְךָ that *it may be well* with you; Gen. 3. 3 פֶּן־תְּמֻתוּן lest *you die*. 2 S. 14. 14. See final Clause.

Rem. 1. The expression מִי יוֹדֵעַ *who knows?* differs little from *perhaps*, and is followed by YIQTOL, 2 S. 12. 22, Joel 2. 14, Jon. 3. 9. In Est. 4. 14 אִם is supplied before the verb.

Rem. 2. On the YIQTOL forms with *paragogic Nun* see Grammars. These are not common and tend to occur in pause, suggesting that they may carry some emphasis. But this is doubtful; it is more likely that they are archaic forms of the kind often attracted to the pausal position. There is some evidence that they belong properly to the long YIQTOL, as they are rare with *Vav* cons. YIQTOL and never occur with jussive. Rather more frequently this *Nun* is retained before suffixes (the so-called *energic* forms) but there is again no discernible function.

THE MOODS. IMPERATIVE, JUSSIVE AND COHORTATIVE

§ 65. In addition to modal YIQTOL Hebr. possesses an Imperative mood and two other partially used volitive moods, the Jussive for the 3rd and, especially in negative commands, the 2nd pers., and the Cohortative for the 1st pers. All these are formed on the YIQTOL base, the imper. dropping the initial תּ of the 2nd pers., the jussive having (where it can) the same form as the short YIQTOL, the cohort. (except in final weak verbs) adding ה. They normally come first in a clause or immediately following *Vav*, which distinguishes them from the long YIQTOL, which avoids these positions. This general rule is not affected by the not infrequent cases where a long YIQTOL is used instead of a special mood (e.g. Gen. 41. 34 יַעֲשֶׂה פ׳ *let Ph. act*); but it may be countermanded in those cases where, out of a desire to focus upon a subj. or obj. or for some other reason, another word precedes the modal form, Gen. 42. 18 זֹאת עֲשׂוּ וִחְיוּ *this* do, and (you shall) live. To all three moods the particle נָא may be added, imparting a mild precative nuance which scarcely needs to be represented in Engl. The regular negative with the moods is אַל.

§ 66. The imper. is used to impress the speaker's will or desire directly upon another person. As in a command, specific or general, Gen. 16. 9 שׁוּבִי אֶל־גְּבִרְתֵּךְ *return* to your mistress; Ex. 20. 12 כַּבֵּד אֶת־ אָבִיךָ וְאֶת־אִמֶּךָ *honour* your father and mother. Or in advice or admonition, Ecc. 11. 9 שְׂמַח בָּחוּר בְּיַלְדוּתֶךָ *rejoice*, young man, in your youth, Hos. 10. 12. Or in giving permission or an invitation, Gen. 24. 33 and he said דַּבֵּר *speak on*, Ex. 10. 24, 2 S. 18. 23. Or making a request or

entreaty, Is. 6. 8 הִנְנִי שְׁלָחֵנִי here am I, *send me;* Ps. 64. 2 שְׁמַע־
אֱלֹהִים קוֹלִי *hear* my voice, O God; 119. 33-39. Imper. may be used
ironically, Am. 4. 4 בֹּאוּ בֵית־אֵל וּפִשְׁעוּ *come to Bethel - and transgress,*
1 K. 2. 22.

The imper. cannot be used with a negative. Either long YIQTOL or
juss. must be used, the first with לֹא and expressing a strong prohibition,
the second with אַל and expressing a specific prohibition or attempt to
dissuade, Ex. 20. 3 לֹא יִהְיֶה לְךָ *you shall not have* other gods; Gen.
45. 9 רְדָה אֵלַי אַל־תַּעֲמֹד come down to me, *do not delay;* Deu. 9. 7
זְכֹר אַל־תִּשְׁכַּח remember, *forget not.* Gen. 2. 17. Gen. 18. 3; 26. 2;
37. 22, Deu. 31. 6, 2 K. 18. 26, 31-32, Is. 6. 9, Jer. 4. 3.

> *Rem. 1.* There is a lengthened imper. with הָ (cf. Gen. 45. 9 above); this
> may (cf. cohort.) have expressed some subjective emphasis on the part of the
> speaker, but it is now difficult to see any difference between the forms, comp.
> Jud. 9. 8 with *vs.* 14, 1 S. 9. 23; and in some verbs the longer form has become
> fixed, as חוּשָׁה *hasten,* עוּרָה *awake,* הַגִּישָׁה *bring near,* הִשָּׁבְעָה *swear,* and
> others.
>
> *Rem. 2.* The imper. has some rhetorical usages, esp. in poetry. It is
> sometimes interjected in descriptions of the fut., the speaker as it were taking
> part in the scene and directly addressing the subj. of the events. This imper. is
> equivalent to a strong subjective expression of fut., e.g. Is. 54. 14 רְחָקִי *be far*
> = *you shall be far.* 2 K. 19. 29, Is. 65. 18, Ps. 110. 2, Job 5. 22. Or it may be used
> as a kind of apostrophe, when no definite subj. is addressed, Is. 13. 2 שְׂאוּ־נֵס
> *lift up* a signal = *let* a signal *be lifted up.* Or in personification, Is. 1. 2
> שִׁמְעוּ שָׁמַיִם וְהַאֲזִינִי אֶרֶץ *hear, O heavens,* and *give ear, O earth.* Ps. 148,
> *passim.*

§ 67. The jussive expresses similarly the will or desire of the speaker
when, not the person addressed, but a third person is the subj. of the
action. It is also used in the 2nd pers., regularly to express a negative
command (see above), occasionally a positive, 1 S. 10. 8 שִׁבְעַת יָמִים
תּוֹחֵל seven days *you shall wait.* In the 3rd pers. it may also be used with
the force of a command, Gen. 1. 3 יְהִי אוֹר *let there be* light; Hos. 4. 4
אַךְ אִישׁ אַל־יָרֵב וְאַל־יוֹכַח אִישׁ yet *let none contend* and *none reprove.*
Gen. 30. 34; 33. 9; 45. 20. Or to give advice, encouragement, or
permission, Jud. 15. 2 תְּהִי־נָא לְךָ תַּחְתֶּיהָ *have her* instead of her; Gen.
41. 33 יֵרֶא פ' ... וִישִׁיתֵהוּ *let Ph. look out ... and place him.* Ex. 8. 25, Deu.

20. 5, 1 K. 1. 2; 22. 13. Or to express a wish, request, or entreaty, 1 S. 1. 23 תָּשָׁב־נָא נֶפֶשׁ הַיֶּלֶד הַזֶּה *may Y. fulfil* his word; 1 K. 17. 21 יָקֶם י' דְּבָרוֹ *may the life* of this child *return;* Gen. 18. 30 אַל־נָא יִחַר לַאדֹנָי *be not angry,* Lord. Gen. 13. 8; 26. 28; 33. 14; 44. 33, Ex. 5. 21, 1 S. 24. 16, 2 S. 19. 38, Ps. 121. 3. Or in pronouncing a benediction or malediction, Nu. 6. 25 יָאֵר י' פָּנָיו אֵלֶיךָ *Y. make* his face *to shine* upon us; Gen. 9. 26 יְהִי כְנַעַן עֶבֶד לָמוֹ *may C. be* his slave. 1 S. 10. 24; Jer. 20. 14.

> *Rem. 1.* A few cases occur of juss. in 1st pers., 1 S. 14. 36, 2 S. 17. 12, Is. 41. 23 (*Ket.*), 28. These, taken together with the frequent cases (though chiefly with אַל) of 2nd. pers. juss. and the few cases (§ 68, R. 1) of the cohort. in 3rd pers., suggest that both moods may at one time have been complete. At present the fragmentary forms supplement each other.
>
> *Rem. 2.* Occasionally לֹא is found with the juss., 3rd or 2nd pers., instead of אַל, Gen. 24. 8, 1 S. 14. 36, 2 S. 17. 12; 18. 14 (cohort.), 1 K. 2. 6, Ez. 48. 14.
>
> *Rem. 3.* The form יוֹסֵף etc. (hiph. of יסף *add, do again* or *more*) occurs with no juss. sense, e.g. Gen. 4. 12, Nu. 22. 19, Hos. 9. 15, Joel 2. 2, Ez. 5. 16, perhaps therefore properly short YIQTOL.
>
> *Rem. 4.* Noteworthy rhetorical usages of juss. are in personification and metonomy, generally in poetry, espec. Pss., Ps. 33. 8; 96. 11-12; 97. 1; 98. 7-8.

§ 68. The cohort. is used to express the will of the speaker in reference to his own action. When the speaker is free the cohort. expresses intention or resolve, Gen. 18. 21 אֵרֲדָה־נָּא *I will go down;* 22. 5 וַאֲנִי וְהַנַּעַר נֵלְכָה עַד־כֹּה while I and the lad *will go* there; Deu. 17. 14 אָשִׂימָה עָלַי מֶלֶךְ *I will set* a king over me. Gen. 12. 2, 3; 24. 57, Ex. 3. 3, Is. 1. 24. When he is dependent on others it expresses a wish or entreaty, Deu. 12. 20 אֹכְלָה בָשָׂר I *would* (*like to*) *eat* flesh; 2 S. 24. 14 נִפְּלָה־נָא בְיַד י' ... וּבְיַד־אָדָם אַל־אֶפֹּלָה *let us fall* into the hand of Y. ... but into the hand of men *let me not fall.* Gen. 33. 14; 50. 5, Nu. 21. 22, Jud. 12. 5, 1 S. 28. 22, 2 S. 16. 19, 1 K. 19. 20, Is. 5. 1, Jer. 17. 18; 18. 18, Jon. 1. 14, Ps. 25. 2; 69. 14-15. In the plur. a note of mutual encouragement is often present, Deu. 13. 3 נֵלְכָה אַחֲרֵי אֱלֹהִים אֲחֵרִים *let us follow* other gods. Gen. 37. 27, Ps. 2. 3. Especially if preceded by, as a kind of auxiliary, the plur. imper. of a verb of motion, Is. 1. 18 לְכוּ־נָא וְנִוָּכְחָה come, and *let us reason together;* Jud. 19. 28 קוּמִי וְנֵלֵכָה get up, *let us be going.* Gen. 11. 3, 4, 7, Jud. 19. 11, 13, 1 S. 9. 9, 2 S. 15. 14, Jer. 46. 16, Ps.

95. 1, 6.

> *Rem. 1.* Exx. of cohort. in 3rd pers., Deu. 33. 16, Is. 5. 19, Ps. 20. 4 (rare).
>
> *Rem. 2.* Occasionally cohort. is used in the protasis of a conditional sent., presumably with a nuance of intention, Ps. 139. 8, Job 16. 6, cf. 19. 18. So following עַד *until,* Ps. 73. 17; cf. Lam. 3. 50 (juss.).
>
> *Rem. 3.* Occasionally cohort. may be translated by Engl. *must* (Is. 38. 10; Jer. 4. 21) or *can* (Ex. 32. 30, Jer. 6. 10) but it is the context which allows this; it is not likely that notions of obligation, compulsion or possibility are present in the form itself. Rather different are the cases in which cohort. carries, not modal, but indicative meaning. In a past context, Ps. 66. 6, Pr. 7. 7. In a present context, Is. 59. 10, Jer. 4. 19, Ps. 42. 5; 55. 3, 18; 57. 5; 77. 4, 7; 88. 16. Cf. also *Vav* cons. with cohort. (§ 83, R. 1). It is uncertain whether these are survivals of a once more widespread usage or later "pseudo" developments based on the analogy of *Vav* cons. YIQTOL with the 3rd pers. which often has (though properly short YIQTOL) forms similar to the juss.

The *VAV* Consecutive Constructions

§ 69. Hebr. has developed a number of syntactical devices for distinguishing among the different linking functions carried out by its ubiquitous conjunction *Vav*. Prominent among these are the two constructions traditionally called *Vav* conversive or consecutive, one in which the *Vav* is attached to a form from the QATAL conjugation (veQATAL) and is commonly preceded by a form from the long YIQTOL conjugation (or one of its associated moods) and one in which the *Vav* is attached to a form from the short YIQTOL conjugation (VAYYIQTOL) and is commonly preceded by a form from the QATAL conjugation. Their chief function is to mark the continuance of a piece of narrative or discourse over at least one but more often several stages. The sequence they establish is essentially chronological, though not necessarily one of strict succession, but it is also frequently logical as well (cf. Engl. *then*). It is their characteristic usage following a form from the *opposite* conjugation that gave rise to the name conversive, as if the constructions involved of necessity not only a change of conjugation but a transfer to the converted form of the initial verb's value. But there is another usage of the constructions which is almost as common and which is triggered not by an antecedent verb but by a previous statement which need not contain a verb of the opposite conjugation or indeed any verb but may simply be a phrase or even a single word. This statement is not, like the antecedent verb, part of the sequence but rather supplies the ground or occasion of it and, being to that extent detached, cannot therefore transfer any meaning to the *Vav* cons. form. The name conversive should therefore be dropped and the primary meanings of veQATAL and VAYYIQTOL sought among the aspectual possibilities offered by their own conjugations. In effect veQATAL denotes a state (or an action so viewed) and VAYYIQTOL denotes a simple (i.e. non-frequentative and non-modal) action which arise out of something that has gone before; and these values remain the same whether that something is a verb of the opposite conjugation or an antecedent clause or phrase. It is important that this fact be fully appreciated if only because Engl. has no means of rendering the aspectual meanings of the two cons. forms but is compelled to translate a sequence containing them as though they were long YIQTOLs or indicative QATALs, and to do this not only when such a verb begins the sequence but also (obviously because the contexts are in other ways so similar) when they are preceded by a clause or phrase. Rem. 1.

If in these two constructions there is no "conversion" of the verb after *Vav* it follows that there can be no "reversion" to a simple YIQTOL or QATAL when a negative or other word or phrase is inserted between *Vav* and the verb. Such a change of word order is not, as the rules in the Grammars seem to assume, a matter of convention but indicates either that the constructions in question are non-consecutive or, if they are consecutive, that they are deliberately highlighting a feature of the connection other than the verb. It is therefore of their own nature and not as variants of cons. forms that the verbs in these constructions belong to the YIQTOL or QATAL conjugations.

The *Vav* cons. constructions are much less used in poetry than in prose. This may suggest that they are not original to poetry, but it may simply be due to the constraints of poetic parallelism which, by the way it divides a narrative or discourse into discrete units, is not conducive to constructions which further their continuity.

    Rem. 1. It is worth emphasizing again (see § 55, R. 2) that tense in Hebr. is signalled by the context and is not a function of the verb, as it is in Engl.

This means that in the case of *Vav* cons. forms as of free-standing verbal forms Engl. is obliged to pick up from the context time references which do not belong to these forms. But there is, as has already been mentioned, a further difficulty with cons. forms. Engl. does not possess such forms and cannot therefore represent their aspectual values, but has in fact to translate them in sequence as though they were "conversive" forms. Thus 1 K. 22. 22 אֵצֵא וְהָיִיתִי רוּחַ שֶׁקֶר which literally means something like "I-go-out and (as a result) I-in-a-state-of-being a lying spirit" must in that context be rendered *I will go out and (will) be a lying spirit* (אֵצֵא is properly cohort., § 68). So also following a non-verbal antecedent, Ex. 16. 6 עֶרֶב וִידַעְתֶּם, lit. "evening and you-in-a-state-of-knowing", must in the context be rendered *at evening you will know*. Similarly in the case of VAYYIQTOL, e.g. Gen. 3. 1 הַנָּחָשׁ הִשִּׁיאַנִי וָאֹכֵל, lit. "the serpent in-a-state-of-deceiving me and I-eat" has in the context to be translated *the serpent deceived me and I ate*. The translation in effect buries the original usage.

Rem. 2. The two *Vav* cons. constructions rarely clash. Since the QATAL conjugation is involved in both, they are most easily distinguished from each other by whether they contain or are associated with a short or long YIQTOL. Short YIQTOL expresses simple indicative action and long YIQTOL iterative or modal action, and it is not therefore surprising that VAYYIQTOL predominates in past narrative and that the two commonest uses of veQATAL are in contexts which describe process in past time or make predictions, commands, etc., in future time. But these are majority usages only, and both constructions are in fact found in all three time settings; in particular VAYYIQTOL should not be called a narrative form.

VAV Consecutive QATAL

§ 70. There is a formal means, to do with moving the stress foward, of identifying *Vav* cons. QATAL, but it applies only to two members of the paradigm instead of the three where it might apply, namely to the 2nd mas. sing. and the 1st sing., but not to the similarly structured 1st plur. Nor is there shift of stress in 1st and 2nd sing. pausal forms, and exceptions are frequent in Hiph. forms and in verbs final Aleph and He. See Grammars.

§ 71. The contexts in which *Vav* cons. QATAL is most clearly seen to possess its own distinctive aspectual meaning are those in which *Vav* joins a main clause to its subordinate clause, the *Vav* functioning as what is called *Vav apodosi* or *Vav* of the apodosis, rather like *then* or *therefore* in similar sentences in Engl. In these constructions there can be no question of QATAL deriving its meaning from an antecedent long YIQTOL. On the other hand, long YIQTOL may replace veQATAL in the main clause, though usually without a linking *Vav* and (see § 63, 64) rarely in initial position, and have, according to the time set by the context, its regular indicative, modal or frequentative meanings. This fact is important, as it indicates the kinds of "stative" value carried by the QATAL; they are the kinds carried by free-standing QATAL in e.g. the passages cited in § 57c, d or § 59b where the two conjugations are also interchangeable - compatible would be a more exact term; the Hebr. forms are not so much interchangeable as drawing attention to different aspects of the same situation; it is only in Engl. translation that they seem interchangeable.

(a) *Vav* cons. QATAL regularly introduces the apodosis of conditional sentences, the QATAL expressing the state of affairs that should result if the condition laid down in the protasis is fulfilled. It is unlikely that the QATAL by nature contains any sense of contingency or modality, these nuances being derived from the context; see § 60. As the apodosis may have either veQATAL or YIQTOL, so may the protasis contain either YIQTOL or QATAL; but the latter choice does not govern the former, each conjugation expressing independently its appropriate aspectual sense.

Jud. 4. 8 אִם תֵּלְכִי עִמִּי וְהָלַכְתִּי *if you (will) go with me, (then) I will go.* Gen. 18. 26 if אֶמְצָא *I find* at Sodom fifty righteous men within the city וְנָשָׂאתִי (*then*) *I will spare* the whole place. Deu. 19. 8-9 if Y. your God יַרְחִיב *enlarges* your border ... וְיָסַפְתָּ (*then*) *do you add* three other cities. With QATAL in prot., Jud. 16. 17 אִם־גֻּלַּחְתִּי וְסָר מִמֶּנִּי כֹחִי *if I be shaved, (then) my strength will leave me.* 2 S. 15. 33.

Two *Vav* cons. QATALs may be juxtaposed to form a conditional sent., the particle being omitted. Gen. 9. 16 וְהָיְתָה הַקֶּשֶׁת בֶּעָנָן וּרְאִיתִיהָ (*if, when*) *the bow is in the cloud, (then) I will see it.* Ex. 33. 10 וְרָאָה *and* (*when*) *all the people saw* the pillar of cloud ... וְקָם (*then*) *all the people would rise up.* 1 K. 8. 30 וְשָׁמַעְתָּ וְסָלָחְתָּ *and (when) you hear, forgive.*

With YIQTOL in apod., Jud. 4. 8 וְאִם־לֹא תֵלְכִי לֹא אֵלֵךְ *but if you (will) not go with me, I will not go.* 1 S. 12. 25 וְאִם־הָרֵעַ תָּרֵעוּ גַּם־ אַתֶּם גַּם־מַלְכְּכֶם תִּסָּפוּ *but if you still act wickedly, both you and your king shall be swept away;* Is. 1. 18 אִם־יִהְיוּ חֲטָאֵיכֶם כַּשָּׁנִים כַּשֶּׁלֶג יַלְבִּינוּ

though your sins be as scarlet, they shall be white as snow; Am. 9. 2-4. If
there is, apart from the aspectual nuances, a difference between veQATAL
and YIQTOL, it may lie in the added force which the *Vav* gives to the
contingency. Note that, though YIQTOL may not, an imper. or juss.
may come first in the apod., Job 19. 28-29 גּוּרוּ ... כִּי תֹאמְרוּ *if you say ...
be afraid.* Ps. 137. 5.

(*b*) *Vav* cons. QATAL is similarly used and with similar YIQTOL
compatible values in the main clause following a subordinate temporal or
causal clause, Gen. 27. 40 כַּאֲשֶׁר תָּרִיד וּפָרַקְתָּ עֻלּוֹ *when you grow
restless, (then) you shall break his yoke;* Ex. 1. 19 בְּטֶרֶם תָּבוֹא *before* the
midwife *comes* to them וְיָלָדוּ *they are delivered.* With YIQTOL in apod.,
Gen. 4. 12 לֹא־תֹסֵף תֵּת־כֹּחָהּ ... כִּי תַעֲבֹד *when you work* the ground,
it shall no longer yield its strength to you. Causal: 1 K. 20. 42 ... יַעַן שִׁלַּחְתָּ
וְהָיְתָה נַפְשְׁךָ תַּחַת נַפְשׁוֹ *because you let go ... (therefore) your life shall be
forfeit for his life,* vs. 28, Gen. 22. 16, Is. 3. 16-17. Deu. 4. 37-39 וְתַחַת כִּי
and because he loved your fathers ... וְיָדַעְתָּ הַיּוֹם *know (therefore) this day.*
Jud. 1. 15.

(*c*) *Vav* cons. QATAL by extension may follow equivalent temporal,
causal, etc. phrases with prep. and infin., Gen. 9. 14 וְזָכַרְתִּי ... בְּעַנְנִי עָנָן
when I bring clouds ... I will remember my covenant, Lev. 26. 26, Jos. 2. 14.
Gen. 3. 5 בְּיוֹם אֲכָלְכֶם מִמֶּנּוּ וְנִפְקְחוּ עֵינֵיכֶם *in the day you eat of it, your
eyes shall be opened,* Ex. 32. 34. Deu. 20. 2 וְנִגַּשׁ ... כְּקָרָבְכֶם *when you
draw near ... the priest shall approach,* Gen. 44. 30-31. With YIQTOL in
apod., Nu. 35. 19 בְּפִגְעוֹ־בוֹ הוּא יְמִתֶנּוּ *when he meets him, he shall put
him to death.* Causal: Is. 37. 29 ... וְשַׂמְתִּי יַעַן הִתְרַגֶּזְךָ אֵלַי *because you
have raged against me ... I will put my hook in your nose,* Jer. 7. 13-14. Cf.
Am. 1. 3-4. With YIQTOL in apod., Is. 30. 12-13 לָכֵן ... יַעַן מָאָסְכֶם
יִהְיֶה לָכֶם הֶעָוֹן הַזֶּה *because you depise ... therefore this iniquity shall be to
you* like, etc. With juss. in apod., 1 S. 24. 11-12 בְּכָרְתִי ... יִשְׁפֹּט י' *in that
I cut off ... may Y. judge between me and you.*

(*d*) So following a great variety of temporal, causal and other
expressions, some very briefly expressed. Hos. 1. 4 עוֹד מְעַט וּפָקַדְתִּי *yet
a little while, and I will visit;* and often with עוֹד, Ex. 17. 4, Is. 10. 25;
21. 16 בְּעוֹד שָׁנָה וְכָלָה *within a year there shall come to an end;* 29. 17; cf.
16. 14 בִּשְׁלֹשׁ שָׁנִים. Ex. 16. 6 עֶרֶב וִידַעְתֶּם *at evening you shall know,* cf.

Nu. 16. 5 (with, unusually, *Vav apodosi* preceding YIQTOL) בֹּקֶר וְיֹדַע
' in the morning *Y. will show.* 1 K. 13. 31 בְּמוֹתִי וּקְבַרְתֶּם אֹתִי when I
am dead, *bury me.* Is. 18. 5 לִפְנֵי קָצִיר ... וְכָרַת before the harvest ... *he
will cut off.* After הִנֵּה, Nu. 14. 40 הִנֶּנּוּ וְעָלִינוּ see, we are here, *and we
will go up,* Jer. 23. 39. 1 S. 2. 31 הִנֵּה יָמִים בָּאִים וְגָדַעְתִּי behold, days are
coming *when I will cut down.* Commonly after extraposed subj. or obj.
(*casus pendens*), Is. 9. 4 כִּי כָל־סְאוֹן סֹאֵן ... וְהָיְתָה for every boot of the
tramping soldier ... *shall be* for burning; 10. 26 וּמַטֵּהוּ עַל־הַיָּם וּנְשָׂאוֹ
and his rod upon the sea, *he shall lift it up,* Nu. 14. 24, 31, 1 S. 25. 27. Ps.
25. 11 לְמַעַן שִׁמְךָ יי וְסָלַחְתָּ for your name's sake, Y., *pardon.*

(*e*) Finally, *Vav* cons. QATAL may be used loosely following various
independent clauses (or their equivalents); some of these may be resolved
into causal or other clauses with in effect *Vav apodosi*, but in others the
logical connection is not obvious and the clauses simply provide the
starting-point of a new development. Gen. 20. 11 there is no fear of God
in this place וַהֲרָגוּנִי *and they will kill me.* 26. 10 one of the people might
easily have lain with your wife וְהֵבֵאתָ *and you would have brought guilt
upon us.* Vs. 22 for now Y. has made room for us וּפָרִינוּ *and we shall be
fruitful* in the land. Ex. 6. 6 I am Y. וְהוֹצֵאתִי *and I will bring you out.*
Deu. 6. 4-5 Y. is your God, Y. alone (§ 49, R. 3) וְאָהַבְתָּ *and you shall
love* Y. your God; cf. 10. 15-16. Jud. 11. 8 now we turn to you וְהָלַכְתָּ *and
do you go with us.* 13. 3 you are barren and have no children וְהָרִית *but
you shall conceive.* 16. 2 until the light of morning וַהֲרַגְנֻהוּ *then we shall
kill him.* 1 S. 15. 28 Y. has today torn the kingdom of I. from you וּנְתָנָהּ
and will give it to a neighbour of yours. 2 S. 14. 7 they have said ... וְכִבּוּ
and (thus) they would quench my coal which is left. Is. 5. 8 until there is
no place וְהוּשַׁבְתֶּם *and you are made to dwell* alone. 6. 7 this has touched
your lips וְסָר *and your guilt is taken away.* Ez. 13. 6 Y. has not sent them
וְיִחֲלוּ *yet they expect* him to fulfil their word. Am. 5. 27 you shall take up
Sakkuth your king ... וְהִגְלֵתִי *therefore I will take you into exile.* Pr. 6. 11 a
little sleep ... וּבָא *and poverty will come upon you.* 9. 14 a foolish woman
is noisy ... וְיָשְׁבָה *so she sits* at the door of her house. Ru. 1. 11 have I yet
sons in my womb וְהָיוּ *who will become* your husbands? 3. 9 I am R. your
maidservant וּפָרַשְׂתָּ *so do you spread* your skirt, etc.

§ 72. The usages of *Vav* cons. QATAL in discourse (descriptive,
predictive or prescriptive) and narrative in general follow the pattern of

§71. The cons. form does not normally occur at the beginning of a passage or, if it is of any length, of significant subdivisions of it, but is a continuation form which is set in motion (as in § 71) by some kind of statement of time, circumstance or intention, etc., or (as in § 73) by the first action, but with the subject coming first followed by YIQTOL; and thoughout the discourse or narrative it in effect follows other *Vav* cons. QATALs. These carry forward the main sequence of the passage, "off-line" statements, e.g. with a negative or a fronted subj. or obj., being non-consecutive or halting the sequence, be it only slightly, to focus attention on a particular person or thing and therefore having the appropriate YIQTOL or imper. or juss. verb. Illumine from the predictive passages Deu. 18. 17-20, introduced by a statement giving the reason for Yahweh's actions and Is. 2. 2-4, introduced by וְהָיָה (see below) and a statement of time; and from the prescriptive passages Ex. 26ff. where the main fittings to be made for the Tabernacle are highlighted by being mentioned first in the clause, Deu. 6. 4-9 beginning with a command, and Ez. 4. 1-8 where the extraposed pronouns אַתָּה and אֲנִי introduce the main instructions to the prophet and the main intentions of Yahweh. In these passages veQATAL, though having its own aspectual nuance, correlates with YIQTOL with fut. indic. or volitive meaning. Descriptive passages in which YIQTOL indicates a process or sequence in the pres. mainly occur in poetry (e.g. Proverbs) and because of the parallelism veQATAL is frugally used, but cf. Jer. 17. 5-8, beginning with a curse formula. Much commoner are passages set in past time in which veQATAL correlates with frequentative YIQTOL, as Ex. 33. 7-11, which has fronted subjects in *vss.* 7-8 identifying the participants and וְהָיָה with a temporal clause in *vs.* 9 introducing the main course of events. For further exx. see § 63, 64 (on the role of YIQTOL in such passages).

The formula וְהָיָה often associated with such passages is significant. It may introduce the chief initial action after an intervening circumstantial or temporal clause of the kind noted in § 71; but in longer passages it can also have an important macro-syntactic role, identifying not only a main event but any important development of it and thus structuring the passage, particularly in terms of time. Like its counterpart וַיְהִי from the other conjugation, it is impersonal and essentially a linking word, with function but no real meaning; and it gives way, after the accompany-ing clause or phrase, either to veQATAL or, without the *Vav*, to YIQTOL.

Thus in fut. contexts, in single statements, 1 S. 3. 9 לֵךְ שְׁכָב וְהָיָה אִם־יִקְרָא אֵלֶיךָ וְאָמַרְתָּ go, lie down; *and it shall be, if he call you, you shall say.* Gen. 27. 40; 44. 31, Jud. 4. 20, 1 S. 16. 16, 1 K. 1. 21. In longer passages with וְהָיָה introducing a new development, Ex. 22. 24-26 (prohibiting usury and the taking of a debtor's garment overnight) וְהָיָה כִּי־יִצְעַק אֵלַי וְשָׁמַעְתִּי *if (then) he cries out to me, I will listen.* Gen. 9. 9-16 (*vs.* 14), Deu. 6. 4-15 (*vs.* 10); 17. 14-20 (*vs.* 18), 1 K. 11. 31-39 (*vs.* 38), Is. 14. 1-3 (*vs.* 3). But וְהָיָה is not always used where one might expect it, Is. 11. 1-9 (e.g. at *vs.* 6); 28. 5 (with *in that day*), Am. 8. 11-14 (at *vs.* 13). And YIQTOL is often used instead of veQATAL, Gen. 4. 14 וְהָיָה כָל־מֹצְאִי יַהַרְגֵנִי *and (it shall happen that) anyone who finds me shall slay me;* 1 K. 2. 37 וְהָיָה בְּיוֹם צֵאתְךָ ... יָדֹעַ תֵּדַע *for (it shall happen that) on the day you go out ... you shall know for certain.* 1 S. 2. 36; 17. 25, 2 S. 15. 35, 1 K. 19. 17, 2 K. 4. 10, Is. 2. 2; 10. 27; 27. 6, Hos. 2. 23.

In past contexts, in single statements, Jud. 19. 30 וְהָיָה כָל־הָרֹאֶה וְאָמַר *then all who saw (it) used to say.* 1 S. 16. 23, 2 S. 14. 25; 15. 5, Am. 4. 7-8. In longer passages describing past events that were customary or habitual, Jud. 6. 2-3 the hand of Midian was strong against Israel ... וְהָיָה אִם־זָרַע יִשְׂרָאֵל וְעָלָה מִ' *and (it used to happen that) whenever I. sowed crops,* M. etc. *would come up,* etc. Gen. 30. 41-42. But oftener וְהָיָה is not used, Gen. 29. 3, 1 S. 17. 34-36; and indeed, since the context is past, וַיְהִי may replace וְהָיָה, the passage moving in and out of normal narrative; thus in 1 S. 1.4 וַיְהִי is continued by *Vav* cons. QATAL while in Jud. 6. 2ff. וְהָיָה is continued in *vs.* 3 by *Vav* cons. QATAL and in *vs.* 4 by *Vav* cons. YIQTOL. 12. 5-6, 1 S. 2. 16. And YIQTOL is often used instead of veQATAL, Ex. 33. 7 (יֵצֵא), 8 (יָקוּמוּ), 9 (יֵרֵד).

Rem. 1. Occasionally *Vav* cons. QATAL seems to begin a completely new passage, but there is always a wider context. Thus 1 K. 9. 25 וְהֶעֱלָה שׁ' *S. sacrificed* three times a year, has no connection with the previous verses, but it comes in a ch. which summarises the king's various activities; and Is. 2. 2ff וְהָיָה בְּאַחֲרִית הַיָּמִים *it will happen in the latter days,* etc., though it is preceded by an editor's rubric, has behind it the general background of the prophet's preaching. Even introduced by כֹּה אָמַר, Ez. 11. 17; 17. 22. Such

apparent new beginnings are even commoner in the case of וַיְהִי (§ 80, R. 3);
it is a mistake, however, to think of the cons. forms acquiring a status of their
own independent of what precedes them.

Rem. 2. Both וְהָיָה and its counterpart וַיְהִי are, as impersonal forms, to
be distinguished from normal uses of the verb in its senses *to be, become* with
subj. and complement, cf. Is. 29. 4, 5, 7. In a few passages, however, the *Vav*
cons. QATAL is exceptionally brought into agreement with the subj., Nu.
5. 27, Jer. 42. 16; cf. *vs.* 17.

Rem. 3. In Is. 40. 6 וְאָמַר need not be emended to וָאֹמַר *and I said;* the
clause attracts its frequ. sense from the previous ptcp. The picture is one of
angels passing the message of God's salvation from the heavenly court down
to Jerusalem, and in such a picture the intrusion of the prophet does not fit;
render *a voice was saying, Cry, and (another) was saying, What shall I cry?* Cf.
the similar context in 6. 3 וְקָרָא זֶה אֶל־זֶה וְאָמַר *and one cried* (continuously)
to another and said.

Rem. 4. Other macrosyntactic devices used in discourse are (וְ)הִנֵּה and
וְעַתָּה. As וְהָיָה plots (chiefly) the time scale of a discourse, (וְ)הִנֵּה signals a
dramatic or noteworthy development and וְעַתָּה introduces a corollary of
what has happened and leads to a fresh statement of intent, command, etc.
They may occur in an extended speech or in smaller portions of an ongoing
conversation. (וְ)הִנֵּה may draw attention either to something that has
happened or to something that is about to happen.

Exx. of (וְ)הִנֵּה referring to past or pres., Gen. 27. 6 הִנֵּה שָׁמַעְתִּי *behold, I
heard* your father speaking to Esau; 1 S. 14. 33 הִנֵּה הָעָם חֹטְאִים *behold, the
people are sinning* against Y. Ex. 1. 9, 1 K. 20. 31; 22. 13. Referring to fut., Ex.
7. 17 הִנֵּה אָנֹכִי מַכֶּה *behold, I will strike.* 4. 23, Deu. 31. 17, 1 S. 3. 11 and
frequently in prophs., Is. 3. 1; 10. 33; 13. 17; 22. 17; 24. 1; 29. 14; 43. 19, Jer.
8. 17, Am. 4. 2; 8. 11. Exx. of וְעַתָּה, Isa. 5. 5 וְעַתָּה אוֹדִיעָה־נָּא *so now I will tell;*
cf. *vs.* 3. Gen. 27. 3, 8; 30. 30; 37. 20; 44. 30, 33; 45. 8, Is. 36. 8; 52. 5, Ps. 2. 10;
39. 8. In many passages the two particles are found together, Gen. 3. 22 הֵן
behold, the man has become like one of us ... וְעַתָּה *and now* ...; 12. 19, Ex.
3. 9-10, Jos. 14. 10, 1 S. 12. 2-3, 1 K. 1. 18, Job 16. 19.

In addition to (וְ)הָיָה, (וְ)הִנֵּה and וְעַתָּה, an extraposed subj. or obj. may set
boundaries to or within a piece of discourse. At the beginning, Is. 27. 2 כֶּרֶם
חֶמֶר *a fruitful vineyard* - sing of it, Gen. 17. 4, 15, Nu. 22. 11. Introducing a
new topic, Lev. 26. 35 (the previous *vss.* were speaking of the land), Gen.
47. 21, Nu. 14. 31. Closing a speech, 1 S. 20. 23. § 149. Such markers combine
with circumstantial clauses, subordinate clauses and other "off-line" features
to delineate the inner structure of a discourse and deserve to be more
carefully studied than they usually are. Narrative structure is not dissimilar; it
employs וַיְהִי instead of וְהָיָה and also uses הִנֵּה and extraposition, but וְעַתָּה is
confined to discourse. § 80.

§ 73. To be distinguished from those many cases, as in § 71, 72, where veQATAL follows a previous clause or phrase or, as in extended discourse, another veQATAL are those cases, equally many, where it follows an antecedent YIQTOL or its equivalent. In the former veQATAL begins (and continues) the sequence while in the latter it merely continues a sequence which is begun by YIQTOL. There are instances from § 71 where a discourse may open with an introductory statement which as well as preparing the scene also describes the first event or situation and which therefore, as in a clause with fronted subj., contains YIQTOL; and such statements may also occur within a discourse identifying or emphasizing the presence of a participant or some object, causing a pause and in effect having a macrosyntactic role of sorts (see further § 72, R. 4). But apart from these and other cases of noun-verb order (e.g. in a circumstantial clause proper; see § 135ff.) veQATAL in discourse only directly follows YIQTOL in dependent (subordinate) clauses or in independent clauses that begin with a negative or other adverb or a particle like אוּלַי *perhaps* or that ask a question or (with the modal verb coming first) that give a command, express an intention, etc. In all such cases the antecedent YIQTOL or its equivalent may have any of the normal indicative, frequentative or modal meanings associated with that conjugation; but, it should again be stressed, these values are not transferred to the succeeding veQATAL, though it may seem that way in Engl. translation.

§ 74. In the aforementioned kinds of context *Vav* cons. QATAL continues YIQTOL

(*a*) in the sense of fut. indic. (§ 64*a*). With subj. first, Is. 49. 7 מְלָכִים יִרְאוּ וְקָמוּ kings shall see *and arise*. Following לָכֵן, Hos. 2. 11 לָכֵן אָשׁוּב וְלָקַחְתִּי therefore I will return *and take*. Or כִּי *surely*, Jud. 6. 16 surely I will be with you וְהִכִּיתָ *and you will smite*. In circumst. clause, Ex. 4. 12 וְאָנֹכִי אֶהְיֶה עִם־פִּיךָ וְהוֹרֵיתִיךָ and (while) I will be with your mouth *and will teach you*. Gen. 18. 18. With interr., Ex. 2. 7 הַאֵלֵךְ וְקָרָאתִי shall I go *and call?* Jud. 15. 18, 1 S. 23. 2, Ru. 1. 11. Within various subord. clauses. With אִם, Ex. 19. 5 if you will indeed obey my voice וּשְׁמַרְתֶּם *and keep* my covenant. Gen. 28. 20, 1 S. 1. 11, Jer. 3. 1. With כִּי *that*, 2 K. 5. 11 I thought that he would surely come out to me וְעָמַד *and stand* etc. With כִּי *when*, Deu. 31. 20 when I bring them into the land ... וְאָכַל *and they eat*, etc. With כִּי *for, because*, Jer. 22. 10 for he shall no more return וְרָאָה *and see*. Is. 13. 7-9. With אֲשֶׁר, Deu. 2. 25 (the people) who shall hear ... וְרָגְזוּ *and shall tremble* etc. Jud. 1. 12 whoever attacks Kiriath Sepher וּלְכָדָהּ *and captures it*. Gen. 24. 14, 1 S. 17. 26. With (אֲשֶׁר) עַד, Is. 32. 15 until the Spirit is poured upon us from on high וְהָיָה *and* the wilderness *becomes*. Gen. 29. 8, Jer. 13. 16, Hos. 5. 15.

(*b*) in the modal and contingent senses mentioned § 64*c*, *d*. E.g. of volition, 1 S. 17. 32 עַבְדְּךָ יֵלֵךְ וְנִלְחַם *your servant will go and fight*. Of command, Ex. 20. 24 מִזְבַּח אֲדָמָה תַּעֲשֶׂה־לִּי וְזָבַחְתָּ *an altar of earth shall you make me, and sacrifice* upon it; vs. 9. With אוּלַי, Gen. 27. 12 אוּלַי יְמֻשֵּׁנִי וְהָיִיתִי *perhaps he may feel me, and I shall be* as one that mocks him. 2 K. 19. 4, Nu. 22. 11, 2 S. 16. 12. With interrog., 2 K. 14. 10 וְלָמָה תִתְגָּרֶה בְּרָעָה וְנָפַלְתָּה *why should you provoke misfortune and fall?* Jer. 40. 15. Gen. 39. 9 אֵיךְ אֶעֱשֶׂה ... וְחָטָאתִי *how should I do this great evil and sin!* With כִּי *that*, Gen. 37. 26 what gain כִּי נַהֲרֹג אֶת־אָחִינוּ וְכִסִּינוּ אֶת־דָּמוֹ *that we should kill our brother and cover* his blood? Following telic particles, Gen. 32. 12 פֶּן־יָבוֹא וְהִכַּנִי *lest he come and smite me*. Is. 28. 13 לְמַעַן יֵלְכוּ וְכָשְׁלוּ וְנִשְׁבָּרוּ *that they may go, and fall and be broken*. With וְלֹא *that not*, Deu. 19. 10; 23. 15. — Gen. 3. 22; 19. 19, Ex. 1. 10, Deu. 4. 16, 19; 6. 15, 1 S. 9. 5, Is. 6. 10, Hos. 2. 5, Am. 5. 6. — Gen. 12. 13, Nu. 15. 40, Deu. 4. 1; 6. 18.

> Rem. 1. It is rare that YIQTOL with simple *Vav* is used instead of veQATAL, as Ps. 2. 12 פֶּן־יֶאֱנַף וְתֹאבְדוּ *lest he be angry and you perish*. In most of the cases the verbs are parallel, Is. 40. 27 (לָמָה); Ex. 23. 12, Is. 41. 20 (לְמַעַן). To be distinguished from YIQTOL (juss.) to express purpose. § 84, 86.
>
> Rem. 2. *Vav* cons. QATAL may continue QATAL when it occurs in a fut. context, following the sense rather than the grammar. So commonly after "performative" QATAL (§ 57*b*), Gen. 17. 20 הִנֵּה בֵּרַכְתִּי אֹתוֹ וְהִפְרֵיתִי אֹתוֹ I bless him *and make him fruitful*. Jer. 31. 33. And sometimes after "prophetic" QATAL, Is. 43. 14 שִׁלַּחְתִּי בָבֶלָה וְהוֹרַדְתִּי I will send to B. *and bring down*. 2. 11; 5. 14. With interr. expressing surprise, Jud. 9. 9. § 59*b*, R. 1.

§ 75. In the appropriate contexts *Vav* cons. QATAL continues YIQTOL expressing what is customary or general (freq.) in pres. or past (§ 63). (*a*) Gen. 2. 24 עַל־כֵּן יַעֲזָב־אִישׁ ... וְדָבַק *therefore a man leaves his father and mother and cleaves* to his wife. Hos. 7. 7 כִּי כֻלָּם יֵחַמּוּ

כַּתַּנּוּר וְאָכְלוּ for they all get heated like an oven, *and devour* their judges. Is. 36. 6 אֲשֶׁר יִסָּמֵךְ אִישׁ עָלָיו וּבָא בְכַפּוֹ on which one leans, *and it goes* into his hand. Am. 5. 19 כַּאֲשֶׁר יָנוּס אִישׁ מִפְּנֵי הָאֲרִי וּפְגָעוֹ הַדֹּב as a man flees from a lion, *and a bear meets him.* Ex. 18. 16, Lev. 20. 18, Is. 29. 8, 11, 12, Jer. 17. 5-8; 20. 9, Ez. 29. 7, Mic. 2. 1, Ps. 90. 6, Pr. 4. 16; 18. 10, 17.

(*b*) In the past, though this usage is commoner in extended passages. Gen. 2. 6 וְעֵד יַעֲלֶה ... וְהִשְׁקָה but a mist used to go up *and water.* 6. 4 וְגַם אַחֲרֵי־כֵן אֲשֶׁר יָבֹאוּ בְּנֵי הָאֱלֹהִים ... וְיָלְדוּ and also afterwards when the sons of God went into the daughters of men, *and they bore children* to them. 1 S. 2. 19, 20 and a little robe תַּעֲשֶׂה־לּוֹ אִמּוֹ וְהַעַלְתָה לוֹ his mother used to make for him, *and bring it up* to him every year. Gen. 29. 2, 3; 31. 8, Ex. 17. 11, Deu. 11. 10, 1 K. 18. 10.

§ 76. *Vav* cons. QATAL continues verbal forms belonging to the sphere of YIQTOL or, in context, equivalent to it in meaning, as (*a*) imper., cohort., juss.; (*b*) infin.; (*c*) ptcp.

(*a*) In discrete commands, requests, etc. Imper., 1 S. 8. 22 שְׁמַע בְּקוֹלָם וְהִמְלַכְתָּ listen to their voice *and appoint a king;* 1 K. 2. 31 פְּגַע־בּוֹ וּקְבַרְתּוֹ fall upon him *and bury him.* Gen. 6. 14; 19. 2; 45. 19, Ex. 14. 13, 1 S. 12. 24; 15. 18, 2 S. 19. 34, 1 K. 2. 36; 17. 13, Jer. 25. 15. So after inf. abs. as imper. (§ 103), Deu. 1. 16; 31. 26, Jer. 32. 14. Cohort., Gen. 31. 44 נִכְרְתָה בְרִית וְהָיָה לְעֵד let us make a covenant *and let it be a witness;* 12. 3, Jud. 19. 13, Ru. 2. 7. After juss., Ex. 5. 7 הֵם יֵלְכוּ וְקֹשְׁשׁוּ תֶבֶן let them go themselves *and gather straw.* Gen. 1. 14; 28. 3, 1 K. 1. 2; 22. 13.

(*b*) Infin. - In reference to fut., 2 K. 18. 32 עַד־בֹּאִי וְלָקַחְתִּי till I come *and take;* Ex. 7. 5 the Egyptians will know that I am Y. בִּנְטֹתִי אֶת־יָדִי עַל־מִצ' וְהוֹצֵאתִי when I stretch my hand over Egypt *and bring forth.* Gen. 27. 45, Ex. 1. 16, Jud. 6. 18, 1 S. 10. 8, 1 K. 2. 42. So inf. abs. for finite verb, Is. 5. 5; 31. 5. After infin. in frequentative sense, Am. 1. 11 עַל־רָדְפוֹ אָחִיו וְשִׁחֵת רַחֲמָיו because he pursued his brother *and stifled his compassion;* Jer. 7. 9, 10 הֲגָנֹב רָצֹחַ וְנָאֹף ... וּבָאתֶם do you steal, murder, commit adultery ... *and then come and stand* before me? 23. 14.

(*c*) Ptcp. - In refer. to fut., Ex. 7. 17 הִנֵּה אָנֹכִי מַכֶּה ... וְנֶהֶפְכוּ לְדָם behold I will strike the waters ... *and they shall be turned* into blood. So *vss.* 27, 28; 8. 17; 17. 6, Deu. 4. 22, Jos. 1. 13, 1 S. 14. 8, 1 K. 2. 2; 13. 2, 3;

20. 36, Jer. 21. 9; 25. 9. So following a ptcp. equivalent to a contingent clause, Ex. 21. 12 מַכֵּה אִישׁ וָמֵת anyone who strikes a man *and he dies; vs.* 16. Nu. 21. 8, 2 S. 17. 17, Is. 29. 15, Am. 6. 7, Hab. 2. 12.

VAV Consecutive Yiqtol

§ 77. The YIQTOL in *Vav* cons. YIQTOL is related to short YIQTOL and the construction is formally recognised, therefore, by the shorter forms which the verb assumes in certain paradigms (§ 61, R. 1); and it is further identified by the *Pathah* vowel after the *Vav* and the doubling of the first consonant of the verb (with the usual modifications when this consonant is א or י with *Sheva*).

> *Rem. 1.* In the paradigms where a shortened form is possible, there is a tendency also for the stress to be retracted, thus וַיָּ֫שָׁב *and he returned* over against juss. יָשֹׁב *let him return* (though retraction may sometimes occur with the juss. too). Cf. short YIQTOL תָּשֵׁב (Ps. 90. 3).

§ 78. The short YIQTOL in *Vav* cons. YIQTOL denotes a "simple" action, and the *Vav* links it as chronologically and sometimes logically sequential to something that has gone before. Its aspectual quality is more readily appreciated as independent when A) the antecedent is an introductory clause or phrase which sets a series of *Vav* cons. YIQTOLs in motion than when B) (§§ 81ff.) it follows a prior QATAL which is itself part of such a series. In context A, however, it may be replaced by QATAL, showing a compatibility, therefore, with certain values of that conjugation, but significantly these do not include the values which in the *Vav* cons. QATAL construction are compatible with long YIQTOL. In effect the "simple" action denoted by VAYYIQTOL is often but not necessarily punctual (see § 62*a* and the exx. there where the action may last a considerable time) but it is not iterative or modal (though in certain cases it may attract a modal nuance from its context). It should also be noted that in context B, though very largely in poetry, *Vav* cons. YIQTOL may continue an antecedent YIQTOL, short or long, another indication that its meaning is not controlled by QATAL.

In addition to expressing what is consequential or simply successive in time, *Vav* cons. YIQTOL has in a number of passages what may be called an *explanatory* or *interpretative* function, a function not obviously carried by its counterpart *Vav* cons. QATAL. In these passages the event or fact expressed by *Vav* cons. YIQTOL may be identical with the preceding event, or synchronous with it, or even anterior to it. Gen. 40. 23 וַיִּשְׁכָּחֵהוּ ... לֹא זָכַר he did not remember Joseph *but forgot him;* Jud. 16. 10 הֵתַלְתָּ בִּי וַתְּדַבֵּר אֵלַי כְּזָבִים you have cheated me, *and told* me lies. So in essence the common וַיֹּאמֶר *saying,* after a verb of speaking and with direct speech following. Frequently after עשׂה *to do,* 1 K. 18. 13 אֵת אֲשֶׁר עָשִׂיתִי ... וָאַחְבִּא what I did when ..., *how I hid.* Gen. 31. 26, Ex. 1. 18; 19. 4, Jud. 9. 16, 1 S. 8. 8, 1 K. 2. 5, 2 Chr. 2. 2, cf. Neh. 13. 17. Spelling out the details or import of a previous clause, Gen. 36. 14 these are the sons of O., daughter of A. ... וַתֵּלֶד לְעֵשָׂו : *she bore* to Esau J., J. and K.; 1 S. 15. 17 are you not the head of the tribes of Isr.? וַיִּמְשָׁחֲךָ יְ׳ *Y. anointed you* king over Isr.; 2 S. 14. 5 I am a widow וַיָּמָת אִישִׁי, my husband *is dead;* Job 10. 22 to a land of darkness etc. וַתֹּפַע כְּמוֹ־ אֹפֶל *and the light* is (lit. *it* [impers.] *shines*) as dark. So *Vav* cons. YIQTOL in its role of summing up the result of a preceding narrative, Jud. 3. 30 וַתִּכָּנַע מוֹאָב *so* Moab *was subdued;* Gen. 2. 1; 23. 20, Jos. 5. 9, Jud. 8. 28.

> *Rem. 1.* Though it has been strenuously denied (Driver), it seems an extension of this explanatory usage when in a few passages *Vav* cons. YIQTOL refers to something that happened before the events being described and calls, therefore, for a transl. with a pluperf. in Engl. Ex. 4. 19 וַיֹּאמֶר יְ׳ אֶל־מֹשֶׁה בְּמִדְיָן *now* Y. *had said* to M. in Midian (he had been instructed to return to Egypt before he had gone back to Jethro, *vs.* 18). 1 K. 13. 12 וַיִּרְאוּ *and* his sons *had seen* the way which the man of God had taken (unless we point as Hiph., i.e. *and his sons showed* (him)). Nu. 1. 48, 1 S. 14. 24, Is. 38. 21, 22; 39. 1, Jer. 39. 11, Zech. 7. 2, Neh. 2. 9. This usage is to be distinguished from that in § 81*b*, where *Vav* cons. YIQTOL continues a QATAL form with plupf. nuance.

§ 79. In usage A *Vav* cons. YIQTOL follows clauses or equivalent phrases or even single words which supply the ground or occasion of the development which it describes. The time setting, usually past or pres., occasionally future, comes from the context. Thus *Vav* cons. YIQTOL begins the main clause after a temporal or causal clause or its equivalent. Hos. 11. 1 כִּי נַעַר יִשְׂרָאֵל וָאֹהֲבֵהוּ when I. was a child, *I loved him.* Ps.

138. 3 בְּיוֹם קָרָאתִי וַתַּעֲנֵנִי in the day I called *you answered me.* Gen. 19. 15. Is. 6. 1 בִּשְׁנַת־מוֹת הַמֶּלֶךְ ע' וָאֶרְאֶה in the year that king Uzziah died *I saw* the Lord. Hos. 13. 6. 2 S. 11. 12-13 ד' וַיִּקְרָא־לוֹ וּמִמָּחֳרָת and on the morrow David *invited him.* Causal: 1 S. 15. 23 ... יַעַן מָאַסְתָּ וַיִּמְאָסְךָ because you have rejected the word of Y., *he has rejected you.* Nu. 14. 16, Is. 45. 4. 1 K. 10. 9 בְּאַהֲבַת י' ... וַיְשִׂימְךָ because Y. loved Israel ... *he has made you* king. Is. 48. 4-5. For exx. with QATAL instead of VAYYIQTOL see § 74, R. 2. *Vav* cons. YIQTOL is rare in apodosis of condit. clause, Ps. 59. 16 אִם־לֹא יִשְׂבְּעוּ וַיָּלִינוּ if they are not satisfied, *they tarry all night.* Job 36. 8-9. Cf. Pr. 25. 4 remove dross from silver וַיֵּצֵא *and* a vessel *comes out* for the smith.

After a question, Is. 51. 12 who are you וַתִּירְאִי *that you are afraid* of man who dies? Ps. 144. 3 (contrast 8. 5 with כִּי). After nominal clause, 1 Chr. 7. 24 his daughter was Sh. וַתִּבֶן *who built* Beth-horon; Ps. 118. 27 Y. is God וַיָּאֶר לָנוּ *he has given* (or, *gives*) us *light.* Hab. 3. 19, Pr. 30. 25. After various kinds of clause or equivalent, sometimes with a connection that is not easy to specify. Gen. 32. 31 I have seen God face to face וַתִּנָּצֵל נַפְשִׁי *yet* my life *is preserved.* Jud. 2. 21 which Jos. left וַיָּמֹת *when* he died. Ps. 55. 18 evening and morning and at noon I complain and moan וַיִּשְׁמַע *but he will hear* my voice; cf. *vs.* 20. Jer. 38. 9 in that they have cast him into the cistern וַיָּמָת *and he is like to die.* Hos. 13. 6 כְּמַרְעִיתָם וַיִּשְׂבָּעוּ the more their pasture, *the more they ate themselves full.* Job 2. 3 he is still holding fast his integrity וַתְּסִיתֵנִי בוֹ *although you incited me* against him.

Commonly after extraposed subj. or obj., Gen. 22. 24 ... וּפִילַגְשׁוֹ וַתֵּלֶד and his concubine, whose name was R., *bore.* 1 K. 15. 13 וְגַם אֶת־מ' אִמּוֹ וַיְסִרֶהָ מִגְּבִירָה and also Maacha his mother *he removed* from being dowager. Nu. 14. 36-37, 1 K. 12. 17, 2 K. 16. 14, Jer. 6. 19. After הִנֵּה, Nu. 22. 11.

§ 80. Narrative prose follows the pattern of usage A. The narrative usually opens with a statement of circumstance, the subj. coming first, or a statement of time, with or without an impersonal (§ 72, R. 2) וַיְהִי. Jud. 11. 1 וְיִפְתָּח הַגִּלְעָדִי הָיָה גִּבּוֹר חַיִל *now Jephthah* the Gil. was a mighty warrior, etc. Gen. 4. 1; 12. 10; 37. 2, 1 S. 28. 3. Gen. 6. 1 וַיְהִי כִּי־הֵחֵל הָאָדָם לָרֹב *(and it happened) when* men began to multiply, etc. 27. 1. Jud. 15. 1 וַיְהִי מִיָּמִים בִּימֵי קְצִיר־חִטִּים *(and it happened) one day* at

harvest time. 16. 40. Without וַיְהִי, Gen. 15. 1, Is. 6. 1. The story line
begins thereafter with *Vav* cons. YIQTOL and is continued with other
Vav cons. YIQTOLs, identifying the main successive events. Thus in
Gen. 24, after the circumst. clause in *vs.* 1, there follow 2 וַיֹּאמֶר ...
וַיִּקַּח ... וַיֵּלֶךְ ... וַיָּקָם וַיֵּלֶךְ 10 ... וַיָּשֶׂם ... וַיִּשָּׁבַע 9 ... וַיֹּאמֶר 5 etc., the
first major break coming at *vs.* 15 with a time clause introduced by וַיְהִי
succeeded by a clause with הִנֵּה and at *vs.* 16 with two circumst. clauses
beginning with the subj. describing Rebekah's beauty before, halfway
through the latter verse, the narrative resumes with וַתֵּרֶד *and she came*
down to the well - or rather, וַתֵּרֶד tells what Rebekah did and is a
continuation of the temporal and הִנֵּה clauses in *vs.* 15, comprising a
subsidiary narrative with the main narrative taking up again in *vs.* 17 with
the action and words of Abraham's servant. These three "off-line"
constructions, often clustering together, show the kind of interruption
that can take place within the narrative flow: וַיְהִי punctuates the
narrative timewise, as later in *vss.* 22, 30 and 52 (cf. 12. 11, 14, Jud. 16. 16,
25); וְהִנֵּה is also macrosyntactic and introduces an unexpected or
important new happening, often with a ptcp. but sometimes otherwise,
as later in *vss.* 30, 45 and 63 (cf. Gen. 1. 31; 6. 12, Ex. 2. 6, Jud. 11. 34);
and the circumst. clause is microsyntactic and describes a concomitant
state of affairs, as later in *vss.* 29, 45 and 62 (cf. 15. 2, 1 S. 4. 12). These
particular circumst. clauses (except the second one in *vs.* 16) are nominal
or contain a ptcp. but others have QATAL, giving background
information, on the story line or prior to it, as the second one in *vs.* 16
וְאִישׁ לֹא יְדָעָהּ *a virgin whom no man *had known,* cf. Gen. 3. 1; 31. 34. A
subordinate clause with QATAL may serve the same purpose, Gen. 6. 6
Y. was sorry כִּי־עָשָׂה *that he had made* man; 28. 11 כִּי־בָא *because* the
sun *had gone down.*

Other macrosyntactic signals are given by וְהָיָה or *Vav* cons. QATAL
introducing repeated or customary action (§ 72) or by extraposition or
subj.-verb (circumst.) order, introducing or reintroducing a character,
e.g. the men of Israel in 1 S. 17. 24 (extrapos.), Elisha in 2 K. 9. 1 (subj.
first); or concluding an episode, e.g. the people who were left in 2 K.
25. 22 (extrapos.), all Israel in 2 S. 18. 17 (subj. first). *Vav* cons. YIQTOL
in its "explanatory" use may also be employed to sum up a narrative
(§ 78). Within a narrative subj.- or obj.-verb order also has micro-

syntactic uses, e.g. in circumst. clauses, Ex. 9. 23 and Moses stretched forth his rod ... וַיהוה נָתַן *while Y.* sent thunder and hail, cf. 10. 13; 1 K. 19. 3-4 and he left his servant there וְהוּא הָלַךְ *but he himself* went into the desert, 2 K. 5. 24-25. So in a chiasmus, Gen. 1. 5 וַיִּקְרָא אֱלֹהִים לָאוֹר וְלַחֹשֶׁךְ קָרָא ... and God *called the light* day, and *the darkness he called* night; 4. 4-5. Note that where in such examples QATAL occurs in the second clause, it is not continued by a successive *Vav* cons. YIQTOL; rather the latter continues the *Vav* cons. YIQTOL in the first clause and QATAL marks an off-line (simultaneous) situation. Similarly in many of the exx. cited earlier. The roles of QATAL and VAYYIQTOL in narrative prose are thus sharply distinguished. In effect Hebr. narrative may be compared to a journey in which the main route is clearly marked by the sequence of *Vav* cons. YIQTOLs, while the beginning and end and any detours in between are signalled by clauses with QATAL or other equally recognisable constructions.

On the role of QATAL in narrative, including some differences in narrative accounts in discourse and poetry, *see* § 58*b, c, d;* and on the rather looser and more varied structure of extended discourse which, probably for that reason, has not received so much attention as that of narrative, *see* § 72.

Rem. 1. See for variety of usage of וַיְהִי with accompanying time clause or phrase or word and VAYYIQTOL Gen. 12. 11-14; 19. 34; 21. 22; 24. 52; 26. 8; 27. 1; 29. 13; 41. 8, Jud. 1. 14; 11. 4, 1 S. 10. 11; 11. 11 end, 2 S. 2. 23.

Exx. of וַיְהִי succeeded by QATAL, Gen. 40. 1 (and it happened) after these things חָטְאוּ (that) the butler of the king of Eg. and his baker *offended,* Ex. 16. 27, Deu. 9. 11, Jos. 10. 27, 1 S. 18. 30, 1 K. 11. 4; 14. 25; 15. 29; 17. 17. The aspectual difference between (VAYYIQTOL) a consequent action and (QATAL) a consequent state-cum-action, which would be felt in Hebr., cannot be caught in Engl.

Sometimes the secution is *Vav* with the subj. preceding the verb, either introducing what is in effect a circumstance or focussing on the subj. Gen. 15. 12 (and it happened) as the sun was going down וְתַרְדֵּמָה נָפְלָה (that) a *deep deep fell* on Abr.; 22. 1 (and it happened) after these things וְהָאֱלֹהִים נִסָּה (that) God *tested* Abr.; 7. 10, Ex. 12. 29, 1 S. 18. 1, 2 S. 3. 6, 2 K. 2. 9.

Rem. 2. A circumstantial or other off-line statement may be of considerable length and contain within it what is in effect a subsidiary narrative in which VAYYIQTOL may be used. Thus in Jud. 11 *vs.* 1 contains two subj. fronted clauses explaining who Jephthah was and these are followed by a short narrative telling of his banishment (*vss.* 2 and 3), the whole being preliminary to the main story of his defeat of the Ammonites which begins in *vs.* 4. Cf. 1 S. 30. 1-2 with the main story being resumed in *vs.* 3; Job 1. 1-5 with VAYYIQTOLs in *vss.* 2-3 and *vs.* 5 (a) and veQATALs in *vs.* 4 and *vs.* 5 (b), a mixture of simple and frequentative action, the whole setting the scene for the main story which opens in *vs.* 6. For little off-line stories within a larger narrative and using VAYYIQTOL cf. Gen. 24. 15-16 (above); 31. 34(a), 2 S. 18. 18.

Rem. 3. It is wrong to regard *Vav* cons. YIQTOL as developing an independent status of its own simply because it begins the biblical books of Lev., Nu., 2 K. and 2 Chr. or (in the form of וַיְהִי) those of Jos., Jud., 1 and 2 S., Ez. and Ru. There is always a connection of sorts, obvious or implied, with previous books. The case is no different from apparently independent narratives within books which open in the same way, e.g. Gen. 6. 1, 5; 11. 1; 35. 1, Ex. 12. 1, etc. See further § 72, R. 1.

§ 81. In usage B *Vav* cons. YIQTOL (or a sequence of such) is triggered not by an antecedent clause (or equivalent) but by an antecedent QATAL (or equivalent) which itself begins and is part of a sequence. This kind of sequence is in prose narrative restricted to off-line statements which begin with a fronted subj. or obj. or adv. (including the negative לֹא) or which comprise a subordinate clause, or where QATAL is used appositionally. In discourse and poetry it occurs additionally in narrative reports and accounts which begin with QATAL and more widely in various kinds of discrete clause which begin with a noun or with an interr. or other particle. It is to be noted also that, though almost always in poetry, *Vav* cons. YIQTOL may continue a compatible YIQTOL, be this a short YIQTOL as in narrative passages or a long YIQTOL (as long as it is not used in a freq. or modal sense) elsewhere.

The sequence QATAL-VAYYIQTOL (or on occasion YIQTOL-VAYYIQTOL) occurs in all three temporal frames; thus in the past

(*a*) in passages where it is most naturally rendered by past tenses in Engl. Gen. 3. 13 הַנָּחָשׁ הִשִּׁיאַנִי וָאֹכֵל the serpent deceived me, *and I ate;* 4. 1. In discourse and poetic narrative, 2 S. 3. 23 בָּא אַבְנֵר ... וַיְשַׁלְּחֵהוּ they told Joab, "Abner ... came to the king, *and he let him go";* Am. 9. 1. With YIQTOL preceding, Ps. 78. 26 יַסַּע ... וַיְנַהֵג he caused the east wind to blow *and led out* the south wind; Deu. 2. 12; 32. 13, 1 K. 20. 33, Ps. 18. 14-15; 95. 10. With neg., Job 3. 10 because לֹא סָגַר he did not shut the doors of my (mother's) womb וַיַּסְתֵּר *and hide* trouble from my eyes; Jer. 20. 17, Job 32. 3. Within sub. clause, 1 S. 15. 24 because I feared the people וָאֶשְׁמַע *and obeyed* their voice; Nu. 14. 36. With interrog;, Jud. 11. 7 הֲלֹא אַתֶּם שְׂנֵאתֶם אוֹתִי וַתְּגָרְשׁוּנִי *did you not hate me, and drive me away?*

(*b*) in passages where Engl., arguing from the broader context, would use pluperfs. (§ 58). Gen. 39. 13 when she saw כִּי־עָזַב בִּגְדוֹ בְּיָדָהּ וַיָּנָס *that he had left his garment in her hand and fled;* 31. 34 ... וְרָחֵל לָקְחָה וַתֵּשֶׁב ... וַתְּשִׂמֵם *now R. had taken the Teraphim and put* them in the camel's saddle *and sat* upon them. Gen. 26. 18-, 27. 1, Nu. 21. 26, Jos. 10. 1, Jud. 4. 11, 1 S. 30. 1, 2, 2 S. 18. 18, 1 K. 2. 41, Is. 39. 1.

(*c*) within conditional clauses (where it is the context, not QATAL, which supplies the modal nuance, § 60). In prot., 1 S. 25. 34 לוּלֵי מִהַרְתְּ וַתָּבֹאי *unless you had made haste and come;* Ps. 138. 8-11 following YIQTOL אִם־אֶסַּק ... אֶשָּׂא ... וָאֹמַר *if I ascend ... (if) I take ... (and if) I say.* Nu. 5. 27, Job 9. 16. In apod. after כִּי עַתָּה, often with suppressed prot., Ex. 9. 15 for by now שָׁלַחְתִּי אֶת־יָדִי וָאַךְ *I could have stretched out my hand and struck.* In a wish with לוּ, Jos. 7. 7 לוּ הוֹאַלְנוּ וַנֵּשֶׁב *would that we had consented to dwell!*

§ 82. In pres. and fut. contexts *Vav* cons. YIQTOL continues QATAL

(*a*) as in § 57*c* describing a typical experience or a common truth. Is. 40. 24 וְגַם־נָשַׁף בָּהֶם וַיִּבָשׁוּ *he blows upon them, and they wither.* Job 7. 9; 14. 2; 24. 2. So in continuance of a ptcp.with this meaning, Am. 5. 8 הַקּוֹרֵא לְמֵי הַיָּם וַיִּשְׁפְּכֵם *who calls the waters of the sea, and pours* them; 9. 15. Gen. 49. 17, 1 S. 2. 6, Jer. 10. 13, Am. 6. 3; 9. 5, Mic. 7. 3, Nah. 1. 4, Ps. 34. 8; 104. 32, Job 12. 18, 22-25, Pr. 21. 22. So not uncommonly continuing YIQTOL, Job 4. 5 כִּי עַתָּה תָּבוֹא אֵלֶיךָ וַתֵּלֶא *but now it reaches you, and you collapse.* Hos. 8. 13, Ps. 42. 6; 52. 9, Job 6. 21; 7. 17-18; 14. 10.

(*b*) in the sense of Engl. pres. perf. (§ 57*d*), Gen. 3. 17 כִּי שָׁמַעְתָּ לְקוֹל אִשְׁתְּךָ וַתֹּאכַל *because you have obeyed the voice of your wife and eaten;* Is. 53. 6, Jer. 8. 6, Job 42. 5. With interr., Deu. 4. 33 הֲשָׁמַע עָם קוֹל א' ... וַיֶּחִי *has a people heard the voice of God ... and lived?* 1 S. 19. 17, Job 9. 4. With neg., 1 S. 15. 19 וְלָמָּה לֹא־שָׁמַעְתָּ בְּקוֹל י' וַתַּעַט *why have you not obeyed, but have flown* upon the spoil? Gen. 32. 5, 1 S.

19. 5.

(c) as so-called "prophetic perf." (§ 59b). Is. 9. 5 ... כִּי־יֶ֣לֶד יֻלַּד־לָ֗נוּ
וַתְּהִי ... וַיִּקְרָא for a boy will be born to us ... *and* the government *shall be*
upon his shoulder, *and they shall call* his name; Ps. 22. 30 אָכְל֬וּ וַיִּֽשְׁתַּחֲו֬וּ
all the fat ones of the earth shall eat *and bow down*. Is. 5. 25; 24. 18;
48. 20, 21, Mic. 2. 13, Jer. 8. 16, Ps. 20. 9. With no preceding QATAL,
but stating the issue of actions just described, Is. 2. 9 וַיִּשַּׁח אָדָם וַיִּשְׁפַּל־
אִישׁ so man shall be humbled, and men brought low, cf. 5. 15. Ps. 37. 40;
64. 8-10, Job 5. 15, 16; 36. 7. (These cases belong properly in § 79.) So
VAYYIQTOL continuing YIQTOL, Ps. 49. 15 מָ֫וֶת יִרְעֵם וַיִּרְדּ֬וּ death
shall shepherd them, *and* the upright *shall rule* over them; 94. 22-23.

> *Rem. 1.* Ex. of *Vav* cons. YIQTOL after stative verb (§ 57a), Is. 3. 16 are
> haughty *and walk*; Ps. 16. 9. The YIQTOL after אָז *then*, referring to the past
> (§ 62, R. 1), is also continued by VAYYIQTOL, Jos. 8. 30, 31; 10. 12; 22. 1,
> 1 K. 3. 16, 2 K. 12. 18. On the other hand the secution after performative
> QATAL (§ 57b) is usually *Vav* cons. QATAL, Gen. 9. 13; 17. 20 and so of
> QATAL in the sense of Engl. fut. perf. (§ 59a), Is. 4. 4, and expressing
> incredulity in a question (§ 59b), Jud. 9. 9, 1 S. 26. 9. So very often the
> "prophetic perf." (§ 59b) is continued by *Vav* cons. QATAL, the gramm.
> construction being abandoned in favour of one following the sense, Nu.
> 24. 17, Is. 2. 11; 43. 14, Ps. 20. 9. On the secution of the so-called "precative
> perf." see § 60, R. 1.

§ 83. *Vav* cons. YIQTOL continues any verbal form, as inf. or
ptcp., which is used in a sense equivalent to QATAL. Gen. 39. 18
כַּהֲרִימִי קוֹלִי וָאֶקְרָא when I lifted up my voice *and cried;* 28. 6, 1 K.
18. 18, Is. 30. 12, Jer. 10. 13, Ps. 50. 16; 92. 8. Gen. 35. 3, לָאֵל הָעֹנֶה אֹתִי
וַיְהִי עִמָּדִי who answered me, *and was* with me; 27. 3, Job 12. 4. See also
exx. § 82a.

> *Rem. 1.* In conversation and in psalms using the 1st pers. *Vav* cons is
> sporadically used with Cohort., perhaps imparting a personal focus to what is
> said, but possibly simply used on the model of the short YIQTOL form
> which in 3rd pers. looks like a juss.; see § 68, R. 3. Gen. 41. 11; 32. 6, 2 S.
> 22. 24, Ps. 3. 6.

The Conjugations and Moods with Simple *VAV*

§ 84. In addition to the *Vav* cons. constructions which express a succession of events or situations over time, Hebr. has greatly developed constructions in which a noun follows *Vav* in each or at any rate one of two clauses in order to relate them non-sequentially. *See* under Chiastic and Contrastive sentences and Circumst. clause. Clauses beginning with a verb may also be coordinated non-sequentially by means of simple instead of cons. *Vav*. Some of these may be fitted into the patterns of Conjunctive and Antithetical sentences (q.v.), but others are different, and require separate examination.

Thus simple *Vav* with QATAL (*a*) repeats on the same time-scale or, it may be, slightly extends the reference of a previous verb, being thus more or less synonymous with it. 1 S. 12. 2 וַאֲנִי זָקַנְתִּי וְשַׂבְתִּי and I am old *and grey;* Is. 1. 2 גִּדַּלְתִּי וְרוֹמַמְתִּי I have nourished *and brought up* children; Gen. 31. 7 he has cozened me, *and changed* (changing) my hire. Deu. 2. 30, 1 S. 17. 38, 1 K. 8. 47, 2 K. 18. 4; 19. 22; 23. 12, Is. 63. 10, Am. 7. 4, Ps. 38. 9, Ecc. 2. 9 (second verb), Lam. 2. 22, 1 Chr. 23. 1. Sometimes the second verb expresses antithesis or contrast, 1 K. 3. 11 you have not asked long life ... וְשָׁאַלְתָּ *but have asked,* etc.; 1 S. 10. 2 he has lost thought of the asses וְדָאַג לָכֶם *and is rather concerned* about you. Jos. 22. 3, 2 K. 8. 10; 18. 36, Jer. 4. 10, Ez. 20. 22

(*b*) or, more generally (almost as though it were a less certain variety of *Vav* cons. QATAL), it identifies an event as going on at roughly the same time as a previous event, 2 K. 14. 10 you have indeed smitten Edom וּנְשָׂאֲךָ *and* your heart *has lifted you up;* Is. 1. 8 your land is desolate וְנוֹתְרָה ... בַּת־צִ׳ *and* the daughter of Zion *is left,* etc. Gen. 21. 25; 34. 5, 1 S. 5. 7; 17. 20, 1 K. 21. 12, Jer. 3. 9, Ecc. 1. 13; 5. 13, Ezr. 3. 10, 1 Chr. 22. 18. So וְהָיָה linking extended situation and accompanying event, 1 S. 1. 12 *and it happened* that, as she made many prayers before Y., Eli was watching (ptcp.) her mouth; 25. 10, 2 K. 3. 15

(*c*) Sometimes simple *Vav* with QATAL seems to restate or resume or sum up what has gone before, Gen. 15. 6 וְהֶאֱמִן בַּי׳ *so did he believe* in Y.; Jud. 7. 13 וְנָפַל הָאֹהֶל *so fell* the tent. 1 K. 20. 21, Is. 22. 14; 28. 26, Ecc. 2. 9 (first verb), 13, 15, Est. 9. 23, Ezr. 6. 22; 8. 30, 36, Neh. 13. 20.

(*d*) Hardly non-sequential, however, though significantly sometimes occuring in general accounts of someone's activities or experiences, are

quite a few cases where *Vav* with QATAL seems merely copulative and it
is not easy to see why *Vav* cons. YIQTOL was not used, 2 K. 23. 10 *and*
(next) *he defiled* Topheth. Jud. 16. 18, 2 S. 16. 5, 2 K. 14. 7, Ez. 9. 7, Ps.
136. 14, 15, 21, Job 16. 12. So וְהָיָה when וַיְהִי would have seemed more
natural, 1 S. 10. 9, 1 K. 12. 32; 13. 3; 14. 27, 2 K. 21. 4; 23. 4. This usage, in
effect in lieu of *Vav* cons. YIQTOL, has often been regarded as late and
due to the influence of Aram. (which does not possess cons. forms), but
its incidence in early texts is not negligible. It is more satisfactorily
explained as an inner Hebr. development out of usages as in *b*, a
development which ultimately led in Mishnaic Hebr. to the abandonment
of *Vav* cons. YIQTOL and its complete replacement by simple *Vav* with
QATAL. But that end result, which turned QATAL into a past tense and
involved also the abandonment of its "stative" character in other than
narrative contexts, is even in the latest strata of Bibl. Hebr. still in the
future.

§ 85. Likewise simple *Vav* with YIQTOL (*a*) joins together on the
same time-scale two events or situations, especially in the expression of
general truths or customary happenings or ongoing experiences. This
usage is found in prose, but is particularly characteristic of poetic
parallelism, the two clauses neatly balancing one another. Ex. 23. 8 for a
bribe blinds the clear-sighted וִיסַלֵּף *and twists* the words of the righteous
(cf. Deu. 16. 19); Ps. 104. 32 he touches the mountains וְיֶעֱשָׁנוּ *and they
smoke.* Ps. 25. 9; 26. 6; 104. 20, 30; 107. 42, Pr. 5. 20; 30. 17(a), Job 13. 27
(short YIQTOL, § 62*b*); 27. 21-23 (*vs.* 22 short YIQTOL); 39. 21.
Expressing antithesis, Pr. 15. 25.

(*b*) In fut. settings, like *Vav* with QATAL in past settings, it relates
two events or situations which take place around the same time or at any
rate are not felt to be fully consecutive. Is. 40. 30 וְיָעֲפוּ נְעָרִים וְיִגָעוּ *and
youths shall faint *and be weary;* Pr. 9. 11 for by me your days will be
multiplied וְיוֹסִפוּ לְךָ *and they* (indef.) *will add,* i.e. years of life will be
added to you. Ex. 15. 17, Lev. 15. 24; 26. 43, Deu. 32. 41, Is. 35. 1, 2; 42. 6;
58. 10, Ez. 14. 7, Zeph. 2. 13 (short YIQTOL), Ps. 32. 8; 69. 36; 78. 6;
91. 4, Job 20. 23 (short YIQTOL), Pr. 23. 15-16; 30. 17(b); 31. 5, Dan.
11. 4, 10, 16-19, etc.

(*c*) This usage is also found in past settings, very largely in poetic
narrative or reminiscence, but in these cases the verbs, though sometimes

marked as long YIQTOLs, are properly perfective short YIQTOLs, § 62*a*. Ps. 107. 20 he sent forth (יִשְׁלַח) his word וְיִרְפָּאֵם *and healed them* וִימַלֵּט *and delivered* (them) from destruction; Is. 43. 28 so I profaned (see below) the princes of the sanctuary וַאֲחַלֵּל (cohort., cf. § 83, R. 1) *and I put* Jacob to the ban. Is. 10. 13; 12. 7 (one formally short YIQTOL); 51. 2; 57. 17; 63. 3 (short YIQTOL), 5-6, Zech. 8. 10, Ps. 18. 38; 107. 20, 27, Job 3. 13. In some of these exx. the difference between happening at roughly the same time and being consecutive is not great, and there are some other instances where it is hardly possible to claim that simple *Vav* with YIQTOL is not an alternative to *Vav* cons.: so the first case in Is. 43. 28 and those in 1 K. 14. 5 (וַיְהִי), Ps. 18. 43, Dan. 8. 12 (one short YIQTOL). There is, however, not a large number of YIQTOLs in past contexts with simple *Vav* compared with the cases where they are in appos. or free-standing, and taken as a whole they seem by a considerable margin to be non-consecutive rather than consecutive.

§ 86. Modal forms are commonly coordinated by simple *Vav* in similar ways to QATAL and YIQTOL. Thus imper., Is. 56. 1 שִׁמְרוּ מִשְׁפָּט וַעֲשׂוּ צְדָקָה *keep* justice *and do* righteousness. Gen. 1. 28, Ex. 9. 1, 8 (imper. and juss.), 13, Is. 65. 18; 66. 10. Juss., Ps. 96. 11 יִשְׂמְחוּ הַשָּׁמַיִם וְתָגֵל הָאָרֶץ *let* the heaven *be glad and* the earth *rejoice*. Gen. 1. 6, 9; 44. 18, 33, Jer. 9. 22, Ps. 107. 21-22; 109. 11, 12, 15. Cohort., Ps. 95. 6 נִשְׁתַּחֲוֶה וְנִכְרָעָה *let us worship and bow down*. Gen. 1. 26 (cohort. and juss.); 11. 4, 2 S. 17. 1, Jon. 1. 14 (cohort. and imper.).

But additionally two moods may be joined with one another in a *logical* sense, simple *Vav* supplying the link. Thus an imper. with simple *Vav* (*a*) after another imper. usually expresses the certain *effect* or consequence of the first. The first imper. in this case virtually expresses a condition which carries with it the second as a consequence. Gen. 42. 18 זֹאת עֲשׂוּ וִחְיוּ *do this and* (you shall) *live;* 2 K. 5. 13 רְחַץ וּטְהָר *wash and* (so) *become clean;* Is. 45. 22 פְּנוּ אֵלַי וְהִוָּשְׁעוּ *turn to me, and be saved*. Ironically, Is. 8. 9 הִתְאַזְּרוּ וָחֹתּוּ *gird* yourselves *and* (but you shall) *be confounded*. 2 K. 18. 31, Jer. 25. 5; 27. 12, Am. 4. 4; 5. 4, 6, Ps. 37. 27.

(*b*) After a juss. or cohort., or their equivalent, as an interr. clause, there is to the imper. often the added nuance of confident expectation or indeed intention. After juss., Gen. 20. 7 וְיִתְפַּלֵּל בַּעַדְךָ וֶחְיֵה *and he can pray for you that you live;* Ps. 128. 5 may Y. bless you from Zion וּרְאֵה

and you then see the prosperity of Jerusalem. Ru. 1. 9; 4. 11. After cohort., Gen. 12. 2 I will bless you and *so* make your name great וְהְיֵה בְּרָכָה *that you* (yourself) *will become* a blessing; 1 K. 1. 12 let me give you counsel וּמַלְּטִי *that you may save* your life. Gen. 45. 18, Ex. 3. 10, 1 S. 12. 17. After a question, 2 S. 21. 3 how can I make amends וּבָרְכוּ *that you may bless* the heritage of Y.? Distinguish the more rhetorical use of a following imper., § 66, R. 2.

§ 87. The juss. and cohort. with simple *Vav* more obviously express *design* or purpose, though the notion of consequence or effect is never far away. If such a purpose-clause be neg., וְלֹא with (presumably modal, § 64c) long YIQTOL is almost always used.

(*a*) After an imper., or anything with imper. sense, as another cohort. or juss. Gen. 27. 4 הָבִיאָה לִּי וְאֹכֵלָה bring to me *that I may eat;* Ex. 14. 12 חֲדַל מִמֶּנּוּ וְנַעַבְדָה leave us alone, *that we may serve* Egypt; Jud. 6. 30 הוֹצֵא אֶת־בִּנְךָ וְיָמֹת bring out your son, *that he may die;* Gen. 42. 2 שִׁבְרוּ־לָנוּ וְנִחְיֶה וְלֹא נָמוּת buy corn for us *that we may live, and not die;* 1 S. 5. 11 שַׁלְּחוּ ... וְיָשֹׁב ... וְלֹא יָמִית send away the ark of the God of Isr., and let it return to its place, *that it may not slay* me, etc.; 2 S. 13. 25 אַל־נָא נֵלֵךְ כֻּלָּנוּ וְלֹא נִכְבַּד עָלֶיךָ (note long YIQTOL for cohort.) let not all of us go, *that we be not burdensome to you.* Rem. 1.

(*b*) After clauses expressing a wish or hope. Jud. 9. 29 מִי יִתֵּן אֶת־ הָעָם הַזֶּה בְּיָדִי וְאָסִירָה would that this people were in my hand, *and I would remove* Abim.; Jer. 8. 23 O that my head were waters and my eyes a fountain of tears וְאֶבְכֶּה *that I might weep;* so 9. 1, Job 13. 5; 16. 20, 21; 23. 3-5. After clause with אוּלַי *perhaps,* Jer. 20. 10; after אוּלַי, Ex. 32. 30.

(*c*) After neg. clause, Nu. 23. 19 לֹא אִישׁ אֵל וִיכַזֵּב God is not a man, *that he should lie;* cf. infin. 1 S. 15. 29 (Rem. 3). Ps. 51. 18 you desire not sacrifice וְאֶתֵּנָה *that I should give* (else would I give) it. 2 K. 3. 11, Is. 41. 28; 53. 2, Ps. 49. 8-10; 55. 13. Without *and,* Job 9. 33 there is no umpire between us, *that he might lay* his hand upon us both; so *vs.* 32. Rem. 5.

(*d*) After interrog. clauses, 1 K. 22. 20 מִי יְפַתֶּה אֶת־אַחְאָב וְיַעַל who will entice Ahab *to get up?* Am. 8. 5 when will the new moon be over וְנַשְׁבִּירָה שֶּׁבֶר *that we may sell corn?* Ex. 2. 7, 1 K. 12. 9 (cf. infin. *vs.* 6), 2 K. 3. 11, Is. 19. 12; 40. 25; 41. 26, Jon. 1. 11, Job 41. 3, Lam. 2. 13.

Rem. 1. Additional exx. of § 87*a.* Gen. 18. 30; 19. 20; 27. 21; 30. 25, 28;

42. 20, Ex. 14. 15, 16, Nu. 14. 42; 21. 7; 25. 4, Deu. 1. 42; 5. 28, 1 S. 9. 27; 11. 3; 15. 16; 17. 10; 18. 21; 28. 7, 2 S. 14. 7, 1 K. 13. 6, 18; 18. 27, 2 K. 5. 8; 6. 22, Is. 2. 3; 5. 19; 55. 3, Jer. 37. 20; 38. 24, Hos. 2. 4, Ps. 45. 12; 81. 9, 11; 90. 14, Job 13. 13.

Rem. 2. Very occasionally Hebr. uses *Vav* with juss. to express design even after the indic. in the past, as Lam. 1. 19 בִּקְשׁוּ אֹכֶל וְיָשִׁיבוּ they sought food *that they might revive* their strength (cf. infin. *vs.* 11). 1 K. 13. 33, 2 K. 19. 25, Is. 25. 9, Jer. 23. 18.

Rem. 3. The idea of *design* expressed by the construction is illustrated by its interchange with לְ and infin., cf. 1 K. 12. 6 infin. with *vs.* 9 juss.; 1 K. 22. 7 with *vs.* 8; Deu. 17. 17 with *vs.* 20 (clause with לְמַעַן). Occasionally *Vav* cons. QATAL may also attract a nuance of design from its context, cf. 1 S. 15. 25 cohort. with *vs.* 30 cons., Ex. 8. 12, 2 S. 21. 6, 1 K. 1. 2. Of course, effect or consequence is often implied by *Vav* cons. QATAL, especially following a neg. clause, Deu. 7. 26 *and so* become curse. Ex. 33. 20, Deu. 19. 10, Ps. 143. 7.

Rem. 4. A second neg. clause is usually introduced by וְלֹא (or לֹא) with (long) YIQTOL. The form וְאַל with juss. rather coordinates its clause to the preceding one, Gen. 22. 12, Deu. 33. 6, Jud. 13. 14, Ps. 27. 9, though some cases may seem dubious, 1 S. 12. 19, Ps. 69. 15.

Rem. 5. The *Vav* is sometimes omitted. Ps. 61. 8 מַן יִנְצְרֻהוּ enjoin *that they keep him*. It is, of course, the juss. or cohort. that supplies the logical connection, the *Vav* merely linking the clauses. Ex. 7. 9, Is. 27. 4, Ps. 55. 7; 103. 5; 118. 19; 119. 17, Job 9. 32, 33, 35.

The Object of the Verb (Direct, Indirect, Complement). Object Clauses

§ 88. Verbs in Hebr. as in other languages are classified as transitive or intransitive according as they take or do not take a *direct object* (§§ 89, 90). The other two kinds of obj. are the *indirect object* (§ 91) and the *object complement* (§ 92) the first occuring like the dir., with trans. verbs and the second with both trans. and intrans. The so-called *cognate object* (§ 93) may be regarded as a special type of obj. complement. The dir. object may consist of a noun (or noun phrase), a pronoun or (§ 90) *a clause* and may, like the subj. be either def. or indef., animate or inanimate. The indirect obj. is usually def. and usually animate. The obj. complement may be either a noun or an adj. (ptcp.) and is most often indef. The dir. obj. may be introduced by a prep., as נָגַע בְּ *touch*, and with many verbs either the indirect obj. or the obj. complement may be replaced by a prepositional phrase. All three kinds of obj. are found in Engl., but there are, as one might expect, many divergencies in usage between the two languages.

The particle אֵת is frequently used before the obj., especially a def. direct obj., but it has other functions which have nothing to do with the obj. The prep. לְ is used non-prepositionally in a similarly manner. See *Excursus*.

> *Rem. 1.* In addition to representing the three kinds of obj., nouns (and adj.) may be used adverbially to modify the action of the verb, e.g. נוֹרָאוֹת *fearfully* (lit. fearful things) in Ps. 139. 4. In Arabic both nouns used objectively and nouns used adverbially are put into the accusative case, and on this analogy they are often treated together in Hebr. Grammars under the heading "accusative". But this is not a wise procedure with a lang. that does not possess case endings, and these two usages are more sensibly distinguished by their functions. In the same way prepositional objects should be distinguished from prep. phrases used adverbially. On the adverbial uses of nouns and prep. phrases see §§ 117, 118.

§ 89. *The direct object.* Classes of verbs governing dir. obj. — (*a*) Numerous verbs trans. in Qal, as נָתַן *give*, לָקַח *take*, שִׂים *put*, פָּתַח *open*, כָּתַב *write*, רָדַף *pursue*, בָּלַע *swallow*, יָרַשׁ *inherit*, עָשָׂה *make, do,* etc. Some stative verbs may also be used transitively, as אָהֵב *love*, שָׂנֵא *hate.*

(*b*) The causatives of verbs intrans. in Qal, as קָדַשׁ *be consecrated, holy,* Piel *sanctify;* כָּבֵד *be heavy,* Piel *honour;* קַל *be light,* Piel *despise;* בּוֹא *come, go in,* Hiph. *bring in;* יָצָא *go out,* Hiph. *bring out;* עָלָה *go up,* Hiph. *bring up;* יָרַד *go down,* Hiph. *bring down;* הָלַךְ *go,* Hiph. *lead,* etc. Some verbs are trans. in both Qal and caus., שָׁלַח and Piel, *send, put forth* (*hand*); שָׁבַר *break,* Piel *shatter;* לָמַד *learn,* Piel *teach;* יָדַע *know,* Hiph. *show.*

(*c*) Verbs of putting on and putting off clothes seem in Hebr. usage mostly trans., but may also be intrans., cf. the alternative forms לָבֵשׁ, לָבַשׁ. For intrans. usages see § 92*a*. Clearly trans. is לָבַשׁ in 1 K. 22. 30 וְאַתָּה לְבַשׁ בְּגָדֶיךָ but you *put on your robes* and פָּשַׁט in 1 S. 19. 24 וַיִּפְשַׁט גַּם־הוּא בְּגָדָיו and he too *stripped off his garments.* Gen. 38. 19, Lev. 6. 4, Deu. 22. 5, 1 S. 28. 8, Song 5. 3. So אָזַר *gird on,* 1 S. 2. 4; חָגַר *id.,* 1 S. 25. 13, Ps. 109. 19; עָדָה, also Hiph., *deck oneself with,* Is. 61. 10,

Ez. 16. 11, Job 40. 10. For *put off* הֵסִיר is often used, Gen. 38. 19.

(*d*) Some intrans. verbs, which are usually construed with a prep., sometimes lack it, and in such cases may be considered trans., as חָפֵץ בְּ *be pleased with* but חָפֵץ *desire*, Is. 1. 11; יָרֵא מִן *be afraid of* but יָרֵא *fear*, Ps. 23. 4; בָּכָה עַל *weep for* but בָּכָה *bewail*, Deu. 21. 13. So in derived stem, קִוָּה לְ *hope for*, קִוָּה *id.*, Job 7. 2. This is probably not the case, however, where the noun is one of place; such nouns are more likely to be adverbial, replacing a prep. phrase; so יָשַׁב (2 S. 6. 11), שָׁכַן (Pr. 2. 21), הָלַךְ (Deu. 1. 19), בּוֹא (Ps. 100. 4), יָצָא Gen. 44. 4. § 117*a*. The verb מָלֵא *be full of, filled with* is generally followed by an obj. complement (§ 92*a*) but also takes a dir. obj. with the transitive sense of *fill*.

(*e*) Some trans. verbs regularly or sometimes reach the direct obj. by means of a prep. and may be compared with Engl. phrasal verbs like *look up, turn down*; the prep. goes with the verb rather than with the obj. and in effect becomes an adverb modifying the verb. Thus נָגַע בְּ *touch*, אָחַז בְּ *catch hold of*, בָּחַר בְּ *choose*, מָאַס בְּ *reject*, נָשָׂא בְּ *bear away*, צִוָּה עַל *approach*, רָאָה בְּ *see one's desire on*, פָּקַד עַל *punish*, צִוָּה עַל *command*, כִּסָּה עַל *cover over*. Some of these verbs may be used without the prep. with the same or similar meaning, e.g. אָחַז *seize*, צִוָּה *command;* others have a different meaning when so used, e.g. פָּקַד *visit*, רָאָה *see*. As in Engl. there are many uncertainties in distinguishing phrasal verbs from verbs followed by a normal prep., and the whole matter requires further investigation.

Rem. 1. Transitivity or the capacity to take a dir. obj. cannot be decided on formal grounds alone. Most *qåṭal/yiqṭōl* forms in Qal are trans., but some are intrans., as עָמַד *stand*, סָבַב *turn*, קוּם *rise;* while most statives (*qåṭēl/yiqṭal* and *qåṭōl/yiqṭal*) are intrans., but some are trans., as אָהֵב *love*, שָׂנֵא *hate*, or both, as לָבֵשׁ/לָבַשׁ *put on, be clothed with.* Similarly, most Niph. and Hithpa. are reflexive/passive, but sometimes they can be used transitively, as Jud. 19. 22 the men of the city נָסַבּוּ אֶת־הַבַּיִת *surrounded* the house, 1 S. 18. 4 וַיִּתְפַּשֵּׁט י' אֶת־הַמְּעִיל and Jon. *stripped from himself* his robe; while most Piels and Hiph. are trans., but some are intrans., as מִהַר *hasten*, יָחַל *wait*, הִשְׁרִישׁ *take root*, הִלְבִּין *become white.*

Rem. 2. With the verbs in *d* a pronom. object more commonly lacks prep. than a nominal, and it may lack a prep. even with the verbs in *e*, e.g. נָגַע, Gen. 26. 29.

Rem. 3. Probably belonging to *e* are a number of trans. verbs like הֵרִים

בַּמַּטֶּה *lift up the rod* (Ex. 7. 20); the בְּ is better explained as used adverbially, as in Engl. *hold with*, than as a prep. of instrument or means. Jer. 12. 8 *give* (forth) (with) the voice; 18. 16 *wag* (with) the head, Ps. 22. 8, Job 16. 9 *gnash* (with) the teeth, Job 16. 10 *open* (with) the mouth, Lam. 1. 17. *Cf.* Pr. 6. 13 (three exx.). So the phrase קָרָא בְשֵׁם *call with* the name, i.e. *invoke*, Gen. 12. 8, *proclaim*, Ex. 34. 5.

Rem. 4. Ellipsis. Many trans. verbs may, as in Engl., omit the direct obj., leaving it to be understood from the context; they do not because of the omission become intrans., Gen. 28. 16 (after *know*); 21. 26 (after *tell*), Ex. 8. 25 (after *sacrifice*). Also frequently omitted, but against Engl. usage, is the pronom. dir. obj. where the person has already been mentioned, especially after verbs of *giving, bringing, putting,* etc., Gen. 2. 19 (after *brought*), 1 S. 19. 13 (after *put*). Gen. 12. 19; 18. 7; 27. 13, 14; 38. 18, Deu. 21. 12. In similar circumstances an indir. obj. may be omitted, Gen. 21. 1 (after *said, spoken*), Jud. 5. 25 (after *give*). A different kind of ellipsis, in effect idiomatic, occurs in the following: נָשָׂא *lift up,* sc. קוֹל, Is. 3. 7; 42. 2; נָשָׂא לְ *forgive,* sc. עָוֺן, Is. 2. 9, Gen. 18. 24; כָּרַת sc. בְּרִית *make covenant,* 1 S. 20. 16, 2 Chr. 7. 18; הִפִּיל sc. גּוֹרָל *cast the lot,* 1 S. 14. 42, Job 6. 27, cf. Jud. 18. 1; שִׂים sc. לֵב *pay attention,* Job 4. 20, so כּוֹנֵן, Job 8. 8; נָטַר, שָׁמַר *retain,* sc. אַף *anger,* Jer. 3. 5, Ps. 103. 9; שָׁלַח sc. יָד, 2 S. 6. 6; הִקְשָׁה sc. עֹרֶף *stiffen neck,* Job 9. 4, cf. Jer. 7. 26.

§ 90. *Object clauses.* Clauses (verbal or nominal) may occupy the place of the subj. (§ 51) or of the dir. obj. They are introduced by the conjunction כִּי, less often אֲשֶׁר, *that.* Pronom. אֲשֶׁר *him who,* etc. may also begin obj. clauses, § 10, as may the pron. מִי, מָה, § 8.

(*a*) After verbs of *perception* and *feeling.* 1 S. 3. 8 וַיָּבֶן עֵלִי כִּי יְ׳ קֹרֵא לַנַּעַר and E. perceived *that Y. was calling* the child. Gen. 8. 11 וַיֵּדַע כִּי קַלּוּ הַמָּיִם knew *that the waters had abated.* Frequently after *see, hear, know.* After *repent,* Gen. 6. 6, 7; after *believe,* Ex. 4. 5, Lam. 4. 12; after *remember,* Ps. 78. 35, Job 7. 7; after *forget,* Job 39. 15. An unmediated כִּי is rare after verbs of *telling, showing,* but it is found with הִגִּיד, Gen. 3. 11; 12. 18, etc. — Not so commonly in earlier, but often in later books, אֲשֶׁר. 1 S. 18. 15 וַיַּרְא שָׁאוּל אֲשֶׁר הוּא מַשְׂכִּיל מְאֹד and S. saw *that he prospered* greatly. Ex. 11. 7, Deu. 1. 31, 1 K. 22. 16 (after *adjure*), Jer. 28. 9, Ez. 29. 26, Neh. 8. 14, 15 (after *find written, command*), Est. 3. 4; 4. 11; 6. 2 (after *find written*), Ecc. 6. 10; 7. 29 (after *find*); 9. 1 (after *lay to heart*), Dan. 1. 8 (id.). Also אֵת אֲשֶׁר *the fact, circumstance that, how that.* 2 K. 20. 3 זְכָר־נָא אֵת אֲשֶׁר הִתְהַלַּכְתִּי *remember how I have walked.* 2 S. 11. 20 הֲלוֹא יְדַעְתֶּם אֵת אֲשֶׁר־יֹרוּ *that they would shoot?* Deu. 9. 7, Jos.

2. 10, 1 S. 2. 22.

It is common for the logical subj. of the object clause to be attracted as obj. into the governing clause. Gen. 49. 15 וַיַּרְא מְנֻחָה כִּי טוֹב he saw *rest that it was good* (that rest was). 1 K. 5. 17 יָדַעְתָּ אֶת־דָּוִד אָבִי כִּי לֹא יָכֹל *that my father D. was unable.* Gen. 1. 4; 31. 5, Ex. 2. 2, 2 S. 17. 8. With אֲשֶׁר, Nu. 32. 23.

(*b*) After the verb *say* quoted or direct speech is to be regarded as dir. obj. Gen. 12. 12 וְאָמְרוּ אִשְׁתּוֹ זֹאת they will say, "*This is his wife,*" vs. 19; 20. 2, 13; 26. 7; 43. 7, Jud. 9. 48, 1 S. 10. 19, 2 S. 3. 13, 1 K. 2. 8, Ps. 10. 11. It is not often that another verb is used without a form of אָמַר (often לֵאמֹר *saying*) intervening, but occasionally this happens, e.g. following דִּבֶּר, Jos. 22. 21; עָנָה, Neh. 8. 6; קָרָא, Lam. 4. 15.

There is a tendency to pass into the semi-oblique form, as Gen. 12. 13 אִמְרִי־נָא אֲחֹתִי אָתְּ say *you are my sister.* Ps. 10. 13; 50. 21 (after דִּמָּה *imagine*); 64. 6, Job 35. 14. But Hebr. does not use conjs. like כִּי to introduce full indirect speech, as Engl. However, כִּי may be used to introduce direct speech (כִּי *recitativum*). 1 K. 1. 30 I swore, saying כִּי שׁ׳בְנֵךְ יִמְלֹךְ אַחֲרַי "*Sol. your son shall reign after me.*" 2 K. 8. 13 and Hazael said כִּי מָה עַבְדְּךָ "*What is your servant, a mere dog, that ...?*" Gen. 29. 33, Jos. 2. 24, Jud. 6. 16, 1 S. 13. 11, 1 K. 11. 22; 21. 6, 1 Chr. 4. 9; 21. 18; 29. 14. (Some, but not all, of these exx. could be rendered with other meanings of כִּי, *when, because, surely,* cf. Gen. 29. 33, 1 S. 13. 11, 1 K. 1. 30).

Rem. 1. The כִּי of obj. clause is sometimes omitted, Ps. 9. 21 know אֱנוֹשׁ הֵמָּה *that they are* (but) *men.* Is. 48. 8, Am. 5. 12, Zech. 8. 23, Job 19. 25, cf. 2 K. 9. 25.

Rem. 2. A clause with *and* occasionally takes the place of an obj. clause (i.e. coordination instead of subordination). Gen. 30. 27 נִחַשְׁתִּי וַיְבָרְכֵנִי י׳ I have divined *and* (*that*) Y. has blessed me. 47. 6 אִם־יָדַעְתָּ וְיֶשׁ־בָּם *if you know and there be* (*that there are*) among them. Cf. Aram., Dan. 2. 13 the law went out *and* (*that*) the wise men were to be slain (ptcp.). A usual brachylogy occurs with *command,* Gen. 18. 19 לְמַעַן אֲשֶׁר יְצַוֶּה ... וְשָׁמְרוּ *that he may charge his sons ... and they will keep* (*to keep*). 42. 25 וַיְצַו יו׳ וַיְמַלְאוּ Jos. commanded *and they filled* (*them to fill*). Nu. 35. 2, 2 S. 4. 12, Jon. 2. 11, cf. Am. 6. 11; 9. 9.

§ **91.** *The indirect object* is usually def. and represents the person (or

animal, rarely thing) at whom the action of a trans. verb upon the dir.
obj. is aimed. Characteristically it precedes the dir. obj. and accompanies
verbs such as *give, teach, show, speak, tell*, etc., but also (unlike Engl.) the
opposites of some of these in meaning, as *take away* (from).

(*a*) In the Qal many such verbs prefer a prep. to an indirect obj., as
נָתַן לְ *give* (something) *to* (someone); קָרָא לְ *call, give* (name) *to*
(someone); שָׁאַל מִן *ask* (something) *from* (someone). So some verbs
whose basic form is Piel or Hiph., as דִּבֶּר אֶל־ *speak to* (someone);
הִגִּיד לְ *tell* (something) *to* (someone). But all may take an indir. obj.
unmediated, especially when it is pronom. suff. Thus נָתַן, Jos. 15. 19
(where the dir. obj. is focussed and precedes); זָבַד *give dowry to*
(someone), Gen. 30. 20 (with cognate obj.); קָבַע *take away* (something)
from (someone), Pr. 22. 23. Is. 58. 2 יִשְׁאָלוּנִי מִשְׁפְּטֵי־צֶדֶק *they ask me
for right judgments*, Ps. 137. 3. 1 K. 12. 13 וַיַּעַן אֶת־הָעָם קָשָׁה *he
returned the people a harsh answer*, 1 S. 20. 10. Cf. הָשִׁיב דָּבָר, Gen.
37. 14 *bring back word to me*, 2 S. 24. 13, 1 K. 12. 6. 1 S. 21. 3 הַמֶּלֶךְ צִוַּנִי
דָּבָר *has entrusted a matter to me*.

(*b*) In the caus. of a number of verbs already trans. in the Qal the
dir. obj. of the verbal action is retained as such and the subj. of the Qal
becomes the person who is affected by the action, i.e. the indirect obj. (it
is in effect the obj. of the idea of causation present in the derived stem).
The verbs concerned now carry the implication of *giving, telling*, etc.
Deu. 8. 3 וַיַּאֲכִלְךָ אֶת־הַמָּן *he fed manna to you;* Jud. 4. 22 אַרְאֶךָּ
אֶת־הָאִישׁ *I will show you the man*. So הוֹדַע *show*, 1 S. 14. 2; הוֹרָה,
הֵבִין *teach, explain*, Is. 28. 9; הִנְחִיל *give as inheritance*, Deu. 3. 29; 31. 7;
לִמַּד *teach*, Jud. 3. 2, Deu. 4. 5; הִשְׁמִיעַ *make, let hear*, 2 K. 7. 6, Song
2. 14. 2 K. 6. 6; 11. 4. An interesting ex. of three obj., direct, indirect and
compl. is 2 K. 8. 13 *showed me you king*.

(*c*) So the caus. of verbs of *putting on, off* clothes (§ 89*c*) where these
are trans. in Qal. 1 S. 17. 38 וַיַּלְבֵּשׁ אֶת־דָּוִד מַדָּיו *he put his garments on
David*, Gen. 41. 42, Ps. 132. 16, 18. Gen. 37. 23 וַיַּפְשִׁיטוּ אֶת־יוֹ' אֶת־
כֻּתָּנְתּוֹ *they stripped his coat from Joseph*, Nu. 20. 26, 28. The dir. obj. is
retained even in the reflexive, 1 S. 18. 4 וַיִּתְפַּשֵּׁט אֶת־הַמְּעִיל *he stripped
his robe from himself* (*himself of*), the indir. obj. being taken into the
verb.

Rem. 1. Of course, not all trans. verbs need take an indir. obj., but only a dir. obj., which may be either animate or inanimate, extending their meaning to another pers. or thing, where required, by means of a prep. (‑אֶל, לְ, מִן, etc.). Noteworthy among these are verbs of *making, taking, bringing,* etc. as עָשָׂה, לָקַח, הֵבִיא, which in Engl. often have an indir. obj. (as *he brought David the scroll*), but in Hebr. prefer a prep. Gen. 2. 22, Ex. 3. 13; 18. 9, 1 S. 2. 19, 1 K. 17. 10, etc. § 89, R. 2.

§ 92. The *object complement* may be a noun or an adj. (ptcp.) and is used in several ways. With some intrans. verbs, e.g. מָלֵא Qal, Niph. *be full of, filled with,* it indicates the result that comes about from the action of the verb (rather than what is done by it), and is retained in this role with their trans. counterparts which have a dir. obj., as מָלֵא Qal, Piel, *fill;* Engl. does not have a compl. with such verbs, but uses *with* or other prep. With some trans. verbs, as שִׂים, עָשָׂה, the obj. compl. specifies what the dir. obj. becomes through the action of the verb, while with other trans. verbs, as רָאָה, שָׁמַע, it describes the condition of the dir. obj. during the action of the verb. When the obj. compl. accompanies a dir. obj., it usually follows it, though its position may vary.

(a) Some intrans. verbs, notably of *fulness* and *want,* take an obj. compl. in Qal, as מָלֵא *be full of,* שָׂבַע *be satisfied with,* חָסֵר *want,* שָׁכֹל *be bereaved of.* Is. 1. 11 שָׂבַעְתִּי עֹלוֹת אֵילִים I am sated *with burnt-offerings of rams; vs.* 15 יְדֵיכֶם דָּמִים מָלֵאוּ *your hands are full of blood;* Deu. 2. 7 לֹא חָסַרְתָּ דָּבָר *you wanted for nothing.* Gen. 18. 28; 27. 45, Ex. 15. 9, Pr. 25. 17. Intrans. usages of לָבֵשׁ/לָבַשׁ may be included here, Ps. 93. 1 גֵּאוּת לָבֵשׁ *he is robed in majesty;* 65. 14 (also עטף); 109. 29 (also עָטָה), Job 7. 5. So other Qal verbs, as שָׁרַץ *swarm with,* Gen. 1. 20, 21; פָּרַץ *overflow with,* Pr. 3. 10; יָרַד *flow down with,* Lam. 3. 48. And suitable passives, Ex. 1. 7, Is. 6. 4.

(b) In caus. of such verbs the subj. becomes the direct obj. and the compl. remains. Gen. 42. 25 וַיְמַלְאוּ אֶת‑כְּלֵיהֶם בָּר they filled (Piel) their sacks *with corn.* 1 K. 18. 13 וָאֲכַלְכְּלֵם לֶחֶם וָמָיִם I sustained them *with bread and water,* Gen. 47. 12, Is. 50. 4. הִשְׂבִּיעַ *satisfy with,* Ps. 132. 15. חִסַּר *make to lack,* Ps. 8. 6. רִוָּה *make saturated with,* Is. 16. 9, cf. הִרְוָה, 55. 10. Lam. 3. 15. So some verbs in Qal: סָעַד *support with,* Jud. 19. 5; סָמַךְ *id.,* Ps. 51. 14; and trans. uses of מָלֵא Qal., *fill,* 1 K. 18. 34.

(c) After trans. verbs of *making, placing, appointing,* etc., an obj. compl. defines what the dir. obj. becomes. Gen. 27. 9 וְאֶעֱשֶׂה אֹתָם

וָאֶבְנֶה אֶת־מַטְעַמִּים I will make them *into savoury food.* 1 K. 18. 32 לֹא תְשִׂימֵנִי קָצִין הָאֲבָנִים מִזְבֵּחַ he built the stones *into an altar.* Is. 3. 7 עָם you will not appoint me *a ruler of the people.* Gen. 17. 5, Ex. 30. 25, Deu. 28. 15, 1 S. 28. 2, 1 K. 14. 7, Is. 5. 6; 28. 15, Mic. 4. 13. אָפָה *bake into,* Ex. 12. 39; בָּרָא *create to be,* Is. 65. 18; הָפַךְ *turn into,* Ps. 114. 8. Cf. 1 K. 11. 30 (*rend into*), Is. 37. 26 (*make collapse into*), Am. 6. 11 (*smite into*), Job 28. 2 (*smelt into*), Ps. 74. 2 (*redeem to be*).

(*d*) After trans. verbs of *seeing, hearing, knowing,* etc., the obj. complement, sometimes a noun, more often an adj. or ptcp., describes the state in which the dir. obj. is seen, heard, known to be. Gen. 15. 6 וַיַּחְשְׁבֶהָ לּוֹ צְדָקָה he counted it *righteousness* to him. 3. 8 וַיִּשְׁמְעוּ אֶת־ קוֹל י׳ א׳ מִתְהַלֵּךְ they heard the voice of Y. God *walking* in the garden (the obj. is a constr. relation and it is properly the second member which is complemented). 7. 1 אֹתְךָ רָאִיתִי צַדִּיק you I have seen (to be) *righteous.* Gen. 21. 9; 27. 6, Nu. 11. 10, 2 K. 14. 26, Is. 6. 1; 53. 4. So after other trans. verbs, as Jos. 11. 6 אָנֹכִי נֹתֵן אֶת־כֻּלָּם חֲלָלִים I shall deliver them all *dead men;* 1 K. 20. 18 (take *alive*), Ps. 124. 3; Is. 20. 4 (lead away *naked*). (Rem. 2).

> *Rem. 1.* Many verbs which take an obj. compl. may also be construed with prep., as שָׂבַע with מִן, Pr. 1. 31, Ps. 104. 13; הִשְׂבִּיעַ with בְּ, Is. 58. 11, Lam. 3. 15; נָתַן with לְ, *make into,* Gen. 12. 2; שִׂים with לְ, *id.,* Mic. 1. 6; חָשַׁב with לְ or כְּ, Job 13. 24; 19. 11.
>
> *Rem. 2.* Definitions of material used in *making, building,* etc. are often added to the verb unmediated by prep., as Gen. 2. 7 (formed man of *dust*). But these usages are adverbial and should be distinguished from the exx. of obj. compl. in *c.* (§ 117*d*) Also, in a few cases of *d* the adj. is sing. following plur. dir. obj., as Is. 20. 4, Job 24. 10 (*naked*), Job 12. 17 (*stripped*); these too should be considered adverbial, the indeclinable adj. operating in effect as adv.

§ 93. The *cognate obj.* is a noun from the same base as the verb it accompanies. Such a verb is usually intrans., though it may be trans., but even in the latter case the cognate obj. is not obviously acted upon as a dir. obj. is, but seems best regarded as a complement of the kind found with the verbs in § 92*a, b.* It is sometimes called the *internal* obj.

(*a*) The cognate obj. sometimes has the almost adverbial effect of strengthening the verb; 1 S. 1. 6 וְכִעֲסַתָּה צָרָתָהּ גַּם־כַּעַס and her rival-wife *continually aggrieved* her; Lam. 1. 8 חֵטְא חָטְאָה יְרוּשָׁלַיִם Jerus. *sinned grievously*; Is. 42. 17 יֵבֹשׁוּ בֹשֶׁת הַבֹּטְחִים בַּפֶּסֶל *they shall be utterly shamed* who trust in a graven image. Is. 21. 7; 24. 16; 66. 10, Ez. 25. 12, Mic. 4. 9, Zech. 1. 2, Job 27. 12, Ps. 14. 5; 106. 14.

(*b*) But more frequently the cognate obj. expresses a concrete instance of the verbal action; 2 K. 12. 21 וַיִּקְשְׁרוּ־קֶשֶׁר they *made a conspiracy*, so 15. 30; Gen. 40. 8 חֲלוֹם חָלַמְנוּ we have *dreamed a dream*. Gen. 9. 14, Ex. 22. 5, Jos. 7. 1; 22. 20, 31, 1 K. 1. 12. In this case it is characteristically in the constr. state before another noun, often with a nuance of comparison; or it is followed by one or more adjectives, which supply the strengthening. 1 S. 20. 17 אַהֲבַת נַפְשׁוֹ אֲהֵבוֹ he loved him *with the love* (he had) *for his own soul*; Jer. 22. 19 קְבוּרַת חֲמוֹר יִקָּבֵר he *shall be buried with the burial of an ass.* Lev. 26. 36, Deu. 16. 18, Jos. 9. 9, Is. 14. 6; 27. 7; 45. 17, Jer. 30. 14, Zech. 7. 9, Ps. 144. 6, *cf.* Ps. 13. 4 (*sleep* the sleep of *death*), Ps. 139. 22 (*with completeness of,* i.e. perfect, *hatred*). With adj., Gen. 27. 34 וַיִּצְעַק צְעָקָה גְדֹלָה וּמָרָה עַד־מְאֹד he cried *with an exceeding loud and bitter cry.* Gen. 12. 17; 50. 10, Deu. 7. 23, Jud. 21. 2, 1 S. 17. 25, 2 S. 13. 15, 36, 1 K. 1. 40, Jer. 8. 5; 14. 17, Jon. 1. 10, Zech. 1. 14, 15; 8. 2, Neh. 2. 10.

> *Rem. 1.* Perhaps it should be considered a form of cognate or internal obj. when verbs of *expression* or *conduct*, esp. the first, subordinate to themselves the organ of expression or acting, 2 S. 15. 23 all the land בֹּכִים קוֹל גָּדוֹל were weeping *with a loud voice*, Pr. 10. 4 עֹשֶׂה כַף־רְמִיָּה he who *works with a slack hand.* Deu. 5. 19, 1 K. 8. 55, Is. 19. 18, Jer. 25. 30, Ez. 11. 13, Ps. 12. 3; 63. 6; 109. 2, Ezr. 10. 12.

Excursus: the Particles אֵת and לְ

§ 94. The particle אֵת is most commonly used before a *def.* nominal or pronom. obj. referring to a person or animal, though it also occurs with a non-animate obj. Gen. 2. 15 וַיִּקַּח אֶת־הָאָדָם he took *the man;* 2. 24 יַעֲזֹב אֶת־אָבִיו וְאֶת־אִמּוֹ he shall leave *his father and mother;* 4. 11 לָקַחַת אֶת־דְּמֵי אָחִיךָ to receive *your father's blood;* 40. 4 וַיְשָׁרֶת אֹתָם he served *them.* However, אֵת is very often wanting in such cases, and (like the Art.) it is much less employed in poetry, espec. earlier poetry, than in prose; thus it occurs not at all or very rarely in the poems in Gen.

49 (once, *vs.* 15), Ex. 15, Deu. 32; 33 (twice, *vs.* 9), Jud. 5, 1 S. 2, Ps. 18 (twice in the parallel in 2 S. 22, *vss.* 20, 28). Moreover, אֵת sometimes marks an indef. dir. obj., often enough an indir. obj. (which is usually def.), and sporadically an obj. compl. (which is usually indef.); it is even used with a noun as adv. ("adverbial accusative"); and in a significant number of passages it accompanies, not the obj., but the *subject* of a clause. This variety of usage suggests that אֵת is not essentially connected with the obj., def. or otherwise, but has a wider, and optional, focussing or specifying function. Mostly a prep., לְ shares some of these functions of אֵת and should be regarded in a similar light.

Rem. 1. When several dir. obj. are coupled with *and,* אֵת is usually repeated before each of them, Gen. 1. 1, but is occasionally confined to the first, Jud. 1. 4.

Rem. 2. The dir. obj., when a pron., is as often appended to the verb as to אֵת. But אֵת must be used in these cases: (*a*) when the dir. obj. is focussed and placed before the verb, Jud. 14. 3 אֹתָהּ קַח־לִי get *her* for me. Gen. 7. 1; 24. 14; 41. 13, 1 S. 8. 7; 21. 10, Hos. 2. 15. (*b*) When the pron. obj. is governed by infin. absol., Gen. 41. 43 וְנָתוֹן אֹתוֹ and set *him* over, 1 S. 2. 28, Jer. 9. 23, Ez. 36. 3. (*c*) When the verb also has a pron. indir. obj. or, in the case of infin. constr., a suffixed subj., 2 S. 15. 25 וְהִרְאַנִי אֹתוֹ and he will let *me* see *it;* Gen. 29. 20 בְּאַהֲבָתוֹ אֹתָהּ because of *his* loving *her.* Gen. 19. 17; 38. 5, Deu. 7. 24; 31. 7, 1 S. 1. 23; 18. 3, 2 K. 8. 13. Similarly when subj. of infin. constr. is a noun, Deu. 22. 2.

Rem. 3. What is an indef. obj. in Hebr. is not simply a matter of the absence of the Art. Pronouns are def., including אֲשֶׁר, as in Hebr. practice are numerals, even אֶחָד *one,* and similar words like כֹּל *all, every,* אַחֵר *another;* and def. nouns frequently in poetry (occasionally in prose) may lack Art.; see § 31, R. 2. All of these may take אֵת (not מָה, § 7*b*). Is. 6. 8 אֶת־מִי *whom,* 1 S. 16. 3 אֵת אֲשֶׁר *the one of whom.* Gen. 44. 1. Gen. 9. 24, 2 K. 20. 3. With numerals, Gen. 21. 30, 2 S. 15. 6. With אֶחָד, Nu. 16. 15, 1 S. 9. 3. With כֹּל, Gen. 1. 21, Deu. 2. 34, 2 S. 6. 1. With אַחֵר, Jer. 16. 13. In poetry, Is. 41. 7; 50. 4, Pr. 13. 21, etc. Such cases should be distinguished from genuine exx. of אֵת with an indef. dir. obj., of which there are rather too many to be explained away as having a particular reference in the context. Thus *a man, a woman* in legal texts, Ex. 21. 28, Lev. 20. 14, Nu. 21. 9. Otherwise 1 S. 24. 5 (*a skirt*); 26. 20 (*a flea*), 2 S. 4. 11 (*a righteous man*).

Rem. 4. Exx. of the other two objects with אֵת. Indirect (not infrequent): Gen. 7. 9 (command *Noah*), Deu. 3. 28 (cause *them* to possess); 4. 5 (teach *you*), 1 S. 14. 12 (make known *to you*); 17. 38 (put garments *on David*); 20. 10

(answer *the people*), Jer. 1. 16 (speak *to them*), etc. Complement (rare): Ex.
8. 17 (filled with *flies*), 1 K. 7. 14 (filled with *wisdom*). When two objs. are
used, it is not often that both are marked with אֵת, though exx. occur, Deu.
3. 28.

Rem. 5. Exx. of אֵת with nouns used adverbially (§ 117): Gen. 17. 11, 14,
25 (not 24) (*in the flesh of his foreskin*), Ex. 13. 7 (*seven days*), Lev. 25. 22 (*in the
eighth year*), Deu. 9. 25 (*forty days and forty nights*), 1 K. 15. 23 (*in his feet*). It
could be argued that this usage survives from a time when Hebr. possessed an
accusative case, thus associating the particle historically with that case; but
that would not cover the usage with subj. (R. 6).

Rem. 6. The subj. of a trans. verb is rarely marked with אֵת, Neh. 9. 34.
It is much commoner with subj. of intrans. verbs, 2 K. 6. 5 וְאֶת־הַבַּרְזֶל נָפַל
the iron (axehead) fell into the water, Jud. 20. 24, 1 S. 17. 34, Ez. 17. 21; 44. 3,
Dan. 9. 13, Neh. 9. 19. Or of passive verbs, Gen. 4. 18 וַיִּוָּלֵד לַחֲנוֹךְ אֶת־עִירָד
and *Irad* was born to Enoch; 21. 5, 2 S. 21. 22. Or with the substantive subj.
(properly in appos. to "it") of impers. verbs, 2 S. 11. 25 אַל־יֵרַע בְּעֵינֶיךָ אֶת־
הַדָּבָר let not *the matter* trouble you (let. let it not be evil in your eyes, *namely
the matter*); 1 S 20. 13 (read יֵיטַב), Neh. 9. 32 (fem. noun). Or with the subj.
or subj. compl. in nominal clauses or of the verb הָיָה, Nu. 35. 7 all the cities
... (shall be) forty-eight cities אֶתְהֶן וְאֶת־מִגְרְשֵׁיהֶן *they* and *their pastoral lands*.
Nu. 3. 26; 5. 10, Jos. 17. 11; 22. 17, 1 S. 26. 16, Jer. 36. 22, Ez. 10. 22; 35. 10,
Zech. 7. 7, Ecc. 4. 3; *cf.* אֵת following יֵשׁ, 2 K. 10. 15; following אֵין, Hag. 2. 17
(or are these obj.?, § 52). It has been remarked that certain of these exx. are
similar to a construction called "ergative", by which in certain languages the
subj. of an intrans. or passive verb is marked in the same way as the dir. obj.
of a trans. verb; compare אֶת־עִירָד as the subj. of *was born* (Gen. 4. 18) with
אֶת־אֱנוֹשׁ as the object of *begat* (5. 6). But, though this is evidence of
"ergative" thinking in Hebr., such an explanation does not apply to, e.g., the
subjects of the nominal clauses cited above where there is no verb which can
change from intrans. to trans. It seems more sensible to regard אֵת
accompanying subjects as (mildly) focussing or emphatic. Note particularly
the exx. where אֵת is used with a noun in app., e.g. 2 S. 11. 25 (above), Ez.
10. 22, and where it marks only the second of two subjects, e.g. 1 S. 17. 34 (the
lion and *also the bear*); 26. 16.

Rem. 7. Rarer uses of אֵת, also apparently with focussing force, are to
mark an extraposed noun (*casus pendens*), Gen. 13. 15 (*as for* all the land), 1 K.
15. 13, Ez. 20. 16; or a noun in appos. to a dir. obj., 1 K. 2. 32 (*namely* Abner,
etc.), Ez. 14. 22, or even to a prepos. phrase, Ex. 1. 14 (*namely* in all their
labours).

Rem. 8. As well as its normal prep. usages, לְ has some non-prepositional
usages similar to those of אֵת: (*a*) to indicate the def. dir. obj. of a trans. verb,
partic. infin. and ptcp., Ex. 32. 13 זְכֹר לְא׳ remember *Abraham*, 1 S. 23. 10

לְשַׁחֵת לָעִיר *to destroy the town*, Is. 11. 9 לַיָּם מְכַסִּים *covering the sea*. Nu. 12. 13; 32. 15, 2 S. 3. 30, Is. 29. 2, Jer. 40. 2, Hos. 10. 1, Am. 6. 3; 8. 9, Job 11. 6, Ps. 69. 6; 73. 18, Ezr. 8. 16, 24, 1 Chr. 16. 37. Further to mark (*b*) an indef. dir. obj. (rare), Job 5. 2; (*c*) the subj. of an intrans. or pass. verb, 2 S. 17. 16 פֶּן יְבֻלַּע לַמֶּלֶךְ *lest the king be swallowed up*, 2 Chr. 7. 21; (*d*) a noun in appos., Ps. 136. 19, 20 (*namely* Sihon), 1 Chr. 5. 26; 13. 1, 2 Chr. 2. 12; 23. 1. On the other hand, with indir. obj. and obj. compl. לְ operates normally as prep., Gen. 3. 17 כִּי שָׁמַעְתָּ לְקוֹל אִשְׁתֶּךָ *because you listened to the voice of your wife*; 12. 2 וְאֶעֶשְׂךָ לְגוֹי גָּדוֹל *that I may make you into a great nation.*

CONSTRUCTION OF THE PASSIVE

§ 95. As in other languages the dir. obj. of a trans. verb becomes the subj. of the equivalent pass., with usual concord. Qal pass.: Gen. 12. 15 וַתֻּקַּח הָאִשָּׁה *the woman was taken;* 4. 24, Job 19. 23(b) (plur.). Niph.: 2 K. 13. 13 וַיִּקָּבֵר יוֹאָשׁ *J. was buried*, Zeph. 3. 8 (fem). Job 19. 23(a) (plur.). Pual: Is. 9. 9 שִׁקְמִים גֻּדָּעוּ *the sycamores have been cut down*, Am. 7. 17 (fem.). Hoph.: Is. 16. 15 כִּסֵּא ... וְהוּכַן *a throne will be established*, Lev. 21. 10. The subj. is not uncommonly marked with אֵת (above, R. 6), Gen. 29. 27 וְנִתְּנָה לְךָ גַּם־אֶת־זֹאת *this one too* will be given to you; 17. 5; 18. 4, Deu. 12. 22, 2 S. 21. 22 (plur.).

The following usages are noteworthy. — (*a*) There are a number of cases where concord is not observed and a plur. or fem. subj. is contrued with 3 mas. sing. verb as the basic form in accordance with § 22, 1. Is. 9. 18 וְנִשְׁאַר־בּוֹ עֹלֵלוֹת *the land is burned;* 24. 12. 17. 6 נֶעְתַּם אָרֶץ *gleanings will be left* in it, Jer. 36. 32. More commonly the subj. is marked with אֵת. Nu. 14. 21 וְיִמָּלֵא כְבוֹד־יְ אֶת־כָּל־הָאָרֶץ *the earth will be filled* with the glory of Y., Hos. 10. 6, Ps. 72. 19. Jer. 35. 14 הוּקַם אֶת־דִּבְרֵי יוֹ׳ *the commands* of Jonadab *have been kept*, Gen. 27. 42, 2 S. 21. 6.

(*b*) The obj. complement is retained when the verb is passive. Thus of intrans. verbs: Is. 6. 4 וְהַבַּיִת יִמָּלֵא עָשָׁן *the house was filled with smoke*, Ex. 1. 7, 1 K. 7. 14, Is. 2. 7, 8; 38. 10, Ps. 80. 11, Pr. 24. 31. Of trans. verbs of *making, appointing*, etc.: Mic. 3. 12 צִיּוֹן שָׂדֶה תֵחָרֵשׁ *Zion shall be ploughed into a field*, Is. 6. 11; 24. 12. 1 K. 14. 6. So cognate obj., Jer. 14. 17. The obj. compl. of verbs of *seeing, estimating*, etc., on the other hand, becomes *subj. compl.* in pass. (§ 50), Gen. 31. 15 הֲלוֹא נָכְרִיּוֹת נֶחְשַׁבְנוּ לוֹ *are we not considered foreigners* by him, Is. 40. 17.

(c) The subj. of a trans. verb becomes the agent of pass., and is usually expressed by prep. לְ. Gen. 14. 9 בָּרוּךְ לְאֵל עֶלְיוֹן blessed *by God Most High;* 31. 15 נֶחְשַׁבְנוּ לוֹ we are counted *by him;* Is. 65. 1 נִמְצֵאתִי לְלֹא בִקְשֻׁנִי I was to be found *by those who sought me not.* Ex. 12. 16, 1 S. 15. 13, Jer. 8. 3, Neh. 6. 1. More rarely by מִן (*from,* of source), Lev. 21. 7 אִשָּׁה גְּרוּשָׁה מֵאִישָׁהּ a woman divorced *from her husband, cf.* Jud. 14. 4, Job 4. 9. Prep. מִן is more usual of *cause* or means, not personal, Gen. 9.11 יִכָּרֵת מִמֵּי הַמַּבּוּל shall be cut off *by the waters of the flood,* Obad. 9, cf. Job 7. 14. Prep. בְּ (of instrument), usually of things (Ez. 26. 6 be slain *by the sword*), may also be used of persons, Gen. 9. 6 בָּאָדָם דָּמוֹ יִשָּׁפֵךְ *through men* shall his blood be shed.

Rem. 1. Traditionally the nouns with אֵת in *a* have been regarded as dir. obj. of the pass. verbs used impersonally, and this interpretation extended to mas. sing. nouns with אֵת, it being in effect denied that אֵת can mark the subj. But this view does not take account of cases where אֵת indicates the subj. of a nominal clause (§ 94, R. 6) or, more appositely, cases like Gen. 29. 27 above, where a fem. subj. or 2 S. 21. 22, where a plur. subj., both with אֵת, have their verbs in concord.

Rem. 2. Though such instances of nouns with אֵת are to be taken as subj., not obj., genuine cases of the *impersonal construction* with pass. (and intrans.) verbs are still found, as Gen. 2. 23 לְזֹאת יִקָּרֵא אִשָּׁה to this one *it shall be called* (this one shall be called) woman; 4. 26 הוּחַל לִקְרֹא *it was begun* (men began) to call on the name of Y.; 12. 13 לְמַעַן יִיטַב־לִי that *it may go well* with me because of you. Nu. 16. 29 (with cognate obj. retained), 1 S. 29. 9, Is. 53. 7, Ps. 68. 15 (fem. verb). See further § 15. See also § 94, R. 6, where in 2 S. 11. 25 the "real" subj., marked with אֵת, is in appos. to the "it" of the verb.

Two Verb Constructions

§ 96. Verbs which regularly govern another verb are of two kinds: (a) those which have a meaning distinct from the other verb, as אָבָה *be willing* (to do), הֵחֵל *begin,* חָדַל *cease,* חָפֵץ *be pleased,* יָדַע *know* (how to do), כִּלָּה *finish* (doing), לָמַד *learn,* מֵאֵן *refuse,* נִסָּה *try.* In some cases the first verb may have a dir. obj., as לִמֵּד *teach* (someone to do), נָתַן *allow.* (b) Characteristic of Hebr., those which merely modify the second verb and have often to be rendered adverbially or otherwise paraphrased in Engl., as הוֹסִיף, יָסַף *add to do,* i.e. *do again* or *more,* שׁוּב *do again,*

הַרְבָּה *do much, greatly, often,* מַהֵר *do quickly,* הֵיטִיב *do well,* הִגְדִּיל *do greatly,* etc.

§ 97. Modes of connection (*Note:* some verbs are found using two or all three modes, others tend to favour only one).

(*a*) The second verb is *infin. constr.* with, less commonly without, לְ or, still less commonly, *infin. absol.* Exx. of § 96*a*: Gen. 11. 8 וַיַּחְדְּלוּ לִבְנֹת הָעִיר they *gave up* building the city; 1 S. 18. 2 וְלֹא נְתָנוֹ לָשׁוּב he did not *allow him to return*; Deu. 10. 10 לֹא אָבָה י' הַשְׁחִיתֶךָ Y. *was unwilling to destroy* you; Is. 1. 16 חִדְלוּ הָרֵעַ לִמְדוּ הֵיטֵב *cease to do evil, learn to do good.* Gen. 4. 26; 6. 1; 24. 15, 19, 22; 37. 35, Ex. 10. 27, Deu. 2. 30; 3. 23; 4. 34, 1 S. 16. 8, Jer. 1. 6, Am. 3. 10; 7. 2, Job 6. 7. Exx. of *b*: Gen. 8. 21 לֹא אֹסִף לְקַלֵּל עוֹד *I shall* never *again curse* the ground; Ex. 8. 24 לֹא־תַרְחִיקוּ לָלֶכֶת *you shall* not *go far away*; 2 K. 2. 10 הִקְשִׁיתָ לִשְׁאוֹל *you have asked a hard thing* (made hard to ask). 1 S. 1. 12; 2. 3; 16. 17, 2 S. 19. 4, 1 K. 14. 9, 2 K. 21. 6, Is. 23. 16; 29. 15; 55. 7, Jer. 1. 12; 16. 12, Hos. 9. 9, Am. 4. 4, Jon. 4. 2, Ps. 55. 8; 113. 5-6, Ezr. 10. 13, 2 Chr. 20. 35. The infin. in these exx. may, following *trans.* verbs, be regarded as dir. obj. and, following *intrans.* verbs or *trans.* verbs already having a dir. obj., as obj. complement. This usage is to be distinguished from other uses of infin., e.g. to express purpose or result, § 126*b*.

(*b*) The verbs are *coordinated* in the same conjugation with *Vav.* Gen. 24. 18 וַתְּמַהֵר וַתֹּרֶד כַּדָּהּ *she quickly let down* her pitcher; 44. 11. 2 K. 6. 3 הוֹאֶל־נָא וְלֵךְ *consent to go*; Jud. 19. 6. Gen. 25. 1 וַיֹּסֶף אב' Abr. *took another wife*; 1 K. 19. 6 וַיֵּשֶׁב וַיִּשְׁכַּב he *lay down again*; 2 K. 1. 11, 13. Or the equivalent *Vav cons.* may be used, Hos. 2. 11 אָשׁוּב וְלָקַחְתִּי *I will take back again.* 2 S. 7. 29, Is. 6. 13, Mal. 1. 4, Job 6. 9. — Jos. 7. 7, Is. 1. 19, Est. 8. 6, Dan. 9. 25.

(*c*) The verbs are *coordinated* without *Vav*, asyndetously. Esp. in imper.: 2 K. 5. 23 הוֹאֶל קַח כִּכָּרַיִם *please take* two talents; 1 S. 3. 5 שׁוּב שְׁכַב *lie down again*, Gen. 19. 22, Deu. 2. 24. Jos. 5. 2, Is. 21. 12, Jer. 13. 18, Ps. 51. 4. — YIQTOL: Hos. 1. 6 לֹא אוֹסִיף עוֹד אֲרַחֵם *I will no more pity*; Gen. 30. 31 אָשׁוּבָה אֶרְעֶה צֹאנְךָ *I will again feed* your flock; 1 S. 2. 3 אַל־תַּרְבּוּ תְדַבְּרוּ *talk no longer.* Mic. 7. 19, Lam. 4. 14, Job 10. 16; 19. 3. Peculiarly with change of pers., Is. 47. 1 לֹא תוֹסִיפִי יִקְרְאוּ־לָךְ רַכָּה *no longer shall people call you* (shall you be called) Tender, Lam. 1. 10. YIQTOL may follow a stative QATAL, Job 32. 22 לֹא יָדַעְתִּי אֲכַנֶּה

I am not good at flattering, Is. 42. 21. — QATAL: Ps. 106. 13 מִהֲרוּ שָׁכְחוּ *speedily they forgot.* Hos. 5. 11; 9. 9, Zeph. 3. 7, Zech. 8. 15. These usages are to be distinguished from normal asyndeton, 1 S. 3. 9, Ps. 88. 11; 102. 14, etc.

Rem. 1. In a few instances the *ptcp.* or *adj.* seems to be substituted for infin., Is. 33. 1 כַּהֲתִימְךָ שׁוֹדֵד when you are done *destroying;* 1 S. 3. 2 וְעֵינָו הֵחֵלּוּ כֵהוֹת his eyes had begun *to be dim.* 1 S. 16. 16, Hos. 7. 4, Neh. 10. 29 (all able *to understand*). So possibly a noun, Gen. 9. 20, Noah was the first (to be) *a tiller of the soil* (*cf.* infin. in 10. 8, 1 S. 14. 35; 22. 15). But אִישׁ הָאֲדָמָה is more likely to be a subj. compl., began *as* and so therefore perhaps כֵהוֹת in 1 S. 3. 2 and its counterparts in Is. 33. 1, Hos. 7. 4. Neh. 10. 29 may be an ex. of normal asyndeton or it and 1 S. 16. 16 cases of appos.

The Syntax of the Infinitive and Participle

———◆———

§ 98. Hebrew has four non-finite forms which share features of both verb and noun, two infinitives traditionally called Absolute and Construct, and two participles, active and passive. The chief uses of the infin. absol. can hardly be called infinitival in the normal sense of the word, but in other uses it shares with the infin. constr. the nominal and verbal functions associated in Engl. with both infinitive and gerund in -*ing*. In these functions they are in effect nouns which may take an obj. and as such cannot operate as full finite verbs. The participles are in effect adjectives which may take an obj. (the pass. ptcp. only an obj. compl.) and are similarly unable to function finitely. The infinitives denote the action or state of the verb from which they are derived, the participles the person involved in such action or state, either as actor or patient. But neither express aspect or mood like the inflected conjugations nor, of course, do they any more than these have implications of "tense".

The Infinitive Absolute

§ 99. The infinitives absol. and constr. were so called because of a surface resemblance to the (longer) absol. and (shorter) constr. states of the noun, but the two are in fact unrelated in origin and, for the most part, in usage. The infin. absol. may, like the infin. constr., be used as the equivalent of an Engl. infin. or gerund, but its three main usages are its own: to be (1) a strengthening complement to finite verbs from the same root, (2) an adverbial compl. to finite verbs from a different root, and (3) a substitute for any form of a finite verb.

§ 100. The infin. absol. as infin./gerund is less common than the infin. constr. and more restricted in usage; it cannot receive suffixes and is only rarely preceded by a prep:, and it cannot be put into the constr. state. It may, however —

(a) Be the subj. in a nominal clause, espec. when the pred. is טוֹב *good* or לֹא טוֹב (in poetry בַּל טוֹב) *not good*, but also otherwise. Pr. 28. 21 הַכֵּר־פָּנִים לֹא־טוֹב *to be partial* is not good. 1 S. 15. 23, Jer. 10. 5, Pr. 24. 23; 25. 27, Job 25. 2. Exceptionally, it may be subj. to a verbal clause, Job 6. 25. In Is. 58. 6 it is in appos. to זֶה as subj.

(b) Or the dir. obj. of a trans. verb, Is. 1. 17 לִמְדוּ הֵיטֵב *learn to do well*. Or the obj. compl. of an intrans. verb, Is. 42. 24 לֹא אָבוּ הָלוֹךְ *they were unwilling to walk*. Is. 7. 15; 57. 20, Pr. 15. 12, Job 9. 18; 13. 3. Lam. 3. 45. In Jer. 9. 23 it is in appos. to בְּזֹאת following the verb יִתְהַלֵּל *glory in*.

(c) It may itself like a finite verb take a dir. obj., Hos. 10. 4 כָּרֹת בְּרִית *making covenants;* Is. 22. 13 הָגֹר בָּקָר וְשָׁחֹט צֹאן *killing oxen* and *slaying sheep*. Is. 5. 5; 21. 5; 59. 4, 13, Pr. 25. 4, 5. Or, like a phrasal finite verb, govern via a "prep", Is. 7. 15 מָאוֹס בָּרָע וּבָחוֹר בַּטּוֹב *to refuse evil* and *choose good*.

(d) It may, though not commonly, follow a prep., 1 S. 1. 9 אַחֲרֵי שָׁתֹה *after* drinking, 2 K. 13. 17, 19, Is. 30. 15. Or, rather more commonly, another noun in constr., Is. 14. 23 בְּמַטְאֲטֵא הַשְׁמֵד *with the broom of* destruction, Pr. 1. 3; 21. 16.

§ 101.   The most characteristic use of the infin. absol. is as complement to a cognate verb. — (a) When *before* its verb, it serves as a strengthening or emphasizing complement. Traditionally this has been spoken of as in the "accusative" case, more particularly as a cognate or internal "accusative" (see § 93); but now that its equivalent in Ugaritic has (in final Aleph verbs) been discovered to carry the nominative -*u* ending, it should rather be regarded as a special kind of *subject* compl. In effect, the subj. of the finite verb is twice described as taking part in a certain action or being in a certain state. The intensification of meaning which results, however, is not of the kind associated with the Piel (e.g. שָׁבַר *break*, שִׁבֵּר *smash*); it does not simply apply to the finite verb but to the whole clause, the appropriate Engl. translation depending on what kind of clause it is. Thus the infin. absol. strengthens the note of certainty in affirmations and in promises or threats, and of contrast in adversative or concessionary statements, while it reinforces any sense of supposition or doubt or volition present in conditional clauses or questions or wishes. It is not often found in narrative. A translation by an

adv. like *indeed, surely, of course, even, really, at all,* etc. or by a modal
should, could, must, may, etc. may catch the nuance, but is often
unnecessarily strong.

Exx. of *affirmation*: Gen. 2. 17 מוֹת תָּמוּת *you shall* (surely) *die;* 16. 10;
18. 10, 2 S. 5. 19. Frequently in injunctions: Ex. 21. 28 סָקוֹל יִסָּקֵל הַשּׁוֹר
the ox *shall be stoned;* 23. 4; Deu. 12. 2, and often. *Antithesis*: Jud. 15. 13
לֹא כִּי אָסֹר נֶאֱסָרְךָ וְהָמֵת לֹא נְמִיתֶךָ *no, we will bind you, but we will*
not kill you. Deu. 7. 26; 13. 10; 21. 14, 1 S. 6. 3, 2 S. 24. 24, 1 K. 11. 22, Is.
28. 28, Jer. 32. 4; 34. 3, Am. 9. 8. *Concession*: Gen. 31. 30 וְעַתָּה הָלֹךְ
הָלַכְתָּ *well, you have gone off* because, etc. (but why steal my gods?), 1 S.
2. 30. *Supposition* (very common): Ex. 21. 5 וְאִם אָמֹר יֹאמַר הָעֶבֶד *but if*
the slave should say; 22. 3, 11, 12, 16, 22, Jud. 11. 30; 14. 12, 1 S. 1. 11; 20. 6,
9, 21, 2 S. 18. 3. *In questions*: Gen. 24. 5 הֶהָשֵׁב אָשִׁיב אֶת־בִּנְךָ *am I, then,*
to bring back your son? 37. 8, 10 הֲמָלֹךְ תִּמְלֹךְ עָלֵינוּ *shall you* (indeed)
rule over us? 43. 7 הֲיָדֹעַ נֵדַע כִּי יֹאמַר *were we* (then) *to know?* Nu.
22. 30, 37, 38, Jud. 11. 25, 1 S. 2. 27, 2 K. 18. 33, Is. 50. 2, Jer. 26. 19, Ez.
14. 3; 18. 23, Zech. 7. 5. *In wishes*: Job 6. 2 לוּ שָׁקוֹל יִשָּׁקֵל כַּעְשִׂי *would*
that my vexation *could be weighed!* 1 S. 14. 30, Job 13. 5.

The peculiar emphasis of infin. absol. is well felt when a speaker gives
a report regarding circumstances, or repeats (directly or indirectly) the
words of another, or his own thoughts. Gen. 43. 3, 7, Jud. 9. 8; 15. 2, 1 S.
10. 16; 14. 28, 43; 20. 3, 6, 28; 23. 22, 2 S. 1. 6. Also when restrictive
particles רַק, אַךְ, are used, Gen. 44. 28, Jud. 7. 19 (*just then*). In
narrative, Gen. 27. 30 (*just*)

(*b*) In negative clause infin. absol. precedes the neg., and the
negation is emphasized. Is. 30. 19 בָּכוֹ לֹא־תִבְכֶּה *you shall* *not* weep. Ex.
8. 24; 34. 7, Deu. 21. 14, 1 K. 3. 27, Jer. 13. 12, Am. 3. 5, Dan. 10. 3. So in
narrative or report, Jud. 1. 28, Jer. 6. 15. With אַל, 1 K. 3. 26, Mic. 1. 10.
Exceptions occur mostly when a denial is given to previous words, Gen.
3. 4, Am. 9. 8, Ps. 49. 8.

(*c*) When placed as a (subj.) compl. *after* its verb, infin. absol. has
often clearly the same force as when before it. 2 K. 5. 11 אָמַרְתִּי אֵלַי יֵצֵא
יָצוֹא I thought, *He will* (certainly) *come out to me,* Nu. 23. 11, 2 S. 3. 24;
6. 20, Jer. 23. 39, Dan. 11. 10, 13. In this case infin. absol. is sometimes
strengthened by גַּם. Gen. 46. 4 וְאָנֹכִי אַעַלְךָ גַם־עָלֹה *I will indeed bring*
you up; 31. 15, Nu. 16. 13. Infin. absol. always stands after *imper.* and

nearly always after *ptcp.*, Nu. 11. 15 הָרְגֵנִי־נָא הָרֹג *kill me rather* (at once), Jud. 5. 23, Is. 6. 9, Jer. 22. 10. Is. 22. 17 הִנֵּה י׳ מְטַלְטֶלְךָ טַלְטֵלָה *behold, Y. will hurl you violently away*, Jer. 23. 17.

But infin. absol. after its verb often seems to suggest an indefinitely prolonged state of the action, and therefore to express continuance, prevalence, etc. This use, however, need not be thought of as different from the intensifying use; rather it is the way in which the intensification works out when the verb is one of motion or implies a lengthy action. By its nature, this use is commoner in narrative. Nu. 11. 32 וַיִּשְׁטְחוּ לָהֶם שָׁטוֹחַ *and they kept spreading them out* (the quails), Jer. 6. 29. The nuance of continuity becomes clearer when an infin. absol. of another verb is added, Jud. 14. 9 וַיֵּלֶךְ הָלוֹךְ וְאָכֹל *he went on, eating as he went;* Gen. 8. 7 וַיֵּצֵא יָצוֹא וָשׁוֹב *and it went out and back.* 1 S. 6. 12, 1 K. 20. 37, 2 K. 2. 11, Is. 19. 22. Significantly this infin. absol. may occur *before* verb, Is. 3. 16, cf. Ps. 126. 6.

> *Rem. 1.* The infin. absol. is oftenest of the same stem as the finite, whether before or after it, *e.g. Qal* Gen. 2. 16, *Niph.* Ex. 22. 3, *Piel* Gen. 22. 17, *Pual* 40. 15, *Hiph.* 3. 16, *Hoph.* Ex. 16. 4, *Hithpa.* Nu. 16. 13. But as infin. absolute of Qal expresses the idea of the verb in general, it may be joined with any other stem, *e.g.* with *Niph.* Ex. 21. 20, with *Piel* 2 S. 20. 18, with *Pual* Gen. 37. 33, with *Hiph.* 1 S. 23. 22, Gen. 46. 4, with *Hoph.* Ex. 21. 12 (and always in this phrase *shall be put to death*), with *Hithpo.* Is. 24. 19. Other combinations are rarer, *e.g.* infin. absol. *Hoph.* with *Niph.* 2 K. 3. 23, and with *Pual* Ez. 16. 4; infin. absol. *Piel* with *Hiph.* 1 S. 2. 16. On occasion the infin. is from another verb, cognate and similar in sound, Is. 28. 28, Jer. 8. 13; 48. 9, Zeph. 1. 2, thus retaining the paranomastic flavour of the construction.
>
> *Rem. 2.* Instead of infin. absol., the verb with cognate obj. or other construction with play on words is sometimes used: Is. 35. 2, Jer. 46. 5, Mic. 4. 9, Hab. 3. 9, Job 27. 12, cf. Is. 29. 14, both infin. absol. and cognate noun.
>
> *Rem. 3.* The verb הָלַךְ with its infin. absol. is followed: (*a*) mostly by another infin. absol. as above in *c*, *e.g.* 2 S. 3. 16 וַיֵּלֶךְ הָלוֹךְ וּבָכֹה, Jos. 6. 9, 2 K. 2. 11; but (*b*) also by ptcp., 2 S. 18. 25 וַיֵּלֶךְ הָלוֹךְ וְקָרֵב, Jer. 41. 6, cf. with other verbs 2 S. 16. 5 (in 1 S. 17. 41 הֹלֵךְ is also ptcp.); and (*c*) by a finite form, 2 S. 16. 13 וַיֵּלֶךְ הָלוֹךְ וַיְקַלֵּל, Jos. 6. 13, 1 S. 19. 23, 2 S. 13. 19, cf. with other verb Is. 31. 5.
>
> But הָלַךְ is often used in a metaphorical sense to express *progress, continuance*, etc. in an action or condition, the latter being expressed by ptcp. or adj., Gen. 26. 13 וַיֵּלֶךְ הָלוֹךְ וְגָדֵל *he grew ever greater*, Jud. 4. 24, 1 S. 14. 19,

2 S. 5. 10, 1 Chr. 11. 9. In the same sense the ptcp. הֹלֵךְ is used in a nominal clause, 2 S. 3. 1 וְדָוִד הֹלֵךְ וְחָזֵק *D. grew stronger and stronger*, Ex. 19. 19, 1 S. 2. 26, 2 Chr. 17. 12, Est. 9. 4. In Pr. 4. 18 הוֹלֵךְ is followed by infin. absol.

Used adverbially with infin. absol. of other verbs infin. absol. of הָלַךְ expresses the same idea of progress or endurance. Gen. 12. 9 וַיִּסַּע הָלוֹךְ וְנָסוֹעַ *he continued always journeying*; 8. 3 *receded more and more*, cf. *vs.* 5.

§ **102.** Adverbial use of infin. absol. — The infin. absol. is used in all genres as a compl. to describe adverbially the manner, degree, etc., of the action expressed by a previous non-cognate verb. This infin. is without *and*, but other infin. may be added to it. Deu. 9. 21 וָאֶכֹּת אֹתוֹ אָקִים אֶת כָּל־אֲשֶׁר טָחוֹן הֵיטֵב and I beat it, *grinding it small;* 1 S. 3. 12 דִּבַּרְתִּי הָחֵל וְכַלֵּה I will fulfil all that I have spoken, *from beginning to end.* Gen. 21. 16; 30. 32, 37, Nu. 6. 23, Jos. 3. 17; 6. 3, 11, 1 S. 17. 16, 2 S. 8. 2, Is. 57. 17, Jer. 3. 15; 12. 17; 22. 19, Mic. 6. 13, Zech. 7. 3. Cf. Is. 31. 5. Some infin. absol. (chiefly Hiph.) have become in effect straightforward adverbs, as הֵיטֵב *well, very* (Deu. 9. 21 above), הַרְבֵּה *much, very* (1 S. 26. 21), הַרְחֵק *far* (Gen. 21. 16, Jos. 3. 16). So Piel מַהֵר *quickly* (Ex. 32. 8).

> *Rem. 1.* Perhaps belonging here with the adv. sense of *earnestly* is the common phrase of Jer., e.g. 7. 13 וָאֲדַבֵּר ... הַשְׁכֵּם וְדַבֵּר I spoke, *earnestly speaking*, in which infin. of first verb is repeated; 11. 7; 26. 5 (oddly with *and*); 29. 19; 32. 33; 35. 14, 15. But הַשְׁכֵּם may rather have the nuance of continuity or repetition, like הָלוֹךְ (§ 101, R. 3) e.g. 7. 13 *over a long period;* 26. 5 *again and again.*

§ **103.** The use of infin. absol. instead of inflected form is also common. — (*a*) Without significant force when an inflected form has already been used, i.e. in connected narrative or discourse. This infin. may follow any inflected form and, unlike the compl. infin., is introduced by *and*. Jud. 7. 19 וַיִּתְקְעוּ בַּשּׁוֹפָרוֹת וְנָפוֹץ הַכַּדִּים they blew the trumpets, *and broke* (there was *breaking* of) the pitchers; 1 K. 9. 25 וְהֶעֱלָה שׁ׳ וְהַקְטִיר Sol. used to offer sacrifice (freq.) *and burn incense;* Jer. 14. 5 גַּם־אַיֶּלֶת בַּשָּׂדֶה יָלְדָה וְעָזוֹב even the hind in the field calves, *and forsakes* (her young); 32. 44 שָׂדוֹת יִקְנוּ וְכָתוֹב בַּסֵּפֶר וְחָתוֹם וְהָעֵד עֵדִים they shall buy fields, *and subscribe deeds, and seal them, and take witnesses.* Rem. 1.

(b) With more force on its own without a preceding finite form, *e.g.* in injunctions, espec. divine or of general application; in proverbial sayings or descriptions of prevailing conduct or condition of things; but also in any case where the action in itself is to be vividly expressed. This use belongs particularly to discourse. Ex. 20. 8 זָכוֹר אֶת־יוֹם הַשַּׁבָּת *remember* the sabbath day!; Hos. 4. 2 אָלֹה וְכַחֵשׁ וְרָצֹחַ וְגָנֹב וְנָאֹף *false swearing, and lying, and murder, and theft, and adultery* (they practise)!; Pr. 15. 22 הָפֵר מַחֲשָׁבוֹת בְּאֵין סוֹד plans *fail* for lack of counsel; Jer. 8. 15 קַוֵּה לְשָׁלוֹם וְאֵין טוֹב *we looked* for peace, but no good (has come)!; 1 K. 22. 30 הִתְחַפֵּשׂ וָבֹא בַמִּלְחָמָה *disguise myself* (will I) *and go* into battle!; 2 K. 4. 43 כֹּה אָמַר י׳ אָכוֹל וְהוֹתֵר thus says Y., *They shall eat and - have some left!*

> *Rem. 1.* Exx. of *a*. After QATAL forms, 1 S. 2. 27, 28, Jer. 19. 13, Hos. 10. 4, Hag. 1. 6, Zech. 3. 4; 7. 5, 1 Chr. 5. 20, 2 Chr. 28. 19, Ecc. 4. 1, 2; 9. 11, Est. 9. 6, 12, 16, cf. 17, Dan. 9. 5. — After YIQTOL, Jer. 32. 44; 36. 23. With אוֹ *or*, Lev. 25. 14, Nu. 30. 3, Deu. 14. 21. — After *Vav* cons. QATAL, Jer. 22. 14, Zech. 12. 10. — After infin. constr., 1 S. 22. 13, Jer. 7. 18. — After ptcp., Hab. 2. 15, Est. 8. 8.
>
> *Rem. 2.* Exx. of *b*. Infin. absol. as imper., Ex. 13. 3, Nu. 4. 2, Deu. 1. 16; 5. 12; 31. 26, Jos. 1. 13, 2 K. 3. 16, Is. 14. 31; 37. 30, Zech. 6. 10, Pr. 25. 4, 5. So הָלוֹךְ *go!* 2 S. 24. 12, 2 K. 5. 10, and often in Jer., 2.2; 3. 12, etc. — As juss., Gen. 17. 10, Ex. 12. 48, Is. 22. 13, Pr. 17. 12. — Of prevailing conduct, etc., Is. 21. 5; 59. 4, 13, Jer. 7. 9; 14. 19, Ez. 21. 31, Hag. 1. 9. — With more or less force, 2 K. 4. 43, Is. 5. 5, Jer. 3. 1 (וְשׁוֹב), Ez. 23. 30, Job 40. 2.
>
> *Rem. 3.* Like infin. constr. (§ 107) but less commonly, infin. absol. when used for finite verb may be continued by finite form, Is. 42. 22; 58. 6.
>
> *Rem. 4.* When infin. absol. is used for finite verb the *subj.* is occasionally expressed with it, Gen. 17. 10, Lev. 6. 7, Nu. 15. 35, Deu. 15. 2, 1 S. 25. 26, Is. 42. 22, Ps. 17. 5, Job 40. 2, Pr. 17. 12, Ecc. 4. 2, Est. 9. 1.

THE INFINITIVE CONSTRUCT

§ 104. The infin. constr. is the normal Hebr. infin.-cum-gerund. It has the qualities of both noun and verb, as the first capable of being put into the constr. state and admitting prepp. and suffixes, as the second of taking an obj. It is defin. but does not, except rarely, have the Art.

> *Rem. 1.* The infin. constr. sometimes has a fem. form, as אַהֲבָה *to love,*

קָרְבָה *to hate,* יְרָאָה *to fear,* קְרָאָה *to meet,* מָשְׁחָה *to anoint* (Ex. 29. 29), קָרְבָה *to approach.* So in verbs initial *Yod* (שֶׁבֶת) or finally weak (עֲשׂוֹת). Or it may have -מ prefix in the Aramaic manner, as מִקְרָא *to call* and מַסַּע *to depart* (Nu. 10. 2), מִקַּח *to take* (2 Chr. 19. 7); with fem. ending מַעֲלָה *to go up* (Ezr. 7. 9). Regardless of form the infin. constr. is usually mas. in gender (Gen. 2. 18, Pr. 25. 24), very occasionally fem. (1 S. 18. 23, Jer. 23. 17).

§ 105. As noun or gerund, the infin. constr. occurs in all syntactic positions. — (*a*) It may be subj. to a nominal clause, espec. when the pred. is "good" or "not good", but also otherwise. Gen. 2. 18 לֹא טוֹב הֱיוֹת הָאָדָם לְבַדּוֹ *the man's being alone* is not good; Is. 7. 13 הַמְעַט מִכֶּם הַלְאוֹת אֲנָשִׁים is *wearying men* too little for you? Gen. 29. 19; 30. 15, Ex. 14. 12, Jud. 9. 2; 18. 19, 1 S. 15. 22; 23. 20; 29. 6, 2 S. 18. 11, Is. 28. 19, Mic. 3. 2, Ps. 118. 8-9, Pr. 10. 23; 13. 19; 16. 6, 12, 16.

(*b*) It may be governed by a noun in constr. state or a prep. Gen. 2. 4 בְּיוֹם עֲשׂוֹת י' *in the day of Y.'s making;* 14. 17 אַחֲרֵי שׁוּבוֹ מֵהַכּוֹת *after his returning* from *smiting* Gen. 2. 17; 21. 5; 24. 30; 29. 7, Is. 7. 17, Hos. 2. 5, 17, etc. Also, though rarely, after an adj. or ptcp. in constr., Is. 56. 10, Jer. 13. 23. After כֹּל *all,* Gen. 30. 41, 1 K. 8. 52, Ps. 132. 1, 1 Chr. 23. 31.

(*c*) It may be dir. obj. to certain trans. verbs as *begin, cease, know* (*how*), *add* (do again), etc. 1 K. 3. 7 לֹא אֵדַע צֵאת וָבֹא I do not know (how) *to go out or come in.* Gen. 8. 10, Ex. 2. 3, Deu. 2. 25, 2 K. 19. 27, Is. 1. 14; 11. 9, Jer. 15. 15, Am. 3. 10, Ps. 101. 3. Or obj. compl. following intrans. verbs as *be willing, return* (do again), Deu. 10. 10. Further exx. § 97*a*. The sign אֵת may be used, 2 K. 19. 27, Is. 37. 28.

However, the infin. constr. with לְ has in usage greatly replaced the simple infin. when *obj.,* Gen. 18. 29 וַיֹּסֶף עוֹד לְדַבֵּר; 11. 8; 13. 6, etc. So when obj. compl., Hab. 2. 16. This form also occurs as subj. in nominal clauses, where it can hardly express the direction of action of a governing verb, 2 S. 18. 11, Ps. 118. 8-9, Pr. 21. 9 (contrast 25. 24). The לְ should therefore be regarded as an ex. of non-prepos. לְ equivalent to אֵת, § 94, R. 8, and distinguished from prepos. uses, § 118, R. 2.

§ 106. The infin. constr. may have its own subj. and obj., both appended either in the nominal or in the verbal manner.

(*a*) The subj. or agent generally follows the infin. constr. in a construct relation. Gen. 2. 4 עֲשׂוֹת י' *Y.'s making;* 16. 16; 24. 11, Ex. 17. 1, Hos. 3. 1. So when suff., Gen. 3. 19 עַד שׁוּבְךָ אֶל־הָאֲדָמָה; 3. 5; 39. 18.

This construction is clearest when the infin. is fem. and reducible, Gen. 19. 16 בְּשִׂנְאַת יְ׳ אֹתָנוּ in *Y.'s* pitying him; Deu. 1. 27 בְּחֶמְלַת יְ׳ עָלָיו because *Y.* hated us. Deu. 7. 8, 1 K. 10. 9, Is. 13. 19.

When, however, the subj. is separated from the infin. by the obj. or other intervening words, the construct relation is broken and the construction is essentially verbal. Perhaps the noun denoting the agent is in appos. to the implied subj. of the infin., or it is simply treated as though it were the subj. of a finite verb, the whole clause then becoming a bound unit and able, e.g., to be construed with a prep. Is. 20. 1 בִּשְׁלֹחַ אֹתוֹ סַרְגוֹן when *Sargon* sent him. Gen. 4. 15, Nu. 24. 23, Deu. 4. 42, Jos. 14. 11, Jud. 9. 2, 1 S. 16. 16, 2 S. 18. 29, Is. 5. 4, Jer. 21. 1, Ez. 17. 10, Ps. 51. 2; 56. 1; 76. 10; 142. 4, Pr. 1. 27; 25. 8, Job 34. 22. There are also indications that this construction is employed in cases where no words come between infin. and subj., Rem. 2.

(*b*) Before an obj., on the other hand, the infin. constr. normally behaves verbally. This is clear in a large number of cases, as when the infin. constr. is followed by אֵת or by a verbal suff. of 1 pers. sing., or is fem. in form and changeable or involves לְ or comes from Hiph. of a medially weak verb (Rem. 2); and may be assumed in most other cases. 1 S. 19. 1 לְהָמִית אֶת־דָּוִד to slay *David*, Gen. 14. 17; 19. 29, Ex. 38. 27, 1 K. 12. 15; 15. 4. Ex. 2. 14 הַלְהָרְגֵנִי אַתָּה אֹמֵר do you intend to kill *me*? 1 S. 5. 10; 27. 1; 28. 9, Ru. 2. 10. Deu. 10. 15 לְאַהֲבָה אוֹתָם to love *them*, Ex. 2.4. Ps. 50. 4 לָדִין עַמּוֹ to judge *his people*, Is. 3. 13. So also when the infin. has a subj. as well as an obj., Gen. 2. 4 בְּיוֹם עֲשׂוֹת יְ׳ א׳ אֶרֶץ וְשָׁמָיִם in the day that Y. God made *earth and heaven*; 39. 18 כַּהֲרִימִי קוֹלִי as soon as I lifted up *my voice*, though in most of these cases אֵת is also used, Hos. 3. 1 כְּאַהֲבַת יְ׳ אֶת־בְּנֵי יִשְׂרָאֵל as Y. loves *the people of Israel*, Gen. 13. 10; 39. 19, 1 K. 11. 24; 13. 31, Is. 10. 15, Am. 1. 3. And by analogy where the subj. is not expressed, Jud. 14. 6 כְּשַׁסַּע הַגְּדִי as one tears *a kid*, 1 K. 18. 28, Is. 10. 14; 17. 5, Ps. 66. 10. Rem. 1.

There are, however, cases where the obj. is expressed though a construct relation, clearest where a 1 pers. sing. suffix has the nominal form or the infin. has a fem. form. Ps. 73. 28 קָרְבַת א׳ to draw near to *God*; Mic. 6. 8 אַהֲבַת חֶסֶד to love *mercy*; 1 S. 17. 48 לִקְרַאת דָּוִד to meet *David*; 25. 32 לִקְרָאתִי to meet *me*. The obj. may be indir., Nu. 22. 13 Y. has refused לְתִתִּי to let *me* go with you. For other suffixes see Rem. 3.

When the finite verb is a phrasal verb or is normally construed with a prep., so is the infin., Deu. 11. 22; 20. 4.

Rem. 1. The subj., especially when a pron. is often omitted: (*a*) when clear from the context, Gen. 24. 30 כִּרְאֹת *when he saw;* 19. 29, Deu. 4. 21, 1 K. 20. 12, Ez. 8. 6. (*b*) When indeterminate, Gen. 33. 10 כִּרְאֹת *as one sees,* Jud. 14. 6, 1 S. 2. 13; 18. 19, 2 S. 3. 34; 7. 29, Is. 7. 22; 10. 14. — Gen. 25. 26, Ex. 27. 7; 30. 12, Nu. 9. 15; 10. 7, Zeph. 2. 2, Zech. 13. 9, Ps. 42. 4 (cf. *vs.* 11), Job 13. 9; 20. 4. The *obj.* is also often omitted, when a pron., in the same circumstances. § 3, R. 3.

Rem. 2. Though it may not be separated from infin. (*a* above), the subj. cannot belong to a construct relation, *e.g.* when לְ of infin. retains prestress *Qameṣ*: 2 S. 19. 20 לָשׂוּם הַמֶּלֶךְ that *the king* should lay (it) to heart, Job 37. 7 (contrast Gen. 16. 3 לְשֶׁבֶת אַבְרָם, 2 K. 6. 1). The infin. Hiph. of verbs medially weak is reduced before suff. (Gen. 39. 18 in *b* above) but never when it is followed by a nominal subj. or obj.; the subj. no less than the obj. must therefore be construed verbally, Is. 10. 15 כְּהָנִיף שֵׁבֶט as though *a rod* should wield him who lifts it; 14. 3 בְּיוֹם הָנִיחַ י' לְךָ in the day that *Y.* gives you rest, 2 S. 17. 14, Ps. 46. 3. With obj., 1 S. 19. 1 (see *b* above), Pr. 8. 27.

Rem. 3. The only verbal suff. regularly used with infin. constr. is that of 1 sing., though others are occasionally found, *e.g.* 3 sing. mas. Jer. 39. 14 לְהוֹצִיאֵהוּ; *energicum* Deu. 23. 5 לְקַלְלֶךָ. On the other hand, the nominal form of the 1 sing. suff. occurs as obj. in לִקְרָאתִי and some other cases; and all the other suffixes have forms which could be either nominal or verbal. It is likely that most suffixes, when obj:, are verbal, espec. where the infin. has another obj. or takes part in a two-verb construction (§ 97*a*) or expresses purpose or accompanies another infin. which has אֵת or behaves verbally, etc. Comp. exx. like Gen. 37. 4 דַּבְּרוֹ (indir.) *to speak to him;* 37. 22, Deu. 1. 27; 9. 28; 26. 19 (Ps. 89. 28), Jud. 13. 23; 14. 8; 18. 2, 1 S. 2. 25; 19. 11, 1 K. 20. 35, 2 K. 9. 35, Ps. 106. 23, 26, 27, etc. But this is not certain, and it is possible that some suffixes (and indeed some nouns) belong to a construct relation, the second member of which may express the obj. as well as the subj. The whole matter of the subj. and obj. of infin. constr. requires more careful investigation.

§ 107. The most characteristic usage of infin. constr. is as a clause substitute after a prep. Such phrases have all the meanings of the finite forms with conjunctions. Thus *temporal*: Gen. 4. 8 בִּהְיוֹתָם בַּשָּׂדֶה *when they were* in the field; 3. 19 עַד שׁוּבְךָ *until you return;* 39. 18 כַּהֲרִימִי קוֹלִי *as soon as I lifted up* my voice. *Causal*: Deu. 1. 27 בְּשִׂנְאַת י' אֹתָנוּ *because Y. hated* us; Is. 30. 12 יַעַן מָאָסְכֶם *because you despise;* Am. 2. 6 עַל־

מִכְרָם *because they sell. Purpose*: Gen. 2. 15 לְעָבְדָהּ *to work it*; Deu. 2. 30 לְמַעַן תִּתּוֹ בְיָדֶךָ *that he might give him* into your hand; Jud. 3. 1 לְנַסּוֹת בָּם אֶת־יִשְׂרָאֵל *to test* Israel by them. *Result*: Deu. 9. 18 לְהַכְעִיסוֹ *so provoking him to anger*; Ru. 2. 10 לְהַכִּירֵנִי *that you should notice me*. The prepp. become conjunctions, taking finite forms, by combination with the rel. אֲשֶׁר. Comp. Gen. 18. 12 with Jud. 11. 36, 2 S. 19. 31; Am. 1. 11 with 2 S. 3. 30; 2 S. 3. 11 with Is. 43. 4. — Gen. 13. 10; 27. 4; 34. 7; 35. 1, Jud. 2. 22, 1 S. 1. 7; 9. 15, Am. 5. 11. See further Adverbial Phrases and Clauses, § 119.

Following such infin. phrases, when new clauses are added with *and*, the infin. is very generally changed into the finite construction. The finite conjugation consecutive to the infin. and the wider context will show the nuances of aspect and time in which the infin. is used. In past context: Gen. 39. 18 כַּהֲרִימִי קוֹלִי וָאֶקְרָא *as soon as I lifted up my voice and cried*. In fut. context: 2 K. 18. 32 עַד־בֹּאִי וְלָקַחְתִּי *till I come and take*. Past frequentative: Am. 1. 11 עַל־רָדְפוֹ בַחֶרֶב אָחִיו וְשִׁחֵת רַחֲמָיו *because he pursued his brother with the sword and cast off pity*. Gen. 27. 45, Jud. 6. 18, 1 S. 24. 12, Is. 5. 24; 10. 2; 13. 9; 30. 12, 26; 45. 1, Jer. 9. 12, Ps. 104. 14, 15. This resolution is necessary with a neg. clause, Am. 1. 9.

§ 108. The prep. לְ, in addition to expressing purpose or result (§ 126*b*), has three other common uses with infin. — (*a*) In a gerundial or adverbial sense to explain the circumstances of a previous action. 1 S. 14. 33 הָעָם חֹטְאִים לֶאֱכֹל עַל־הַדָּם *the people are sinning in eating* with the blood; 1 K. 5. 23 תַּעֲשֶׂה אֶת־חֶפְצִי לָתֵת לֶחֶם בֵּיתִי *you will meet my wishes by giving* bread for my household. Gen. 18. 25; 19. 19; 29. 26; 34. 7; 43. 6, 1 S. 12. 17, 19; 19. 5; 20. 20, 2 S. 14. 20, 1 K. 8. 32; 14. 8; 16. 19. So the ubiquitous לֵאמֹר *saying*. Similarly in explanation of a comparison, Gen. 3. 22 the man has become like one of us לָדַעַת טוֹב וָרָע *to know good and evil*. 2 S. 14. 25, Is. 21. 1, Ez. 38. 16, Pr. 26. 2, 1 Chr. 12. 8.

(*b*) In nominal clauses as a periphrastic fut., Gen. 15. 12 וַיְהִי הַשֶּׁמֶשׁ לָבוֹא *and it was, the sun was about to set*, Jos. 2. 5. Is. 38. 20 י׳ לְהוֹשִׁיעֵנִי *Y. is* (ready, about) *to save me*. Is. 10. 32, Ps. 25. 14; 49. 15, Pr. 19. 8, Ecc. 3. 15, 1 Chr. 9. 25.

(*c*) Or as a gerundive, in the sense of *is to be, must be, ought to be*. 2 K. 4. 13 מֶה לַעֲשׂוֹת לָךְ הֲיֵשׁ לְדַבֶּר־לָךְ *what is to be done for you? should one speak for you* to the king? 2 K. 13. 19 לְהַכּוֹת חָמֵשׁ אוֹ־שֵׁשׁ

פְּעָמִים *you should have struck* five or six times. Is. 5. 4, Jer. 51. 49, Hos. 9. 13, Ps. 22. 9, Job 30. 6. Or in the sense of *can be*, Jud. 1. 19 (§ 109*b*), 2 S. 14. 19 (יֵשׁ = אֵשׁ).

§ 109. The *negative* infin. is formed — (*a*) Usually by particle בִּלְתִּי with לְ. This negatives non-prepos. לְ with infin. (§ 105*c*) after, *e.g.,* verbs of *commanding, agreeing, swearing,* Gen. 3. 11 צִוִּיתִיךָ לְבִלְתִּי אֲכָל־מִמֶּנּוּ I commanded you *not to eat of it,* Deu. 4. 21, Jos. 5. 6, 1 K. 11. 10, 2 K. 12. 9. It also negatives prepos. לְ with infin. in its various uses, *e.g.* when it expresses purpose, Gen. 4. 15 לְבִלְתִּי הַכּוֹת־אֹתוֹ כָּל־מֹצְאוֹ *lest* any who found him *should kill him;* 38. 9; and frequently in its gerundial or explicative sense, Ex. 8. 25 only let not Ph. deal falsely again לְבִלְתִּי שַׁלַּח אֶת־הָעָם *by not letting the people go.* Gen. 19. 21, Deu. 8. 11; 17. 12, Jud. 2. 23; 8. 1, Jer. 16. 12; 17. 23, 24, 27. On מִן as negative, Rem. 1

(*b*) The infin. in nominal clauses (above *b, c*) is negatived by לֹא לְ or אֵין לְ. Am. 6. 10 לֹא לְהַזְכִּיר בְּשֵׁם י׳ the name of Y. *must not be mentioned;* Jud. 1. 19 כִּי לֹא לְהוֹרִישׁ but *he could not dispossess* the inhabitants of the plain, 1 Chr. 5. 1. Est. 4. 2 כִּי אֵין לָבוֹא אֶל־הַשַּׁעַר for *no one might enter* the gate. Ps. 40. 6, Ecc. 3. 14, Ezr. 9. 15, 2 Chr. 5. 11; 20. 6, 17; 22. 9, Est. 8. 8. There seems no difference in sense between לֹא לְ and אֵין לְ, though the latter is common in later style; cf. 1 Chr. 15. 2 with 23. 26.

> *Rem. 1.* The infin. with מִן is used after verbs of *restraining, ceasing,* etc., Gen. 16. 2 Y. has prevented me מִלֶּדֶת *from bearing children;* 20. 6, Ex. 23. 5; 34. 33. Occasionally with causal force, Deu. 7. 8, negatived by מִבִּלְתִּי, Nu. 14. 16. מִן *away from* may also negative an infin., as Is. 5. 6 command *not to rain* (מֵהַמְטִיר). So after *to swear,* Is. 54. 9, cf. Deu. 4. 21, and *to beware,* Gen. 31. 29 (cf. *vs.* 24), 2 K. 6. 9.
>
> *Rem. 2.* The infin. constr. with *and* is used, particularly in poetry and later texts, in continuation of a preceding finite form (or ptcp.). This is not, strictly speaking, a substitute for a finite form (as infin. absol., § 103), but rather an extension of the nominal uses in § 108*b, c;* there is often a nuance of purpose. Several times וְלָתֵת Ex. 32. 29, Jer. 17. 10; 19. 12, Dan. 12. 11. Other exx.: Is. 44. 28, Jer. 44. 19, Ez. 13. 22, Hos. 12. 3, Am. 8. 4, Ps. 104. 21, Job 34. 8. Lev. 10. 10, 1 S. 8. 12, Ecc. 9. 1, Neh. 8. 13, 1 Chr. 6. 34; 10. 13, 2 Chr. 7. 17; 8. 13. Prep. לְ omitted, 1 Chr. 21. 24.
>
> *Rem. 3.* Though Niph., Pual, Hoph. have their proper infin., the Qal (or sometimes other active) infin. is often used where pass. infin. might be expected. Gen. 4. 13 my punishment is greater מִנְּשֹׂא *than can be borne* (or

my iniquity ... *than can be forgiven*), Jos. 2. 5, 1 S. 18. 19, Is. 8. 3, Jer. 25. 34; 41. 4, Hos. 10. 10, Hag. 2. 15, Ps. 67. 3, Job 20. 4, Ecc. 3. 2, Est. 7. 4.

The Participles

§ 110. The ptcp. also partakes of the nature of the noun (adj.) and the verb. The *active* ptcp. presents the person or subj. in the exercise or exhibition of the action or condition denoted by the verb. In many contexts and with suitable verbs it implies continuity, but this is not a necessary part of its meaning, as in other contexts and with other verbs it indicates a simple punctual action. The *passive* ptcp. describes the subj. as having the action exercised upon him; if it differs from the adj. it is in presenting the state of the subj. as the result of an action.

> *Rem. 1.* Act. ptcps. expressing conditions or operations which are habitual come to be used as nouns, as אֹהֵב *friend*, אֹיֵב *enemy*, שֹׁפֵט *judge*, שֹׁמֵר *watchman*, חֹזֶה *seer*, etc. Pass. ptcps. likewise in usage become adjectives. The ptcp. Niph. in particular has the sense of the Latin gerundive and adj. in -*bilis*, as נוֹרָא *to be feared, terrible*, נֶחְשָׁב *to be accounted*, נֶחְמָד *desirable*, נִתְעָב *detestable*, נִכְבָּד *honourable*. Occasionally ptcp. Pual, מְהֻלָּל *to be praised*, Ps. 96. 4. Possibly Qal, Ps. 137. 8. See Is. 2. 22, Ps. 18. 4; 19. 11; 22. 32; 76. 8; 102. 19, Job 15. 16. Such nouns and adj. are distinguished from proper ptcps. by coming first in a classifying nominal clause, Gen. 42. 14 מְרַגְּלִים אַתֶּם you are *spies*, Ps. 96. 4 נוֹרָא הוּא he is *to be feared*, § 49*d*. Ptcps. normally follow the subj., § 113*b*.

§ 111. Construction of ptcp. The ptcp. is construed — (*a*) Verbally, with a dir. obj. Gen. 32. 12 כִּי יָרֵא אָנֹכִי אֹתוֹ for *I fear him*; 25. 28 רִבְקָה אֹהֶבֶת אֶת־יַעֲקֹב *Reb. loved Jacob*. Gen. 27. 8; 37. 7, 16; 40. 8, 17; 41. 9; 42. 29, 1 S. 11. 3, 2 S. 14. 18, 1 K. 18. 3, Am. 5. 8, 9, 18. With a prep., if the finite verb takes one. Gen. 26. 11 הַנֹּגֵעַ בָּאִישׁ הַזֶּה *whoever touches this man*; 16. 13 הַדֹּבֵר אֵלֶיהָ Y. *who spoke to her* 1 S. 17. 19, 2 S. 23. 3, Ps. 89. 10. A ptcp. of a trans. verb may take two obj., indir. and dir., 2 S. 1. 24 הַמַּלְבִּשְׁכֶם שָׁנִי *who clothed you in scarlet*. Or dir. and compl., Zeph. 1. 9 הַמְמַלְאִים בֵּית אֲדֹנֵיהֶם חָמָס וּמִרְמָה *those who fill their master's house with violence and fraud*. The ptcp. of intrans. verb or a pass. ptcp. take obj. compl. Deu. 6. 11 מְלֵאִים כָּל־טוּב *full of every good*, Am. 2. 13. 1 S. 2. 18 חָגוּר אֵפוֹד *girt with an ephod*, Jud. 18. 11, Ez. 9. 2, 3, Neh. 4. 12.

Cogn. obj., 1 K. 1. 40.

(*b*) Or nominally, being in the constr. state. Gen. 3. 5 יֹדְעֵי טוֹב וָרָע *knowing good and evil;* Hos. 2. 7 נֹתְנֵי לַחְמִי וּמֵימַי *who give my bread and water.* This construction is very common; the second member indicates the dir. obj. of an *active* ptcp. or the agent or instrument of a *passive* ptcp. Gen. 22. 12 יָדַעְתִּי כִּי־יְרֵא א' אַתָּה I know that *you fear God;* 19. 14, 2 S. 4. 6; 6. 13, 1 K. 12. 21, Is. 5. 8, 18; 19. 8, 9; 28. 6; 29. 21, Jer. 23. 30, Hos. 5. 10; 6. 8; 11. 4, Ps. 19. 8, 9, 136. 4-7. Pass. ptcp., Gen. 24. 31 *blessed by,* 2 S. 5. 8 *hated by,* Is. 53. 4, Job 14. 1. Is. 1. 7 שְׂרֻפוֹת אֵשׁ *burnt with fire.* Gen. 20. 3; 41. 6, Deu. 32. 24, Is. 14. 19; 22. 2; 28. 1 *overcome with wine,* Jer. 18. 21, Hos. 4. 17.

(*c*) In like manner suff. to ptcp. may be verbal or nominal. It is verbal when the ptcp. has the Art. or the suff. has the forms נִי ָ or הוּ ָ or has the *energicum* form or is preceded by אֵת, etc. Deu. 8. 16 הַמַּאֲכִלְךָ מָן *who fed you with manna;* 8. 5 מְיַסְּרֶךָ *your God disciplines you;* 13. 6 הַמּוֹצִיא אֶתְכֶם *who brought you out;* Job 31. 15 הֲלֹא־בַבֶּטֶן עֹשֵׂנִי עָשָׂהוּ did not *he who made me* in the womb make him? Deu. 13. 11, Is. 9. 12; 10. 20; 47. 10; 63. 11, Jer. 9. 14; 23. 15, Ps. 18. 33; 81. 11, Job 40. 9. On the other hand, it is nominal when the ptcp. is obviously constr. or has the suff. ָי, and in other cases. Gen. 27. 29 מְבָרְכֶיךָ *they who bless you;* 4. 14 כָּל־מֹצְאִי *anyone finding me.* Ex. 20. 5, 6, 1 S. 2. 30, Is. 50. 8, Ps. 7. 5; 55. 13, Job 7. 8.

> *Rem. 1.* A number of verbs, usually intrans. and construed with a prep., may omit prep. (89*d*), as בָּא *go into,* יָצָא *come out of,* יָשַׁב *dwell in* (Ps. 100. 4, Gen. 44. 4, 2 S. 6. 11) and their act. ptcp. may therefore be put in the constr. state, Gen. 9. 10 מִכֹּל יֹצְאֵי הַתֵּבָה *of all who came out of* the ark; 19. 25; 23. 10, 18; 34. 24; 46. 26, Ex. 1. 5, Jud. 1. 19; 8. 30. Cf. ptcp. of הָלַךְ Jud. 5. 6, of יָרַד Is. 38. 18, even of אָכַל *eat from,* 1 K. 2. 7. In poetry this forcible construction, omitting the prep., is not uncommon with other ptcp., Is. 22. 2 חַלְלֵי־חֶרֶב *slain by the sword,* Mic. 2. 8 *returned from war,* Ps. 88. 6 *lying in the grave.* Particularly with suff., Ps. 18. 40 קָמַי *those rising against me,* cf. Ps. 3. 2. Deu. 33. 11, Is. 22. 3, Ps. 53. 6; 73. 27; 74. 23; 102. 9, Pr. 2. 19.

> *Rem. 2.* Following pass. ptcp. in constr. the second member often has adverbial force (like the so-called "adverbial accus." with a finite verb), Is. 3. 3 נְשׂוּא פָנִים *he whose face is lifted up;* Ps. 32. 7 כְּסוּי חֲטָאָה *he whose sin is covered.* 2 S. 13. 31, Is. 33. 24, Pr. 14. 2. So with ptcp. of intrans. verb, Is. 1. 30 נֹבֶלֶת עָלֶהָ *fading in its leaf.* With noun first, the whole phrase is adverbial, Ex. 12. 11 מָתְנֵיכֶם חֲגֻרִים *your loins girt,* cf. Jer. 30. 6.

§ 112. The ptcp. becomes virtually a noun, as Is. 19. 20 מוֹשִׁיעַ *a saviour*, and may be subj. or obj. of a clause. When in appos. to a noun it is used as an adj., Deu. 4. 24 אֵשׁ אֹכְלָה *a devouring fire;* 4. 34 *an outstretched arm*, Is. 18. 2. Or subj. compl., Gen. 22. 13 a ram was behind (him) נֶאֱחַז בַּסְּבַךְ בְּקַרְנָיו *caught* in a thicket by its horns (נֶאֱחַז, QATAL is also read). Or obj. compl., Jud. 1. 24 וַיִּרְאוּ אִישׁ יוֹצֵא they saw a man *coming out*. With the Art. the ptcp. may like the adj. designate a class, Am. 5. 13 הַמַּשְׂכִּיל *the prudent* (man), Is. 14. 8; 28. 16, Mic. 4. 6; or have the sense of *he who, whoever*, 2 S. 14. 10 הַמְדַבֵּר אֵלַיִךְ *whoever* (if anyone) *speaks* to you, Gen. 26. 11; and so in constr., Ex. 21. 12 מַכֵּה אִישׁ *whoever strikes* a man, *vs.* 15.

When in appos. to a preceding def. subj. the ptcp. with Art. has the meaning very much of a relative clause. Gen. 12. 7 י׳ הַנִּרְאָה אֵלָיו Y. *who had appeared* to him; 1 S. 1. 26 אֲנִי הָאִשָּׁה הַנִּצֶּבֶת I am the woman *who stood*, cf. Jud. 16. 24. This usage is very common: Gen. 13. 5; 27. 33; 35. 3; 43. 12, 18; 48. 15, 16, Ex. 11. 5, Jud. 8. 34, 1 S. 4. 8, 2 S. 1. 24, 2 K. 22. 18, Is. 8. 6, 17, 18; 9. 1, Am. 4. 1; 5. 3, Mic. 3. 2, 3, 5, Ps. 113. 5-7. With pass ptcp., Nu. 21. 8, Jud. 6. 28 the altar *that had been* built; 20.4, the woman *who was murdered*, 1 K. 18. 30, Ps. 79. 10. — Ps. 19. 11 resumes *vs.* 10 (they) *which are more desirable.* Ps. 18. 33; 49. 7.

> *Rem. 1.* The ptcp. with Art. is exceptionally used after *indef.* noun, Jer. 27. 3, Ez. 2. 3; 14. 22, Ps. 119. 21, Dan. 9. 26, though in some of these cases the preceding word may be considered def., though formally undetermined. In other cases the preceding subj. receives a certain definiteness from being connected with *all*, Gen. 1. 21, 28, or a numeral, Jud. 16. 27, cf. 1 S. 25. 10, or from standing in a comparison, Pr. 26. 18, cf. Ps. 62. 4, or from being described by an adj. or ptcp. with Art., Is. 65. 2, cf. *vs.* 3.
>
> *Rem. 2.* When in adjacent clauses another ptcp. succeeds one with Art. it is often without Art., Is. 5. 20, Am. 6. 4, Job 5. 10. But sometimes the clauses are made parallel and the Art. used, Is. 40. 22, 23, Mic. 3. 5. Occasionally the rel. pron. takes the place of the Art., Deu. 1. 4, Jer. 38. 16, Ez. 9. 2, Ps. 115. 8. Both are used, 1 K. 12. 8; 21. 11.

§ 113. (*a*) The ptcp. as pred., unlike the finite verb, does *not* contain the subj., which must be expressed. 1 S. 19. 11 מָחָר אַתָּה מוּמָת *tomorrow you shall be slain;* Gen. 38. 25 הוּא מוּצֵאת *she was brought forth;* 1 S. 9. 11

הֵמָּה עֹלִים *they were going up*. The pron., however, is often omitted if the subj. has just been mentioned, particularly after הִנֵּה, Gen. 24. 30 וַיָּבֹא אֶל־הָאִישׁ וְהִנֵּה עֹמֵד *he came to the man, and behold, he was standing*. Gen. 37. 15; 41. 1, 1 S. 30. 3, 16, Is. 29. 8, Am. 7. 1. With גַּם, Gen. 32. 7.

(*b*) The ptcp. as pred. nearly always follows the subj., distinguishing it both from a finite verb in a verbal clause and from a classifying noun or adj. in a nominal clause, both of which come first. § 110, R. 1. Gen. 2. 10 וְנָהָר יֹצֵא *now, a river went forth*; 24. 21 וְהָאִישׁ מִשְׁתָּאֵה לָהּ *and the man gazed at her*; 39. 23 וַאֲשֶׁר־הוּא עֹשֶׂה יְ׳ מַצְלִיחַ *and whatever he did, Y. made it prosper*; Deu. 26. 16 today יְ׳ אֱלֹהֶיךָ מְצַוְּךָ לַעֲשׂוֹת *Y. your God is commanding you to do*. Gen. 33. 13, Ex. 9. 24, Deu. 4. 12, etc. So commonly after הִנֵּה and in rel. clauses, Gen. 24. 13 הִנֵּה אָנֹכִי נִצָּב *behold, I am standing*; 28. 20 in this way אֲשֶׁר אָנֹכִי הוֹלֵךְ *which I am going*. 18. 17; 24. 37; 31. 43, Ex. 14. 25, etc. In a minority of cases the ptcp. comes first, sometimes after אִם, Deu. 5. 22 אִם־יֹסְפִים אֲנַחְנוּ לִשְׁמֹעַ *if we hear anymore* the voice of Y., Jud. 11. 9, 1 S. 7. 3, 2 K. 10. 6; often after כִּי, Gen. 42. 23 they did not know כִּי שֹׁמֵעַ יוֹסֵף *that Jos. was listening*; 1 S. 3. 9 כִּי שֹׁמֵעַ עַבְדֶּךָ *for your servant hears*, Gen. 3. 5; 15. 14; 19. 13, Is. 12. 4. With interr., Gen. 4. 9 הֲשֹׁמֵר אָחִי אָנֹכִי *am I my brother's keeper?*; 18. 17, Nu. 11. 29. The pass. ptcps. בָּרוּךְ and אָרוּר, when used precatively, usually precede the subj. See further Nominal Clauses, § 49*d*.

(*c*) The ptcp. is found in all three time settings, in past and pres. often with the implication of continuous action, in fut. more often describing a punctual action. 1 S. 1. 12 she prayed long וְעֵלִי שֹׁמֵר אֶת־פִּיהָ *while Eli watched her mouth*. Gen. 4. 10 צֹעֲקִים דְּמֵי אָחִיךָ *your brother's blood is crying*. 19.13 כִּי מַשְׁחִיתִים אֲנַחְנוּ *for we are going to destroy*. See exx., Rem. 1.

(*d*) The ptcp. clause is negatived by אֵין, revealing its nominal character. The place of the neg. varies, § 52. Gen. 41. 8 אֵין פּוֹתֵר אֹתָם *there was no one to interpret* them; cf. different order, 40. 8; 41. 15. Ex. 5. 16 תֶּבֶן אֵין נִתָּן *straw is not given*; 1 K. 6. 18 אֶבֶן אֵין נִרְאָה *no stone was seen*. The אֵין often takes suff. of subj., Gen. 43. 5 אִם אֵינְךָ מְשַׁלֵּחַ *if you do not send*, Ex. 5. 10 (so commonly יֵשׁ in a positive clause, Gen. 43. 4). — Gen. 20. 7; 39. 23; 41. 24, Ex. 3. 2, Deu. 4. 22; 22. 27, Jos. 6. 1, Jud. 3. 25, 1 S. 3. 1; 22. 8; 26. 12, 1 K. 6. 18, Is. 5. 27; 17. 2; 22. 22, Jer. 9. 21,

Hos. 5. 14, Am. 5. 2, 6. See Rem. 3.

(*e*) When additional clauses are joined by *and* to a participial construction, the appropriate finite verb is usually employed, consec. unless other words are interposed. Gen. 35. 3 לָאֵל הָעֹנֶה אֹתִי וַיְהִי עִמָּדִי the God who answered me, *and was* with me; 27. 33 הַצָּד צַיִד וַיָּבֵא who hunted venison *and brought* it; 7. 4 אָנֹכִי מַמְטִיר עַל־הָאָרֶץ ... וּמָחִיתִי I will send rain upon the earth ... *and will blot out;* Mic. 3. 5 הַמַּתְעִים אֶת־עַמִּי ... וְקָרְאוּ שָׁלוֹם the prophets who mislead my people ... *and cry* "Peace"; *vs.* 9 הַמְתַעֲבִים מִשְׁפָּט וְאֵת כָּל־הַיְשָׁרָה יְעַקֵּשׁוּ who abhor justice *and pervert* all equity. In poetry appos. is common, often with chiasmus, Is. 5. 8 מַגִּיעֵי בַיִת בְּבַיִת שָׂדֶה בְשָׂדֶה יַקְרִיבוּ who join house to house, *lay* field to field; cf. Ps. 147. 14-16. — Gen. 17. 19; 27. 33; 35. 3; 48. 4, Deu. 4. 22, 1 S. 2. 6, 8, 31; 2 S. 20. 12, 1 K. 13. 2, 3, Is. 5. 23; 14. 17; 29. 21; 30. 2; 31. 1; 44. 25, 26; 48. 1, Jer. 13. 10, Hos. 2. 16, Am. 5. 7-12; 8. 14; 9. 5, Ps. 18. 33. This change to the finite is *necessary* when the additional clause is neg., Ps. 15. 2-3.

(*f*) The ptcp. is greatly employed in describing scenes of a striking kind and in circumstantial clauses. Much of the picturesqueness of prose historical writing is due to it. Thus it is used with such particles as הִנֵּה *behold,* עוֹד *still, while.* 1 K. 22. 10 the kings יֹשְׁבִים אִישׁ עַל־כִּסְאוֹ מְלֻבָּשִׁים בְּגָדִים וְכָל־הַנְּבִיאִים מִתְנַבְּאִים were sitting, each on his throne, clothed in their robes, and all the prophets were prophesying before them; cf. *vss.* 12, 19. 2 S. 15. 30 David's ascent of Olivet, cf. *vss.* 18, 23. Is. 6. 2, 2 S. 12. 19, 1 S. 9. 11, 14, 27, Is. 5. 28, Nu. 11. 27, 1 K. 12. 6, 2 K. 2. 11. With הִנֵּה, adding colour to a description or intention. Gen. 25. 32; 37. 7; 41. 1-3, 1 S. 10. 22; 12. 2, 2 K. 17. 26, and often in poetry. With עוֹד, Gen. 18. 22, Ex. 9. 2, 17, 1 K. 1. 14, 22, 42, 2 K. 6. 33, Jer. 33. 1, Job 2. 3. So with יֵשׁ and אֵין, Gen. 24. 42, 49; 43. 4, Deu. 29. 14, Jud. 6. 36.

Rem. 1. The *time* of ptcp. Exx. of *present* time: Gen. 16. 8; 19. 15; 32. 12; 37. 16; 43. 18, Deu. 4. 1; 12. 8 and often, Jud. 7. 10; 18. 3, 1 S. 14. 11, Is. 1. 7, Hos. 3. 1. Exx. of *past* time: Gen. 37. 7, 15; 40. 6; 41. 7ff., Ex. 18. 5, 14, Deu. 4. 12, Jud. 4. 22; 14. 4; 19. 27, 1 S. 2. 13; 9. 11, 1 K. 3. 2; 4. 20; 6. 27, 2 K. 13. 21. Exx. of *future* time: Gen. 7. 4; 17. 19; 41. 25, 28; 49. 29, Ex. 33. 15, Jud. 11. 9; 15. 3, 1 S. 20. 36, 2 S. 12. 23, 2 K. 4. 16, Ps. 22. 32; 102. 19. Particularly with הִנֵּה, as Gen. 15. 3; 20. 3; 24. 13, 1 S. 3. 11, 1 K. 13. 2, Is. 3. 7; 7. 14, Am. 8. 11. The ptcp. with הִנֵּה, however, may refer to any time, as pres.: Gen. 38. 24, Jud. 9. 36, 1 S. 10. 22, 1 K. 1. 25; 17. 12, or past: Gen. 40. 6; 41. 1, Am. 7. 1, 4, 7.

Rem. 2. The verb הָיָה is sometimes used with the ptcp., often indicating the state in which a person (or thing) is found, sometimes expressing the idea of continuity, but in other cases a punctual action. The reference is usually to the past, but occasionally to the future. The הָיָה usually precedes the ptcp., coming after the subj., if there is one. Gen. 1. 6 וִיהִי מַבְדִּיל and *let it separate;* 4. 17 וַיְהִי בֹּנֶה עִיר *and he built* a city; 37. 2 יוֹסֵף הָיָה רֹעֶה *Jos. was herding;* 1 S. 2. 11 וְהַנַּעַר הָיָה מְשָׁרֵת אֶת־יְ׳ and *the child ministered* to Y.; Ps. 122. 2 עֹמְדִים הָיוּ רַגְלֵינוּ *our feet have been standing.* Gen. 39. 22, Ex. 3. 1, Deu. 9. 7, 22, 24; 28. 29, Jud. 1. 7, 1 S. 18. 29, 2 S. 3. 6, 17; 7. 6, 2 K. 17. 25-41; 18. 4, Is. 2. 2; 59. 2, Jer. 26. 18, 20, Hos. 9. 17, Job 1. 14. Pass. ptcp., Lev. 13. 45, 1 K. 22. 35, Jer. 14. 16; 36. 30, Zech. 3. 3. The usage is more common in later books, sometimes substituting more or less for a regular verbal form (it becomes a straightforward tense in postbiblical Hebr.). Neh. 1. 4; 2. 13, 15, 1 Chr. 6. 17; 18. 14, 2 Chr. 30. 10; 36. 16, Est. 2. 15, Dan. 1. 16; 5. 19; 10. 9.

Rem. 3. The ptcp. is negatived by לֹא when an attributive. Jer. 2. 2 אֶרֶץ לֹא זְרוּעָה a land *not sown* (cf. adj. Deu. 32. 6, Hos. 13. 13). Jer. 18. 15, Hab. 1. 14 in an attributive clause, Job 29. 12. Cf. 2 S. 1. 21, Hos. 7. 8. But also in a number of cases where *pred.,* Nu. 35. 23, Deu. 19. 4; 28. 61, 2 S. 3. 34, Jer. 4. 22, Ez. 4. 14; 22. 24, Zeph. 3. 5, Ps. 38. 15, Job 12. 3. In Hos. 1. 6 לֹא רֻחָמָה and Is. 54. 11 לֹא נֻחָמָה the forms are QATAL (Pual).

Rem. 4. The ptcp., perhaps because it has weaker force than finite verb, sometimes uses prep. לְ for obj., espec. when obj. precedes. Is. 11. 9 לַיָּם מְכַסִּים waters *covering the sea.* Nu. 10. 25, Deu. 4. 42, Am. 6. 3 (cf. Is. 66. 5), Is. 14. 2.

Rem. 5. The ptcp. without subj. tends to be used occasionally for 3rd pers. like finite verb. Jos. 8. 6, Neh. 6. 6; 9. 3, 5, Is. 13. 5, and in Psalms. So for infin., Jer. 2. 17 עֵת מוֹלִיכֵךְ *the time when he led you.* Gen. 38. 29, Mal. 1. 7. Both uses are common in postbiblical Hebr.

Rem. 6. The pass. ptcp. appears in some cases to express a state which is the result of the subject's own action. Is. 26. 3 בָּטוּחַ *trusting,* Ps. 103. 14 זָכוּר *mindful,* Is. 53. 3 יָדוּעַ *acquainted with.* Song 3. 8.

Syntax of the Adverb and Adverbial Phrases and Clauses

———◆———

§ 114. Adverbs are optional elements of clause structure. They extend the meaning of (modify) either a verbal clause or the verb itself or either a nominal clause or a single noun or adjective. In the latter cases they should strictly speaking be called adnominals.

Hebr. possesses relatively few individual adverbs compared with Engl. with, e.g. its large open class formed with an adj. and -ly. But it has other ways of expressing adverbial function which are not found in Engl., notably by the use of verbs like הוֹסִיף, שׁוּב, etc., with an accompanying infin. constr. or finite verb (§ 96b, 97) or through the infin. absol. (§ 102), or which are exceptional in Engl., as by the use of simple nouns or adjectives (§ 117 below). Circumstantial clauses may also function adverbially (§ 137), as more directly may (see §§ 118, 119 below) prepos. phrases, infin. phrases and certain subordinate clauses.

In function, adverbs and other adverbial expression between them negate or affirm an action or situation, locate it in space or time, indicate the manner in which it occurs, the circumstances or causes which give rise to it, the purpose behind it, the result which flows from it, the restrictions which apply to it, and so on.

Independent Adverbs

§ 115. In *form*, independent adverbs are very varied; they may be of unknown derivation, as לֹא *not*, שָׁם *there;* or composed of demonstr. (deictic) elements, as כֹּה *thus, here,* הֵנָּה *hither;* or have the ending ם /ַם, as אָמְנָם *truly,* פִּתְאֹם *suddenly;* or be frozen infinitives absol., as הַרְבֵּה *greatly;* or they may be nouns and adjectives which by their use or frequency are more appropriately classified as adverbs than under § 117 below, as שָׁוְא *falsely,* שֵׁנִית *a second time, again.* A few adverbs also do duty as conjunctions, as כִּי *indeed* (adv.), *that, because, but* (conj.) or as prepp., as אַחַר *afterwards* (adv.), *after* (prep.). Some adverbs may themselves take prepp.; where they are derived from nouns, the result is formally a prepos. phrase, as כָּעֵת *as of now*, מִבַּיִת *inside*, but where they are not, the result is in effect another adv., as מִשָּׁם *hence*. Combinations of prep. and pron. זֶה, זֹאת may also be considered adverbs, as מִזֶּה *hence*, כָּזֹאת *thus, accordingly*.

§ 116. *Function.* — (*a*) Most individual adverbs modify the verbal predicate and may be broadly divided into adverbs of place, time, degree and manner. See classification in Rem. 1. Some may belong to more than one category, as אַחַר both *behind* of place and *afterwards* of time, or be also clausal adverbs, as כֹּה both *here* of place and *thus* clausally, אָז and עַתָּה both *then, now* of time and clausally in a logical sense. On clausal uses see *b*. Gen. 22. 13 וְהִנֵּה אַיִל אַחַר and behold there was a ram *behind*. 24. 55 אַחַר תֵּלֵךְ *after that* she may go. Ru. 2. 8 וְכֹה תִדְבָּקִין עִם־נַעֲרֹתָי but keep close *here* to my maidens. Nu. 24. 17 אֶרְאֶנּוּ וְלֹא עַתָּה I shall see him, but not *now*. 1 S. 26. 21 וָאֶשְׁגֶּה הַרְבֵּה מְאֹד I have erred *exceedingly*. Ps. 127. 1 שָׁוְא עָמְלוּ בוֹנָיו בּוֹ those who build it labour *in vain*.

(*b*) Adverbs modifying clauses are fewer in number. Interrogatives are properly clausal adverbs (see Questions, § 152), as are אָז and עַתָּה used logically. Pr. 2. 5 (if you seek ...) אָז תָּבִין *then* you will understand. Ps. 119. 22 (*in that case*). Ecc. 2. 15 (*that being so*). עַתָּה is used of reaching a conclusion, Gen. 27. 2-3 see, I am old ... וְעַתָּה שָׂא־נָא כֵלֶיךָ *now, then,* take your weapons, Is. 5. 3, 5, and is common as a macro-syntactic signal in discourse; see further § 72, R. 4. But most clausal adverbs may be broadly divided into *negative* and (see *c* below) *affirmative*. The negative לֹא is used by and large in objective statements and solemn commands. Gen. 45. 1 וְלֹא יָכֹל יוֹסֵף לְהִתְאַפֵּק and J. *was unable* to restrain himself. 3.1 לֹא תֹאכְלוּ מִכֹּל עֵץ הַגָּן *you shall eat of no tree* of the garden. The neg. אַל is the subjective neg., used sometimes in commands, oftener in dissuasion, deprecation, expression of a wish, etc. (see Cohort., Jussive). Gen. 19. 7 אַל־נָא אַחַי תָּרֵעוּ my brothers, please *do not do wrong*, cf. *vs.* 8. 1 S. 17. 32, 2 S. 24. 14, Jer. 9. 22, Ps. 51. 13. The usual place of the neg. is before the verb, but it may be placed before the emphatic word in the neg. clause; either way, it properly modifies the whole clause. Gen.

45. 8 לֹא אַתֶּם שְׁלַחְתֶּם אֹתִי *it was not you* that sent me. 32. 29, 1 S. 2. 9; 8. 7, Neh. 6. 12. Both לֹא and אַל are used only with QATAL and YIQTOL forms. On imper. with neg., § 66. The negatives with infin. (לְבִלְתִּי, § 109a) and with participial (§ 113d) and with nominal clauses in general (both אֵין) function adnominally, as in effect forming a constr. relation, though אֵין (and its affirmative counterpart יֵשׁ) show verbal features. On the usage of אֵין and יֵשׁ, § 52. The neg. טֶרֶם *not yet*, is a temporal, not a clausal, adv., though it is peculiar in that it is usually joined to (long) YIQTOL; see § 62, R. 1. The telic neg. פֶּן *lest*, is a conjunction, § 128.

(c) *Affirmative* clausal adverbs are אֲבָל *truly* (Gen. 42. 21, 1 K. 1. 43), though in later Hebr. it becomes a strong adversative conjunction, *howbeit, but* (Dan. 10. 7, Ezr. 10. 13). — אַךְ *surely, no doubt* (Gen. 29. 14, Is. 63. 8), otherwise an exclusive or antithetical conjunction, *except, only yet, but* or an adnominal (see *d* below). So אָכֵן (Gen. 28. 16, Is. 40. 7; 53. 4), also used as a conj. — אָמְנָם *truly, indeed* (Job 12. 2, Ru. 3. 12), אֻמְנָם idem. (only in questions, Gen. 18. 13, 1 K. 8. 27), אָמְנָה idem. (Gen. 20. 12). — כִּי is usually a conj., *for, because, that, but* and so in usages like אַף כִּי, lit. *furthermore* (it is a fact) *that*, though often translated *indeed* (Gen. 3. 1 in a question), or in its meaning *so much the more, less* (§ 143c), cf. הֲכִי (Job 6. 22), אַךְ כִּי *only* (1 S. 8. 9), לֹא כִּי *no but* (Gen. 18. 15, Is. 30. 16). But sometimes it functions adverbially, espec. when it occurs internally, but also otherwise, Gen. 18. 20 the outcry against Sodom כִּי רַבָּה is *surely* great, 1 S. 20. 26, Is. 32. 13, Hos. 6. 9; 8. 6; 9. 12, Am. 3. 7, Ps. 76. 11; 77. 12, Pr. 30. 2, Ecc. 4. 16; 7. 7, 20, Lam. 3. 22. So also when כִּי introduces the apod., Gen. 31. 42; 43. 10, Is. 7. 9. — The clausal adverbs כֹּה and כֵּן *thus* have respectively a forward and a backward reference: כֹּה in Ex. 3. 14 (say *this*) and often with אָמַר, Is. 24. 13; כֵּן in Gen. 1. 7 (and it was *so*), Jud. 5. 31, Jer. 14. 10. כָּכָה *thus* has reference both ways, Ex. 12. 11, Nu. 8. 26. לָכֵן and עַל־כֵּן are best regarded as conjunctions.

אוּלַי *perhaps* may be included here as expressing an emphatic hope or doubt, Gen. 16. 3, Jer. 20. 10; Gen. 24. 5, 39, Job 1. 5. Ironic, Is. 47. 12, Jer. 51. 8.

(d) *Adnominal usages*. The commonest Hebr. adnominal, used mostly with adjectives, is מְאֹד *very*, Gen. 1. 31 טוֹב מְאֹד *very good*, though it is also used with stative verbs, i.e. the verbs most like an adj., 7. 18 *were very strong*, i.e. *prevailed greatly*. With noun, 13. 13 (*great sinners*), with Niph. ptcp., Ps. 46. 2 (a help *greatly* to be found), with infin. constr., Jos. 9. 13 (from *the very long journey*), with another adv., 1 K. 10. 10 (*in very great quantity*). The directional ending ה is adnominal, following the noun, cf. Engl. *-wards*. פְּנִימָה *inside*, sometimes with prep. לְ or מִן, is construed adnominally, following its noun, 1 K. 6. 18, 2 K. 7. 11, Ps. 45. 14. So occasionally other adverbs, as מְעַט in Ez. 11. 16 (a sanctuary *but little*, perhaps *for a little while*). Cf. the adverbial prepos. phrases Deu. 4. 39 (heaven *above*), Ez. 41. 9 (the *outside* wall), Ps. 15. 24 (Sheol *beneath*).

The neg. לֹא forms compounds with nouns, Deu. 32. 21 לֹא אֵל a *no-god*, Is. 10. 15; 31. 8, Am. 6. 13. With adj., Hos. 13. 13 לֹא חָכָם a son *not-wise*, Ps. 43. 1, Pr. 30. 25. So אִי in Job 22. 30 (the *non-innocent*) and perhaps in 1 S. 4. 21 (*inglorious*), though here אִי may mean *where?* (cf. Ugar. *iy zbl*, *where is the prince*, i.e. Baal, and the names Ichabod and Jezebel). So the frozen constructs בְּלִי and אֶפֶס: 2 S. 1. 21 בְּלִי מָשִׁיחַ *not anointed*, Deu. 32. 36, Is. 5. 8, Job 8. 11.

The inclusive particles גַּם and אַף and the restrictive particles אַךְ and רַק are best treated as conjunctions linking either two nouns (§ 38*a, b*) or two clauses (§§ 143, 144). But when there is no coordination they may serve as emphasizing or limiting adverbs or adnominals. Thus גַּם before infin. absol., § 101*c*, or גַּם or אַף before another adverb (Gen. 18. 13; 20. 12, *truly indeed*) or noun or pron. (Ex. 12. 32 and bless *even* me; 1 S. 22. 7 *indeed* all of you; 1 K. 2. 14 he *himself*); אַךְ and רַק before infin. absol., § 101*a*; before a noun or adj. (Gen. 6. 5 *nothing but* evil; 18. 32 *just this once*; Ex. 8. 5 *only* in the Nile; 12. 15 on the *very first* day; 1 S. 18. 8 *nothing less than* the kingship; Is. 19. 11 *utterly* foolish).

> *Rem. 1.* Independent adverbs other than clausal may be divided as follows (some place and time adverbs may have the directional ה). — *Of place:* אַחַר *behind*, אָחוֹר אֲחֹרַנִּית *backwards*, הָלְאָה *forward, beyond*, הֲלֹם *hither*, הֵנָּה *hither*, הַרְחֵק *at a distance*, חוּץ *outside*, כֹּה *here*, מַטָּה *downwards*, מַעַל *above*, מַעְלָה *upwards*, מֵסַב סָבִיב *around*, פֹּה *here*, פְּנִימָה *inside*, קָדִימָה/קֵדְמָה *eastwards*, שָׁם *there*, שָׁמָּה *thither*.
>
> *Of time:* אָז/אֲזַי *then*, אַחֲרֹנָה/אַחַר *afterwards, at the last*, אֶמֶשׁ *last night*, אֶתְמוֹל שִׁלְשׁוֹם *previously* (lit. *yesterday and the day before*), הָלְאָה *henceforth*, מְהֵרָה/מָהָר הֵנָּה *now*, טֶרֶם *not yet*, כְּבָר *already*, לַיְלָה *by night*, יוֹמָם *daily*,

tomorrow, עֲדֶנָה/עֶדֶן *previously,* עוֹד *still, again,* עוֹלָם *forever,* עַתָּה *now,*
רִאשׁוֹנָה *before, formerly,* רַבַּת *for a long time,* רֶגַע *for a moment.*

Of degree: הַרְבֵּה *very, greatly,* יֶתֶר, יוֹתֵר *to excess, overmuch,* מְאֹד *very,*
מְעַט *a little, almost,* רַב, רַבָּה, רַבַּת *much, abundantly.*

Of manner: אַחַת *once,* אַט *gently,* הֵיטֵב *well,* חִנָּם *in vain,* חִישׁ *quickly,* חֶרֶשׁ
secretly, יַחְדָּו/יַחַד *together,* מַהֵר, מְהֵרָה *quickly,* פִּתְאֹם *suddenly,* פֶּתַע *suddenly,*
רֶגַע *in a moment, suddenly,* רֵיקָם *vainly,* שָׁוְא *falsely,* שֵׁנִית *again* (see also
multiplicatives, § 48, R. 3), תָּמִיד *continually.*

Adverbs with prepp. (selected exx.; see Lexx.). Before other adverbs:
אַחֲרֵי־כֵן *afterwards,* מִשָּׁם *hence,* עַד־הֵנָּה *hither, hitherto,* עַד־מְאֹד *exceedingly.*
Before pron.: כָּזֹאת *thus, accordingly,* מִזֶּה *hence.* Before nouns: בַּסֵּתֶר *secretly,*
בִּשְׁגָגָה *inadvertantly,* בִּשְׁלָוָה *unawares,* כָּעֵת *now, at the present time,* לָבֶטַח
securely, לָנֶצַח *forever,* לְעוֹלָם (also עַד־) *forever,* מִבַּיִת *inside,* מִחוּץ *outside,*
מִנֶּגֶד *in front, straight away,* מִקֶּדֶם *of old,* מִקָּרוֹב *recently, soon,* מֵרָחוֹק *afar off.*

Rem. 2. Word-order. Clausal adverbs normally come first in a clause.
Adverbs (and prep. phrases) modifying the verb usually follow the verb and, if
it has one, its object; but if they refer back to some person, thing or place in a
previous clause (anaphoric), they generally precede the object; and if they are
given special prominence, they may come first in the clause, espec. in poetry.
Ps. 16. 8 שִׁוִּיתִי י׳ לְנֶגְדִּי תָמִיד *I keep Y. before me continually.* Gen. 2. 7 וַיִּפַּח
בְּאַפּוֹ נִשְׁמַת חַיִּים *and he breathed into his nostrils the breath of life; vs.* 8 וַיָּשֶׂם
שָׁם אֶת־הָאָדָם *and he placed there the man whom he had formed.* Gen. 3. 18
בְּעִצָּבוֹן תֹּאכְלֶנָּה כֹּל יְמֵי חַיֶּיךָ *in pain you shall eat of it all the days of your life.*
Ps. 127. 1. But usage varies.

NOUNS AND ADJECTIVES AS ADVERBS

§ 117. Nouns and adjectives may be freely used in an adverbial
function (adnominal if they modify nominal clauses). They should not
be called adverbial "accusatives", § 88, R. 1. — (a) In definitions of *place*.
Indicating *where.* This use is common with the words בַּיִת *house,* פֶּתַח
door, and some others, especially following verbs like יָשַׁב *dwell, sit,* etc.
Gen. 24. 23 הֲיֵשׁ בֵּית־אָבִיךְ מָקוֹם *is there room in your father's house?*
2 S. 9. 4 וְהוּא הִנֵּה־הוּא בֵּית מָכִיר *he is at the house of* M.; Gen. 18. 1, 10
יֹשֵׁב פֶּתַח־הָאֹהֶל *as he sat at the door of* the tent. Gen. 38. 11; 45. 16. Ex.
33. 10, Jos. 1. 4, 15; 12. 1; 23. 4, 1 K. 19. 13, 2 K. 2. 3, Is. 3. 6, Jer. 36. 10.
Gen. 28. 11 *at the place of his head,* 1 S. 26. 7; Ru. 3. 8, 14 *at the place of his
feet.* Proper names compounded with בֵּית are similarly construed, 2 S.
2. 32, Hos. 12. 5. Sometimes a prep. is used, cf. Jer. 27. 18 (בְּ) with *vs.* 21.

Indicating *whither, to where*. Gen. 27. 3 צֵא הַשָּׂדֶה go out *to the field;*
45. 25 וַיָּבֹאוּ אֶרֶץ כְּנַעַן and they came *to the land of* C.; Ps. 100. 4
בֹּ֫אוּ שְׁעָרָיו go *into his gates*. The ה of direction is frequently appended,
Gen. 24. 16 וַתֵּ֫רֶד הָעַ֫יְנָה and she went down *to the fountain;* 12. 5; 39. 1,
12; 42. 38; 43. 17. Prepp. (אֶל־, עַד־, etc.) may of course be used before
noun of *place*, but must be used with names of *persons*. The directional ה
cannot be appended to the latter. Gen. 45. 25 וַיָּבֹאוּ אֶרֶץ כְּנַעַן אֶל־
יַעֲקֹב and they came *to the land of C. to J.*, Jer. 27. 3. The prep. is used
also with creatures, Gen. 31. 4 הַשָּׂדֶה אֶל־צֹאנוֹ *to* the field *to* his flock.
— Gen. 13. 10; 24. 27, Ex. 4. 9; 17. 10, Jos. 6. 19, 24, Jud. 1. 26; 19. 18,
1 S. 1. 24; 17. 17, 20, 2 S. 20. 3, Is. 14. 11, Jer. 16. 8; 18. 2; Nah. 2. 6. — In
Ez. 11. 24; 23. 16 כַּשְׂדִּים is the name of the country, Jer. 50. 10; 51. 24, 25.

Indicating *how far*. 1 K. 19. 4 and he went into the desert דֶּ֫רֶךְ יוֹם a
day's journey, Gen. 7. 20, Ez. 41. 22, Jon. 3. 4.

(*b*) In definitions of *time*. Indicating *when*. Hos. 7. 5 יוֹם מַלְכֵּ֫נוּ *on
the day* of our king; 2 S. 21. 9 תְּחִלַּת קְצִיר שְׂעֹרִים *at the beginning* of
barley harvest; Ps. 127. 2 יִתֵּן לִידִידוֹ שֵׁנָא he gives to his beloved *in sleep*.
Gen. 14. 15; 27. 45; 40. 7, Hos. 1. 2; 7. 6; Ps. 91. 6 (*at noon*; elsewhere
with prep. בְּ); Ps. 119. 62 חֲצוֹת לַ֫יְלָה *at midnight*; Ps. 5. 4; 6. 11.
Indicating *how long*, Gen. 3. 14 כָּל־יְמֵי חַיֶּ֫יךָ *all the days* of your life;
Hos. 3. 4 יָמִים רַבִּים יֵשְׁבוּ *many days* shall they abide. Gen. 7. 4, 24;
14. 4; 15. 13; 21. 34; 27. 44.

(*c*) In definitions of *manner* (how). Zeph. 1. 14 מַר צֹרֵחַ גִּבּוֹר *bitterly*
cries the mighty man; Ez. 27. 30 וְיִזְעֲקוּ מָרָה they shall cry *bitterly;* 1 S.
12. 11 וַתֵּשְׁבוּ בֶּ֫טַח and you dwelt *in confidence;* Hos. 14. 5 אֹהֲבֵם נְדָבָה
I will love them *freely*, 1 S. 15. 32 וַיֵּ֫לֶךְ אֵלָיו אֲגַג מַעֲדַנֹּת and Agag came
to him *cheerfully;* Zeph. 3. 9 לְעָבְדוֹ שְׁכֶם אֶחָד to serve him *with one
accord* (lit. shoulder). Rem. 3.

(*d*) In definitions of *material* (with what?). Gen. 2. 7 וַיִּ֫יצֶר אֶת־
הָאָדָם עָפָר he made man *out of dust*. Deu. 27. 6 אֲבָנִים שְׁלֵמוֹת *of whole
stones* you shall build the altar. Gen. 27. 9 (suff.), Ex. 20. 25, 25. 18, 28;
38. 3, Deu. 27. 6, 1 K. 7. 15, 27, Song 3. 10. Of *instrument, means*, etc. Is.
5. 2 וַיִּטָּעֵ֫הוּ שֹׂרֵק he planted it *with choice vines*, Jud. 9. 45. Ps. 45. 8 God
has anointed you שֶׁ֫מֶן שָׂשׂוֹן *with the oil of gladness;* Mic. 7. 2 hunts his
brother *with a net;* Mal. 3. 24 smite the earth *with a curse;* Ps. 64. 8 shoot
at them *with arrows*. 2 K. 19. 32, Ps. 88. 8, Pr. 13. 24. Jos. 7. 25 וַיִּרְגְּמוּ

אֹתוֹ אֶבֶן they stoned him *with stones*, Lev. 24. 23, 2 Chr. 24. 21; also with בְּ of instrum., and so סָקַל *stone* always, Jos. 7. 25, Deu. 13. 11, 1 K. 21. 13.

(*e*) In *specifying* definitions. When to the general statement of the action there is added the point of its incidence, or the respect in which it holds, this secondary limitation is expressed by nouns used adverbially. Gen. 3. 15 הוּא יְשׁוּפְךָ רֹאשׁ he shall bruise you *on the head;* 37. 21 לֹא נַכֶּנּוּ נֶפֶשׁ let us not smite him *as to life* (mortally); 1 K. 15. 23 חָלָה אֶת־רַגְלָיו he was diseased *in his feet*. Gen. 17. 25; 41. 40, Ex. 16. 16, Deu. 19. 6, 11; 33. 11, Jud. 15. 8, 2 S. 21. 20, Jer. 2. 16, 28, Ps. 3. 8; 17. 11, Job 21. 7.

Rem. 1. The force of the ה of direction has in many cases become enfeebled; thus שָׁמָּה *there*, Jer. 18. 2, and following בְּ or מִן, Jos. 15. 21, Jer. 27. 16. It sometimes seems little more than an ornate ending, Hos. 8. 7; 10. 13, Ps. 3. 3; 116. 14, 15, 18; 124. 4; 125. 3.

Rem. 2. Adjectives indicating the *manner* of an action may be mas. or fem. (Is. 5. 26), sing. or plur., esp. fem. plur. (Ps. 139. 14, Job 37. 5). If a noun: (1) in principal any noun may be used, Mic. 2. 3 רוֹמָה, Ps. 56. 3 מָרוֹם *haughtily*, Is. 60. 14 שְׁחוֹחַ *bowing down*, Pr. 31. 9 צֶדֶק *in righteousness*, Jud. 5. 21 עֹז *in power;* Lev. 19. 16, Nu. 32. 14, Is. 57. 2. (2) The noun may be plur., Lam. 1. 9 פְּלָאִים she came down *wonderfully*, Hos. 12. 15 תַּמְרוּרִים *bitterly*, Ps. 58. 2; 75. 3. (3) a nominal phrase may be used, Jos. 9. 2, 1 K. 22. 13 פֶּה אֶחָד *unanimously;* Lev. 26. 21, 23, 24, Pr. 7. 10. 2 S. 23. 3 ruling יִרְאַת א' *in the fear of* God. This usage of the noun is mostly poetical, prose rather employing a prep., Lam. 1. 5 שְׁבִי *into captivity*, elsewhere בַּשְּׁבִי; Ps. 119. 78, 86 שֶׁקֶר *falsely, in vain*, usually לַשֶּׁקֶר, 1 S. 25. 21. Jer. 23. 28, Ps. 73. 13; 119. 75, Job 21. 34. Comp. Is. 30. 7 with 49. 4; 65. 23; Ps. 119. 75 אֱמוּנָה with 2 K. 12. 16.

PREPOSITIONAL PHRASES

§ 118. Prepos. phrases function adverbially in verbal clauses and adnominally in nominal clauses and phrases.

(*a*) *Form*. Some prepp. like some adverbs fall outside the root system, consisting of a single consonant (בְּ, כְּ, לְ) or of two (מִן); like the monocons. prepp. מִן is usually attached directly to its noun, though it sometimes takes Maqqeph, as usually do the fuller forms לְמוֹ, כְּמוֹ, בְּמוֹ, almost exclusively poetical. The prepp. אֶל, עַד, עַל are derived from triconsonantal roots, the final root letter appearing in the poet. forms אֱלֵי, etc., and before suffixes, עָלֶיךָ, etc. The shortened forms are usually

attached to their noun via Maqqeph. Other prepp. are in effect nouns in
the construct state, as תַּחַת, בֵּין, אַחֲרֵי. Combinations of two simple
prepp., as מֵאֵת, or of a simple prep. with a constr. noun, as לִפְנֵי, are
common, rather less so more complicated combinations, as לְמִתַּחַת לְ
(1 K. 7. 32). Rem. 3.

(b) *Usage.* The prep. defines the kind of relationship which the
phrase of which it is part has with the verb, Ex. 6. 10 Y. spoke אֶל־מֹשֶׁה
to Moses; or with the wider context, Is. 5. 25 בְּכָל־זֹאת *for all this* his
anger is not turned away; or with the subj. of nominal clause, Ps. 36. 6
your faithfulness (is, reaches) עַד־שְׁחָקִים *to the clouds;* or with a noun or
adj. (ptcp.), Pr. 21. 14 מַתָּן בַּסֵּתֶר a gift *in secret;* Ps. 113. 4 רָם עַל־כָּל־
גּוֹיִם high *above all nations.* In most (but not all) cases the basic
relationship seems to be spatial or directional, this being extended
metaphorically to take in temporal and a variety of other relationships
(agency, instrumentality, advantage or disadvantage, reason, etc.), Rem. 1.
In the case of the three monoconsonantal prepp. the primary relationship
seems to be more general, and the local uses as well as other kinds to be
secondary, Rem. 2. As relational terms prepp. are, more than most
grammatical entities, dependent for their precise meaning on the context
in which they occur, especially on the kind of noun which they govern
and the kind of verb with which they are used. The perspective of the
speaker may also be relevant, Rem. 4.

Prepp. can differ widely in their usage as between Hebr. and Engl.
Some uses are similar in both languages, notably the overlap between
locative לְ go *to* and possessive לְ belong *to,* or between agentive and
instrumental בְּ *by, with* or both of these and comitative בְּ *(along) with.*
In other features, however, Hebr. usage is markedly different from Engl.,
employing the same prep. where Engl. would employ several. Thus Hebr.
makes no distinction between בְּ of presence *in,* e.g., a house and בְּ of
presence *at,* e.g., a place, or between אֶל of presence *at, near* and אֶל of
direction *to, towards,* or between the static usages of בְּ *in, at,* אֶל *at, near,*
עַל *over* and the dynamic (involving motion) usages of בְּ *into,* אֶל
towards, עַל *upon.* It is the verb and sometimes the kind of noun
governed which in effect decide these distinctions. Unlike Engl. but like
the Latin dative לְ carries the double sense of, e.g., give *to* and act *for.*
Some prepp. also express, depending on the context, both the ideas of

advantage *for* and disadvantage *against*.

The static-dynamic relationship is sometimes clarified if a more appropriate verb than the one used is understood (*pregnant* construction). 1 S. 7. 8 אַל־תַּחֲרֵשׁ מִמֶּנּוּ *be not silent* (turning away) *from us*. Ps. 22. 22 מִקַּרְנֵי רֵמִים עֲנִיתָנִי *heard* (and delivered) *me from* the horns of wild oxen. Gen. 19. 27 וַיַּשְׁכֵּם ... אֶל־הַמָּקוֹם *he rose early* (and went) *to* the place, Song 7. 13. Gen. 42. 28 וַיֶּחֶרְדוּ אִישׁ אֶל־אָחִיו *they trembled* (and looked) *towards* one another; and often with verbs of *fearing, wondering*, etc., Gen. 43. 33, Is. 13. 8, Hos. 3. 5, Mic. 7. 17. So the brief language, 1 S. 15. 23 rejected you מִמֶּלֶךְ *from* (being) *king*, cf. *vs.* 26 מִהְיוֹת מ׳, 1 K. 15. 13. Ps. 55. 19 פָּדָה בְשָׁלוֹם *has redeemed* (so as to be) *in peace*.

(*c*) *Phrasal verbs*. A number of trans. verbs govern a dir. obj. via a prep., and may be compared with so-called Engl. phrasal verbs like *turn in, sum up*, etc. The prep. does not function adverbially within the clause, modifying the verb in terms of place, time, manner, etc., but rather adverbially within the verbal phrase itself, telling us something about the mode of action. See for exx., § 89*e*. These verbs should be distinguished from verbs, trans. or intrans., with which, however often attached to it, a prep. functions normally, *e.g.*, הֶאֱמִין בְּ *believe in*, נִלְחַם אֶת/בְּ *fight with*, עַל both *for* and *against*, רָצָה עִם/בְּ *be pleased with*.

> *Rem. 1.* The following prepp. are primarily of place or direction and secondarily applied to other relationships:
>
> The prepp. אַחַר and אַחֲרֵי are *behind* of location (Ex. 11. 5), *after* with a verb of motion (Gen. 44. 4), often in a figurative sense implying a way of behaviour (Deu. 8. 19, 2 K. 13. 2); of time, *after* (Gen. 15. 1; 35. 12).
>
> The prep. אֶל (אֶל־) is occasionally locational, *at, near* (1 K. 13. 20), but more often directional, *towards*, whether the goal be reached or not (Gen. 2. 19; 3. 19; 6. 18 *into* the ark). After verbs of speaking, *to* (especially דִּבֶּר אֶל־) but also in the sense of *with reference to, of* (Gen. 20. 2, Ps. 2. 7), cf. לְ. After other verbs with nuance of advantage (*on behalf of, for*, 1 S. 1. 27; *over*, 15. 35; 1 K. 19. 3 (fled) *for* his life), or disadvantage (*against*, Gen. 4. 8, Is. 2. 4). In the sense of *in addition to, over and above* (Lev. 18. 18, 1 K. 10. 7). In the last two senses אֶל overlaps with עַל, and there is some evidence of interchange (2 S. 2. 9 has three exx. of אֶל and three of עַל following the same verb) and, less commonly, of one being used for the other in a sense where they do not usually overlap, e.g. 1 S. 1. 10 pray *to* God with עַל, *vs.* 26 אֶל.

The confusion should not be exaggerated.

The prep. אֵצֶל is always spatial, *beside* (Gen. 41. 3).

The prepp. אֵת (אֶת־, suff. אִתּוֹ, sometimes אוֹתְךָ as if from אֵת of the object) and עִם are hardly distinguishable. They may be used of being *near* a place (Jud. 4. 11, Gen. 25. 11), but are much commoner in a comitative sense, *with* persons (Gen. 6. 18; 13. 1), *along with* things (Gen. 6. 13, Deu. 12. 33). עִם is occasionally used of time, Ps. 72. 5 *as long as* the sun. Both occur frequently with verbs of personal intercourse, עָשָׂה אֶת/עִם *do*, e.g. kindness, *with*, i.e. *deal kindly with*, הֵיטִיב עִם, רָצָה עִם; Mic. 6. 8; also quarrel, fight *with* (Is. 45. 9, Gen. 32. 29). Adnominally, blameless *before* (Deu. 18. 13), at peace *with* (2 S. 21. 4). In comparisons, *like* (Job 9. 26, Ecc. 2. 16), *besides, except* (Ex. 20. 20, Deu. 32. 39). With senses like *in the possession, care, knowledge* of, 1 S. 9. 7, Is. 49. 4, Pr. 2. 1; 11. 2; Gen. 24. 25, 1 S. 9. 23, Ps. 130. 7. With words like *heart*, denoting the locus of feelings and emotions, 2 K. 10. 15; Deu. 8. 5, 1 K. 8. 17, Ecc. 1. 16. In Gen. 4. 1 אֵת is usually rendered *with the help of*, but in the context *as well as* may fit better.

The prep. בֵּין (also בֵּינוֹת and, only with suff., בֵּינַי) is *between* (Ex. 13. 9) and more generally *among* (Song 2. 2). If two places or people or things are involved, the prep. is repeated before each (Gen. 13. 3), or בֵּין ... לְ is used (Gen. 1. 6). Metaphorically of judging, knowing (difference), adnominally of a covenant, *between*, etc., Gen. 9. 12; 16. 5; 31. 49, Jos. 22. 27, 2 S. 19. 36, Is. 2. 4.

The prep. בַּעַד is basically *behind* (Gen. 7. 16) or more loosely, *around* (Job 1. 10) or *through* (with the back towards) (Jos. 2. 15, Jud. 5. 28). Metaphorically, *on behalf of* (Gen. 20. 7, Ex. 8. 24)

The prep. מוּל is spatial, *in front of*, Deu. 1. 1.

The prep. מִן expresses separation, including the direction in which someone or something is placed or situated, Gen. 12. 8 *on* the west, east, but more commonly the place of origin, *from* (1 S. 1. 1). *Away from*, Gen. 27. 39. With verbs of motion, deliverance, ceasing, etc. it expresses movement *away from*, Ex. 19. 14, 1 S. 2. 8, Ex. 14. 12. In pregnant construction, Ps. 43. 1 judge (and save) *from*. In causative sense, *because of*, Gen. 48. 10 *from* old age, Is. 6. 4 *at* the voice; 53. 5 *because of* our transgressions. With verbs of fearing, Ps. 27. 1 be afraid *of*. With verbs of removing, speaking, looking, etc., *out of*, Ex. 2. 10, Song 2. 9. Pregnantly, Mic. 7. 17 *tremble* (come trembling) *out of*. Adnominally, Job 4. 13 thoughts (arising) *out of*. Often of time, *since*, marking the *terminus a quo* (1 S. 7. 2) or *after* a previous period (Jos. 23. 1). Sometimes *on, at*, referring to a future time, Gen. 19. 34 *on* the morrow; or a past time, Jos. 24. 2 *of* old. Idiomatically, מִיָּמֶיךָ *since* you were born, *all your days* (1 S. 25. 28, Job 38. 12). Other uses are *partitive*, Gen. 7. 8 two by two *from*, *of*, with number omitted, *some of*, Gen. 30. 14, *not ... any of*, Deu. 16. 4; *comparative*, Jud. 14. 18 sweeter *than*, Ex. 12. 4 *too* small *for*, Hos. 6. 6

rather than; privative, Job 11. 15 *without* spot. On the use of מִן to negate an infin. (*so as not to*), § 109, R. 1 and, less commonly than לְ, to express the agent of the passive, § 95c.

The prep. עַד *as far as, up to,* more often includes the limit than אֶל, which is rather *towards.* Gen. 11. 31 *to* Haran, Hos. 14. 2 return *to* Y. Common in the phrase (וְ)עַד ... מִן, Gen. 10. 19; inclusively, Gen. 19. 4 *both* young *and* old. עַד is not, like אֶל, used of location but it is, unlike אֶל, used of time, *until* (Gen. 19. 37), espec. with infin., both in past (Gen. 8. 7) and future (3. 19) contexts. With the nuance of *against* (a time), Gen. 43. 25 *against* (for) Joseph's coming. *While, as long as,* 2 K. 9. 22.

The prep. עַל is *above, over, upon,* whether of rest or motion, Gen. 2. 5; 24. 30, 2 K. 4. 34. And in figurative senses, Gen. 16. 5 my wrong be *upon you;* 41. 33 set him *over* the land, Jud. 3. 10, 1 S. 15. 17. With verbs like *stand, sit,* it can mean *beside, by,* Gen. 18. 2, 2 S. 9. 10, Is. 6. 2, Ps. 1. 3. Other senses: to express addition, Gen. 31. 50 *besides* my daughters; 32. 12 *along with,* Am. 3. 5. Or obligation, 2 S. 18. 11 *incumbent upon,* Jud. 19. 20, Pr. 7. 14. Or advantage, Gen. 19. 17 *for* your life, Jud. 9. 17 fight *for,* 1 K. 2. 18 *on your behalf;* or disadvantage, Deu. 20. 10 fight *against,* Gen. 34. 25, Ex. 15. 24. In the expression of one's own feelings, Jer. 8. 18 sick *upon me,* Ps. 42. 6, 7 *within* me; 143. 4, Job 10. 1. Sometimes the prep. is almost untranslatable, Gen. 48. 7 Rachel died עָלַי *to my sorrow.* In a logical sense עַל is used to express the condition, circumstances in which an action is performed, on which it rests or which underlie it. Engl. has to translate variously, *amidst, although, notwithstanding, according to, concerning,* etc. Jer. 8. 18 *in, amidst* trouble, Job 10. 7 *although* you know, Is. 53. 9 *in spite of the fact that,* Gen. 41. 15 *concerning* you. Ex. 12. 8, Is. 1. 1; 38. 15; 60. 7 *with acceptance,* Jer. 6. 14, Ps. 50. 5. On עַל with phrasal verbs see § 89e.

For עִם see אֵת

The prep. תַּחַת is *under, below* (Gen. 7. 9, Nu. 5. 19, Jud. 3. 20); idiomatically, 1 S. 14. 9 תַּחְתֵּינוּ (note plur. form, as usually before suff.) *where we stand* (under us), *on the spot,* Jos. 5. 8; 6. 5. In the sense *instead* (Gen. 4. 25) or *in return, exchange for* (Gen. 44. 4, Ex. 21. 23); ת' אֲשֶׁר *because* (Deu. 21. 14), conj.

Rem. 2. The three monoconson. prepp. בְּ, כְּ, לְ seem non-locational in their primary meanings. This is certainly true of כְּ, and is the most satisfactory way to account for the wide spread of meanings of בְּ and לְ. The only other simple prep. which does not build on a locational origin is יַעַן *because of,* usually with infin. (1 K. 21. 20), rare with a noun (Ez. 5. 9).

The prep. בְּ is *in, within,* e.g. a city (Gen. 18. 24), a field (30. 14), gates (Ex. 20. 10), as well as *at, on,* e.g. a spring (1 S. 29. 1), a mountain (Ex. 24. 18), an altar (Nu. 23. 2). *Among* people (2 S. 15. 31), sometimes implying pre-eminence, Song 1. 8 fair(est) *among* women. With verb of motion, *into* the shelter of (Gen. 19. 8), *through* a land (12. 6). Figuratively of a state or condition, *in* peace (Gen. 15. 15), *in* distress (Ps. 91. 15). Of time only *on, at* a particular time (Gen. 1. 1; 2. 2); with infin., *when*. Connected with the meaning *in* is the so-called *Beth essentiae, in the capacity of, as,* Ex. 6. 3 I appeared *as* El Shaddai; 18. 4 (was) *my help,* Nu. 26. 53 *as* an inheritance, Ps. 68. 5 his name is *Yah*. Similarly בְּ with certain verbs, as הֶאֱמִין בְּ believe *in*. It is difficult, however, to see how its common meanings *by, with, through* (of instrument, agent or means) or *with* (of accompaniment) or *for* of exchange (*Beth pretii*) can derive from any sense of *in*. Gen. 9. 6 *by* men, Ex. 5. 2 *with* many men, Jer. 11. 19 *with* its fruit, Job 40. 29 play *with*. 2 S. 24. 4 buy *for*, Deu. 21. 14 sell *for*, Ex. 34. 20 redeem *with*, 2 S. 23. 17 *at peril of* their lives, Deu. 19. 21 life *for* life. Likewise its meanings *because of, on account of* (Gen. 18. 28, 2 S. 3. 27) and *although, in spite of* (Nu. 14. 11, Is. 5. 25). Some broader idea is required to encompass these meanings along with the locational, e.g. inclusive or (Jenni) unifying.

The prep. כְּ expresses similarity or comparison. Gen. 1. 26 *according to* our likeness; 3. 5 *as* gods, Is. 61. 10, Ps. 19. 6; כְּ ... כְּ, Ps. 139. 12 (*as*) darkness is *as* light, Lev. 24. 16. With infin., Jud. 14. 6 *like* the rending of a kid, and very commonly *when*, cf. בְּ. Often כְּ is used in a quasi-nominal way, cf. Engl. *the like(s) of*, Deu. 4. 32 *the like of* this great thing, Ru. 1. 4 *about* ten years. It is also commonly used in a pregnant sense, Ps. 95. 8 כִּמְרִיבָה *as at* M.; 83. 10 do to them *as to* M., Gen. 34. 31, Hos. 2. 5.

The prep. לְ combines the meanings of Engl. *at, near* (Gen. 4. 7) and *to*, the latter sometimes in the sense of אֶל, expressing direction, לְאָחוֹר *backwards* or, with verbs of motion, *towards* (Gen. 30. 25), but predominantly in non-local senses; thus give *to* (as alternative to the indirect obj.), make *into*, appoint *as* (as alternative to the obj. complement), belong *to* (of possession), be good *to*, (too) much *for*, etc. It is used both of advantage (*for*) and disadvantage (*against*). Gen. 19. 8 do *to, with*, Ps. 16. 10 abandon *to* Sheol. Gen. 2. 22 built the rib *into* a woman, *vs.* 7 (הָיָה לְ) *became*. Gen. 31. 16 it is *mine*, Is. 2. 12 Y. *has* a day. Is. 6. 8 who will go *for* us?, Ps. 137. 7 *against* the Edomites, Jud. 16. 2 lie in wait *for*. 2 S. 1. 26 be pleasant *to*, Hos. 2. 9 better *for*. Of time: Gen. 8. 11 *at* evening, Ex. 34. 2 *by* morning, Deu. 16. 4 *until* morning, Deu. 7. 9 *for* a thousand generations. In the so-called *Dativus ethicus* the action is reflected back upon the agent, Gen. 12. 1 get *you*; 22. 5 sit *you* here, Am. 7. 12, Ps. 120. 6. But in a large number of cases לְ seems to mean simply *in relation to, with reference to, concerning*. Gen. 20. 13 say *of* me, Ps. 3. 3, Lev. 19. 27 *on account of* the dead person, Deu. 12. 30 enquire *about*, Gen. 41. 19 *for* badness, Deu. 1. 10 *for* multitude, Lev. 5. 4 be guilty *in, as regards*, Jos. 9. 24 fear *for* our lives, Gen. 42. 25 provisions *for* the way; 1. 11 *according to* its kind; 17. 20 *as for* Ishmael. And this broad relational sense may be original. Jenni suggests diversifying over against unifying for בְּ. This sense is elastic enough to take in the local and non-local and the temporal meanings above as well as several prepos. uses already noted, e.g. to express the agent of the passive, Engl. *by* (§ 95*c*) or, with the infin., to express purpose or result, or the gerundial sense *in eating*, or the meanings *about to* and *must be, ought to be* (§ 108). (לְ also has usages which are best regarded as non-prepos., as normally before the infin., and as when it equates with the "object" marker אֵת, §§ 105*c*, 94, R. 8).

Rem. 3. Compound prepositions. The first element is usually אֶל (occasionally עַד) or מִן, adding a nuance of either direction towards or separation from the second element, אֶל־מַחוּץ, אֶל־מוּל, אֶל־בֵּין, אֶל־אַחֲרֵי, עַד־מְאֹד. Prep. לְ *in reference to* adds little to the meaning, עַד לְ, מֵעַל לְ, לִפְנֵי. See Lexx.

Rem. 4. The perspective of the speaker is a feature of the use of some prepp., particularly where location is involved; thus the meaning *into* for בְּ, of *to* for לְ or of *onto* for עַל may be seen as indicating location *after* movement, Ru. 2. 18 she entered *into* (= went and ended up *in*) the city, Gen. 30. 25 that I may go *to* (and end up *at*) my own land, 2 K. 4. 34 he lay down *upon* the child. In a small number of cases these three prepp. have the meaning *from*, the perspective being *before* movement, Ps. 18. 9 smoke went up בְּאַפּוֹ *from* his nostrils; 68. 21 to Y. belongs escape לַמָּוֶת *from* (when *near*) death, Job 30. 2 עָלֵימוֹ *from* them vigour is gone. Ps. 4. 7 (Dahood); 40. 11; 84. 12, Pr. 9. 5, Job 5. 21. Cf. French, ils mangent *sur* la table, they ate *from* the table. It is significant not only that these three prepp. are frequently used in this manner in Ugar. (see Pardee), but that Ugar. (like Phoen.) does not possess מִן. The Hebr. exx. are, therefore, not surprisingly rare and found only in poetry; they may be regarded as archaisms surviving from a period when מִן was missing also from Hebr. Neither in Ugar. nor in Hebr. should these usages be taken to indicate ambiguity or interchangeability within the prepos. system.

ADVERBIAL CLAUSES AND INFINITIVE PHRASES

§ 119. Adverbial clauses are subordinated to a main clause, modifying it or the verb in it in much the same way as an adverb or prep. phrase. The main clause (apodosis) and the subordinate clause (protasis) together form what is traditionally called a *complex* sentence (§ 131), but it is the adverbial function of the subordinate clause which is significant syntactically. Other subordinate clauses function nominally, taking the place of a noun (see subj. and obj. clauses, §§ 51, 90) or adnominally, qualifying a noun (see relative clauses, §§ 9ff.). Clauses of place are usually adnominal (in, to the place שָׁם ... אֲשֶׁר *where*). Temporal clauses may be adnominal (on the day *when*), but are often adverbial. Other common types of adverbial clause are conditional, causal, final or purpose, result, etc. Each has its appropriate conjuction(s), but some conjunctions, notably כִּי, אֲשֶׁר (§ 125, R. 2), are found with several types, including nominal or adnominal. The verbs in adverbial clauses have their normal values, stative or quasi-stative or active or (in the case of YIQTOL only) modal. QATAL may, however, attract modal nuances from its context, § 60.

The place of adverbial clauses is commonly taken by phrases with a prep. and infin., § 107. When they precede the main clause, adverbial clauses and infin. phrases are often linked to the larger context by וַיְהִי or וְהָיָה and to the main clause by *Vav apodosi* with the appropriate consec. form. See further §§ 71, 72, 79, 80.

Conditional Clauses

§ 120. These are the most complicated of adverbial clause constructions, frequently employing modalities which spill over into the accompanying main clause. The clause expressing the condition (protasis) is subordinated to the main clause (apodosis) which indicates the result dependent upon it. Either or both clauses may be verbal or nominal. The apodosis, in particular, may assume many forms. *Real* conditions are those which have already been fulfilled or which are judged capable, even hypothetically, of being fulfilled in the pres. or future. These are introduced by אִם or כִּי, less commonly by אֲשֶׁר or הֵן; negative, אִם לֹא or אִם אֵין. Depending on the context, Engl. may prefer to render by *when* (of time) or *although* (of concession) rather than the strictly conditional *if*. *Unreal* (irreal) conditions are those where stress is laid on the fact that they have *not* been fulfilled in the past or on the impossibility (or at least unlikelihood) of their being fulfilled in the pres. or future. These are introduced by לוּ, neg. לוּלֵי.

§ 121. (*a*) In *real* conditions capable of being fulfilled in the future, the most common form is YIQTOL in prot. and *Vav* consec. QATAL or simply YIQTOL in apod., the YIQTOL having indicative or other modal value (§ 64). YIQTOL may be a straight replacement of VeQATAL in apod., coming first, but more often it resists that position,

§ 71. Jud. 4. 8 אִם תֵּלְכִי עִמִּי וְהָלַכְתִּי וְאִם־לֹא תֵלְכִי לֹא אֵלֵךְ *if you go*
with me *I will go*, but *if you do not go* (with me) *I will not go.* 2 K. 4. 29
כִּי תִמְצָא־אִישׁ לֹא תְבָרֲכֶנּוּ *if you meet* anyone, *you shall not salute* him.
Gen. 18. 28 לֹא אַשְׁחִית אִם־אֶמְצָא *I will not destroy if I find.* 13. 16 אִם
יוּכַל אִישׁ לִמְנוֹת ... גַּם זַרְעֲךָ יִמָּנֶה *if one could count* the dust of the
earth, your seed *also might be counted.* Am. 9. 2 אִם יַחְתְּרוּ בִשְׁאוֹל מִשָּׁם
יָדִי תִקָּחֵם *though they dig* into Sheol, from there my hand *will take them.*
Preceded by וְהָיָה, Ex. 4. 9 וְהָיָה אִם־לֹא יַאֲמִינוּ ... וְלָקַחְתָּ and it will be
that *if they do not believe ... you shall take.* Deu. 11. 14; 20. 11. A ptcp. may
take the place of YIQTOL, Gen. 43. 4, 5 אִם־יֶשְׁךָ מְשַׁלֵּחַ גֵרְדָה וְאִם־
אֵינְךָ מְשַׁלֵּחַ לֹא נֵרֵד *if you will let* our brother *go we will go down,* but *if
you will not let him go we will not go down.* 24. 42; 34. 15-17, Ex. 8. 17,
Jud. 6. 36, 1 S. 19. 11. So without יֵשׁ Deu. 5. 22, Jud. 9. 15; 11. 9, 1 S. 6. 3;
7. 3, 1 K. 21. 6, 2 K. 10. 6. But the prot. may be a purely nominal clause,
and the apod. may take almost any form, 1 K. 18. 21 אִם יהוה הָאֱלֹהִים
לְכוּ אַחֲרָיו *if Y. be God, follow him;* Ex. 7. 27 אִם מָאֵן אַתָּה הִנֵּה אָנֹכִי
נֹגֵף *if you refuse,* behold, *I will strike.* Gen. 42. 19; 44. 26, Ex. 1. 16; 21. 3,
Jos. 17. 15, Jud. 6. 31, 2 K. 1. 10; 10. 6, Mal. 1. 6.

(b) In real conditions QATAL may be used in prot. instead of
YIQTOL, denoting a state or an action so regarded which is set in fut.
time (§ 59b). Jud. 16. 17 אִם גֻּלַּחְתִּי וְסָר כֹּחִי *if I be shaved* my strength
will depart; 2 S. 15. 33 אִם עָבַרְתָּ אִתִּי וְהָיִתָ עָלַי לְמַשָּׂא *if you go on* with
me *you shall be* a burden to me. Deu. 32. 41, 2 K. 7. 4, Is. 4. 4; 16. 12,
Mic. 5. 7, Jer. 14. 18; 23. 22; 37. 10; 49. 9, Obad. 5, Job 7. 4; 10. 14; 11. 13;
21. 6, Ru. 1. 12. Comparison of cases like Gen. 43. 9 and 42. 37 or Lev.
13. 53 and 56 show that there is no difference between QATAL and
YIQTOL except in aspectual nuance, which Engl. cannot express. Cf.
Job 31 throughout. This QATAL may also appear in apod., 1 S. 2. 16 וְאִם
לֹא לָקַחְתִּי *and if not I will take it.* Nu. 32. 23, Jud. 15. 7, Ps. 127. 1, Job
20. 14.

In other cases QATAL in prot. refers back to something that has
already happened, and has the value of Engl. perfect with *have* or Engl.
future perf. (§ 59a), indicating a pres. or fut. state arising from a previous
action. 1 S. 26. 19 אִם י׳ הֱסִיתְךָ יָרַח מִנְחָה *if Y. has incited you,* let him
accept (smell) an offering; Jud. 9. 19 אִם בֶּאֱמֶת עֲשִׂיתֶם שְׂמְחוּ *if you have
dealt* justly, *rejoice.* Ex. 22. 1, 2 אִם יִמָּצֵא הַגַּנָּב ... אִם זָרְחָה הַשֶּׁמֶשׁ *if a*

thief be found ... (but) *if the sun has risen*, etc.; cf. Deu. 17. 2, 3 with *Vav* consec. YIQTOL וַיֵּלֶךְ ... כִּי יִמָּצֵא אִישׁ אֲשֶׁר יַעֲשֶׂה *if a man be found who does* evil ... *and he has gone* and served (having gone). With Ex. 22. 2 cf. 21. 36 (אוֹ). Lev. 4. 23; 5. 1, Nu. 5. 19, 20, 27; 15. 24; 22. 20, Deu. 22. 20, 21, 1 S. 21. 5, Is. 28. 25, Am. 3. 3, 4; 7. 2, Ps. 41. 7; 44. 21; 50. 18, Job 8. 4; 9. 15, 16; 31. 5, 9, 21, 24, 33; 34. 32.

In narrative contexts following וְהָיָה *and it used to happen* אִם with QATAL is usual, though peculiar. Gen. 38. 9 וְהָיָה אִם בָּא אֶל־אֵשֶׁת אָחִיו וְשִׁחֵת אַרְצָה *so whenever he went* into his brother's wife, *he would spoil* (the act by spilling his seed) on the ground. The וְהָיָה and the *Vav* consec. QATAL sufficiently mark the context as frequentative. Nu. 21. 9, Jud. 2. 18; 6. 3. When there is no וְהָיָה the more appropriate YIQTOL is used in prot. Gen. 31. 8, Ex. 40. 37.

(*c*) The prot. in *a, b* is often of considerable length, and has its own verbal secution, which must be distinguished from that of the apod. Gen. 28. 20 וְהָיָה י' ... וְשַׁבְתִּי ... וְנָתַן ... עִמָּדִי וּשְׁמָרַנִי ... אִם יִהְיֶה א' *if God will be* with me, *and will keep* me ... *and give* me ... *and I return* ... *then* Y. *shall be* my God. Deu. 13. 1-3 ... וְנָתַן אֵלֶיךָ אוֹת כִּי יָקוּם בְּקִרְבְּךָ נָבִיא ... וּבָא הָאוֹת ... לֹא תִשְׁמַע *if a prophet arises* among you ... *and gives* you a sign ... *and the sign come true* ... *you shall not listen.* Gen. 43. 9 אִם־לֹא הֲבִיאֹתִיו אֵלֶיךָ וְהִצַּגְתִּיו לְפָנֶיךָ וְחָטָאתִי לְךָ *if I do not bring him* to you *and set him* before you, *I shall be guilty of sinning* against you. Nu. 5. 27 וּבָאוּ ... אִם נִטְמְאָה וַתִּמְעֹל *if she has been defiled and acted unfaithfully* ... the waters that bring the curse *shall enter* into her. Gen. 46. 33, Jud. 4. 20, 1 S. 1. 11; 12. 14, 15; 17. 9, 2 S. 15. 34, 1 K. 9. 6; 11. 38; 12. 7.

Rem. 1. Additional exx. of real conditions. With אִם and YIQTOL in prot. and *Vav* consec. QATAL in apod.: Gen. 24. 8; 32. 9, Ex. 13. 13; 21. 5, 6, 11, Nu. 21. 2, Jud. 14. 12, 13; 21. 21, 1 S. 12. 15; 20. 6, 1 K. 6. 12; cohort. after אִם Job 16. 6. With YIQTOL in apod.: Gen. 30. 31; 42. 37, Ex. 20. 25, 1 S. 12. 25, 1 K. 1. 52, Is. 1. 18-20; 7. 9; 10. 22, Am. 5. 22; 9. 2-4, Ps. 50. 12. With כִּי in prot.: Gen. 32. 18; 46. 33, Ex. 21. 2, 7, 20, 22, 26, 28; 22. 4, 6, 9, Deu. 13. 13; 15. 16; 19. 16 *seq.*, Jos. 8. 5, 1 S. 20. 13, 2 S. 7. 12, 1 K. 8. 46, 2 K. 18. 22, Jer. 23. 33, Hos. 9. 16, Ps. 23. 4; 37. 24; 75. 3, Job 7. 13. With אֲשֶׁר: Lev. 4. 22, Jos. 4. 21, 1 K. 8. 31. Various forms of apod.: Gen. 4. 7; 24. 49; 27. 46; 30. 1; 31. 50, Ex. 8. 17; 10. 4; 33. 15, Jud. 9. 15, 1 S. 19. 11; 20. 7, 21; 21. 10, Is. 1. 15; 43. 2, Jer. 26. 15, Ps. 139. 8. הֵן in prot., Ex. 8. 22.

Rem. 2. The prot. is often strengthened by infin. absol., but only with

אִם and YIQTOL, not with כִּי nor with QATAL. Ex. 21. 5; 22. 3, 11, 12, 16, Nu. 21. 2, Deu. 8. 19, Jud. 11. 30, 1 S. 1. 11; 20. 6, 7, 9, 21 (§ 101a). So with הֵן, Is. 54. 15. The apod. may be strengthened by כִּי, Is. 7. 9, Jer. 22. 24, cf. Ex. 22. 22 where כִּי precedes אִם.

Rem. 3. In the casuistry of the Law the *subj.* sometimes precedes the conjunction, i.e. is extraposed and located in the main clause. Lev. 4. 2 נֶפֶשׁ כִּי־תֶחֱטָא if anyone sins; 5. 1, 4, 15; 7. 21; 12. 2; 13. 2 and often; Nu. 9. 10; 27. 8; 30. 3, 4; cf. 1 K. 8. 37, Is. 28. 15, 18, Ez. 14. 9, 13; 18. 5, 18; 33. 2, 6, 9. Cf. Ps. 62. 11. In secondary conditions the usual order is found, Lev. 13. 42, etc. The older order is general in Exodus, 22. 4, 5, 6, 9, 13, and often. In the group of laws in Ex. 21 *seq.* the principal condition is introduced by כִּי and the subordinate details follow with אִם or וְאִם, Ex. 21. 2-5, 7-11, etc.

§ 122.   *Irreal* conditions. Actions not realised in the past, or considered not realisable (or unlikely) in the pres. or fut. may be made the subject of a condition. In this case לוּ (לֻא) *if*, and לוּלֵי (לוּלֵא) *if not, unless*, are used. The adverbs אָז, עַתָּה or כִּי are not uncommonly used in apod. (Rem. 2).

(*a*) In the case of actions set in the past QATAL stands both in prot. and apod. (§ 58a, b). Jud. 13. 23 לוּ חָפֵץ לַהֲמִיתֵנוּ לֹא לָקַח *if he had meant* to kill us *he would not have accepted* a burnt offering, 8. 19; Gen. 31. 42 לוּלֵי אֱלֹהֵי אָבִי הָיָה לִי כִּי עַתָּה שִׁלַּחְתָּנִי *unless* the God of my father *had been* on my side, surely now *you would have sent me away empty*, 43. 10. — Nu. 22. 33 (*rd.* לוּלֵי for אוּלַי?), Jud. 14. 18, 1 S. 14. 30 (apod. interr.); 25. 34, 2 S. 2. 27, Is. 1. 9, Ps. 94. 17; 119. 92 (both nominal prot.); 106. 23. Nu. 22. 29 (unless a wish with לוּ, § 155).

(*b*) When the context is pres. or fut. the apod. is usually YIQTOL, 2 S. 18. 12 לֹא אָנֹכִי שֹׁקֵל ... לֹא־אֶשְׁלַח יָדִי *if I weighed* a thousand shekels on my palm, *I would not put forth* my hand, 2 K. 3. 14; Deu. 32. 29 לוּ חָכְמוּ יַשְׂכִּילוּ *if they were wise they would understand* this, Job 16. 4. Mic. 2. 11, Ps. 81. 14. 2 S. 19. 7 (nominal prot. and apod.).

Rem. 1. Occasionally (to our way of thinking) the wrong conjunction seems to be used. Thus Ez. 14. 15 אִם = לוּ, Ps. 73. 15 לוּ = אִם.

Rem. 2. Exx. of אָז, עַתָּה, כִּי in apod.: Gen. 31. 42 (above); 43. 10, 2 S. 2. 27, Job 8. 6; 11. 15, 16, Pr. 2. 5. This kind of apod. may occur with no formal prot., the prot. having to be supplied; e.g. after neg., 1 S. 13. 13 you have not kept ... (if you had) *then Y. would have established*; or an interr., Job 3. 13 why breasts that I should suck? (if not) *then I should have lain down*; or a gerundive infin., 2 K. 13. 19 you should have struck ... *then you would have smitten* Aram. Ex. 9. 15, Job 13. 19.

§ 123. What is equiv. to a cond. sent. may be expressed though coordination of clauses without any cond. conjunction. Particularly common is the use of two clauses both introduced by *Vav* cons. QATAL. Gen. 44. 22 וְעָזַב אֶת־אָבִיו וָמֵת *if he leave* his father *he will die.* Ex. 4. 14 וְרָאֲךָ וְשָׂמַח בְּלִבּוֹ *when he sees you he will be glad* in his heart. Gen. 33. 13; 42. 38; 44. 4, 29, Ex. 16. 21, Nu. 14. 15; 23. 20, 1 S. 16. 2; 19. 3; 25. 31, 1 K. 8. 30; 18. 10 (*and if they should say*), 2 K. 7. 9, Is. 21. 7, Jer. 18. 4, 8; 20. 9, Pr. 3. 24. This *Vav* cons. QATAL may have any of the senses proper to it, e.g. in past contexts, frequentative. Ex. 33. 10, 1 S. 14. 52, 1 K. 18. 10. Where *Vav* is not joined to the verb, YIQTOL will be used in either clause, Nu. 23. 20 וּבֵרֵךְ וְלֹא אֲשִׁיבֶנָּה *if he blesses I cannot reverse it;* 2 K. 18. 21 אֲשֶׁר יִסָּמֵךְ אִישׁ עָלָיו וּבָא *on which if one lean it goes* into his hand. Deu. 22. 3, 1 S. 20. 13, Jos. 22. 18, Is. 29. 11, 12, Pr. 6. 22. Imper. for second QATAL, 1 S. 29. 10.

Two corresponding imper. may form a virtual condit. sent., Gen. 42. 18, Is. 8. 9. Cohort. in place of imper., Gen. 30. 28. Indeed, almost any form of expression wth two clauses and lacking a condit. conj. may be equivalent to what in other languages could be put conditionally. Rem. 1.

> *Rem. 1.* Such words as אֲשֶׁר *he who, whoever,* מִי, מִי אֲשֶׁר *whoever,* and similar phrases in effect form condit. clauses, Jud. 1. 12; 6. 31, Mic. 3. 5. And the conj. *and* without any particle may introduce a condit. cl., e.g. with יֵשׁ, לֹא, עוֹד, etc. Jud. 6. 13 וְיֵשׁ י' עִמָּנוּ *if then Y. be* with us, 2 K. 10. 15. Similarly the neg. וְלֹא *if not,* 2 S. 13. 26, 2 K. 5. 17. Is. 6. 13 וְעוֹד בָּהּ *if there still be* in it a tenth.
>
> Otherwise clauses with 1. YIQTOL, Hos. 8. 12 *were I to write,* Is. 26. 10. Ps. 139. 18 *were I to count them,* Jud. 13. 12, Ps. 104. 22, 27-30, Pr. 26. 26. Two YIQTOLs, Song 8. 1. Short YIQTOL (§ 62*b*), Is. 41. 28, Job 10. 16. Cohort., Ps. 139. 8, 9, Job 19. 18. With הִנֵּה, 1 S. 9. 7. Cf. Ps. 46. 4; 109. 25; 146. 4.
>
> 2. QATAL, Job 7. 20, *be it I have sinned,* Ps. 139. 18 *if I awake.* Nu. 12. 14, Ps. 39. 12, Pr. 26. 12, Job 3. 25; 19. 4; 23. 10. With הִנֵּה, 2 S. 18. 11, Hos. 9. 6, Ez. 13. 12; 14. 22; 15. 4. And if QATAL naturally also *Vav* cons. YIQTOL, Jer. 5. 22, Ps. 139. 11. Ex. 20. 25, Job 23. 13, Pr. 11. 2. Two QATALs, Pr. 18. 22.
>
> 3. The ptcp., Is. 48. 13 קֹרֵא אֲנִי *if, when I call,* 2 S. 19. 8. Ptcp. with Art.

whoever, 2 S. 14. 10 *if anyone says*, Gen. 9. 6, Ex. 21. 12, 16 and often. Frequently in Pr., e.g. 17. 13; 18. 13; 27. 14; 29. 21, etc. Particularly ptcp. with כֹּל, 1 S. 2. 13, *when any man made a sacrifice*, Ex. 19. 12, Nu. 21. 8, Jud. 19. 30, 2 S. 2. 23, 2 K. 21. 12. With הִנֵּה, 1 K. 20. 36, 2 K. 7. 2.

    4. Infin. absol., Pr. 25. 4, 5. Infin constr. with prep. (rare compared with temporal and other adv. types), Pr. 10. 25.

Temporal Clauses and Infinitive Phrases

§ 124. Many temporal statements are formed with a prep. and infin., e.g. בְּ, כְּ, לְ, מִן, לִפְנֵי, אַחֲרֵי, עַד, etc. These prepp. become conjunctions when the rel. אֲשֶׁר, כִּי is added to them, forming adverbial clauses. The rel. element אֲשֶׁר, however, is often omitted, the prep. directly introducing the clause. Temporal clauses or phrases are commonly preceded by וַיְהִי or וְהָיָה, punctuating a narrative or discourse time-wise.

    (*a*) *When* is expressed by בְּ, כְּ with infin., or by כִּי, אֲשֶׁר, כַּאֲשֶׁר with finite verb (or nominal cl.). Gen. 39. 18 כַּהֲרִימִי קוֹלִי *when* I lifted up my voice, 24. 30. 4. 8 בִּהְיוֹתָם בַּשָּׂדֶה *when* they were in the field, 45. 1. Hos. 11. 1 כִּי נַעַר יִשׂ׳ *when* Isr. (was) a child, Gen. 44. 24, Jos. 17. 13. Gen. 24. 22 כַּאֲשֶׁר כִּלּוּ לִשְׁתֹּת *when* they had done drinking, Jud. 8. 33; 11. 5. The form כְּמוֹ once as conj. (without אֲשֶׁר), Gen. 19. 15. After a time word אֲשֶׁר may be *when* (adnominal), Hos. 2. 15, Ps. 95. 9. And אִם may often be translated *when* (see Cond. Cl.).

    (*b*) *After* by אַחֲרֵי with infin. or אַחֲרֵי אֲשֶׁר with finite verb. Gen. 14. 17 אַחֲרֵי שׁוּבוֹ *after* he returned (his returning), 13. 14; 24. 36. Deu. 24. 4 אַחֲרֵי אֲשֶׁר הֻטַּמָּאָה *after* she has been defiled. Jos. 9. 16, Jud. 11. 36; 19. 23, 2 S. 19. 31. Without אֲשֶׁר, Lev. 25. 48, 1 S. 5. 9.

    (*c*) *Before* by לִפְנֵי with infin., Gen. 13. 10 לִפְנֵי שַׁחֵת י׳ אֶת־סְדֹם *before* Y. destroyed Sodom, 36. 31, 1 S. 9. 15, 2 S. 3. 35. As conj. Pr. 8. 25 (לִפְנֵי אֲשֶׁר is not found). Very often by בְּטֶרֶם, followed by YIQTOL even when referring to the past, prob. a conditioned usage. See for exx., § 62, R. 1. Rarely by QATAL, Ps. 90. 2, Pr. 8. 25.

    (*d*) *Since* by מֵאָז with QATAL, Ex. 9. 24 מֵאָז הָיְתָה לְגוֹי *since* it became a nation. Gen. 39. 5, Ex. 5. 23, Jos. 14. 10, Is. 14. 8, Jer. 44. 18. Cf. אָז, adv. *then* (§ 62, R. 1). It has nominal force in מֵאָז adv. *formerly, long ago* (Is. 16. 13, Ps. 93. 2, etc.) and prob. therefore in מֵאָז with infin., Ex. 4. 10, or with following noun, Ru. 2. 7 (*since* morning).

(e) *Until* by עַד with infin., or עַד אֲשֶׁר‎, עַד כִּי‎, עַד אִם‎, עַד אֲשֶׁר
אִם with finite verb, with reference to past or fut., §§ 59a, 64a. Gen.
24. 19 עַד אִם־כִּלּוּ לִשְׁתּוֹת *until* they (shall) have done drinking. 27. 45
עַד־שׁוּב אַף־אָחִיךָ *till* your brother's anger turn away. 27. 44 ‫עַד־‬
אֲשֶׁר־תָּשׁוּב חֲמַת אָחִיךָ *till* your brother's rage shall turn away. Gen.
28. 15; 29. 8, Ex. 23. 30, Deu. 3. 20, Jud. 4. 24, 1 S. 22. 3; 30. 4, 1 K.
17. 17. Exx. of עַד כִּי Gen. 26. 13; 41. 49; 49. 10, 2 S. 23. 10. Of עַד אִם
Gen. 24. 33, Is. 30. 17. Of עַד אֲשֶׁר אִם Gen. 28. 15, Nu. 32. 17, Is. 6. 11.
Of simple עַד with finite verb Gen. 38. 11, Jos. 2. 22, 1 S. 1. 22, 2 K. 7. 3,
Ps. 110. 1, Pr. 7. 23.

(f) *As often as* by מִדֵּי with infin., 1 S. 1. 7; 18. 30, 1 K. 14. 28, 2 K.
4. 8, Is. 28. 19; once YIQTOL, Jer. 20. 8.

> Rem. 1. *After* in some cases = *seeing that*, Gen. 41. 39, Jos. 7. 8, Jud.
> 11. 36, 2 S. 19. 31, cf. Ezr. 9. 13 (common in post bibl. Hebr.). *After* has also a
> pregnant sense = *after the death*, or *departure of*. Gen. 24. 67 אַחֲרֵי אִמּוֹ *after*
> his mother's *death*. Job 21. 21, Pr. 20. 7. Frequently in Ecc., אַחֲרַי *when I am*
> *gone*. Cf. לְפָנַי *before I came*, Gen. 30. 30.
>
> Rem. 2. Time statements by coordination. Circumst. clauses may be
> rendered by *when, while*, § 137. On the expression of sentences like *and when*
> *you overtake* them *you shall say* (Gen. 44. 4) by two *Vav* cons. QATALs, cf.
> § 123.

Causal Clauses and Infinitive Phrases

§ 125. Causality may, in suitable contexts, be expressed by
coordination, especially by circumst. cl., § 137. Ex. 23. 9 you shall not
oppress a stranger וְאַתֶּם יְדַעְתֶּם נֶפֶשׁ הַגֵּר *because you yourselves know* the
feelings of a stranger; cf. Neh. 2. 3.

Commonly used is כִּי *because*, Gen. 8. 9. Similarly אֲשֶׁר Gen. 30. 18,
1 S. 26. 16, 1 K. 3. 19, 2 K. 17. 4, Jer. 20. 17, Zech. 11. 2 (both). Also the
prep. יַעַן coupled with rel. אֲשֶׁר or כִּי‎. Is. 7. 5 יַעַן כִּי־יָעַץ רָעָה *because*
he has purposed evil. Often in Is., 3. 16; 8. 6; 29. 13; elsewhere, Nu. 11. 20,
1 K. 13. 21; 21. 29. Very common יַעַן אֲשֶׁר‎; 1 S. 30. 22 יַעַן אֲשֶׁר לֹא הָלְכוּ
עִמִּי *because they went not* with me. Gen. 22. 16, Deu. 1. 36, Jud. 2. 20,
1 K. 3. 11; 14. 7, 15. Also יַעַן alone as conj., Nu. 20. 12 יַעַן לֹא הֶאֱמַנְתֶּם
because you believed not, 1 K. 14. 13, 2 K. 22. 19. As prep. with infin., Is.
30. 12 יַעַן מָאָסְכֶם *because of your rejecting*, 37. 29, Jer. 5. 14; 7. 13; 23. 38,
Am. 5. 11, etc. (only in prophets and 1 K. 21. 20).

Rem. 1. Several prepp. have causal force, as בְּ, עַל, תַּחַת, mostly in composition with אֲשֶׁר or כִּי. Gen. 39. 9, 23 (בַּאֲשֶׁר). Is. 43. 4 (מֵאֲשֶׁר). More commonly עַל אֲשֶׁר, Deu. 29. 24, 2 S. 3. 30, 1 K. 9. 9. So עַל כִּי, Deu. 31. 17, Jud. 3. 12, Ps. 139. 14. With rel. omitted in neg. clause, Gen. 31. 20, Ps. 119. 136. Often עַל with infin., Am. 1. 3, 6, 9, 11, etc. תַּחַת אֲשֶׁר, Deu. 28. 47, 1 S. 26. 21, 2 K. 22. 17, Is. 53. 12. So תַּחַת כִּי, Deu. 4. 37. עֵקֶב אֲשֶׁר, Gen. 22. 18; 26. 5, 2 S. 12. 6 (עַל אֲשֶׁר in next clause). So עֵקֶב כִּי, 2 S. 12. 10, Am. 4. 12. Without rel., Nu. 14. 24. Cf. Deu. 23. 5.

Rem. 2. The causal relation expressed by כִּי is not always easy to define. Thus rather than giving a precise cause or reason for what has happened (or is about to happen), it supplies what we would call a justification for it (Is. 2. 6; 3. 8) or an explanation of it (Is. 1. 30; 5. 7). Engl. *for* may be compared. But beyond that כִּי is used as an adverb *surely* and to introduce subj. and obj. clauses (*that*), conditional clauses (*if*) and temporal clauses (*when*) as well as causal. There must be some underlying relational meaning which connects all of these. Further study is needed. So in the case of אֲשֶׁר, which has a similar range of usages.

Final or Purpose Clauses and Infinitive Phrases

§ 126. Purpose may be expressed (*a*) by the use of וְ (simple *Vav*) with jussive, cohort., e.g. after an imper., or anything with similar modal meaning, as another juss., cohort. Gen. 24. 14 הַטִּי־נָא כַדֵּךְ וְאֶשְׁתֶּה let down your pitcher *that I may drink*. Cf. Is. 5. 19 after לְמַעַן in first clause. Similarly after a wish, or a neg. or interr. clause. See § 87. In this case the neg. purpose is expressed by וְלֹא with YIQTOL.

(*b*) by infin. constr. with לְ. Jud. 3. 1 לְנַסּוֹת בָּם אֶת־יִשְׂ׳ *in order to prove* Israel by them. The neg. purpose in this case is expressed by לְבִלְתִּי. Gen. 4. 15 לְבִלְתִּי הַכּוֹת־אֹתוֹ *that* whoever found him *might not kill him*. Cf. §§ 107, 109.

§ 127. More formal telic conj. are לְמַעַן אֲשֶׁר with YIQTOL, more commonly לְמַעַן. Jer. 42. 6 לְמַעַן אֲשֶׁר יִיטַב־לָנוּ *that it may be well* with us. Gen. 18. 19, Lev. 17. 5, 2 S. 13. 5. Gen. 27. 25 לְמַעַן תְּבָרֶכְךָ נַפְשִׁי *in order that I may bless you*. Gen. 12. 13, Ex. 4. 5, Deu. 4. 1, Hos. 8. 4, Is. 41. 20. Or לְמַעַן with infin. Jud. 2. 22 לְמַעַן נַסּוֹת בָּם *in order to prove* by them, cf. simple לְ, Jud. 3. 1 (in *b* above). Gen. 37. 22, Jud. 3. 2, Jos. 11. 20, Am. 2. 7, etc. The simple אֲשֶׁר is also common, Deu. 4. 10 אֲשֶׁר יִלְמְדוּן לְיִרְאָה אֹתִי *that they may learn* to fear me. Nu. 23. 13, Deu. 4. 40; 6. 3 (cf. *vs.* 2); 32. 46. The neg. clause is usually made by אֲשֶׁר לֹא,

Gen. 11. 7, Ex. 20. 26; but also by לְמַעַן אֲשֶׁר לֹא, Deu. 20. 18, Nu. 17. 5, and by לְמַעַן לֹא, Ez. 19. 9, Ps. 119. 11, 80.

In the same sense בַּעֲבוּר אֲשֶׁר with YIQTOL, Gen. 27. 10; more usually בַּעֲבוּר with YIQTOL, Gen. 27. 4, or infin., 2 S. 10. 3.

> *Rem. 1.* The conjs. לְמַעַן, etc. are properly telic, and do not express merely result. But sometimes the purpose seems to animate the action rather than the agent, Am. 2. 7, Mic. 6. 16, Ps. 30. 13; 51. 6. In many instances purpose and result clauses are not easily distinguished.
>
> *Rem. 2.* On occasion *Vav* cons. QATAL may attract a nuance of design or, more frequently, of effect or consequence from the wider context. § 87, R. 3.

§ 128. The special telic neg. פֶּן־ *lest, that not* expresses *motive* or a note of precaution, and hence is much used after (*a*) imper.(juss., cohort.) and neg. clause. Gen. 3. 3 you shall not touch it פֶּן־תְּמֻתוּן *lest you die*, 19. 17; 38. 23, Ex. 5. 3, Jud. 18. 25, 2 S. 1. 20, Is. 6. 10.

(*b*) words of *fearing*, expressed or understood. Gen. 32. 12 I fear him פֶּן־יָבוֹא וְהִכַּנִי *lest he come* and smite me, 26. 7, 9. Gen. 3. 22 וְעַתָּה פֶּן־יִשְׁלַח יָדוֹ and now (I am concerned) *lest he put forth* his hand, 19. 19. Frequently in this sense introduced by a verb of *saying*, Gen. 38. 11 כִּי אָמַר פֶּן־יָמוּת גַּם הוּא for he thought, *Lest he die too*, 31. 31; 42. 4, Nu. 16. 34, Deu. 32. 27. After *beware*, Gen. 31. 24 הִשָּׁמֶר לְךָ פֶּן־תְּדַבֵּר take care *not to speak*, 24. 6, Deu. 4. 23, and often in Deu. Sometimes in the sense of Latin *ne* in independent cl., giving a warning, Ex. 34. 15 פֶּן־ תִּכְרֹת בְּרִית *avoid making* a covenant. Is. 36. 18, Jer. 51. 46, Job 32. 13.

Result Clauses

§ 129. Consequence may be expressed by simple *Vav* with jussive. After neg. clause, Nu. 23. 19 לֹא אִישׁ אֵל וִיכַזֵּב God is not a man *that he should die*. Or interr. cl., Hos. 14. 10. § 87.

More formal particles of consequence are כִּי *that*, אֲשֶׁר *that, so that*. 2 K. 5. 7 הַאֱלֹהִים אָנִי ... כִּי זֶה שֹׁלֵחַ אֵלַי am I God ... *that this person sends* to me? And often in questions, Gen. 20. 10, Ex. 3. 11, Nu. 16. 11, Job 6. 11; 7. 12, Ps. 8. 5. Or after neg., Gen. 40. 15 I have done nothing כִּי־שָׂמוּ אֹתִי בַּבּוֹר *that they should have put* me in the dungeon. With אֲשֶׁר, 2 K. 9. 37 אֲשֶׁר לֹא־יֹאמְרוּ זֹאת אִיזָבֶל *so that none can say*, This is

Jez. Gen. 22. 14, Deu. 28. 27, 51, Mal. 3. 19, Ps. 95. 11. Cf. 1 K. 3. 12, 13.

Comparative Clauses and Infinitive Phrases

§ **130.** These clauses usually have כַּאֲשֶׁר and are followed by כֵּן in apod. Gen. 41. 13 כַּאֲשֶׁר פָּתַר־לָנוּ כֵּן הָיָה *as* he interpreted to us, *so* it was. Ex. 1. 12, Jud. 1. 7, Is. 31. 4; 52. 14, 15; 65. 8, Ps. 48. 9; cf. transposed order, Gen. 18. 5, Ex. 10. 10, 2 S. 5. 25. Or prep. כְּ with infin. (or noun) is used, Hos. 4. 7 כְּרֻבָּם כֵּן חָטְאוּ־לִי *as* they multiplied, *so* they sinned against me (*the more ... the more*). Ps. 48. 11; 123. 2, Pr. 26. 1, 8, 18, 19. 1 S. 9. 13 (temporal).

In the prot. כַּאֲשֶׁר may be omitted. Hos. 11. 2 קָרְאוּ לָהֶם כֵּן הָלְכוּ (the more) they were called, *the more* they went from me. Jud. 5. 15, Jer. 3. 20, Is. 55. 9, Ps. 48. 6. Sometimes the particle may be omitted from both clauses, the comparison being implied, Is. 62. 5. More frequently the two clauses are equated by *Vav*, especially in proverbial comparisons. Pr. 26. 14 the door turns on its hinges וְעָצֵל עַל־מִטָּתוֹ *and* (so) a sluggard on his bed. Pr. 11. 16; 17. 3; 25. 3, 20, 25; 26. 7, 9, 21, Job 5. 7; 12. 11; 14. 11, 12. Sometimes without *and*, Pr. 25. 26, 28.

Rem. 1. In some passages כֵּן *so* expresses the corresponding *time* of the two clauses and almost indicates result or consequence, Ps. 48. 6 they saw *so* they feared (as soon as they saw, etc.). Cf. 1 K. 20. 40, Nah. 1. 12.

Syntax of the Sentence

———◆———

Simple, Complex, Compound and Incomplete Sentences

§ 131. A sentence may be broadly defined as a stretch of language which is syntactically independent. It may express a command (which does not have a subject) or an exclamation (which usually lacks a grammatical structure), but in most cases it presupposes a subject and a predicate (which may be verbal or nominal and include additional elements like a verbal object or an adverb or prep. phrase). A clause, the unit one below a sentence, also contains a subj. and pred., but it need not be independent. When it is independent, it in effect forms a *simple* sentence. When it is dependent (subordinate), it and the main clause together make up a *complex* sentence. When it and another clause are closely coordinated by *Vav* or another conjunction, or are in apposition to each other, the two clauses together make up a *compound* sentence. (Sometimes, in both complex and compound sentences, more than two clauses may be involved).

The syntax of independent and dependent clauses (and therefore of simple and complex sentences) has already been largely covered, the former *passim* via their component parts (pronoun, noun, adjective, verb, object, adverb) and the latter under the headings relative clauses (§§ 9ff.), subj. and obj. clauses (§§ 51, 90) and adverbial clauses (§§ 119ff.). The coordination of verbs (strictly of clauses) by means of the *Vav* consecutive constructions to indicate sequence, or of simple *Vav* to indicate non-sequence, has also been treated (§§ 69ff., 84ff.). There remain to be considered: (*a*) circumstantial clauses (in some cases better, sentences), which are linked by (simple) *Vav* to their context to give various kinds of background or concomitant information; (*b*) a number of compound sentences recognised by their structures, in which the constituent clauses are coordinated by (simple) *Vav* or other conj., and related to each other in terms of equivalence, contrast, inclusion, exclusion, etc.; (*c*) compound

sentences involving clauses in apposition or with asyndeton (i.e. without
Vav); (*d*) sentences with an extraposed element (*casus pendens*); and
(*e*) some other sentence types, simple or otherwise, not so far formally
dealt with, viz. questions, wishes and oaths, and exclamations.

§ 132. *Incomplete* sentences occur when a normal element of
structure is missing and has to be understood. Such an ellipsis is to be
assumed in most exclamations (§ 157), or it may be of a stereotyped
formula as commonly before אִם or אִם לֹא in oaths (§ 157); see also the
"pregnant" construction, § 118*b;* but it is more likely to take place when
there is something in the context which can supply what is missing. This
is the case in a short answer or response to a previous question or
statement, Jud. 13. 11 are you the man ... ? אָנִי *I* (am the man ...). Cf. 1 S.
1. 15 לֹא (I am) *not* (drunk); 9. 12 (יֵשׁ); 12. 5 עֵד (he is) *witness;* 27. 10
(a prep. phrase), 1 K. 18. 10 (אַיִן). Or when the prot. of a conditional
sentence has to be supplied from what goes before, especially when the
apod. is introduced by אָז, עַתָּה or כִּי, § 122, R. 2. So commonly following
וְאִם לֹא *and if not,* Gen. 24. 49, 1 S. 2. 16. See also Antithetical, Exclusive
and Disjunctive sentences. And more generally when in two connected
clauses an element in the first is dispensed with in the second. So a
shared subj. in a second nominal clause, Jos. 5. 13 הֲלָנוּ אַתָּה אִם לְצָרֵינוּ
are *you* for us or (are you) for our enemies? Even when the pred. is a
ptcp., § 113*a.* Also when הִנֵּה begins the second clause, § 54. In a second
verbal clause a common subj. is similarly often not repeated, but this is
not a strict ellipsis, as it is still represented within the verbal form.
Frequently, however, there is ellipsis (or *gapping,* as it is sometimes
called) of an obj. from the first clause or a pronom. suffix referring back
to it, particularly after certain verbs. Exx, §§ 3, R. 3; 89, R. 4. The ellipsis
of a verb is not common in prose, except where two clauses are in a
particularly close relationship, e.g. after the conj. אַף כִּי *how much the
more, less* (§ 143*c*) or in the second half of an alternative condition, 1 S.
26. 19 אִם יְהוָה הֱסִיתְךָ בִי ... וְאִם בְּנֵי הָאָדָם if Y. *has incited you against me ...*
but if human beings (have incited you against me). Of the pred. in a
nominal clause in a similar case, 1 K. 18. 21.

Ellipsis or gapping of the verb or indeed of other clausal elements is
much more characteristic of poetry, where it is commonly exploited in
the interests of the metre or the parallelism. In contradistinction to prose,

however, the ellipsis may occur in a first clause (colon) rather than a second, and the name *double-duty* has been coined to account for this. Ellipsis of a verb, Hos. 5. 8 תִּקְעוּ *blow* the trumpet in G., (blow) the horn in R.; Ps. 18. 42 (also of prepos. object) ... עַל־יְ' ... יְשַׁוְּעוּ *they cried for help* (to Y.), but there was none to save; (they cried for help) *to Y.*, but he did not answer them. Jer. 51. 31, Ps. 56. 14. Of the subj., Ps. 121. 7 יִשְׁמֹר ... יְ' יִשְׁמָרְךָ ... *Y.* will keep you from all evil, he will keep your soul; 29. 5. Frequently of possessive suffix to noun or object suffix to verb; exx, § 3, R. 3. Of interr. pron., a negative, or various particles, Ps. 9. 19 כִּי לֹא לָנֶצַח יִשָּׁכַח אֶבְיוֹן תִּקְוַת עֲנָוִים תֹּאבַד לָעַד for *not* for ever shall the needy be forgotten; the hope of the poor shall (not) perish for aye; 89. 7 כִּי מִי for *who* in the heavens can be compared to Y.? (Who) is like Y. among the sons of God?; 2. 1 (לָמָּה); 13. 5 (פֶּן־); 92. 6 (מַה). Of prepp., Ps. 36. 7 (כְּ) your righteousness is *like* the divine mountains, your judgments (like) the great deep; 18. 42 (עַל־); 65. 5 (בְּ); 114. 8 (לְ).

The Syntactic Role of Sentence Word-Order and of *VAV*

§ 133. For word-order in nominal clauses, which is dependent on the definiteness or indefiniteness of the predicate, the subj. coming first in the first case and the pred. in the second, see § 49*a, b*. In verbal clauses, whether independent or dependent, the normal order is verb first followed by the subj. and then the rest of the pred. (except that long YIQTOL, espec. in prose, tends to avoid initial position, §§ 63, 64). On the placing of the verbal obj. see §§ 91, 92. Of adverbs and prepos. phrases, § 116, R. 2. When, overriding these patterns, the subj. or the obj. or, on occasion, an adverb or prepos. phrase is put first, they are naturally being focussed upon or emphasized; but there is more to it than that. As many of the sentence types treated below show, such word-order often has a syntactic function as well, macrosyntactic in supplying a longer stretch of text with a variety of means to give structuring signals or make off-line remarks (see for narrative §§ 58*b*, 80 and for discourse §§ 64*a*, 72; see also Circumstantial clauses and Sentences with extraposition), and microsyntactic in assisting to relate clauses within a compound sent. for similarity, contrast, etc. Properly, therefore, the so-called normal order should rather be regarded as the *unmarked* order, used only when these macrosyntactic or microsyntactic ends are not being promoted.

§ 134. The conj. *Vav* is by far the commonest coordinator in Hebr., being an essential element in all but a few (§§ 143-145) of the afore-mentioned sentence types and in addition, as *Vav* cons., serving to link clauses in sequential narrative or discourse. By comparison subordinating clauses are less frequently employed. This preference for coordination rather than subordination and for coordination by *Vav* rather than by other conjunctions has sometimes led to Hebr. being compared to its disadvantage with other languages, which are supposed to show more variety and flexibility in their syntax. This is not a fair assessment, often being based, via a tradition of rather literal translation, on versions in Engl. and other western languages rather than on the Hebr. text. Thus western languages cannot distinguish between sequential and non-sequential coordination as Hebr. with its use of *Vav* cons. on the one hand and simple *Vav* on the other does. Nor can they easily reproduce the differences in word-order in adjacent clauses linked by *Vav* through which, rather than by using another conj., Hebr. differentiates among most of the sentence types being considered here. Only the "and" survives in translation, and its different forms and the different constructions which accompany it are suppressed. In short, the very features of its syntax which supply Hebr. with *its* brand of variety and flexibility are set aside. It is yet another instance of translated Hebr. being made the standard of judgment. See §§ 55, R. 2; 69, R. 1.

> *Rem. 1. Discontinuous elements.* Disruption of normal word-order may also take place when a phrase considered to be too long is split, part of it occupying its expected slot and the rest being shifted to the end of a clause, Jud. 7. 8 they took the provisions of the people in their hand וְאֶת־שׁוֹפְרֹתֵיהֶם *and their trumpets.* An adnominal phrase may be similarly separated from its noun, Jud. 14. 1 he saw a woman in Timnah מִבְּנוֹת פְּלִשְׁתִּים *from the daughters of the Ph.* So with list-like phrases in nominal clauses, 2 S. 14. 9 on me, O king, be the guilt וְעַל־בֵּית אָבִי *and on my father's house.* 1 K. 20. 1.
>
> *Rem. 2.* Ill-considered comparisons, whether based on gramm. matters like the use of "and" or on vocabulary, between biblical Hebr. and New Testament Greek should in particular be avoided, e.g. that Hebr. is a simple and concrete lang. and Greek a philosophical and involved one. Such comparisons either do not appreciate the adaptability of Hebr. or are too fond of transferring to the lang. what really belongs to cultures at different stages

of development. When, in a period much later than the biblical, Hebr. was required to express philosophical thought, it proved perfectly capable of doing so.

Rem. 3. Adding to its remarkable range are a number of other usages of *Vav*, where "and" would not normally be used in translation. See §§ 37, 78 (explanatory), § 71 (*apodosi*), § 86, 87 (with modal verbs to express effect or purpose).

CIRCUMSTANTIAL CLAUSES (SENTENCES)

§ 135. Circumstantial clauses, as they have traditionally been called, are very varied. They may be either verbal or nominal, particularly the latter. They nearly always begin with *Vav* and after it the subj., though not in either case exclusively (§ 137*d*, R. 1). They usually follow the statement to which they have reference, but may precede it. They are mostly contemporary with their context, but may describe an event or situation prior to it. They occur in both sequential and non-sequential genres, though they are not so common in poetry as in prose. They are sometimes appended loosely to their context, as in effect simple sentences, and sometimes linked to a preceding clause, making up a kind of compound sentence. But whatever their precise form, they are essentially (or, at any rate, ideally) marginal to what precedes or follows, giving additional or incidental information of various kinds.

§ 136. In formal prose narrative they often have a macrosyntactic function, beginning a narrative or an episode within it by introducing a new topic or character or reintroducing an old, or by providing a necessary backward reference; accompanying a time statement; or bringing a narrative or episode to a close. When two (or more) circ. clauses occur together, the second may continue the first or itself be circumstantial to the first. On occasion a circ. clause that opens a story or episode or that follows a time reference may seem, oddly to our way of thinking, to describe an on-line action or happening rather than an off-line leading up to it. Rem. 1. Circ. clauses are also found with similar functions, but much less frequently, in sequential discourse.

(*a*) At the start of a story, etc., Gen. 3. 1 וְהַנָּחָשׁ הָיָה עָרוּם *now the serpent was more cunning*, etc., and he said to the woman; 4.1 וְהָאָדָם יָדַע אֶת־חַוָּה (*and*) *the man had intercourse with Eve his wife*, and she

conceived; Jud. 3. 20 וְאֵהוּד בָּא אֵלָיו וְהוּא יֹשֵׁב (and) *Ehud came to him,
as he was sitting.* Gen. 2. 20(*b*) (cf. *vss.* 18, 19); 14. 10; 24. 29 (beginning
with וּלְרִבְקָה, cf. § 137*d*); 39. 1; 41. 56; 43. 1; 45. 16; 48. 10, Ex. 3. 1;
14. 10, 18, Deu. 4. 21; 10. 6, Jud. 6. 19, 33, 1 K. 20. 1, 23, 35, 2 K. 4. 1, 38,
42. With backward reference, Gen. 1. 2 וְהָאָרֶץ הָיְתָה תֹהוּ וָבֹהוּ *now the
earth had been waste and void* (if the sense is that God did not create the
chaos; other circ. clauses follow, with the first "act" coming at *vs.* 3);
24. 62 וְיִצְחָק בָּא *now Isaac had come* from B. (another circ. clause
follows). Gen. 16. 1; 31. 34, Ex. 12. 35.

(*b*) Accompanying a structuring time statement, the whole
beginning either with or without וַיְהִי (§ 80), Gen. 2. 4(*b*)-6 בְּיוֹם עֲשׂוֹת
י' א' אֶרֶץ וְשָׁמָיִם וְכֹל שִׂיחַ הַשָּׂדֶה טֶרֶם יִהְיֶה ... *in the day when Y. God
made earth and heaven and there was as yet no plant of the field* in the
earth, nor had ... (other circ. clauses follow, the narrative proper beginning at *vs.* 7); 22. 1 וַיְהִי אַחַר הַדְּבָרִים הָאֵלֶּה וְהָא' נִסָּה אֶת־אַבְרָהָם
and it was, after these things, God tested Abraham; 29. 9 עוֹדֶנּוּ מְדַבֵּר
עִמָּם וְרָחֵל בָּאָה *he was still speaking with them when Rachel came.* Gen.
6. 1; 7. 6; 15. 12, 17; 19. 4, 23; 27. 30; 37. 2; 42. 35, Jud. 18. 3, 1 S. 9. 27,
1 K. 18. 7; 20. 39, 2 K. 8. 5; 13. 21.

(*c*) Closing a story, etc., Gen. 6. 8 וְנֹחַ מָצָא חֵן *but (meanwhile) N.
found grace* in the eyes of Y.; 25. 26 וְיִצְחָק בֶּן־שִׁשִּׁים שָׁנָה *(and) Is. was
sixty years old* when she bore them (infin. phrase). Gen. 16. 16; 18. 33;
24. 21; 30. 36; 37. 36, Ex. 7. 7; 11. 10, Jud. 4. 3; 16. 31.

(*d*) In future discourse, Gen. 44. 30 when I come to your servant my
father וְהַנַּעַר אֵינֶנּוּ אִתָּנוּ *and the lad is not with us.* Gen. 42. 16 (imper.),
1 K. 18. 12 (with וְהָיָה).

§ 137. More tied to its immediate context, whether within a story or
a piece of future discourse or, very frequently, in various kinds of mixed
discourse, a circ. clause describes a concomitant action or condition or
has functions similar to relative or adverbial, espec. causal, clauses. The
varied usages are often reflected in Engl. by other conjunction: *if, but,
with, while, when, seeing that,* etc.

(*a*) Nominal clauses, Gen. 11. 4 let us build a tower וְרֹאשׁוֹ בַשָּׁמַיִם
with its head in the heavens; 18. 12 shall I have pleasure וַאדֹנִי זָקֵן *when my
husband is old?;* 24. 15 behold Reb. came out ... וְכַדָּהּ עַל־שִׁכְמָהּ *her
pitcher on her shoulder;* Ex. 21. 28 the ox shall be stoned וּבַעַל הַשּׁוֹר

... נָקִי *while the owner of the ox* (shall be) *free* (of liability); 1 S. 18. 23 is it a light thing to be son-in-law of the king וְאָנֹכִי אִישׁ־רָשׁ *seeing that I am a poor man?* Gen. 2. 12; 13. 2; 18. 27; 20. 3; 24. 10; 37. 2; 44. 26, 30, Ex. 17. 9; 24. 17; 25. 20; 34. 29, Deu. 9. 15, Jos. 17. 14, Jud. 19. 27, Jer. 2. 11, 37, Hos. 6. 4, Am. 3. 4, 5.

(*b*) Participial clauses, Gen. 1. 2 וְרוּחַ אֱלֹהִים מְרַחֶפֶת *and the spirit of God* (was) *sweeping;* 15. 2 וְאָנֹכִי הוֹלֵךְ עֲרִירִי *seeing I go childless;* 1 S. 4. 12 there ran a man of Benj. ... וּמַדָּיו קְרֻעִים *with his garments rent;* Is. 6. 1 I saw Adonai ... וְשׁוּלָיו מְלֵאִים אֶת־הַהֵיכָל *while his train filled the temple;* 11. 6 וְנַעַר קָטֹן נֹהֵג בָּם *a little child leading them.* Gen. 14. 12, 13; 18. 1, 8; 19. 1; 24. 62; 25. 26; 28. 12; 32. 32; 37. 25; 44. 14, Ex. 2. 5; 14. 27, 29; 18. 14, Deu. 9. 15, Jud. 3. 20; 4. 1; 6. 11; 13. 9, 20, 1 S. 10. 5; 22. 6, 1 K. 1. 48; 22. 16, Is. 49. 21; 60. 11.

(*c*) Verbal clauses, with stative QATAL, Gen. 26. 27 why have you come to me וְאַתֶּם שְׂנֵאתֶם אֹתִי *when you hate me?;* 18. 13; 29. 17. With QATAL in backward reference, Gen. 24. 56 delay me not וַיהוה הִצְלִיחַ דַּרְכִּי *when Y. has prospered my journey;* 1 K. 1. 41 A. and his guests heard it וְהֵם כִּלּוּ לֶאֱכֹל *having just finished feasting.* Gen. 24. 31; 39. 8, Lev. 5. 1, Jud. 8. 11, Am. 3. 6, Ru. 1. 21. With YIQTOL, Nu. 14. 3 why does Y. bring us into this land ... וְטַפֵּנוּ יִהְיוּ לָבַז *if our children are to become a prey?* Am. 3. 6.

(*d*) There are a few anomalies in word-order when something other than the subj. comes after *Vav.* Thus אֵין *there is not,* Is. 17. 2 they shall lie down וְאֵין מַחֲרִיד *none making them afraid.* Gen. 39. 11, Lev. 26. 6, Is. 13. 14, Jer. 9. 21, Pr. 28. 1 (in Ps. 35. 8, Pr. 5. 6 similar clauses are put in apposition). So anaphoric prep. phrases as pred., Jud. 3. 16 he made a dagger וְלָהּ שְׁנֵי פֵיוֹת *having two edges;* Is. 6. 6 there flew one of the Seraphim וּבְיָדוֹ רִצְפָּה *with a hot stone in his hand.* 2 S. 16. 1, Ez. 40. 2, Am. 7. 7, Zech. 2. 5. So the adv. שָׁם *there,* Ex. 15. 27. Cf. עוֹד, Gen. 29. 9 (§ 136*b*), 1 K. 1. 14 (fut.), Job 1. 16-18.

> *Rem. 1.* It is peculiar that an initial clause or a clause following a time statement should have circ. form when they seem in both cases to be part of the story and not, as a circ. clause should be, off the story line, cf. Gen. 4. 1, Jud. 3. 20 in § 136*a;* Gen. 22. 1 in § 136*b.* It also seems odd to us that in the second case the time reference (whether or not preceded by וַיְהִי) should, while beginning with the subj., usually lack *Vav.* The clause stating the time

may contain either a QATAL verb, indicating that its action took place or at any rate began prior to the action of the second, or a ptcp., indicating that its action is simultaneous with that of the second.

Exx. with QATAL: Gen. 44. 3 הַבֹּקֶר אוֹר וְהָאֲנָשִׁים שֻׁלְּחוּ *morning had broken and the men were sent away* (i.e. when, etc.); 1 S. 20. 41 הַנַּעַר בָּא וְדָוִד *when the lad had gone, David arose.* With *Vav*, Jud. 3. 24 וְהוּא יָצָא וַעֲבָדָיו קָם בָּאוּ *when he had gone, the servants came.* Neg., 2 K. 20. 4 ... וַיְהִי י' לֹא יָצָא וּדְבַד־יי' הָיָה אֵלָיו *and it was, before Isaiah had left ... the word of Y. came to him.* Gen. 19. 23, Jos. 2. 8 (with טֶרֶם and YIQTOL, § 62, R. 1), Jud. 15. 14, 1 S. 9. 5; 20. 36, 2 S. 2. 24; 6. 16; 17. 24. With הִנֵּה in second clause, Gen. 24. 15, Jud. 18. 22.

Exx. with ptcp.: 1 S. 9. 27 הֵמָּה יֹרְדִים וּשׁ' אָמַר *as they were coming down, Samuel said;* 1 K. 20. 40 וַיְהִי עַבְדְּךָ עֹשֵׂה הֵנָּה וָהֵנָּה וְהוּא אֵינֶנּוּ *and it was, as your servant was busy here and there, he was no more.* 1 S. 7. 10; 9. 11; 17. 23; 23. 26-27, 1 K. 1. 22; 20. 39. With הִנֵּה in second clause, Jud. 19. 22, 1 S. 9. 14; 17. 23; 25. 20. With nominal clause instead of ptcp., Jud. 19. 11. With עוֹד and ptcp., Gen. 29. 9, 1 K. 1. 14.

That the first clause, that setting the time, is genuinely circ. is probably shown by the minority of cases where *Vav* is present. It is not so certain that the second is, though it has *Vav*, as it can be substituted by an independent הִנֵּה clause or even a *Vav* cons., e.g. 1 K. 13. 20. The same is true of initial clauses that seem on-line. The whole problem requires further study.

Rem. 2. The circumstantial use of *and*, though particularly characteristic of Hebr., is found in many languages,

> And shall the figure of God's majesty
> Be judged, and he himself not present!

> How can ye chaunt, ye little birds,
> An' I sae weary, fu' o' care!

COMPOUND SENTENCES WITH *VAV*

§ 138. In these sentences the constituent clauses are coordinated with (simple) *Vav* and are therefore normally on the same time scale; but it is the different ways in which they are patterned that enable them to be classified as Conjunctive, Chiastic, Contrastive, or Antithetical (Andersen). They are found piecemeal in extended narrative or discourse where, like circumst. clauses, they break the chain of sequence established by the *Vav* cons. forms to bring in a non-sequential statement; but they occur more often and more freely in more heterogeneous passages of prose discourse and in poetry. With their (on the whole) careful patterning they are particularly suited for use in poetic parallelism.

Conjunctive Sentences

§ 139. Conjunctive sents. are the least specific of the four types, simply coordinating by *Vav* clauses which are broadly symmetrical in their structure and similar in their function. Two clauses are general but, unlike in the other types, there may be three or more. The clauses may begin with an identical verb or, though focussing, other clausal element, especially the subj., but often a synonym is used. All the elements of the first clause may be repeated in the second but, because of the similarity in context, ellipsis is not unusual. Many of the cases of like conjugations or moods linked by simple *Vav* are properly conjunctive sents., § 86.

(*a*) Nominal conj. sents., Gen. 28. 17 אֵין זֶה כִּי אִם־בֵּית אֱלֹהִים וְזֶה שַׁעַר הַשָּׁמָיִם *this is* none other than *the house of God, and this the gate of heaven;* 42. 36 יוֹסֵף אֵינֶנּוּ וְשִׁמְעוֹן אֵינֶנּוּ Jos. *is no more, and* Sim. *is no more;* Ex. 9. 27 יְיָ הַצַּדִּיק וַאֲנִי וְעַמִּי הָרְשָׁעִים *Y. is the one in the right, and I and my people are the ones in the wrong;* Jer. 48. 37 עַל כָּל־יָדַיִם גְּדֻדֹת וְעַל־מָתְנַיִם שָׂק *upon all the hands are gashes, and on (all) loins is sackcloth;* Pr. 3. 17 דְּרָכֶיהָ דַרְכֵי־נֹעַם וְכָל־נְתִיבֹתֶיהָ שָׁלוֹם *(all) her ways are ways of pleasantness, and all her paths are peace;* 8. 19 טוֹב פִּרְיִי מֵחָרוּץ וּתְבוּאָתִי מִכֶּסֶף ... *better is my fruit than gold,* even five gold, *and (better is) my income than* choice *silver.* Gen. 3. 6 (3 clauses); 18. 20; 31. 43 (4 clauses), Ex. 16. 31, Deu. 10. 31, Pr. 17. 25; 18. 7, Song 8. 6, Ecc. 7. 1.

(*b*) Verbal conj. sents., Ex. 23. 8 כִּי הַשֹּׁחַד יְעַוֵּר פִּקְחִים וִיסַלֵּף דִּבְרֵי הַצַּ׳ for *a bribe blinds officials, and (a bribe) subverts the words* of those in the right; Deu. 2. 30 ... כִּי־הִקְשָׁה יְיָ ... וְאָמֵּץ for *Y. your God hardened his spirit and (Y.) made his heart obstinate;* Ps. 37. 30 ... פִּי־צַדִּיק יֶהְגֶּה ... וּלְשׁוֹנוֹ יְדַבֵּר *the mouth of the righteous utters wisdom, and his tongue speaks justice;* 96. 11 יִשְׂמְחוּ הַשָּׁמַיִם וְתָגֵל הָאָרֶץ *let the heavens rejoice, and let the earth be glad;* 103. 9 לֹא לָנֶצַח יָרִיב וְלֹא־לְעוֹלָם יִטּוֹר *he will not always chide, nor will he keep (his anger) for ever.* Gen. 3. 14; 22. 17; 27.40; 41. 40; 49. 11, Ex. 9. 29; 34. 13, Deu. 2. 28; 6. 13, Is. 43. 6; 56. 1; 66. 8, Hos. 7. 1; Joel 2. 1; Ps. 19. 3, 5; 25. 9; 26. 5, 6; 85. 13; 91. 7; 104. 30, 32; 138. 7, Pr. 2. 21; 3. 13; 5. 8; 8. 1; 10. 1; 14. 19; 19. 5, 9.

(*c*) There are many cases of mixed conj. sents., e.g. with a nominal and a verbal clause, Pr. 16. 15; 19. 6; and in others the parallism of elements is rather imprecise, Pr. 11. 2; 16. 21; 18. 19; 30. 30, Job 9. 25, 26. When this goes too far, it is hardly possible any longer to speak of a conj. sent., but only of a loose compound sent.

Chiastic Sentences

§ 140. Chiastic sent. are, unlike conjunctive, strictly two clause structures. They are not simply for variety or rhetorical effect, but have a definite purpose. By reversing in the second clause the word-order of the first, they tie the two clauses more closely together than conj. sents. and make the events or situations of which they speak in effect two sides of a single whole. Chiasmus can occur with the same end in a contrastive or antithetical sent. when it overshadows, though it does not remove, the opposition. The first clause may be worked into a prose sequence, in which case the second halts it; but the construction is also common in more independent sentences in prose discourse and in poetry. Any clausal element - verb, subj., obj. or other - may be chosen for reversal. Ellipsis is found, but it is not so common as in the looser structured conj. sentence.

(*a*) In prose. Narrative: Gen. 1. 5 וַיִּקְרָא אֱלֹהִים לָאוֹר יוֹם וְלַחֹשֶׁךְ קָרָא לָיְלָה *God called the light day and (but) the darkness he called night;* וַי' פָּקַד אֶת־שָׂרָה ... וַיַּעַשׂ י' לְשָׂרָה ... 21. 1 *and Y. visited S. as he had said, and Y. did to S. as he had spoken;* 37. 11 וַיְקַנְאוּ־בוֹ אֶחָיו וְאָבִיו שָׁמַר אֶת־הַדָּבָר *and his brothers were jealous of him, while (but) his father kept the saying in mind;* Ex. 40. 34 ... וַיְכַס הֶעָנָן ... וּכְבוֹד י' מָלֵא *and the cloud covered the tent of meeting, and the glory of Y. filled the tabernacle.* Gen. 7. 10 and 11, 12, 18-19; 14. 10(*b*), 16; 25. 5-6, 28; 31. 47; 39. 4; 40. 21-22; 41. 51-52, 54; 43. 15; 45. 14, Ex. 3. 7; 9. 23; 14. 6; 20. 18; 24. 6, Deu. 3. 6-7; 6. 22-23, Jud. 7. 25. Negative, Ex. 16. 18.

Predictive discourse: Gen. 12. 3 וַאֲבָרְכָה מְבָרְכֶיךָ וּמְקַלֶּלְךָ אָאֹר *and I shall bless those who bless you and curse him who curses you;* 34. 16 וְנָתַנּוּ אֶת־בְּנוֹתֵינוּ לָכֶם וְאֶת־בְּנֹתֵיכֶם נִקַּח־לָנוּ *and we shall give our daughters to you and take your daughters to ourselves.* Gen. 47. 24, Ex. 12. 12; 15. 26; 21. 35; 25. 21, Lev. 4. 7; 5. 9, Deu. 10. 16.

Precative discourse: Gen. 44. 33 וְעַתָּה יֵשֶׁב־נָא עַבְדְּךָ ... וְהַנַּעַר יַעַל *and now, let your servant remain in place of the lad ... and let the lad go up with his brothers.* Gen. 1. 20; 14. 21; 22. 5; 44. 1. Prohibition, Gen. 37. 22.

(b) In poetry, espec. proverbial, Jer. 4. 5 הַגִּידוּ בִיה׳ וּבִיר׳ הַשְׁמִיעוּ
declare in Judah and in Jer. proclaim; Ps. 107. 16 כִּי־שִׁבַּר דַּלְתוֹת נְחֹשֶׁת
וּבְרִיחֵי־בַרְזֶל גִּדֵּעַ for he shatters the doors of bronze and the bars of iron
he cuts in two; Pr. 9. 10 תְּחִלַּת חָכְמָה יִרְאַת י׳ וְדַעַת קְדֹשִׁים בִּינָה the fear
of Y. is the beginning of wisdom, and knowledge of the Holy One is
understanding. Is. 2. 11; 5. 7; 22. 22; 40. 12; 42. 4, Jer. 2. 19; 6. 25, Am.
4. 7, Hab. 2. 1, Zeph. 3. 19, Ps. 7. 17; 22. 13; 147. 4, Pr. 3. 18; 4. 14; 6. 23;
10. 3, 4, 11, 12; 12. 4, 22; 25. 26, Job 20. 6.

Contrastive Sentences

§ 141. These, like chiastic sents., are essentially binary in structure.
They achieve their end by highlighting in initial position in each clause
the two persons or other entities which are brought into opposition.
These may be either subj. or obj., or a prepos. phrase may be used. The
opposition is relatively mild, rarely total as in antithetical sents., and need
not always be rendered by Engl. but. Where but is used, it has the sense
of on the other hand rather than on the contrary.

Gen. 3. 15 הוּא יְשׁוּפְךָ רֹאשׁ וְאַתָּה תְּשׁוּפֶנּוּ עָקֵב he will crush you in
the head, and you will crush him in the heel; 13. 12 וְלוֹט ... אַבְרָם יָשַׁב
יָשַׁב ... Abram dwelt in the land of Can., while Lot dwelt among the cities
of the valley; Ex. 16. 12 ... וּבַבֹּקֶר ... בֵּין הָעַרְבַּיִם at twilight you shall eat
flesh, and in the morning you shall be filled with bread. Gen. 27. 11;
29. 17; 42. 13, 32, 33; 44. 10, 17, Ex. 1. 22; 4. 16; 7. 12; 13. 13; 14. 14, 16, 17;
16. 13; 21. 4, Deu. 3. 9, 12-13; 4. 21, Ecc. 2. 13. Very common in poetry,
especially in sayings contrasting God and man, the wise and the foolish,
etc. Ps. 119. 113 סֵעֲפִים שָׂנֵאתִי וְתוֹרָתְךָ אָהָבְתִּי double-minded men I hate,
but your law I love; Pr. 10. 1 ... וּבֵן כְּסִיל ... בֵּן חָכָם a wise son makes a
glad father, but a foolish son is a sorrow to his mother. Is. 1. 27-28; 42. 9;
53. 6; 64. 7, Ps. 18. 26; 96. 5; 102. 27; 103. 15, 17, Pr. passim (e.g. all but a
few vss. in ch. 10), Ecc. 7. 4.

Antithetical Sentences

§ 142. Hebr. lacks the variety of adversative particles possessed by
Engl. (but, yet, however, nevertheless, etc.) and has to make do mostly
with Vav, though other conjunctions are occasionally used. Antithesis is
expressed by the use of antonyms in both clauses or, more frequently, by

negation of the first or the second clause. When, following a strong positive statement, it is the second clause that has a negative, the prominent word in the antithesis is usually highlighted by being placed first. Sents. of this kind, like sents. with antonyms, may be chiastic or contrastive in form; in the first the antithesis is not cancelled out by bringing the two clauses together, while in the second the contrast is enhanced. The subj. or obj. also occupy first position when a preceding negative clause is implied but not actually written (ellipsis). When, however, a first clause has the negative, there is no need for a special order in the second; it is in this type of sent. that the *Vav* may be replaced by another conjunction, notably כִּי or כִּי אִם. Antithetical relationships do not greatly differ from exclusive (§ 144), and the two kinds of sent. sometimes overlap.

(*a*) Antithesis by antonyms. Ex. 10. 23 וַיְהִי חֹשֶׁךְ־אֲפֵלָה *and there was thick darkness* in all the land of Egypt, *but* to all the children of Israel הָיָה אוֹר *there was light* in their dwellings. Gen. 29. 31, Ex. 20. 10, Deu. 2. 11, Ps. 1. 6 (also chiastic); 18. 27; 145. 20, Pr. 10. 1 and frequently (many also contrastive).

(*b*) Antithesis by negation after positive statement. Gen. 4. 5 and Y. had regard for Abel and his offering וְאֶל־קַיִן וְאֶל־מִנְחָתוֹ לֹא שָׁעָה *but for Cain and his offering he had no regard* (with chiasmus); Ex. 19. 24 Go down ... וְהַכֹּהֲנִים וְהָעָם אַל־יֶהֶרְסוּ *but let not the priests and the people break through*. Gen. 2. 16-17; 3. 3-4; 42. 4, Ex. 9. 6; 24. 2, Deu. 4. 12, Is. 5. 12 (first clause implied), Gen. 2. 20, Am. 4. 6.

(*c*) Antithesis after implied negation, in some cases clearly with ellipsis of whole first clause. Gen. 6. 8 וְנֹחַ מָצָא חֵן *but N. found grace* (also circumst., § 136*c*); Ps. 27. 10 (my mother and father have not taken me up) וַיְיָ יַאַסְפֵנִי *but Y. will take me up*. Gen. 17. 21; 31. 5, 29; 41. 15, Deu. 4. 20, Ps. 2. 6; 22. 10, Is. 1. 2.

(*d*) Antithesis after negation. Introduced by *Vav*, Gen. 2. 6 Y. God had not caused it to rain ... וְאֵד יַעֲלֶה *but a mist* went up (circumst.). Gen. 42. 10, Ex. 5. 18; 12. 10. By *Vav* cons., Gen. 40. 23 the chief butler did not remember Jos. וַיִּשְׁכָּחֵהוּ *but* forgot him; Is. 11. 4 he shall not judge by what his eyes see ... וְשָׁפַט בְּצֶדֶק *but* he shall judge in righteousness the poor. Gen. 17. 5; 40. 23, Ex. 1. 17, Ps. 78. 68; 106. 8. After a question, Ps. 8. 6.

Introduced by כִּי. Is. 11. 9 they shall not hurt or destroy in all my
holy mountain כִּי־מָלְאָה הָאָרֶץ *but* (not *for*) the earth shall be full of
the knowledge of Y. Gen. 3. 5; 17. 15; 18. 15, Ex. 4. 10, Deu. 4. 22; 5. 3, Ps.
103. 11. The antithetical meaning of כִּי following a neg. is not sufficiently
taken into account by translators. Introduced by כִּי אִם. Ps. 1. 2 blessed is
the man who does not walk ... כִּי אִם־בְּתוֹרַת יִ׳ חֶפְצוֹ *but* his delight is
in the law of Y. (also *vs.* 4). Gen. 32. 29; 35. 10, Nu. 10. 30, Deu. 7. 5 (cf.
vs. 3), 1 S. 21. 5, 2 K. 23. 9, Jer. 16. 14, 15.

> *Rem. 1.* A more pronounced adversative conj. is אוּלָם, וְאוּלָם *but,*
> *howbeit;* it need not follow a negative. Gen. 28. 19, Ex. 9. 16, Nu. 14. 21, 1 K.
> 20. 23, Mic. 3. 8, Job 2. 5; 5. 8; 11. 5; 13. 3, 4; 14. 18. So אֲבָל in later passages
> (§ 116*c*).

Compound Sentences with Other Conjunctions

The relationships of inclusion (*also*), exclusion (*except*) and disjunction
(*or*) are expressed by other conjunctions.

Inclusive Sentences

§ 143. On גַּם and אַף joining nouns (גַּם even across clauses) see
§ 38*a*. When the verb is included in the reference they coordinate clauses.
The sequence גַּם(וְ) ... גַּם is *both ... and*, with a neg. *neither ... nor;* גַּם ... וְ
is also found, but אַף ... אַף does not occur with nouns, though it does
occasionally with verbs. The role of the two conjs. is broadly to bring the
second clause within the reference of the first. As in the case of
antithetical sents., there may be ellipsis of the first clause (or part of
either clause). Sometimes גַּם and אַף imply *addition* rather than
inclusion, cf. Engl. *also = moreover* rather than *also = as well.* There is a
special usage of אַף כִּי *how much the more, less.*

(*a*) Inclusion by גַּם. In a conjunctive sent. גַּם enhances the similarity
between the two clauses, 1 S. 26. 25 גַּם עָשֹׂה תַעֲשֶׂה וְגַם יָכֹל תּוּכָל *you*
will *both* do much *and* succeed therein. Ex. 34. 3, Nu. 23. 25, Is. 44. 12;
49. 25, Mal. 3. 15, Pr. 14. 13. So in a chiastic sent., Gen. 4. 3-4. In a
contrastive sent. גַּם neutralises the contrast, Gen. 44. 9 with whomever
... וְגַם־אֲנַחְנוּ נִהְיֶה *and we also shall be* my lord's slaves. Gen. 13. 5 (cf.
vs. 2); 24. 44, Ex. 21. 25. Otherwise, Gen. 3. 22 lest he put forth his hand

וְלָקַח גַּם מֵעֵץ הַחַיִּים *and take also of the tree of life.* Gen. 29. 27, 30; 32. 19, Ex. 7. 11 (twice), Nu. 11. 4 (cf. *vs.* 2), Deu. 3. 3, 20, Is. 49. 15, Jer. 2. 33, Hos. 4. 6 (a complex sent.), Pr. 16. 7 (complex); 22. 6. With the first clause implicit, Gen. 3. 6 וַתִּתֵּן גַּם־לְאִישָׁהּ *and she also gave to her husband* (it is implied but not said that she gave to herself); Deu. 12. 31 כִּי גַם אֶת־בְּנֵיהֶם וְאֶת־בְּנֹתֵיהֶם יִשְׂרְפוּ *for they even (also) burn their sons and daughters in the fire to their gods* (i.e. as well as their animals). Is. 14. 10, Jer. 2. 6; 4. 12, Nah. 3. 11.

Exx. of אַף, Gen. 40. 16 אַף־אֲנִי בַּחֲלוֹמִי *I also (had a dream, and) in my dream;* Is. 41. 26 אַף אֵין־מַגִּיד אַף אֵין מַשְׁמִיעַ אַף אֵין־שֹׁמֵעַ אִמְרֵיכֶם *there was none who declared it nor any who proclaimed it nor any who heard your words.* Deu. 15. 17, 1 S. 2. 7, Is. 40. 24; 41. 10; 46. 11, Ps. 16. 9.

(*b*) With additional but no obvious inclusive force. גַּם: Gen. 27. 3 גַּם־בָּרוּךְ יִהְיֶה *yes, and he shall be blessed.* Jud. 20. 48, Is. 13. 3; 14. 8; 43. 13; 48. 8, Jer. 46. 16. Am. 4. 6, 7, Ps. 107. 5. אַף: Gen. 18. 24 הַאַף תִּסְפֶּה *shall you then destroy the place?* Gen. 48. 13 (RSV *indeed*) Deu. 33. 3, 28 (RSV *yea*), Ps. 18. 49 (RSV *yea*); 65. 14; 93. 1 (RSV *yea*), Job 14. 3.

(*c*) A particular kind of inclusion (or addition) is expressed by אַף כִּי. The original sense may appear in Gen. 3. 1 אַף כִּי־אָמַר א׳ *is it also (a fact) that God said?* But the double conj. is mostly used in the sense *how much the more* or (after a neg.) *less.* The reference is to what was said in the previous (relevant) clause, which is to be assumed if necessary. There is usually ellipsis of this clause in the clause with אַף כִּי. The whole statement is often introduced by הֵן or הִנֵּה. Pr. 11. 31 *behold, the righteous is requited on earth* אַף כִּי־רָשָׁע וְחוֹטֵא *how much more the wicked and the sinner (will be requited).* 1 S. 14. 30, 2 S. 16. 11, Pr. 15. 11; 19. 7. 1 K. 8. 27 *behold, heaven and the heaven of heavens cannot contain you* אַף כִּי־הַבַּיִת הַזֶּה *how much less can this house (contain you).* Pr. 17. 7, Job 9. 14; 15. 16; 25. 6.

> Rem. 1. Both גַּם and אַף mean *also* or *in addition.* The nuance of emphasis carried by renderings like *even, indeed, yea,* etc. is, strictly speaking, illegitimate. See § 38*a*.

Exclusive Sentences

§ 144. The conjunctions רַק and אַךְ exclude the second clause from the reference of the first; or, when there is nothing in it from which exclusion may be made, they may simply limit or restrict it adverbially. Commonly the antithetical כִּי אִם (§ 142*d*) may, after a neg., express an exclusive relationship, while the exclusive אַךְ may express an antithetical relationship. On nominal exclusion, where not only רַק and אַךְ but a (surprising) variety of adverbs (adnominals) or prepp. may be used, see § 38*b*. Some of these may, with אֲשֶׁר or אִם added, become conjunctions and coordinate clauses.

(*a*) Exclusion by רַק or אַךְ. Gen. 47. 22 and Jos. bought all the land of Eg. ... רַק אַדְמַת הַכֹּהֲנִים לֹא קָנָה *except that* he did not buy the land of the priests. Gen. 9. 4 every moving thing shall be food for you אַךְ־בָּשָׂר בְּנַפְשׁוֹ דָמוֹ לֹא תֹאכֵלוּ ... *except that* (*only*) you shall not eat flesh with its life, its blood. Ex. 8. 25; 12. 16, Lev. 21. 23, Nu. 1. 49, Deu. 20. 16, Jos. 3. 4; 11. 13, 2 S. 3. 13, 1 K. 2. 3.

(*b*) As adverbs of limitation. רַק: Gen. 24. 8 then you will be free from this oath of mine רַק אֶת־בְּנִי לֹא תָשֵׁב שָׁמָּה *only* you must not take my son back there. Gen. 19. 8; 20. 11, Deu. 2. 28; 10. 15, Is. 4. 1, Job 2. 6. More frequently אַךְ, with (apparently) sometimes an asseverative force like *surely*: Gen. 26. 9 אַךְ הִנֵּה אִשְׁתְּךָ הִוא *but* see, she is your wife; 29. 14 אַךְ עַצְמִי וּבְשָׂרִי אָתָּה *surely* you are my bone and my flesh. Gen. 34. 23 (*only*); 44. 28 (*surely*), Nu. 14. 9 (*only*), Jud. 3. 24 (*just*); 7. 19 (*just*), 1 S. 1. 23 (*only*), 1 K. 22. 32 (*surely*), Is. 63. 8 (*surely*), Jer. 3. 13 (*only*); 5. 4 (*only*), Hos. 12. 9 (*but*).

(*c*) Antithesis (*however, nevertheless*) expressed by אַךְ. 2 S. 2. 10 Ishbosheth was forty years old when he began to reign over Israel אַךְ בֵּית יְהוּדָה הָיוּ ... אַחֲרֵי דָוִד *but* the house of Jud. followed D. Deu. 18. 20, 1 S. 29. 6, 2 S. 3. 13, 1 K. 17. 13, 2 K. 13. 6; 22. 7, Is. 14. 15; 43. 24, Jer. 28. 7; 30. 11, Ez. 46. 17, Zech. 1. 6.

(*d*) Exclusion expressed by כִּי אִם after neg. Gen. 32. 27 I will not let you go כִּי אִם־בֵּרַכְתָּנִי *except* you bless me. Gen. 28. 17; 42. 15, Lev. 22. 6, Is. 55. 10, Am. 3. 7, Ru. 3. 18. After interr., Mic. 6. 8.

(*e*) Exclusion (antithesis) with other conjunctions. אֶפֶס כִּי, Nu. 13. 28 (*yet*), Deu. 15. 4 (*but*), Jud. 4. 9 (*nevertheless*), Am. 9. 8 (*except*); אֶפֶס alone, 1 S. 12. 14 (*nevertheless*). בִּלְתִּי אִם, Am. 3. 3 (*unless*); בִּלְתִּי alone, Gen. 43. 3 (*unless*), Is. 10. 4 (*except*).

Disjunctive Sentences

§ 145. The conj. אוֹ coordinates at sentence as well as at phrase level; on nominal disjunction see § 38c. Ellipsis is common. There is indeed properly ellipsis of the subj. and verb even in "nominal" disjunction; thus Ex. 21. 4 וְיָלְדָה־לּוֹ בָנִים אוֹ בָנוֹת *and (if) she bears him sons or (if she bears him) daughters.* But since the verb is the same, the disjunctive weight is carried by the nominal alternatives. A fully disjunctive sentence has different verbs in each clause. Most occur in alternative conditions in legal texts. Note that כִּי but not אִם may be preceded by אוֹ, though אוֹ may be used when אִם is omitted. Ex. 21. 33 וְכִי *if (when)* ... אוֹ כִי *or if (when)* ..., cf. *vs.* 36, Lev. 5. 1-4, Nu. 5. 30; 35. 16-23. Other exx. of אוֹ, Nu. 11. 8 they gathered (the manna) וְטָחֲנוּ בָרֵחַיִם אוֹ דָכוּ בַּמְּדֹכָה and ground it in mills *or* beat it in a mortar. Ex. 4. 11 (the same verb in two senses), Mal. 2. 17, Job 16. 3.

COMPOUND SENTENCES WITH APPOSITION. ASYNDETON

§ 146. As in the case of nouns (§ 39) *apposition* links clauses more closely than coordination and (Andersen) should not be regarded as a mere stylistic variation of it. Apposition presupposes some kind of equivalence or overlap in reference between two (sometimes more) clauses. The clause in apposition repeats or is broadly synonymous with the preceding clause, or by means of a negative or an antonym sets up an antithesis to it. Or it extends the preceding clause by making specific or explicit something hinted at or merely implied in it, or more generally by spelling out or interpreting its significance. Chiasmus goes well with all kinds of apposition.

Asyndeton, on the other hand, is simply the omission of *Vav*. It applies when, as in heterogeneous discourse, there is no obvious semantic connection between the clauses or when, as in consecutive passages, particularly in poetry, there is merely continuity between them.

§ 147. *Apposition* (*a*) enhances the similarity between two clauses. Gen. 3. 16 הַרְבָּה אַרְבֶּה עִצְּבוֹנֵךְ ... בְּעֶצֶב תֵּלְדִי בָנִים *I will greatly multiply your pain* in childbearing, *in pain you shall bring forth children;* Ex. 18. 18 כָּבֵד מִמְּךָ הַדָּבָר לֹא־תוּכַל עֲשֹׂהוּ לְבַדֶּךָ *the matter is too heavy for you; you cannot do it alone.* Gen. 15. 1; 31. 36; 43. 9, Ex. 1. 14; 14. 3; 22. 26,

Lev. 2. 13, Deu. 7. 6. Sometimes the second clause distributes as well as repeats, Gen. 41. 12 he interpreted to us our dreams אִישׁ כַּחֲלֹמוֹ פָּתָר (*to*) *each man according to his dream he interpreted.* Ex. 12. 4; 16. 8. In some older narrative passages such an apposition seems used to slow the pace of the story, a survival perhaps from the parallelism of a poetic original, Gen. 41. 48 he put food in the cities נָתַן ... אֹכֶל שְׂדֵה־הָעִיר בְּתוֹכָהּ *food from the field*(*s*) *which surround* (every) *city he put in it.* Gen. 7. 7-9, 21-22; 8. 18-19. In future discourse, Gen. 6. 17 I shall bring the flood of waters upon the earth to destroy all flesh כֹּל אֲשֶׁר־בָּאָרֶץ יִגְוָע ... *all who are in the earth shall perish.* Ex. 12. 8, 14.

(*b*) When a negative or antonym is present, apposition enhances the opposition between the clauses, Gen. 42. 31 כֵּנִים אֲנָחְנוּ לֹא הָיִינוּ מְרַגְּלִים *we are honest men; we are not spies.* Gen. 11. 30; 31. 39; 45. 9; 48. 10; 50. 20, Ex. 8. 27; 10. 26, Deu. 9. 7.

(*c*) Apposition is also used for purposes of explanation. Thus specifying or making explicit the first clause, Gen. 21. 14 and he gave (them) to Hagar שָׂם עַל־שִׁכְמָהּ *he placed* (placing) (*them*) *upon her shoulder;* 47. 9 the days of the years of my sojourning are 130 years מְעַט וְרָעִים הָיוּ יְמֵי שְׁנֵי חַיַּי *few and evil have been the days of the years of my life.* Gen. 1. 27; 6. 9, 19; 15. 15; 18. 11; 23. 11; 42. 9, Ex. 19. 12; 23. 15; 36. 35, Deu. 9. 16. Or interpreting it in various ways, Gen. 44. 12 and he searched בַּגָּדוֹל הֵחֵל וּבַקָּטֹן כִּלָּה *he began with the eldest and finished with the youngest;* Deu. 7. 5 but thus shall you deal with them מִזְבְּחֹתֵיהֶם תִּתֹּצוּ *you shall break down their altars,* etc. Gen. 3. 15; 9. 2, 5; 16. 12; 27. 36; 41. 13; 42. 36, Ex. 9. 27; 20. 8-10.

In headings or introductions and in summaries or conclusions what follows or precedes is in effect in apposition. Gen. 9. 13 this is the sign of the covenant ... אֶת־קַשְׁתִּי נָתַתִּי בֶּעָנָן *I will set my bow in the clouds.* Gen. 5. 1; 10. 1; 11. 10; 17. 10; 20. 13; 43. 11. Gen. 6. 22 and N. did (this); all that God commanded him כֵּן עָשָׂה *so he did.* Gen. 2. 4 (if 4(a) refers to what has gone before); 10. 20; 22. 23; 25. 18; 35. 26, Ex. 19. 6. Similarly, in curses and blessings the second clause details what will happen as a result, Gen. 9. 25 אָרוּר כְּנָעַן עֶבֶד עֲבָדִים יִהְיֶה לְאֶחָיו *cursed be Canaan; a slave of slaves shall he be to his brothers.* Gen. 3. 14, 17.

Sometimes apposition is used in place of qualifying subordinate clauses, causal or relative. In place of כִּי, Gen. 17. 14 any uncircumcised male ... shall be cut off from his people אֶת־בְּרִיתִי הֵפַר *he has broken my covenant.* Ex. 12. 11. In place of אֲשֶׁר, Gen. 48. 7 and I buried her there on the way to Ephrath הוא בֵּית לָחֶם *that is, Bethlehem.* Gen. 2. 11, 13, 14; 15. 13; 4. 20, 21; 36. 1, and frequently in poetry (see *d*).

(*d*) In poetry apposition is ubiquitous. The parallelistic structure favours it, especially the synonymous and antithetic. The ellipsis of the relative אֲשֶׁר, which is so characteristic of poetry, supplies many examples. Synonymous: Is. 1. 2 יִשְׂרָאֵל לֹא יָדַע עַמִּי לֹא הִתְבּוֹנָן *Isr. does not know, my people does not consider.* Is. 9. 5, Ps. 2. 7; 6. 6, 7, Job 4. 5, 6; 9. 21, etc. Antithetic: Is. 1. 2 the ox knows its owner .. (*but*) *Israel does not know,* etc. (as above); 43. 17 יִשְׁכְּבוּ בַּל־יָקוּמוּ *they lie down, they cannot rise.* Pr. 10. 15, 20; 12. 5 and *passim.* Explanatory: Is. 13. 4 hark, a tumult on the mountains ... צְבָאוֹת מְפַקֵּד צְבָא מִלְחָמָה 'י *Y. of hosts is mustering a host for battle.* Is. 5. 5; 9. 18, Am. 4. 12, Ps. 64. 2; 84. 11; 100. 3, Job 9. 13, Lam. 2. 17, etc. For exx. of omission of אֲשֶׁר see § 11, 12.

§ 148. *Asyndeton.* (*a*) In prose it is found in loosely structured discourse, as e.g. Gen. 4. 9-12; 18. 24-25; 47. 5-6; Deu. 5. 2-5; Jon. 1. 6; Ecc. 4. 13-16. Espec. in precative discourse; so regularly in the use of an imper. like *come, arise,* etc. along with another imper. or a cohort., Gen. 11. 3, 4, 7; 13. 14; 19. 32, Ex. 6. 11, 2 S. 1. 15. But also in lists of instructions, etc., as in the Ten Commandments (Ex. 20. 2-14) or the Aaronic bene-diction (Nu. 6. 24-26). Two questions without clear common content may also be set out without *Vav,* Ex. 17. 2. On the whole, however, asyndeton is not a frequent feature of prose style, hardly occurring instead of *Vav* cons. constructions in sequential narrative, or in predictive or even precative discourse.

(*b*) On the other hand asyndeton, whether arising from the omission of simple or consec. *Vav,* is as characteristic of poetry as is apposition. It is, of course, the (relative) independence of each unit of parallelism which leads to this. The best way of distinguishing the two is to go through a number of poems of different kinds marking off examples of each. Thus in Ps. 19 *vss.* 4 (synon.), *vss.* 9-11 and 12 (explan.) are app., *vss.* 8-11 are asynd.; in Ps. 51 *vss.* 3 and 19 are app. (synon.), *vss.* 9-11 and 20 are asynd.; in Ps. 90 *vss.* 6-9 (synon.) and 10 (explan.) are app., *vss.* 13-16 are asynd.; in Pr. 3 *vss.* 7 (explan.), 16 and 18 (synon.) and 21 (antith.) are app., *vss.* 3, 19-20, 24 and 27-31 are asynd.; in Is. 40. 1-11, *vss.* 3 and 7 are app.

(synon.), *vss.* 9 and 11 are asynd. Note how in a series of clauses the intrusion of a *Vav*, usually between the last two clauses, is a give-away sign of asynd. rather than app., cf. Ps. 5. 11, Pr. 3. 31, Is. 40. 11. The above exx. are discourse; for asyndeton in poetic narrative or report see Ex. 15. 4-10, Ps. 74. 4-8, 12-17, Lam. 3. 43-66 (also some fut. discourse); contrast Ps. 78, which mainly uses *Vav* cons. (though in several *vss. Vav* is omitted, e.g. 12, 13, 15, 25, 30, etc.).

Sentences with Extraposition (*CASUS PENDENS*)

§ 149. Extraposition is simply a descriptive term and avoids the "case" implications of the traditional Latin term *casus pendens*. It refers to a construction, found in many languages, by which the prominent word (the chief semantic subject) in a sent. is "extraposed" or isolated at the beginning and followed by a full sent. in which it is resumed by a pronoun or pronom. suffix. This sent. may be verbal or nominal. Emphasis or focussing is involved, but the construction fulfils a number of roles beyond this, serving to pattern in various ways both individual sents. and longer passages (Kahn).

§ 150. *Form.* The resumptive pron. may be the subj. or obj. of the following sent. or figure as a suff. to a noun or in a prepos. phrase. As subj.: Gen. 42. 11 כֻּלָּנוּ בְּנֵי אִישׁ אֶחָד נָחְנוּ we are *all of us* sons of one man; Pr. 10. 22 בִּרְכַּת י' הִיא תַעֲשִׁיר *the blessing of Y. (it)* makes rich; Ecc. 3. 15 מַה־שֶּׁהָיָה כְּבָר הוּא *what is* has already been. As obj.: Gen. 24. 27 אָנֹכִי בַּדֶּרֶךְ נָחַנִי י' Y. led *me* in the way; 28. 13 הָאָרֶץ ... לְךָ אֶתְּנֶנָּה *the land* on which you lie I will give *(it)* to you; Is. 1. 7 אַדְמַתְכֶם זָרִים אֹכְלִים אֹתָהּ *your land* strangers devour *(it)* in your sight. So objective suff. after אֵין, Gen. 37. 30 הַיֶּלֶד אֵינֶנּוּ *the lad (he)* is no more; after עוֹד, Gen. 18. 22 וְאַבְרָהָם עוֹדֶנּוּ עֹמֵד and *Abr.* was still standing before Y. Otherwise: Gen. 34. 8 שְׁכֶם בְּנִי חָשְׁקָה נַפְשׁוֹ בְּבִתְּכֶם *Shechem my son - his* heart desires your daughter; Jud. 17. 5 וְהָאִישׁ מִיכָה לוֹ בֵּית א' *the man Micah* had a shrine.

Sometimes the extraposition is partial, Gen. 4. 15 כָּל־הֹרֵג קַיִן שִׁבְעָתַיִם יֻקָּם *anyone who slays Cain* - (on him) vengeance shall be taken sevenfold. Or instead of a pron. the noun may be repeated, Deu. 18. 19-20 הַנָּבִיא ... וּמֵת הַנָּבִיא הַהוּא *the prophet* who ... *that prophet* shall die;

or a synonym used, Jer. 13. 27 *your adulteries and neighings, your lewd harlotries* ... רָאִיתִי שִׁקּוּצָיִךְ I have seen *your foul deeds*. As in Deu. 18. 19-20 above, the following clause may begin with *Vav* cons. (*Vav apodosi*, §§ 71*d*, 79), especially if a relative or other clause intervenes. Ex. 9. 19, Nu. 21. 8, Is. 9. 4, Pr. 9. 16. Commonly הִנֵּה comes between, Gen. 17. 4 אֲנִי הִנֵּה בְרִיתִי אִתָּךְ behold, *my* covenant is with you. 6. 17; 9.9, Ecc. 1. 16.

Rem. 1. Though formally resumptive, הִיא/הוּא often functions as a mere copula, § 1*b*.

Rem. 2. טֶרֶם *not yet* is commonly preceded by the subj. in extraposition, Gen. 2. 5; 24. 15, 45, 1 S. 3. 3, 7.

Rem. 3. Sometimes the extraposed element is itself used with אֵת or a prep., which is resumed later. Kahn calls this pronominal agreement, and distinguishes it formally from extraposition, though it has more or less the same functions. Gen. 13. 15 כִּי אֶת־כָּל־הָאָרֶץ ... לְךָ אֶתְּנֶנָּה for *all the land* which you see I will give (*it*) to you (contrast 28. 13); 2 S. 6. 23 וּלְמִיכַל בַּת־שָׁאוּל לֹא הָיָה לָהּ יָלֶד *to M.*, d. of S. - there was no child *to her* (she had); Gen. 2. 17 וּמֵעֵץ הַדַּעַת ... לֹא תֹאכַל מִמֶּנּוּ but *from the tree of knowledge* ... you shall not eat (*from it*). 2 S. 6. 22, 2 K. 22. 18, Jer. 50. 21, Ez. 18. 24. Pronominal agreement may also be anticipatory, Ex. 2. 6 וַתִּרְאֵהוּ אֶת־הַיֶּלֶד she saw *him - the child;* Nu. 32. 33 וַיִּתֵּן לָהֶם מֹשֶׁה לִבְנֵי־גָד and M. gave *to them - to the sons of Gad*, etc. - the kingdom of Sihon. Ex. 35. 5, Jer. 51. 56.

§ 151. *Function.* (*a*) At sentence level extraposition is extensively used in the various types of sent., usually to facilitate the syntax when a noun or noun equivalent is required in initial position. In conjunctive sent.: Pr. 16. 20 he who considers a matter will find prosperity וּבוֹטֵחַ בַּי' אַשְׁרָיו and (but?) *he who trusts* in Y. - happy is he; Is. 9. 1 the people that walk in darkness ... יֹשְׁבֵי בְּאֶרֶץ צַלְמָוֶת אוֹר נָגַהּ עֲלֵיהֶם *they that dwell in the land of the shadow of death - on them* light has shone (appos.). Is. 1. 7 (app.), Ez. 30. 18; 32. 7, Ps. 125. 2, Job 22. 8, Ecc. 10. 8. In chiastic sent.: Pr. 11. 26 מֹנֵעַ בָּר יִקְּבֻהוּ לְאוֹם *he who keeps back* grain - the people curse him, but a blessing is on the head of him who sells it. Is. 3. 12, Pr. 12. 16, Job 38. 19. In contrastive sent.: 1 S. 25. 29 the life of my lord will be bound up in the bundle of life with Y. your God וְאֵת נֶפֶשׁ אֹיְבֶיךָ יְקַלְּעֶנָּה but *the life of your enemies* he will sling (*it*) out. Gen. 49. 8 (app.), Deu. 1. 38-39; 4. 3-4; 18. 14, Pr. 13. 3 (app.); 14. 21, Ecc. 2. 14. In antithetic sent.: Gen. 15. 4 this one shall not be your heir כִּי־אִם אֲשֶׁר

יֵצֵא מִמֵּעֶיךָ הוּא יִירָשֶׁךָ but *he who comes out* from your own loins - *he* shall be your heir. Gen. 2. 16-17; 42. 11 (app.); 44. 17, Deu. 1. 37-38 (app.), 2 K. 1. 4; 17. 36, Is. 8. 12-13 (app.), Ez. 33. 13, Pr. 11. 4, 2 Chr. 23. 6. In exclusive sent.: Ex. 12. 16, Nu. 22. 20, 35.

(*b*) In more extended passages of narrative or discourse its role (cf. Circumst. cl.) is macrosyntactic. Opening a speech (occasionally comprising a single sent.) or poem: Gen. 17. 15 שָׂרַי אִשְׁתְּךָ לֹא־תִקְרָא אֶת־ שְׁמָהּ שָׂרָי *as for S. your wife* - you shall not call *her* name S. Gen. 31. 12 (single sent.); 17. 4; 24. 27 (after initial blessing); 28. 13 (after initial self-identification); 34. 8, 1 K. 22. 14 (single sent.), Is. 27. 2, Jer. 50. 21, 1 Chr. 22. 7. Closure of speech or poem (or major sect.): Gen. 21. 13 וְגַם אֶת־ בֶּן־הָאָמָה לְגוֹי אֲשִׂימֶנּוּ and *the son of the slave woman* I will also make (*him*) into a nation; Ps. 18. 31 הָאֵל תָּמִים דַּרְכּוֹ (this) *God - his* way is perfect. Gen. 28. 22; 30. 33; 31. 16; 45. 20, Ex. 4. 9, Nu. 16. 11, Jer. 13. 27, Ps. 10. 5; 35. 8; 67. 5, Ecc. 1. 11. Within a speech or poem, marking a change of topic or theme: Jer. 12. 6 כִּי גַם־אַחֶיךָ וּבֵית־אָבִיךָ גַּם־הֵמָּה בָּגְדוּ בָךְ for *your brothers* too *and your father's house* - *they* too have dealt treacherously with you (shift from land in general to the prophet's family); Gen. 31. 40 (rare extrap. of verbal form) הָיִיתִי בַיּוֹם אֲכָלַנִי חֹרֶב *as for my situation*, by day the heat consumed *me* (shift from Jacob's conduct to his suffering). Lev. 25. 44; 26. 36, Nu. 14. 31, 1 S. 12. 23, Is. 4. 3. Extrap. may also indicate a new episode in narrative: Jud. 4. 4 וּדְבֹרָה אִשָּׁה נְבִיאָה ... הִיא שֹׁפְטָה now *Deb., a prophetess ...* (*she*) was judging Israel at that time. 1 S. 17. 24, 2 S. 21. 16, 1 K. 11. 26, Ez. 44. 15, 2 Chr. 15. 1. Sometimes a climax seems to be highlighted, Gen. 13. 15, Nu. 17. 3, 20, Jos. 1. 3, 1 K. 15. 13. Or an additional piece of information, Gen. 48. 7 וַאֲנִי בְּבֹאִי מִפַּדָּן מֵתָה עָלַי ר' *much to my sorrow*, when I came from P., R. died (lit. *I ... upon me*). Gen. 47. 21, Deu. 14. 27, Jos. 11. 3, Jud. 17. 5, 2 S. 6. 23, 1 K. 12. 17.

(*c*) Extraposition is used commonly in legal texts to identify clearly the person to whom a ruling applies; the word extraposed (with a relative clause) is usually אִישׁ or אִשָּׁה, occasionally another noun. Lev. 17. 3-4 אִישׁ אִישׁ מִבֵּית י' אֲשֶׁר יִשְׁחַט שׁוֹר ... דָּם יֵחָשֵׁב לָאִישׁ הַהִיא *any man of the house of I.* who kills an ox (if any man kills ...) ... blood guilt shall be imputed *to that man*. Gen. 17. 14 (*any uncircumcised male* who ...), Ex. 30. 33, 38, Lev. 7. 20 (הַנֶּפֶשׁ אֲשֶׁר), 27 (id.); 13. 45 (*the leper who ...*);

15. 18; 17. 8, 10, 13; 22. 3, 18. Similarly נֶפֶשׁ *person* is frequently extraposed before כִּי *if, when,* Lev. 2. 1; 4. 2; 5. 1, 4, 15, 21; אָדָם, Lev. 1. 2; אִישׁ or אִשָּׁה, Lev. 12. 2; 13. 29, 38, 40.

QUESTIONS

§ 152. On interrogative pronouns (מִי, מָה) see § 7; on interr. adverbs (*why? where? when?* etc.), § 154, Rem. 3 below. The simple polar or *Yes - No* question

(*a*) May be asked without any particle, presumably by tone of voice. 2 S. 18. 29 שָׁלוֹם לַנַּעַר *is the child well?* 2 S. 11. 11 וַאֲנִי אָבוֹא אֶל־בֵּיתִי *shall I then go to my house?* 1 S. 21. 16 חֲסַר מְשֻׁגָּעִים אָנִי *am I in want of madmen?* Gen. 18. 12; 27. 24, Jud. 4. 16, 1 S. 16. 4; 22. 7, 15; 25. 11, 2 S. 9. 6; 16. 17; 19. 23; 23. 5, 1 K. 1. 24; 21. 7, Jon. 4. 11, Song 3. 3. Less frequently in *neg.* sent., 1 S. 20. 9, 2 K. 5. 26, Job 2. 10. Omission of particle is perhaps most common in rhetorical contexts, as when a previous statement is being strongly repudiated, Jud. 14. 16, 2 S. 11. 11, 2 K. 19. 11, Jer. 25. 29, Ez. 20. 31, Jon. 4. 11.

(*b*) But more commonly it uses the particle הֲ. Gen. 4. 9 הֲשֹׁמֵר אָחִי אָנֹכִי *am I my brother's keeper?* 24. 58 הֲתֵלְכִי עִם־הָאִישׁ הַזֶּה *will you go with this man?* Gen. 18. 17; 43. 27, 29; 45. 3, 2 S. 7. 5, etc. So before יֵשׁ and אַיִן, Gen. 24. 23 הֲיֵשׁ בֵּית אָבִיךְ מָקוֹם לָנוּ לָלִין *is there room* for us to lodge in your father's house? Jud. 14. 3 הַאֵין בִּבְנוֹת אַחֶיךָ אִשָּׁה *is there not a woman* among your brother's daughters? Gen. 43. 7; 44. 19, Ex. 17. 7, Jud. 4. 20, 1 S. 9. 11, 2 K. 4. 13; 10. 15. — 1 K. 22. 7, 2 K. 3. 11, Jer. 7. 17.

In a question expecting the answer *No*, often used rhetorically, אִם may replace הֲ, Is. 29. 16 אִם־כְּחֹמֶר הַיֹּצֵר יֵחָשֵׁב *shall the potter be regarded as the clay?* Jud. 5. 8, 1 K. 1. 27, Lam. 2. 20, Job 6. 12, 28; 39. 13. There is (ideally) suppression of a prot., cf. אִם in Oaths.

(*c*) The *neg.* question is put by הֲלֹא, הֲלֹא, Gen. 13. 9 הֲלֹא כָל־הָאָרֶץ לְפָנֶיךָ *is not all the land* before you? 4. 7; 20. 5; 44. 5, Ex. 14. 12, Nu. 23. 26, Deu. 31. 17. Or by הַאֵין when the existence of the subj. is questioned (§ 52) or when the pred. is a ptcp. (§ 113*d*). 1 K. 22. 7, Jud. 14. 3 (above, *b*), Jer. 7. 17, Am. 2. 11. Occasionally the elements of הֲלֹא are separated, Gen. 18. 25.

Rem. 1. The interr. particle, positive or negative, may be strengthened by אַף, Gen. 18. 13, 24, Am. 2. 11, Job 40. 8, or גַּם, Gen. 16. 13. These particles are properly inclusive, though often translated *indeed*, etc.

Rem. 2. The particle הֲלֹא implying an affirmative answer is in effect equivalent to הִנֵּה, Gen. 37. 13, Deu. 3. 11 and often. In Chr. הִנֵּה is sometimes used for הֲלֹא of earlier books, comp. 2 Chr. 16. 11 with 1 K. 15. 23. See 1 Chr. 29. 29, 2 Chr. 27. 7; 32. 32, and Sept. ἰδού for הֲלֹא, Deu. 3. 11, Jos. 1. 9, Jud. 6. 14, Est. 10. 2.

§ 153. The disjunctive or alternative question is put by הֲ in first clause, and אִם or וְאִם in second. Jos. 5. 13 הֲלָנוּ אַתָּה אִם לְצָרֵינוּ *are you for us or for our enemies?* 1 K. 22. 15 הֲנֵלֵךְ אִם נֶחְדָּל *shall we go or forbear?* Or if negative, by אִם לֹא in second clause (or אִם אַיִן if יֵשׁ be in the first), commonly with ellipsis, Gen. 27. 21 הַאַתָּה זֶה בְּנִי אִם־לֹא *are you my son or not?* Ex. 17. 7 הֲיֵשׁ י׳ בְּקִרְבֵּנוּ אִם־אָיִן *is Y. in our midst or not?* Gen. 17. 17, Jud. 9. 2; 20. 28, 1 K. 22. 6, 15, 2 K. 20. 9, Jer. 2. 14, Am. 6. 2, Job 7. 12. — 2 S. 24. 13, Joel 1. 2, Job 11. 2; 21. 4; 22. 3, cf. Pr. 27. 24. The second half of the alternative is often merely the first in a varied form. Nu. 11. 12, Job 8. 3; 22. 3. Gen. 37. 8, Jud. 11. 25, 2 S. 19. 36.

Rem. 1. *Answers* are usually made by repeating part of the question, or by the use of some word suggested by it. See ellipsis, § 132. Gen. 24. 58; 29. 6; 30. 34, Jos. 2. 4, 1 S. 17. 58; 23. 11, 12; 26. 17, 2 S. 2. 20; 9. 2; 12. 19, Am. 6. 10, Hag. 2. 12, 13.

Rem. 2. The question form is much used rhetorically, requiring assent or notice to be taken rather than reply. On interr. prons. so used, § 7. Gen. 27. 45, 1 S. 19. 17, 2 S. 2. 22; 20. 19, Is. 40. 21, Ecc. 5. 5, 2 Chr. 25. 16. See above § 152*a, b*; below R. 3, *a, c.*

Rem. 3. Interr. adverbs are mostly formed on the pron. מָה or the locative אֵי:

(*a*) *Why? wherefore?* לָמָה, וְלָמָה, לָמָה, מַדּוּעַ, וּמַדּוּעַ; *why not?* לָמָה לֹא, מַדּוּעַ לֹא. 1 S. 19. 17 לָמָה כָכָה רִמִּיתָנִי *why have you cheated me thus?* Gen. 12. 18 לָמָה לֹא הִגַּדְתָּ לִי *why did you not tell me?* 1 S. 26. 15, 2 S. 16. 17; 19. 26. Exx. of מַדּוּעַ, Gen. 27. 45, Ex. 32. 11, Nu. 20. 4, Jud. 12. 3, 1 K. 2. 22. The pron. מָה (§ 7*b*) and combinations like עַל מָה are often used in the sense of *why?* Nu. 22. 32, Is. 1. 5, Jer. 9. 11, Job 13. 14.

Like the interr. pronouns, לָמָה is often strengthened by זֶה (but not מַדּוּעַ). Gen. 18. 13 לָמָה זֶּה צָחֲקָה שׂ׳ *why* (in the world) *did Sarah laugh?* Gen. 25. 22, 32, Ex. 5. 22, 2 S. 18. 22; 19. 43, Job 27. 12, cf. Jud. 18. 24, 1 K. 21. 5, 2 K. 1. 5. Rem. 4.

All these interr. may be used rhetorically as words of remonstrance, surprise, etc., and as exclamations.

(b) *Where?* אֵי, אַיֵּה, אֵי זֶה, אָנָה, אֵיפֹה; *whither?* אָנָה, אֵי זֶה; *whence?* אֵי מֵאַיִן, מִזֶּה. Gen. 4. 9 אֵי הֶבֶל אָחִיךָ *where* is Abel? Deu. 32. 37, 1 S. 26. 16. With suff., Ex. 2. 20 אַיּוֹ *where is he?* Gen. 3. 9, Is. 19. 12, Mic. 7. 10, Nah. 3. 17. Gen. 19. 5 אַיֵּה הָאֲנָשִׁים *where are* the men? 18. 9; 22. 7; 38. 21, Jud. 9. 38, 2 S. 9. 4, 2 K. 2. 14. Exx. of אֵיפֹה, Gen. 37. 16, 2 S. 9. 4, Is. 49. 21. Exx. of אָנָה, Gen. 16. 8; 37. 30, 2 S. 2. 1, Is. 10. 3; cf. 1 K. 22. 24 (אֵי זֶה). Exx. of מֵאַיִן, Gen. 42. 7; 29. 4, Nu. 11. 13, Jos. 2. 4, Jud. 17. 9, Is. 39. 3, Ps. 121. 1, Job 1. 7. Exx. of אֵי מִזֶּה, Gen. 16. 8, Jud. 13. 6, 1 S. 25. 11, 2 S. 1. 13.

(c) *How?* אֵיךְ, אֵיכָה; בַּמֶּה (*by what?* Gen. 15. 8); *how not?* אֵיךְ לֹא. 2 S. 1. 5 אֵיךְ יָדַעְתָּ כִּי־מֵת שׁ׳ *how do you know* that Saul is dead? vs. 14 *how not?* Deu. 18. 21, Jud. 20. 3, 1 K. 12. 6, 2 K. 17. 28, Ru. 3. 18. These adverbs are often used rhetorically, in remonstrance, Gen. 26. 9, Jer. 2. 23; repudiation or refusal, Gen. 39. 9; 44. 8, 34, Jos. 9. 7; the expression of hopelessness, Is. 20. 6, and so on. The form אֵיכָה *how!* usually raises the elegy, Is. 1. 21, Lam. 2. 1; 4. 1; but also אֵיךְ, 2 S. 1. 19, 25, 27.

(d) *How many?* כַּמָּה. 2 S. 19. 35 כַּמָּה יְמֵי שְׁנֵי חַיַּי *how many years have I still to live?* Gen. 47. 8, 1 K. 22. 16, Zech. 7. 3, Job 13. 23. Also *how much?* Zech. 2. 6; *how long?* Ps. 35. 17, Job 7. 10; *how often?* Ps. 78. 40, Job 21. 17, 2 Chr. 18. 15. *How long?* is also expressed by עַד־אָנָה, Ex. 16. 8, Nu. 14. 11; and (see below) by עַד־מָתַי.

(e) *When?* מָתַי. Am. 8. 5 מָתַי יַעֲבֹר הַחֹדֶשׁ *when will the new moon be over?* Gen. 30. 30, Ps. 42. 3; 101. 2, Pr. 6. 9, Job 7. 4. *Until when? how long?* עַד־מָתַי. Ex. 10. 7, 1 S. 1. 14, 1 K. 18. 21, Jer. 4. 14, Ps. 6. 4; 74. 10; 82. 2, Pr. 1. 22.

Rem. 4. The particle אֵיפֹה is (cf. זֶה) used to strengthen the question *who?* or *where?* etc. Gen. 27. 33, Ex. 33. 16, Jud. 9. 38, Is. 19. 12; 22. 1, Hos. 13. 10, Job 17. 15; 19. 23.

WISHES AND OATHS

§ **154.** The *wish* may be expressed by juss. or cohort. (§§ 67, 68). 2 S. 18. 32 יִהְיוּ כַנַּעַר אֹיְבֵי אֲדֹנִי *may* the enemies of my lord *be as (that) young man.* With or without נָא, 2 S. 24. 14 נִפְּלָה־נָא *let us fall;* 1 S. 1. 23 יָקֵם י׳ דְּבָרוֹ *may Y. establish.* The passive ptcp. may also be used precatively, espec. in curse and blessing (§ 113b). Gen. 3. 14 אָרוּר אַתָּה *may you be cursed;* Is. 12. 5 מוּדַעַת זֹאת *may this be known.* The verb may be omitted, Gen. 27. 13 *on me* (be) *your curse!* 1 S. 25. 24, Ps. 3. 9.

§ **155.** More formal wishes are expressed (a) by the conditional לוּ,

less usually אִם. Both QATAL and YIQTOL may follow. Nu. 14. 2 לוּ־מַתְנוּ בְּאֶרֶץ מ׳ *would we had died* in the land of Egypt; Nu. 20. 3, Jos. 7. 7. Is. 63. 19 לוּא קָרַעְתָּ שָׁמַיִם *O that you would rend* the heavens (§ 60c). Gen. 17. 18 לוּ יִשׁ׳ יִחְיֶה *O that* Ishmael *might live*; Job 6. 2 לוּ שָׁקוֹל יִשָּׁקֵל כַּעְשִׂי *O that* my vexation *could be weighed*. With imper., Gen. 23. 13; ptcp., Ps. 81. 14. Ps. 139. 19 אִם תִּקְטֹל רָשָׁע *O that you would slay* the wicked. Ps. 81. 9; 95. 7, Pr. 24. 11.

(*b*) By an interr. sent. with מִי *who?* 2 S. 23. 15 מִי יַשְׁקֵנִי מַיִם *O that I had water to drink!* (lit., who will let me drink!). Ps. 4. 7 מִי יַרְאֵנִי טוֹב *O that we might see* some good! Nu. 11. 4, 2 S. 15. 4, cf. Mal. 1. 10. Particularly the phrase מִי יִתֵּן *who will give?* 2 S. 19. 1 מִי יִתֵּן מוּתִי אֲנִי תַחְתֶּיךָ *would that I had died* instead of you! Ex. 16. 3. With verb, Job 6. 8 מִי יִתֵּן תָּבוֹא שֶׁאֱלָתִי *O that* my request *might come!* Job 13. 5; 14. 13. Rem. 3.

> *Rem. 1.* לוּ and אִם properly introduce condit. sents. without an apodosis, though it is not always possible to recover this; cf. Engl. *if only!* Passages like Gen. 24. 42, Ex. 32. 32 show the transition.
>
> *Rem. 2.* The particle אַחֲלֵי, אַחֲלַי *would that* (derivation unknown) is only found in 2 K. 5. 3, Ps. 119. 5.
>
> *Rem. 3.* The construction of מִי יִתֵּן varies. (1) Direct obj., Deu. 28. 67, Jud. 9. 29, Ps. 14. 7; 55. 7, Job 14. 4; 29. 2 (suff.); 31. 35. (2) Two obj., direct and indir. or compl., Nu. 11. 29, Jer. 8. 23; 9. 1. (3) Infin. constr., 2 S. 10. 1, Ex. 16. 3; as obj. compl., Job 11. 5. (4) A verb: obj. clause (no conjunction) with YIQTOL, Job 6. 8; 13. 5; 14. 13 (§ 90, R. 1); YIQTOL with *Vav*, Job 19. 23 (§ 90, R. 2); *Vav* cons. QATAL, Deu. 5. 26 (§ 71a); stative QATAL, Job 23. 3; ptcp., Job 31. 31.

§ **156.** The *oath* does not need to have a special formula (Jud. 21. 1, 2 S. 21. 17), but two exist, commonly used together. These are —

(*a*) The introductory formula (of divinity) חַי יהוה, אֱלֹהִים, אֵל or (God speaking) חַי אָנִי (invariably so pointed); (of humans) חֵי נַפְשָׁךְ, חֵי פַרְעֹה. The formula is translated *as Y., Phar.,* etc. *lives,* but it is gramm. independent of what follows; the forms חֵי/חַי are variously interpreted as verbal, adjectival or nominal. Jud. 8. 19 חַי יהוה; 2 S. 2. 27 חַי הָאֱלֹהִים; Jer. 44. 26 חַי־אֵל; Job 27. 2 חַי אֲדֹנָי י׳. Cf. 1 K. 18. 10, 15. Nu. 14. 21, 28 חַי אָנִי (Deu. 32. 40 אָנֹכִי). Gen. 42. 15 חֵי פַרְעֹה; 2 S. 15. 21 חַי י׳ וְחֵי; 1 S. 20. 3 חֵי י׳ וְחֵי נַפְשָׁךְ. Interestingly Am. 8. 14 חֵי אֱלֹהֶיךָ; אֲדֹנִי הַמֶּלֶךְ.

דָּן *as your god*, O Dan, *lives.*

(b) Following this formula or without it, a clause introduced by the conjunctions אִם, אִם לֹא or כִּי. With the conditionals an apod. (*May Y. do so to me*, etc., Rem. 3) sometimes precedes but is usually understood (ellipsis), so that a clause with אִם לֹא *if not* becomes the oath of affirmation and one with אִם *if* becomes the oath of denial. On the other hand, כִּי is used affirmatively, *surely, indeed,* properly (it is a fact) *that* (§ 116c); like כִּי *recitativum* (§ 90b), it in effect introduces the oath as direct speech, and is gramm. independent of what goes before, even if that should be, strangely, the clause *May Y. do so to me.* When there is a subordinate clause before the oath-clause, it commonly precedes each.

1 S. 19. 6 חַי י' אִם יָמוּת *he shall not be put to death;* 1 K. 1. 51 יִשָּׁבַע־לִי כַיּוֹם אִם יָמִית *let him swear to me first (that) he will not kill* me. Gen. 42. 15, 1 S. 24. 22; 30. 15. Jos. 14. 9 אִם־לֹא הָאָרֶץ ... לְךָ תִהְיֶה לְנַחֲלָה *and Moses swore, saying, The land ... shall be an inheritance for you;* Job 1. 11 אִם לֹא יְבָרֲכֶךָ (I swear) *he will curse* (lit. bless) *you to your face.* 2 K. 9. 26. 1 K. 18. 15 חַי י' כִּי הַיּוֹם אֵרָאֶה אֵלָיו *as Y. lives, surely I will show myself* to him today; Is. 45. 23 בִּי נִשְׁבַּעְתִּי ... כִּי לִי תִכְרַע כָּל־בֶּרֶךְ *I have sworn by myself ... (that) to me every knee shall bow.* 1 S. 14. 44; 20. 3; 29. 6.

Rem. 1. Further exx. of אִם, Gen. 21. 23, Nu. 14. 23, 1 S. 3. 14, 17; 14. 45; 17. 55; 28. 10, 2 S. 11. 11; 14. 11, 2 K. 2. 2; 3. 14; 6. 31, Is. 22. 14, Ps. 89. 36; 132. 3, 4. Of אִם לֹא, Nu. 14. 28, 2 S. 19. 14, 1 K. 20. 23, Is. 5. 9; 14. 24, Jer. 15. 11. Of כִּי, Gen. 42. 16, 1 S. 14. 39 (repeated), 2 S. 3. 9 (repeated), 2 K. 5. 20, Jer. 22. 5. In many cases one can hardly speak of a formal oath, and the particles merely express strong denial or affirmation.

Rem. 2. It sometimes happens that כִּי אִם fall together. In 2 S. 3. 35 כִּי simply strengthens אִם which follows the clause *May Y. do so to me*, etc.; so in 1 S. 25. 34, where כִּי occurs twice, before subord. and main clause, but אִם carries the negative weight. In 1 S. 14. 39 כִּי first introduces the formula חַי י', then a subord. clause with אִם *if*, then an oath of affirmation, cf. Jer. 22. 24. Cf. in non-oath contexts כִּי אִם *for if* (Ex. 9. 2), *for though* (Is. 10. 22), (know) *that if* (Jer. 26. 15). All these cases should be distinguished from כִּי אִם as an antithetical or exclusive conjunction, *but, unless* (§§ 142d, 144d).

Rem. 3. The full formula כֹּה יַעֲשֶׂה־לִי אֱלֹהִים וְכֹה יוֹסִיף *so may may God* (or יהוה) *do to me and more also* (lit. so may he add) occurs only in Sam., Kgs., Ruth, followed properly by אִם or אִם לֹא, conventionally by כִּי, e.g. 1 S. 3. 17 (אִם); 14. 44 (כִּי), 2 S. 19. 14 (אִם לֹא), 1 K. 2. 23 (כִּי), 2 K. 6. 31 (אִם), Ru.

1. 17 (כִּי). Usually לִי or לְךָ or the speaker's own name (1 S. 20. 13, 2 S. 3. 9) is used; it may have dropped out in 1 S. 14. 44; 25. 22 and been restored by Sept., but cf. 1 K. 19. 2.

Exclamations

§ **157.** The particle הִנֵּה often has exclamatory force (§ 54), as have the interr. prons. מָה/מִי (§ 7) and the interr. adverbs, espec. אֵיךְ/אֵיכָה *how!* (§ 154, R. 3), and in general wishes and oaths.

Nouns in direct address (the vocative) are in effect exclamations, as אֲדֹנִי הַמֶּלֶךְ *O king!* אֲדֹנִי הַמֶּלֶךְ *my lord the king!* Cf. the particle of entreaty בִּי *excuse me*, always at the beginning of a speech with אֲדֹנִי or אֲדֹנִי, Gen. 44. 18. But many nouns and nomin. phrases may be uttered elliptically (without a verb) as exclamations, Gen. 43. 23, Jud. 6. 23 and often שָׁלוֹם לְךָ *peace* (be) *to you!* Gen. 44. 7 חָלִילָה לַעֲבָדֶיךָ מֵעֲשׂוֹת *far (be) it from* (lit. profanity to) *your servants that they should do!* With מִי added to the phrase, 1 S. 26. 11 *Y. forbid that I should put forth!* 1 K. 22. 36 *every man to his city!* 2 K. 4. 19 רֹאשִׁי רֹאשִׁי *my head!* 11. 14 *treason!* Is. 13. 4 and often קוֹל *voice, sound of, hark, listen!* 29. 16 הַפְכְּכֶם *you turn things upside down!* Jer. 4. 19 מֵעַי מֵעַי *my bowels!* 37. 14 שֶׁקֶר (it's) *a lie!* Hos. 8. 1 *to your lips the trumpet!* Very commonly אַשְׁרֵי (plur. constr.) *O the joys of, blessed is!* Ps. 1. 1, etc. So adverbs: לֹא *no!* טוֹב *good! well!* 2 S. 13. 12 אַל־אָחִי *don't, my brother!* Also imper. of some verbs, as הָבָה (lit. *permit*) *go to! come now!* (Gen. 38. 16, Ex. 1. 10) or לְךָ, לְכָה (even to a woman, Gen. 19. 32) *come!* See § 68.

More strictly exclamations are הַס *hush! silence!* Jud. 3. 19, Am. 6. 10, Hab. 2. 20, Zeph. 1. 7, Zech. 2. 17. — אוֹי *woe!* with prep. לְ, Is. 6. 5 אוֹי־לִי; 3. 9, 11, Jer. 4. 31. Without prep., Ez. 24. 6. Ps. 120. 5 אוֹיָה־לִּי. With the same meaning אַלְלַי לִי, Mic. 7. 1, Job 10. 15. — הוֹי *woe! alas!* in lament for the dead, 1 K. 13. 30 הוֹי אָחִי, cf. Jer. 22. 18; in the form הוֹ, Am. 5. 16. In a more general sense, Jer. 48. 1; 50. 27. Also in threatening remonstrance, Is. 1. 4 הוֹי גּוֹי חֹטֵא *ah! sinful nation*, and often in Is. — Other forms, Joel 1. 15 אֲהָהּ לַיּוֹם *alas! for the day.* Ez. 30. 2 הָהּ לַיּוֹם; 6. 11 אָח. — An exclamation of pleasure, הֶאָח, Is. 44. 16 *aha!;* by the horse in battle, Job 39. 25; of malicious pleasure, Ez. 25. 3; 26. 2, Ps. 35. 21; 40. 16; 70. 4.

Index of Passages Referred to

(References are to pages)

———◆———

Genesis

1
1............... 12, 116, 150
2 .... 37, 46, 167, 168
3.................56, 81, 167
4............................ 111
5..................... 99, 171
6 .... 105, 138, 148
7 141
9 105
11....................9, 150
14....................21, 94
16............................ 47
20.................113, 171
21 ....44, 113, 116, 135
24..................... 24, 29
26.........19, 105, 150
27 178
28 .... 105, 135
29 59
31...............44, 98, 141

2
1......................... 96
2 150
4 ....29, 128, 129, 178
4-6............................167
5............ 57, 73, 149, 181
6 ....73, 94, 173
7 ......114, 143, 144, 150, 167
8 ....9, 66, 143
9 17
10 136
11...............28, 55, 179
12 .... 53, 54, 168
13 .... 55, 179
14 .... 52, 55, 179
15 ....17, 32, 115, 131
16............................125
16-17................173, 182
17 .... 79, 81, 124, 128, 181
18 .... 39, 52, 128, 167
19 .... 4, 8, 37, 74, 79, 110, 147, 167
20...................167, 173
21 46
22 .... 19, 113, 150
23 .... 5, 6, 28, 51, 119
24..................93, 115
25 74

3
1....... 14, 45, 55, 65, 85, 98, 140, 141, 166, 175
2 79
3.................9, 79, 160

Genesis

3
3-4..................... 173
4 124
5.........31, 87, 128, 134, 136, 150, 174
6 ......30, 38, 170, 175
7 13
8....... 13, 19, 22, 56, 114
9 ....4, 185
10 12
11.....7, 62, 64, 110, 132
12 62
13 .... 3, 8, 11, 100
14 .....55, 62, 77, 144, 170, 178, 185
15 ...2, 77, 145, 172, 178
16 ....77, 125, 177
17 ....101, 118, 178
18 143
19 .....128, 130, 147, 149
20.............................29
21 32
22.... 46, 59, 63, 91, 93, 131, 160, 174
23 10
24 31

4
1...3, 97, 100, 148, 166, 168
2..............................40
3-4..................... 174
4 37
4-5.............65, 99
5 173
6 ....61, 62, 63
7 .... 150, 154, 183
8....... 4, 40, 130, 147, 157
9 ....136, 183, 185
9-12 179
10 .... 3, 7, 20, 30, 62, 136
11.............................115
12 .... 82, 87
13 .... 45, 132
14 ....14, 90, 134
15 ....51, 129, 132, 159, 180
17 138
18 117
19 12
20.................. 31, 179
21 179
22 2
23 3

Genesis

4
24..................... 51, 118
25 ....58, 149
26.........2, 72, 119, 120

5
..............................49
1 178
5 23
6 117
15 49
29 5
32 36

6
1 .... 97, 100, 120, 167
2..............................32
4 .... 6, 9, 37, 73, 94
5.........39, 53, 100, 142
6 .... 66, 98, 110
7 .... 9, 62, 110
8 .... 167, 173
9 .... 52, 178
12 .... 29, 98
13 148
14 .... 32, 94
15.....................5, 54, 56
17 .... 40, 178, 181
18 .... 147, 148
19 178
22 178

7
1 .... 2, 114, 116
2.................9, 42, 51, 52
3..............................37, 51
4 .... 50, 58, 137, 144
6 167
7 22
7-9 178
8..............................148
9 ....51, 116, 149
10 ....99, 171
11 .... 6, 36, 171
12 171
13...................13, 48
14 29
15...............................51
16 148
18 142
18-19 171
20....................65, 144
21-22 178
23 ....10, 38
24 144

8
3 126
5.................50, 126
7 .... 27, 125, 149
8..............................27

GENESIS

8   9 .... 4, 32, 158
   10 128
   11 .... 110, 150
   18-19 178
   19 65
   21 .... 13, 120
   22 .... 21, 58
9   2 178
   3 9
   4 176
   5 .... 14, 178
   6 .... 119, 150, 157
   9 181
   9-16 90
   10 .... 31, 44, 134
   11 119
   12 148
   13 .... 61, 102, 178
   14 .... 87, 90, 115
   16 86
   17 5
   19 48
   20 .... 26, 121
   23 .... 22, 27
   24 .... 10, 45, 116
   25 .... 46, 55, 178
   26 82
10   1 178
   8 121
   9 46
   19 .... 14, 149
   20 178
   21 .... 2, 45
   25 12
   30 14
11   1 .... 42, 47, 100
   3 .... 14, 28, 82, 179
   4 .... 82, 105, 167, 179
   6 .... 46, 59
   7 .... 82, 160, 179
   8 .... 120, 128
   9 13
   10 .... 49, 178
   13-25 49
   24 49
   28 40
   29 .... 12, 35, 55
   30 .... 57, 178
   31 .... 34, 40, 149
12   1 .... 9, 150
   2 .... 82, 106, 114, 118
   3 .... 82, 94, 171
   4 49
   5 .... 40, 144
   6 150
   7 135
   8 .... 110, 148
   9 126
   10 97
   11 .... 33, 98
   11-14 99
   12 .... 77, 111

GENESIS

12   13 .... 4, 93, 111, 119, 159
   14 .... 45, 98
   15 118
   17 115
   18 .... 62, 110, 184
   19 .... 5, 59, 91, 110, 111
13   1 .... 22, 148
   2 .... 28, 53, 168, 174
   3 .... 9, 148
   5 .... 135, 174
   6 128
   7 28
   8 82
   9 183
   10 .... 14, 42, 129, 131,
         144, 157
   11 14
   12 .... 65, 172
   13 142
   14 .... 157, 179
   15 .... 117, 181, 182
   16 .... 14, 79, 153
14   2 12
   3 12
   4 144
   6 40
   9 .... 48, 119
   10 .... 36, 42, 167, 171
   12 168
   13 .... 35, 168
   15 144
   16 171
   17 .... 12, 128, 129, 157
   18 53
   19 .... 29, 37, 54
   21 171
   22 .... 35, 61
   24 38
15   1 .... 98, 147, 177
   2 .... 7, 56, 98, 168
   3 .... 59, 137
   4 181
   6 .... 103, 114
   7 9
   8 .... 7, 32, 185
   10 14
   12 .... 21, 59, 99, 131, 167
   13 .... 11, 144, 179
   14 .... 77, 136
   15 .... 78, 150, 178
   17 .... 21, 167
   18 .... 6, 40, 61
   21 28
16   1 .... 21, 167
   2 .... 79, 132
   3 .... 36, 40, 130, 141
   5 .... 2, 3, 32, 148, 149
   7 31
   8 .... 76, 137, 185
   9 80
   10 124
   12 .... 32, 178

GENESIS

16   13 .... 133, 184
   14 13
   16 .... 128, 167
17   4 .... 91, 181, 182
   5 .... 91, 114, 118, 173
   10 .... 127, 178
   11 117
   12 47
   14 .... 117, 178, 182
   15 .... 174, 182
   17 184
   18 .... 79, 186
   19 137
   20 .... 59, 93, 102, 150
   21 173
   24 117
   25 .... 117, 145
   46 58
18   1 .... 143, 168
   2 .... 31, 59, 149
   3 81
   4 .... 32, 118
   5 161
   6 41
   7 .... 5, 26, 27, 28, 110
   8 .... 26, 66, 168
   9 .... 59, 185
   10 .... 124, 143
   11 .... 21, 178
   12 .... 67, 131, 167, 183
   13 .... 2, 63, 141, 142,
         168, 184
   14 .... 14, 45
   15 .... 62, 141, 174
   17 .... 136, 183
   18 92
   19 .... 111, 159
   20 .... 141, 170
   21 .... 3, 29, 82
   22 .... 4, 58, 137, 180
   24 .... 49, 57, 110, 149,
         175, 184
   24-25 179
   25 .... 79, 131, 183
   26 .... 49, 63, 86
   27 .... 1, 168
   28 .... 49, 50, 113, 150,
         153
   29 .... 48, 58, 79, 128
   30 .... 82, 106
   32 .... 39, 142
   33 .... 66, 167
19   1 168
   2 94
   4 .... 73, 149, 167
   5 185
   7 140
   8 .... 38, 47, 150, 176
   9 45
   10 24
   11 28
   13 .... 63, 136

GENESIS

19 14 134
    15 .... 97, 137, 157
    16 ....47, 129
    17 ....116, 149, 160
    19 .... 36, 93, 131, 160
    20 106
    21 132
    22 120
    23 ....167, 169
    25 ....31, 134
    27 ....10, 147
    28 66
    29 ....129, 130
    32 ....179, 188
    33 6
    34 .... 59, 99, 148
    37 149
20 2 ....III, 147
    3 ....58, 134, 137, 168
    4 65
    5 ....4, 183
    6 132
    7 ......57, 105, 136, 148
    9 ....43, 68, 79
    10 160
    11 ....39, 57, 88, 176
    12 ....38, 141, 142
    13 ..... 5, 10, 23, 43, III,
    ....150, 178
    14 36
    16 50
    17 18
21 1 .... 110, 171
    2 9
    3 29
    5 .... 117, 128
    7 68
    8 .... 43, 63
    9 114
    10 40
    13 182
    14 ....32, 65, 178
    16 126
    17 ....8, 10
    20 40
    22 99
    23 187
    24 2
    25 103
    26 ....8, 39, 110
    29 44
    30 116
    31 13
    32 22
    34 144
22 1 ....58, 99, 167, 168
    2 ....46, 63
    5 ....82, 150, 171
    6 27
    7 185
    12 .... 14, 54, 62, 107,
   134

GENESIS

22 13 ....135, 140
    14 161
    16 ....61, 87, 158
    17 ....125, 170
    18 159
    23 ....48, 178
    24 97
23 1 ....30, 49
    6 ....26, 46
    10 ....31, 134
    11 ....61, 178
    13 ....61, 186
    15 8
    18 134
    20 96
24 98
    1 .... 63, 98
    2 98
    3 .... 9, 35
    4 40
    5 ....10, 79, 98, 124, 141
    6 160
    8 .... 6, 82, 154, 176
    9 ....5, 98
    10 .... 34, 98, 168
    11 ....29, 128
    12 40
    13 ....58, 136, 137
    14 .... 3, 93, 116, 159
    15 ....98, 120, 167, 169,
   181
    15-16 100
    16 ....33, 98, 144
    17 98
    18 120
    19 ....67, 120, 158
    20 .... 27, 58
    21 .... 136, 167
    22 .... 32, 50, 98, 120,
   157
    23 .... 7, 143, 183
    25 ....37, 148
    27 ....144, 180, 182
    29 ....98, 167
    30 .... 30, 59, 98, 128,
    .... 130, 136, 149, 157
    31 ....134, 168
    33 .... 80, 158
    34 26
    35 36
    36 157
    37 136
    39 141
    42 .... 57, 137, 153, 186
    44 ....38, 174
    45 .... 13, 73, 98, 181
    49 ....39, 137, 154, 163
    50 .... 22, 39
    52 ....98, 99
    54 22
    55 ....14, 22, 140
    56 168

GENESIS

24 57 82
    58 ....183, 184
    59 40
    60 ....2, 49
    62 ....98, 167, 168
    63 .... 16, 98
    64 27
    65 ....1, 7, 26, 27
    67 ....26, 158
25 1 120
    5-6 171
    6 .... 36, 58
    7 49
    8 56
    11 148
    18 178
    22 184
    25 56
    26 ....130, 167, 168
    28 ....133, 171
    32 ....137, 184
26 2 81
    5 159
    7 ....33, III, 160
    8 ....27, 99
    9 ....160, 176, 185
    10 ....69, 88
    11 ....133, 135
    12 51
    13 ....125, 158
    15 ....3, 65
    16 .... 45, 63
    18 101
    20 14
    21 38
    22 .... 62, 88
    27 ....63, 168
    28 .... 63, 82
    29 ....39, 52, 109
27 1 ....59, 97, 99, 101
    2 ....61, 63
    2-3 140
    3 ....91, 102, 144, 175
    4 ..63, 72, 106, 131, 160
    6 ....91, 114
    8 ....91, 133
    9 ....63, 113, 144
    10 160
    11 .... 58, 172
    12 93
    13 ....5, 110, 185
    14 ....5, 110
    15 35
    20 8
    21 .... 6, 106, 184
    22 52
    24 183
    25 159
    29 .... 23, 134
    30 ....124, 167
    32 54
    33 ....38, 45, 73, 135,

GENESIS

27 33 .... 137, 185
34 .... 2, 38, 115
36 .... 6, 51, 178
39 148
40 .... 87, 90, 170
41 32
42 118
44 .... 14, 144, 158
45 ...... 79, 94, 113, 131,
.... 144, 158, 184
46 154

28 3 .... 9, 94
5 35
6 102
11 .... 28, 66, 98, 143
12 .... 23, 168
13 .... 180, 182
13-15 78
15 .... 67, 158
16 .... 57, 110, 141
17 .... 7, 39, 52, 170, 176
20 .... 92, 136, 154
22 182

29 2 .... 13, 73, 94
3 .... 90, 94
4 185
6 184
7 .... 58, 128
8 .... 77, 93, 158
9 ... 36, 167, 168, 169
11 59
12 .... 26, 53
13 .... 33, 99
14 .... 41, 141, 176
16 45
17 ... 33, 43, 53, 168, 172
19 .... 45, 128, 174
20 .... 14, 47, 116
21 63
26 .... 74, 131
27 .... 5, 38, 118, 119, 175
30 .... 45, 175
31 .... 53, 173
33 .... 5, 111
34 47

30 1 154
8 46
13 68
14 .... 14, 148, 149
15 128
16 6
18 158
20 .... 2, 47, 112
25 .... 106, 150, 151
27 111
28 .... 106, 156
30 .... 91, 158, 185
31 .... 120, 154
32 126
33 .... 31, 182
34 .... 81, 184
35 44

GENESIS

30 36 167
37 .... 44, 126
38 22
41 128
41-42 90

31 1 10
2 57
3 91
4 44
5 .... 111, 173
7 103
8 .... 23, 94, 154
9 3
12 182
13 .... 10, 26
14 22
15 ... 56, 118, 119, 124
16 .... 150, 182
18 30
19 65
20 159
24 .... 132, 160
26 96
29 .... 73, 132, 173
30 124
31 160
33 65
34 ...... 43, 65, 98, 100,
.... 101, 167
36 .... 7, 68, 177
38 6
39 178
40 182
41 6
42 .... 141, 155
43 .... 52, 136, 170
44 .... 37, 94
47 171
49 148
50 .... 149, 154

32 5 101
6 102
7 136
9 .... 46, 154
10 63
12 ..... 93, 133, 137, 149,
.... 160
13 79
15 47
16 .... 3, 16, 47, 49
17 42
18 .... 7, 154
19 175
20 37
21 38
23 .... 6, 48
24 10
27 176
28 .... 7, 8
29 .... 141, 148, 174
30 76
31 .... 29, 97

GENESIS

32 32 168

33 3 .... 2, 51
5 7
8 8
9 .... 57, 81
10 130
13 .... 136, 156
14 82
16 6
17 13
19 50

34 5 103
7 131
8 .... 180, 182
15 39
15-17 153
16 171
19 63
21 53
23 176
24 .... 22, 134
25 149
31 150

35 1 .... 100, 131
3 .... 33, 102, 135, 137
6 22
7 .... 23, 43
10 174
12 147
13 10
15 10
17 27
26 178

36 1 179
6 30
7 45
8 1
14 96
31 157

37 2 .. 44, 97, 138, 167, 168
4 .... 45, 130
6 62
7 .... 22, 133, 137
8 .... 124, 184
9 48
10 124
11 171
13 .... 55, 184
14 112
15 .... 59, 136, 137
16 .... 133, 137, 185
18 .... 4, 73
19 33
20 .... 8, 91
21 145
22 .... 81, 130, 159, 171
23 112
24 57
25 168
26 .... 8, 93
27 82
29 57

GENESIS

37	30	180, 185
	33	125
	35	56, 120
	36	167
38	5	116
	9	132, 154
	11	56, 143, 158, 160
	12	22
	16	188
	17	2
	18	5, 110
	19	108, 109
	21	185
	23	160
	24	137
	25	9, 135
	28	13, 27
	29	138
39	1	65, 144, 167
	4	11, 171
	5	11, 15, 157
	6	33
	8	168
	9	52, 57, 93, 159, 185
	11	57, 168
	12	144
	13	101
	18	102, 128, 129, 130, 131, 157
	19	14, 129
	20	12
	21	3
	22	13, 138
	23	136, 159
40	1	22, 30, 35, 99
	3	12
	4	4, 14, 115
	5	35
	6	137
	7	144
	8	57, 115, 133, 136
	9	59
	12	5, 32, 47
	13	9, 58, 77
	14	69
	15	68, 125, 160
	16	2, 38, 175
	17	133
	18	47
	21-22	65, 171
	23	96, 173
41	1	41, 136, 137
	1-3	137
	2-6	33
	3	59, 148
	5	51
	6	31, 134
	7	43, 137
	8	35, 57, 99, 136
	9	133
	9-10	66
	10	4

41	11	102
	12	14, 35, 178
	13	116, 161, 178
	14	13
	15	136, 149, 173
	19	150
	24	136
	25	55, 137
	26	44
	26-36	78
	28	137
	31	45
	33	81, 149
	34	80
	35	6
	38	14
	39	158
	40	39, 45, 145, 170
	42	26, 112
	43	18, 36, 116
	44	39
	48	178
	49	158
	50	47, 73
	51-52	171
	54	171
	56	167
	57	22
42	1	57
	2	106
	4	160, 173
	7	13, 17, 76, 185
	8	2
	9	54, 178
	10	66, 173
	11	1, 52, 53, 55, 63, 180, 182
	13	45, 48, 57, 172
	14	133
	15	5, 176, 186, 187
	16	167, 187
	18	5, 80, 105, 156
	19	2, 44, 153
	20	107
	21	141
	23	2, 136
	25	14, 111, 113, 150
	28	147
	29	133
	30	66
	31	63, 178
	32	172
	33	44, 172
	34	54
	35	14, 20, 167
	36	3, 170, 178
	37	153, 154
	38	144, 156
43	1	167
	3	124, 176
	4	57, 136, 137, 153
	5	136, 153

43	6	131
	7	57, 58, 79, 111, 124, 183
	8	22, 37
	9	2, 153, 154, 177
	10	6, 51, 141, 155
	11	178
	12	51, 52, 135
	14	44
	15	51, 171
	16	10
	17	144
	18	135, 137
	23	188
	25	77, 149
	27	183
	29	4, 45, 183
	33	147
	34	51
44	1	10, 116, 171
	3	169
	4	65, 109, 134, 147, 149, 156, 158
	5	74, 183
	7	14, 76, 188
	8	39, 79, 185
	9	79, 174
	10	172
	11	120
	12	65, 178
	14	22, 34, 58, 168
	15	8, 14, 79
	16	37
	17	172, 182
	18	105, 188
	18-34	78
	19	39, 66, 183
	22	156
	24	157
	26	57, 153, 168
	27	2
	28	124, 176
	29	156
	30	91, 167, 168
	30-31	87
	31	90
	33	82, 105, 171
	34	79, 185
45	1	13, 14, 140, 157
	3	183
	4	9, 62
	6	6, 9, 39
	8	2, 91, 141
	9	81, 178
	11	41
	14	171
	16	143, 167
	18	46, 106
	19	94
	20	81, 182
	22	50
	23	47

GENESIS

45 25.....144
    28.....72
46 3-4.....77
    4.....124, 125
    26.....39, 134
    27.....29
    31.....62
    32.....63
    33.....154
    34.....63
47 1.....66
    2.....47
    3.....19, 37, 54
    4.....36
    5-6.....179
    6.....111
    8.....185
    9.....178
    12.....113
    13.....52, 57
    15.....79
    19.....37
    21.....91, 182
    22.....38, 176
    24.....23, 171
    26.....3
    30.....2
    31.....27
48 1.....13
    4.....137
    5.....14
    6.....67
    7.....149, 179, 182
    8-9.....54
    9.....62
    10.....21, 148, 167, 178
    13.....40, 175
    14.....65
    15.....4, 58, 135
    16.....135
    19.....45
49 116
    4.....20, 72
    6.....19
    8.....181
    9.....12, 52, 55
    10.....158
    11.....24, 170
    15.....44, 111, 116
    17.....73, 101
    18.....63
    20.....53
    22.....23
    27.....76
    29.....137
    31.....13
50 3.....74
    5.....82
    10.....115
    14.....22
    15.....79
    20.....178

GENESIS

50 22.....22

EXODUS

1 5.....134
   7.....113, 118
   9.....59, 91
   10.....93, 188
   12.....161
   14.....117, 177
   16.....3, 94, 153
   17.....32, 173
   18.....96
   19.....72, 87
   20.....22
   21.....3
   22.....172
2 2.....111
   3.....58, 128
   4.....8, 79, 129
   5.....168
   6..5, 42, 54, 59, 98, 181
   7.....92, 106
   9.....3
   10.....148
   12.....36, 57
   13.....76
   14.....129
   15.....27
   20.....4, 185
3 1.....138, 167
   2.....136
   3.....76, 82
   6.....35, 52
   7.....171
   8.....31, 33
   9-10.....91
   10.....106
   11.....7, 79, 160
   13.....113
   14.....3, 79, 141
   15.....58
   16.....35
4 1.....77
   5.....35, 79, 110, 159
   9.....144, 153, 182
   10.....33, 55, 157, 174
   11.....177
   12.....92
   13.....11
   14.....156
   15.....78
   16.....172
   17.....9
   18.....58
   19.....96
   22.....52
   23.....59, 91
   26.....72
   31.....22
5 1.....22
   2.....7, 150

EXODUS

5 3.....29, 39, 160
   7.....13, 94
   10.....4, 57, 136
   11.....10
   14.....62
   16.....136
   18.....173
   19.....13
   21.....82
   22.....184
   23.....157
6 1.....77
   2.....1
   3.....150
   5.....9
   6.....88
   7.....52
   10.....146
   11.....179
   12.....33, 59
   28.....12
   30.....59
7 5.....94
   7.....167
   9.....107
   11.....42, 175
   12.....172
   14.....63
   17.....91, 94
   18.....78
   20.....22, 110
   27.....94, 153
   28.....94
8 5.....142
   10.....42
   12.....107
   17.....94, 117, 153, 154
   20.....74
   22.....154
   24.....120, 124, 148
   25.....81, 110, 132, 176
   27.....178
9 1.....105
   2.....137, 187
   6.....173
   8.....41, 105
   13.....105
   15.....101, 156
   16.....174
   17.....137
   19.....181
   23.....99, 171
   24.....136, 157
   27.....55, 170, 178
   29.....170
   32.....20
10 1.....6
   4.....154
   5.....13
   7.....185
   8.....7, 36

EXODUS

10	10.........161
	11.........3
	13.........99
	23.........173
	24.........81
	26.........8, 178
	27.........120
11	5.........135, 147
	7.........110
	8.........6
	10.........167
12	1.........100
	4.........148, 178
	8.........149, 178
	10.........173
	11.........134, 141, 179
	12.........171
	14.........178
	15.........39, 44, 142
	16.........38, 119, 176, 182
	18.........51
	29.........99
	32.........142
	34.........72, 73
	35.........167
	37.........39
	39.........114
	48.........127
	49.........21
13	3.........6, 127
	7.........117
	8.........7
	9.........148
	13.........154, 172
	15.........75
14	3.........177
	6.........171
	10.........167
	12.........55, 106, 128, 148, 183
	13.........31, 94
	14.........172
	15.........7, 107
	16.........107, 172
	17.........172
	18.........167
	20.........6
	22.........53
	25.........136
	27.........44, 168
	29.........168
15	116
	1.........72
	3.........11, 55
	4.........22, 46
	4-10.........71, 180
	5.........71
	6.........53
	9.........113
	10.........71
	11.........7
	13.........7

EXODUS

15	15.........72
	16.........45
	17.........104
	20.........23
	23.........13
	24.........149
	26.........171
	27.........48, 49, 168
16	1.........50
	3.........186
	4.........125
	5.........51
	6.........85, 87
	8.........178, 185
	12.........172
	13.........172
	15.........14
	16.........145
	18.........171
	19.........14
	21.........156
	22.........50, 51
	27.........99
	31.........170
	33.........25, 41
17	1.........128
	2.........179
	4.........87
	5.........14
	6.........94
	7.........183, 184
	9.........168
	10.........144
	11.........23, 94
	12.........14, 43, 51, 53
	14.........27
18	3.........12
	4.........150
	5.........137
	9.........113
	14.........137, 168
	15-16.........75
	16.........94
	18.........45, 177
	19.........2
	20.........11
	22.........2
19	4.........96
	5.........92
	6.........178
	12.........157, 178
	13.........39
	14.........148
	19.........126
	24.........173
20	2-14.........179
	3.........81
	5.........134
	6.........134
	8.........127
	8-10.........178
	9.........93

EXODUS

20	10.........44, 149, 173
	12.........80
	18.........171
	19.........2
	20.........148
	21.........10
	24.........32, 93
	25.........144, 154, 156
	26.........160
21	155
	2.........154
	2-5.........155
	4.........172, 177
	5.........124, 154, 155
	6.........154
	7.........154
	7-11.........155
	11.........48, 154
	12.........95, 125, 135, 157
	13.........10
	15.........135
	16.........95, 157
	18.........39
	20.........27, 125, 154
	22.........154
	23.........149
	25.........174
	26.........154
	28.........116, 124, 154, 167
	29.........19
	31.........39
	32.........39, 49
	33.........177
	35.........171
	36.........74, 154, 177
	37.........39
22	1.........153
	2.........153, 154
	3.........51, 56, 124, 125, 155
	4.........154, 155
	5.........115, 155
	6.........51, 154, 155
	8.........23, 51
	9.........154, 155
	11.........124, 155
	12.........124, 155
	13.........155
	16.........124, 155
	19.........39
	22.........124, 155
	24-26.........90
	26.........177
23	4.........124
	5.........132
	8.........74, 104, 170
	9.........158
	12.........93
	15.........178
	17.........51
	30.........42, 158
24	2.........173
	4.........48, 50

Exodus

24	5	40
	6	171
	7	33
	8	59
	10	13
	14	8
	17	168
	18	149
25	7	32
	12	47
	18	144
	20	168
	21	171
	28	144
26		89
	3	14
	5	14
	19	50
	26	48
	33	32, 46
27	7	130
	12	54
	15	49
	16	41
	17	53
	21	29
28	3	23
	17	41
29	29	33, 128
	40	41
30	12	130
	25	114
	33	182
	38	182
31	14	23
32	1	6
	8	126
	9	33
	11	184
	13	13, 117
	26	8
	27	14
	28	49
	29	132
	30	83, 106
	32	186
	33	8
	34	10, 59, 87
33	7	90
	7-11	89
	7-8	89
	8	90
	9	89, 90
	10	86, 143, 156
	11	74
	14	13
	15	137, 154
	16	185
	20	107
34	2	150
	3	174
	5	110

Exodus

34	6	55
	7	124
	13	170
	14	52
	15	160
	20	150
	28	33
	29	168
	33	132
35	5	42, 181
36	24	50
	30	51
	35	178
38	3	144
	24	49
	27	129
39	10	41
	14	34
	17	40
40	34	171
	37	154

Leviticus

1	2	183
2	1	183
	6	52
	13	178
3	12	52
4	2	14, 155, 183
	7	171
	21	26, 53
	22	154
	23	154
5	1	154, 155, 168, 183
	1-4	177
	2	39
	4	150, 155, 183
	9	171
	15	155, 183
	21	183
	24	10
6	3	4, 41
	4	108
	7	127
	13	41
7	20	182
	21	155
	27	182
10	3	3
	10	132
12	2	155, 183
	4	49
	5	49
13	2	46, 155
	9	23
	12	29
	29	183
	38	183
	40	183
	42	155
	45	138, 182

Leviticus

13	46	12
	53	153
	56	153
	57	42
14	34	26
	46	12
15	2	53
	18	183
	20	53
	24	104
16	4	52
17	3-4	182
	5	159
	8	183
	10	183
	13	183
	14	23
18	15	4
	18	147
19	6	44
	8	23
	16	145
	27	150
	36	32
20	14	116
	18	94
21	7	119
	10	118
	23	176
22	3	183
	6	176
	18	183
	27	44
23	32	50
24	16	150
	22	46
	23	145
25	10	51
	11	51
	14	127
	22	117
	33	23
	44	182
	48	157
26	6	168
	21	51, 145
	23	145
	24	51, 145
	26	87
	35	91
	36	115, 182
	39	38
	42	41
	43	104
27	23	26
	24	10

Numbers

1	2	20
	4	52
	48	96

Numbers

1   49 176
2   17 54
3   1 12
   26 117
   39 49
   43 49
   46 48
   47 36
4   2 127
5   10 117
   18 44
   19 ...... 149, 154
   20 154
   27 ...... 91, 101, 154
   30 177
6   9 13
   23 126
   24-26 179
   25 82
7   88 49
8   26 141
9   6 21
   10 155
   13 ...... 9, 58
   14 37
   15 130
   18 ...... 12, 73
   20 41
10   2 128
   4 51
   7 130
   25 138
   30 174
   33 33
11   2 175
   4 ...... 175, 186
   5 73
   8 177
   9 73
   10 114
   12 ...... 28, 184
   13 185
   15 125
   16 52
   20 ...... 41, 158
   25 44
   27 137
   29 ...... 136, 186
   32 125
   35 73
12   1 22
   2 39
   4 48
   8 29
   13 118
   14 156
13   2 51
   19 52
   27 10
   28 ...... 43, 176
14   1 3
   2 ...... 69, 186

14   3 168
   7 ...... 45, 53
   9 176
   11 ...... 150, 185
   15 156
   16 ...... 97, 132
   18 55
   20 61
   21 ...... 118, 174, 186
   22 51
   23 187
   24 ...... 10, 88, 159
   28 ...... 77, 186, 187
   31 ...... 77, 88, 91, 182
   32 ...... 2, 77
   35 22
   36 101
   36-37 97
   37 44
   40 ...... 59, 88
   42 ...... 57, 107
15   4 41
   24 154
   35 127
   40 93
16   3 54
   5 87
   7 1
   9 46
   11 ...... 160, 182
   13 ...... 124, 125
   15 ...... 46, 116
   29 119
   34 160
   35 48
17   3 182
   5 160
   14 49
   17 14
   20 182
   27 59
18   3 37
   23 2
19   18 63
20   3 186
   4 184
   8 22
   10 22
   11 22
   12 158
   17 77
   26 112
   28 112
21   2 ...... 154, 155
   5 57
   7 ...... 22, 107
   8 ...... 95, 135, 157, 181
   9 ...... 116, 154
   17 72
   22 82
   26 101
22   2 66

22   11 ...... 91, 93, 97
   13 ...... 63, 129
   18 ...... 17, 41
   19 82
   20 ...... 154, 182
   27 27
   28 6
   29 155
   30 ...... 4, 9, 124
   32 184
   33 155
   34 62
   35 182
   37 124
   38 124
23   2 149
   3 ...... 7, 8
   4 47
   8 11
   9 59
   10 68
   11 124
   13 159
   19 ...... 3, 32, 39, 106, 160
   20 156
   23 68
   24 59
   25 174
   26 183
   27 79
24   1 42
   5 63
   6 11
   9 23
   13 17
   17 ...... 68, 102, 140
   20 46
   23 129
25   3 34
   4 107
   14 35
26   22 49
   35 39
   53 150
   59 13
27   7 3
   8 155
   9 57
   16 36
29   6 34
   14 49
   15 49
   26 47
30   2 ...... 5, 36
   3 ...... 127, 155
   4 155
31   13 22
   32 49
   38 49
32   14 145
   15 118
   17 158

NUMBERS

32	23	III, 153
	33	181
33	38	51
34	2	40
	18	51
35	2	III
	6	49, 50
	7	117
	16-23	177
	19	87
	22	14
	23	138

DEUTERONOMY

1	1	148
	2	50
	3	50
	4	135
	6	66
	10	58, 150
	11	51
	14	52
	16	94, 127
	19	6, 109
	22	9
	23	49
	27	129, 130
	31	74, 110
	36	39, 158
	37-38	182
	38-39	181
	41	33
	42	107
	44	28, 74
2	7	14, 113
	11	73, 74, 173
	12	100
	20	38, 73, 74
	24	120
	25	93, 128
	27	42
	28	170, 176
	30	103, 120, 131, 170
	34	116
3	3	175
	6-7	171
	9	172
	11	47, 184
	12-13	172
	18	56
	20	158, 175
	23	120
	28	2, 116, 117
	29	112
4	1	93, 137, 159
	3-4	181
	5	112, 116
	6	3, 52
	7	8
	10	159
	12	136, 137, 173

DEUTERONOMY

4	13	47
	16	93
	19	93
	20	173
	21	52, 130, 132, 167, 172
	22	94, 136, 137, 174
	23	160
	24	53, 135
	26	61, 77
	27	56
	30	132
	32	150
	33	101
	34	120, 135
	35	1
	37	13, 23, 159
	37-49	87
	39	58, 142
	40	79, 159
	41	72
	42	129, 138
	47	29
5	2-5	179
	3	2, 174
	7-18	79
	12	127
	13	47, 79
	14	39, 44
	19	115
	22	136, 153
	23	43
	26	186
	28	107
	29	6
6	2	159
	3	159
	4	47, 55
	4-15	90
	4-5	88
	4-9	89
	10	90
	11	133
	13	55, 170
	15	93
	18	93
	22-23	171
7	3	23, 174
	5	29, 78, 174, 178
	6	178
	7	45
	8	129, 132
	9	50, 150
	10	78
	17	13
	20	78
	21	78
	23	115
	24	116
	25	26, 78
	26	107, 124
8	2	6

DEUTERONOMY

8	3	112
	5	134, 148
	8	35
	11	132
	13	21
	16	134
	19	147, 155
9	1	43
	2	7
	6	33
	7	81, 110, 138, 178
	11	99
	13	33, 59
	15	168
	16	178
	18	131
	21	126
	22	138
	24	138
	25	117
	28	130
10	4	47
	6	167
	9	52
	10	120, 128
	15	129, 176
	15-16	88
	16	171
	17	19, 46, 52, 74
	31	170
11	10	94
	12	29
	14	153
	18	6
	22	130
	23	45
12	1	5
	2	124
	8	137
	11	46
	16	38
	18	36
	20	82
	22	118
	29	77
	30	150
	31	175
	33	148
13	1-3	154
	2	39
	3	82
	6	134
	7	9
	10	124
	11	134, 145
	13	154
	17	58
14	5	36
	21	127
	22	42
	27	182
15	2	127

DEUTERONOMY

15 4 176
    9 51
    16 154
    17 .... 27, 38, 175
    20 42
16 4 .... 47, 148, 150
    8 47
    9 47
    13 47
    15 39
    16 47
    18 115
    19 .... 74, 104
    20 42
    21 .... 14, 40
17 2 154
    3 154
    5 20
    6 47
    8 45
    9 6
    12 132
    14 82
    14-20 90
    15 9
    17 107
    18 90
    20 107
18 3 39
    10 36
    11 36
    13 148
    14 181
    17-20 89
    19-20 .... 180, 181
    20 176
    21 185
19 2 47
    4 .... 52, 138
    6 145
    8-9 86
    9 48
    10 .... 93, 107
    11 145
    13 44
    16 154
    21 150
20 2 87
    4 130
    5 .... 8, 82
    10 149
    11 153
    16 176
    18 160
21 1 .... 8, 56
    3 45
    7 23
    8 40
    10 23
    11 36
    12 .... 5, 110
    13 .... 41, 109

DEUTERONOMY

21 14 ....124, 149, 150
22 2.......................55, 116
    3 156
    5 108
    8 13
    17 27
    19 26
    20........................ 154
    21 154
    22 56
    23 40
    26........................ 14
    27 .... 57, 136
23 5 .... 130, 159
    8 53
    15 93
24 4 157
    7 56
25 7 63
    8 63
    13 .... 37, 42
    14 42
    15 33
    16 5
26 3 61
    5 34
    15 40
    16 136
    19 130
27 6 144
    25 44
28 73
    3 54
    8 73
    14 14
    15 114
    21 .... 29, 73
    22 29
    27 161
    29 .... 74, 138
    36 73
    43 42
    47 159
    48 44
    49 9
    51 161
    61 138
    67 186
29 14 137
    24 159
30 3 10
    15 .... 6, 61
    18 61
    19 61
31 6 81
    7 .... 112, 116
    10 47
    17 .... 6, 91, 159, 183
    20 92
    21 72
    26 .... 94, 127
32 116

DEUTERONOMY

32 4 .... 52, 53
    6 138
    7 37
    8 .... 18, 71
    8-20 71
    11 76
    13 100
    15 10
    17 11
    18 71
    19 35
    21 142
    24 134
    27 160
    29 155
    30 48
    35 .... 12, 21
    36 142
    37 .... 11, 185
    39 148
    40 186
    41 .... 104, 153
    46 159
33 116
    3 175
    6 107
    9 116
    11 .... 134, 145
    16 83
    22 55
    28 175
34 4 5

JOSHUA

1 3 182
    4 143
    9 184
    11.......................... 47
    13 .... 94, 127
    14 .... 20, 56
    15 143
    16 10
2 4 .... 23, 184, 185
    5 .... 131, 133
    8 .... 73, 169
    10 111
    14 .... 6, 87
    15 .... 27, 148
    17 6
    22 158
    23 17
    24 111
3 1 73
    4 .... 44, 176
    5 17
    7 6
    12 .... 42, 51
    16 126
    17 126
4 4 48
    8.......................... 48

JOSHUA

4	20	50
	21	154
5	2	120
	6	132
	8	149
	9	96
	13	163, 184
6	1	136
	3	47, 51, 126
	4	47
	5	149
	8	47
	9	125
	11	126
	13	125
	19	144
	23	47
	24	144
7	1	115
	3	47
	7	101, 120, 186
	8	158
	20	14
	21	26, 49
	25	144, 145
8	5	154
	6	138
	12	47
	22	6
	29	27
	30	72, 102
	31	102
	33	26
9	2	145
	7	185
	8	76
	9	115
	11	4
	12	6
	13	6, 142
	16	157
	24	150
10	1	101
	12	72, 102
	13	3
	16	47
	24	29
	27	99
	33	72
11	3	182
	6	114
	13	176
	20	159
12	1	143
	24	49
14	6	2
	9	187
	10	6, 91, 157
	11	129
15	3	75
	14	47
	19	112

JOSHUA

15	21	145
	41	49
16	8	75
17	11	117
	13	157
	14	168
	15	153
19	30	49
	51	36
21		47
	39	49
22	1	72, 102
	3	103
	17	117
	18	156
	20	115
	21	111
	27	148
	31	72, 115
	32	22
23	1	148
	4	143
24	2	35, 148
	14	44
	15	8
	19	19

JUDGES

1	4	116
	7	19, 35, 49, 138, 161
	9	35
	12	93, 156
	14	8, 99
	15	87
	19	132, 134
	22	22
	24	31, 135
	26	144
	28	124
2	1	71
	2	8
	10	22
	18	154
	19	45
	20	158
	21	97
	22	131, 159
	23	132
3	1	131, 159
	2	112, 159
	3	47
	10	149
	12	159
	14	49
	15	33
	16	13, 47, 168
	17	45
	19	27, 188
	20	27, 149, 167, 168
	24	169, 176
	25	27, 57, 136

JUDGES

3	29	47
	30	96
	31	27
4	1	168
	3	65, 167
	4	25, 182
	6	47
	8	86, 153
	9	3, 176
	11	101, 148
	13	47
	14	5, 9
	16	183
	18	27
	19	27
	20	90, 154, 183
	21	27
	22	112, 137
	24	125, 158
5		116
	1	22
	3	2
	5	6
	6	134
	8	74, 183
	10	34
	11	31, 72
	15	161
	19	72
	21	145
	22	36, 42
	23	125
	25	110
	27	10, 29
	28	148
	29	38, 44
	31	141
6	2	90
	2-3	90
	3	90, 154
	4	39, 73, 90
	5	73
	8	25
	11	26, 168
	12	27
	13	156
	14	6, 184
	15	45
	16	92, 111
	18	2, 94, 131
	19	32, 167
	20	26
	22	26
	23	188
	24	26
	25	36
	28	135
	30	106
	31	153, 156
	33	167
	36	57, 137, 153
	38	27

JUDGES

7 2 45
3.......................8, 49
5....................28, 74
7 ....14, 49
8 ....14, 165
10 ....2, 137
11............................2
12 12
13 ....32, 103
19 ....124, 126, 176
22 ....49, 50
25 171
8 1....................8, 11
2............8, 37, 44
3.........................72
6...................68, 79
8 132
11.......................168
18 ....14, 26
19 ....155, 186
20.........................58
21 ....2, 22
23 2
25 27
28 96
30 ....49, 134
33 157
34 135
9 2 ....46, 128, 129, 184
3.......................4, 53
8 ....81, 124
9 ....67, 93, 102
11.........................68
13 68
14 81
15 ....153, 154
16 ....44, 96
17 149
19 153
28 ....68, 79
29 ....106, 186
34 47
36 ....22, 137
37 22
38 185
43 59
45 144
48 ....22, 27, 111
53 25
55 ....14, 22
10 1...........................26
2 49
3.............................49
4.............................49
10 62
18 8
11 99
1...............32, 97, 99
2 100
2-3 100
3...........................100
4 ....99, 100

JUDGES

11 5 ....100, 157
6 100
7 ....62, 101
8 88
9 ....2, 136, 137, 153
12 8
15 66
25 ....124, 184
29 34
30 ....124, 155
34 98
35 19
36 ....20, 131, 157, 158
38 2
39 ....3, 9
12 3 184
5 ....52, 54, 82
5-6 90
7 20
14 49
13 2 25
3.............................88
4.............................14
6 185
7 33
8 29
9 168
10 28
11 163
12 156
14 107
17 8
20 168
23 ....69, 130, 155
14 1...........................165
3............116, 183
4 ....3, 119, 137
6 ....28, 129, 130, 150
8 130
9 125
11-13 49
12 ....47, 124, 154
13 154
14 44
16 ....61, 183
18 ....45, 73, 148, 155
15 1 97
2..............45, 81, 124
3.................63, 68, 137
4 49
7 153
8 145
11....................47, 54
13 124
14 169
18 92
16 2..................88, 150
8 47
9 28
10 96
15 ....6, 79
16 98

JUDGES

16 17 ....86, 153
18 104
20...................10, 42
21 27
24 135
25 98
27 135
30 9
31 167
40 98
17 3 49
5 ....180, 182
6 73
8 79
9 ....76, 185
10 50
18 1..........................110
2 130
3..................137, 167
7 47
11........................133
16 50
17 50
19 128
22 169
23 68
24 ....8, 184
25 ....29, 33, 160
19 4 47
5....................50, 113
6 120
11...................82, 169
13.................82, 94
17 76
18 144
20........................149
22 ....109, 169
27 ....137, 168
28 82
30 .....14, 62, 90, 157
36 157
20 3.........................185
4..........................135
15..........................49
16 18
21 49
24 117
28 184
35 49
46 49
48 175
21 1 186
2..........................115
5 8
8 7
12 ....19, 50
19 44
21 154
22 39
25 ....6, 57

1 Samuel

1	1................II, 25, 148
	1-2............................55
	2.........................12, 47
	4.......................28, 90
	5............................73
	6...........................114
	7.........42, 73, 131, 158
	8.........................47, 76
	9...........................123
	10......................74, 147
	11......92, 124, 154, 155
	12............103, 120, 136
	13................13, 21, 74
	14..........................185
	15..........................163
	16............................33
	22...........................158
	23.......82, 116, 176, 185
	24..........................144
	25............................13
	26....................135, 147
	27...........................147
	28............................67
2	116
	1............................63
	2............................39
	3................20, 42, 120
	4......................23, 108
	5..........................8, 33
	6....................101, 137
	7...........................175
	8....................137, 148
	9...........................141
	10............................73
	11..........................138
	13....40, 130, 137, 157
	14............................39
	15............................73
	16.......90, 125, 153, 163
	18..........................133
	19..............73, 94, 113
	20............................94
	22...........................III
	23............................44
	24............................55
	25..........................130
	26....................37, 126
	27...................124, 127
	28...................116, 127
	30...................124, 134
	31...................88, 137
	33............................22
	34............................46
	36............................90
3	1...................40, 136
	2...................43, 121
	3.................73, 181
	4............................59
	5..........................120
	7..........................181
	8...................51, 110

3	9...........90, 121, 136
	11................91, 137
	12....................6, 126
	13............................54
	14..........................187
	17..........................187
4	8.......................7, 135
	10............................42
	12............26, 98, 168
	15................21, 23, 33
	21..........................142
5	1............................26
	5............................74
	7..........................103
	9..........................157
	10..........................129
	11..........................106
6	3...................124, 153
	5............................79
	7..............................3
	10..............................3
	12..........................125
	18............................44
	19............................66
7	2..........................148
	3...................136, 153
	8..........................147
	9............................25
	10..........................169
	12............................25
	14..............................9
8	7...................116, 141
	8............................96
	9..........................141
	12..........................132
	22.....................14, 94
9	1............................II
	2........................II, 45
	3...................46, 116
	5...................93, 169
	6............................75
	7...................148, 156
	9...................27, 82
	11......135, 137, 169, 183
	12..........................163
	13................72, 161
	14...................137, 169
	15..........65, 131, 157
	21............................45
	23................81, 148
	24............................29
	27....107, 137, 167, 169
10	2...................9, 103
	5..........................168
	8................81, 94
	9..........................104
	11.............8, 11, 99
	16..........................124
	19..........................III
	22..........................137
	24............................82
	25.....................14, 27

II	2..............................5
	3...................107, 133
	4............................34
	5..............................8
	II............................99
	15............................22
12	2...................103, 137
	2-3............................91
	3........................7, 62
	4............................14
	5....................62, 163
	II..........................144
	14............63, 154, 176
	15..........................154
	17...................106, 131
	19...................107, 131
	22............................43
	23...................44, 182
	24............................94
	25................86, 154
13	2............................14
	5............................49
	6............................22
	7............................58
	II...........................III
	13..........................155
	15....................22, 43
	16............................22
	17............................44
	17-18........................74
	19............................74
14	1............................28
	2...........................II2
	8............................94
	9..........................149
	II..........................137
	12..........................116
	15............................46
	16............................35
	19..........................125
	24............................96
	25............................22
	28..........................124
	29............................62
	30............124, 155, 175
	33...................91, 131
	35..........................121
	36............................82
	39.......................4, 187
	40............................22
	42..........................110
	43..........................124
	44...................187, 188
	45..........................187
	47....................10, 74
	49............................12
	52................33, 156
15	9...................44, 46
	10............................30
	13..........................119
	15............................46
	16..........................107

1 SAMUEL

15   17 .... 96, 149
     18 94
     19 101
     22 128
     23 .... 97, 123, 147
     24 101
     25 107
     26 147
     28 88
     29 106
     30 107
     32 144
     35 147
16   2 156
     3 116
     4 183
     7 .... 45, 74
     8 .... 39, 120
     9 39
     10 47
     11 58
     12 52
     16 .... 90, 121, 129
     17 120
     18 .... 35, 46
     20 32
     23 .... 44, 90
17   4 11
     5 .... 41, 49
     7 49
     8 .... 35, 76
     9 154
     10 .... 61, 107
     12 .... 11, 47
     13 47
     14 .... 45, 47
     16 126
     17 .... 32, 50, 144
     19 133
     20 .... 103, 144
     23 .... 11, 169
     24 .... 98, 182
     25 .... 90, 115
     26 .... 7, 43, 68, 93
     31 4
     32 .... 93, 140
     33 53
     34 .... 28, 117
     34-36 90
     38 .... 103, 112, 116
     40 45
     41 125
     45 34
     46 .... 22, 57
     48 129
     55 .... 26, 187
     56 8
     58 .... 26, 27, 184
18   1 .... 13, 99
     2 120
     3 .... 13, 22, 116
     4 .... 13, 109, 112

1 SAMUEL

18   5 74
     8 142
     15 110
     17 45
     18 .... 7, 79
     19 .... 130, 133
     21 .... 51, 107
     23 .... 128, 168
     25 49
     29 138
     30 .... 45, 99, 158
19   1 .... 129, 130
     3 .... 8, 54, 156
     4 44
     5 .... 102, 131
     6 187
     10 6
     11 .... 130, 135, 153, 154
     13 .... 5, 27, 43, 110
     16 43
     17 .... 101, 184
     20 56
     23 .... 2, 125
     24 .... 74, 108
20   2 79
     3 .... 124, 186, 187
     5 79
     6 .... 124, 154, 155
     7 .... 154, 155
     8 .... 2, 57
     9 .... 124, 155, 183
     10 .... 8, 112, 116
     13 ...... 117, 154, 156, 188
     16 110
     17 115
     20 131
     21 .... 124, 154, 155
     23 .... 22, 91
     26 141
     27 37
     28 124
     36 .... 137, 169
     41 169
     42 .... 2, 48
21   3 .... 14, 112
     4 50
     5 .... 57, 154, 174
     8 36
     9 37
     10 .... 27, 116, 154
     16 .... 5, 183
22   2 33
     3 158
     6 168
     7 .... 142, 183
     8 136
     13 127
     14 7
     15 .... 121, 183
     18 50
23   2 92
     10 117

1 SAMUEL

23   11 184
     12 184
     13 .... 10, 56, 79
     20 128
     22 ...... 13, 74, 124, 125
     26-27 169
     28 13
24   5 116
     11-12 87
     12 131
     15 7
     16 82
     18 45
     22 187
     24 74
25   2 47
     3 33
     10 .... 7, 63, 103, 135
     11 .... 183, 185
     13 108
     15 12
     18 49
     19 40
     20 169
     21 .... 65, 145
     22 188
     24 .... 2, 185
     26 127
     27 88
     28 .... 3, 148
     29 181
     31 156
     32 129
     34 .... 101, 155, 187
     36 26
     43 48
26   2 47
     7 143
     9 .... 68, 102
     11 188
     12 136
     14 11
     15 184
     16 .... 33, 117, 158, 185
     17 184
     18 8
     19 .... 153, 163
     20 .... 13, 28, 116
     21 .... 126, 140, 159
     22 .... 26, 46
     25 174
27   1 .... 13, 129
     5 13
     8 22
     10 163
28   2 114
     3 97
     7 .... 34, 36, 107
     8 .... 13, 108
     9 .... 2, 129
     10 187
     11 7

1 SAMUEL

28　16......76
　　20......66
　　22......82
29　1......149
　　3......6, 8
　　6......128, 176, 187
　　9......119
　　10......156
30　1......101
　　1-2......100
　　2......101
　　3......136
　　4......158
　　7......40
　　15......187
　　16......136
　　21......49
　　22......33, 158
31　9......20

2 SAMUEL

1　3......76
　5......185
　6......124
　13......185
　14......185
　15......179
　19......185
　20......160
　21......138, 142
　22......74
　23......45
　24......133, 135
　25......185
　26......150
　27......185
2　1......46, 185
　8......26, 36
　9......42, 147
　10......176
　13......6
　17......45
　20......184
　21......46
　22......79, 184
　23......66, 99, 157
　24......169
　26......17
　27......155, 186
　28......74
　30......49
　32......143
3　1......126
　6......99, 138
　7......11, 138
　9......187, 188
　11......131
　13......2, 111, 176
　14......49
　16......125
　20......49

2 SAMUEL

3　22......21
　23......100
　24......124
　27......150
　30......118, 131, 159
　31......40
　33......79
　34......130, 138
　35......157, 187
4　4......33
　6......134
　11......116
　12......111
5　8......74, 134
　10......34, 126
　19......124
　24......67
　25......161
6　1......116
　3......44
　6......110
　9......79
　11......109, 134
　12......66
　13......134
　16......169
　19......14
　20......124
　22......45, 181
　23......181, 182
7　5......183
　6......138
　9......10
　12......154
　28......2
　29......120, 130
8　2......24, 126
　4......49
　5......24
　6......10, 24
　8......41
　10......31
9　1......57
　2......184
　4......143, 185
　6......183
　8......14
　10......48, 49, 149
　13......33
10　1......186
　　3......160
　　7......40
　　9......23
　　11......24
　　17......23
11　11......183, 187
　　12-13......97
　　20......110
　　25......74, 117, 119
12　3......73
　　4......44
　　6......51, 159

2 SAMUEL

12　7......1
　　10......159
　　19......137, 184
　　22......7, 80
　　23......8, 137
　　27......66
　　28......2
　　31......73
13　5......159
　　12......188
　　15......115
　　17......5
　　19......125
　　20......37
　　23......41
　　25......106
　　26......156
　　31......134
　　36......115
14　2......6
　　4......27
　　5......25, 96
　　7......88, 107
　　9......165
　　10......135, 157
　　11......187
　　14......79
　　18......133
　　19......132
　　20......131
　　25......90, 131
　　26......18, 49
15　4......186
　　5......90
　　6......25, 116
　　7......9
　　14......82
　　18......137
　　20......10
　　21......12, 39, 186
　　23......22, 115, 137
　　25......116
　　26......59
　　30......137
　　31......13, 149
　　33......67, 86, 153
　　34......154
　　35......90
　　37......74
16　1......49, 168
　　4......61
　　5......104, 125
　　7......33
　　10......8
　　11......175
　　12......93
　　13......125
　　15......21
　　17......183, 184
　　19......82
　　20......41
　　23......13, 31

2 SAMUEL

17 1 105
   1-3 78
   3 .... 28, 42
   5 2
   7-13 78
   8 .... 2, 111
   9 13
   10 ....28, 38
   11 ....13, 61
   12 82
   14 130
   15 14
   16 118
   17 .... 27, 73, 95
   19 14
   24 169
   28 20
18 3 ....56, 124
   8 45
   11 .... 128, 149, 156
   12 .... 8, 155
   13 14
   14 82
   17 .... 65, 98
   18 ....100, 101
   22 184
   23 ....8, 81
   24 27
   25 125
   29 ....129, 183
   32 185
19 1 ....2, 186
   4 120
   7 ....61, 155
   8 .... 45, 156
   14 187
   18 49
   20 130
   23 .... 8, 183
   25 9
   26 184
   27 27
   29 8
   30 61
   31 .... 131, 157, 158
   34 94
   35 185
   36 ....148, 184
   38 82
   43 184
20 3 ....44, 144
   5 45
   6 45
   10 21
   11 8
   12 137
   18 .... 73, 125
   19 ....36, 184
   21 11
21 3 106
   4 148

2 SAMUEL

21 6 .... 47, 107, 118
   9 ....48, 144
   12 28
   16 182
   17 186
   20 ....42, 145
   22 ..47, 48, 117, 118, 119
22 7 71
   12 71
   14 71
   16 25
   20 116
   23 41
   24 102
   28 116
23 3 ....133, 145
   5 183
   8 19
   10 ....74, 158
   15 186
   16 47
   17 150
   23 48
24 3 .... 21, 51
   4 150
   9 24
   12 127
   13 .. 8, 23, 41, 112, 184
   14 .... 82, 140, 185
   23 61
   24 ....34, 41, 124

1 KINGS

1 2 .... 82, 94, 107
   4 45
   5 50
   6 13
   12 ....106, 115
   13 63
   14 ....137, 168, 169
   18 ....63, 91
   21 .... 2, 22, 90
   22 ....137, 169
   24 183
   25 137
   26 2
   27 183
   30 111
   33 36
   34 22
   38 36
   40 .... 115, 134
   41 ....22, 168
   42 137
   43 ....19, 141
   48 168
   51 187
   52 ....18, 154
2 2 94
   3 176
   5 ....2, 96

1 KINGS

2 6 82
   7 134
   8 111
   14 142
   15 2
   18 .... 2, 149
   22 ....81, 184
   23 187
   31 ....34, 94
   32 117
   36 94
   37 90
   38 43
   39 35
   41 101
   42 ....61, 94
3 2 137
   4 49
   6 ....2, 6
   7 128
   9 6
   11 ....103, 158
   12 161
   13 ....61, 161
   16 ....25, 47, 72, 102
   18 ....36, 48
   19 158
   23 6
   25 14
   26 ....37, 124
   27 124
4 1 40
   2 36
   20 137
5 2 51
   6 .... 18, 49
   9 41
   10 .... 30, 45
   11 45
   12 ....18, 19, 50
   17 111
   23 131
   25 73
   28 73
   30 47
6 7 41
   8 75
   12 154
   18 ....136, 142
   27 137
   36 32
   38 51
7 2 13
   4 47
   7 77
   12 44
   14 ....25, 40, 117, 118
   15 ....75, 144
   20 49
   23 75
   26 75
   27 .... 47, 144

1 Kings

7 30........47
   32........146
   44........50
8 1........72
   5........22
   8........74
   9........39
   10........57
   13........51
   17........148
   27........46, 141, 175
   30........86, 156
   31........154
   32........131
   37........155
   46........74, 154
   47........103
   52........128
   55........115
   59........6
   64........45
9 6........154
   9........159
   11........72
   25........90, 126
   26........18
10 5........73
   6........42
   7........147
   8........6
   9........31, 97, 129
   10........142
   15........32
   16........50, 75
   17........49, 50
   19........47
   22........51
   23........45
   27........28
11 3........18, 21, 47, 49
   4........99
   5........16
   7........72
   9........29, 66
   10........132
   12........3
   16........47
   22........III, 124
   24........129
   26........182
   30........114
   31-39........90
   38........90, 154
12 6........106, 107, 112, 137, ...185
   7........154
   8........135
   9........106, 107
   13........112
   15........129
   16........8
   17........97, 182

1 Kings

12 21........134
   26........13
   32........104
13 2........94, 137
   3........94, 104, 137
   6........107
   11........25
   12........11, 96
   13........27
   18........107
   20........147, 169
   21........158
   27........27
   30........188
   31........88, 129
   32........20
   33........107
14 2........13
   5........105
   6........118
   7........114, 158
   8........131
   9........45, 120
   13........158
   15........28, 158
   25........36, 99
   27........104
   28........158
15 4........129
   8........13
   13........97, 117, 147, 182
   19........61
   23........36, 117, 145, 184
   25........51
   28........51
   29........99
16 8........51
   10........51
   11........19
   15........51
   16........29
   18........29
   19........131
   21........40, 51, 72
   24........40, 41
   29........51
17 9........25
   10........113
   12........47, 137
   13........94, 176
   16........23
   17........99, 158
   21........82
   24........6
18 3........133
   4........49
   5........79
   7........167
   10........73, 94, 156, 163, ...186
   12........10, 32, 167
   13........96, 113

1 Kings

18 14........32
   15........186, 187
   18........102
   21........14, 153, 163, 185
   23........46, 47
   26........13, 27, 46
   27........46, 107
   28........129
   30........135
   31........49
   32........41, 114
   34........113
   36........35
   39........1, 22
   44........51
   46........14
19 2........46, 188
   3........147
   3-4........99
   4........25, 144
   5........6, 59
   6........120
   7........45
   11........44
   13........143
   17........90
   19........51
   20........82
20 1........19, 50, 165, 167
   12........130
   16........50
   18........114
   20........23
   21........103
   23........167, 174, 187
   28........87
   29........6
   31........32, 91
   33........100
   35........32, 130, 167
   36........95, 157
   37........125
   38........13
   39........167, 169
   40........57, 161, 169
   42........87
21 5........8, 184
   6........III, 153
   7........183
   10........29
   11........135
   12........103
   13........29, 37, 42, 47, 145
   19........2, 12
   20........149, 158
   29........158
22 6........184
   7........107, 183
   8........75, 107
   9........25
   10........56, 137
   12........137

1 Kings

22 13 .... 46, 59, 82, 91, 94,
...........................145
14......................182
15......................184
16........51, 110, 168, 185
17..........................5
19......................137
20..................6, 106
22......................85
23..........................6
24......................185
25..........................9
27......................41
28......................42
30............13, 108, 127
32......................176
35......................138
36......................188
41......................51
46......................58
47......................19

2 Kings

1 2 7
4......................182
5......................184
8......................33
9......................48
10......................153
11......................120
13..............48, 120
14......................48
2 2 187
3......................143
9 99
10......................120
11..............125, 137
14......................185
16..............49, 50
17..............47, 50
24............16, 47, 49
3 1 51
4 ....41, 49
7 66
8......................11
11..............106, 183
14..............155, 187
15......................103
16..............42, 127
18......................21
23......................125
25......................74
26......................21
4 1............2, 25, 167
6......................58
8 ....28, 73, 158
10......................90
11......................28
13..............131, 183
16......................137
18......................28

2 Kings

4 19 188
29......................153
34..............149, 151
38......................167
42......................167
43............5, 8, 127
5 3 186
4......................14
6......................61
7......................160
8......................107
9......................36
10......................127
11..............92, 124
12............17, 44
13 105
17............41, 156
20............59, 187
21......................27
22..............6, 47
23............41, 120
24-25......................99
26......................183
6 1......................130
3......................120
5......................117
6......................112
8......................14
9............23, 132
10......................51
12............46, 75
16......................10
18......................29
22......................107
31......................187
33......................137
7 1......................41
2......................157
3............7, 67, 158
4............69, 153
6......................112
8......................25
9......................156
11......................142
13 26
16......................41
18......................41
8 1......................10
4......................17
5......................167
6......................25
8......................7
9......................7
10......................103
12......................77
13 ....8, 28, 111, 112, 116
17......................50
22......................72
25............51, 63
29............40, 75
9 1............40, 46, 65, 98
3......................61

2 Kings

9 4......................40
5......................27
12......................14
15......................75
18............3, 7, 8
19......................8
20......................74
22......................149
25............36, 111
26......................187
31......................28
32......................48
35......................130
37......................160
10 1......................49
4 2
6 ....36, 45, 136, 153
14......................49
15......44, 117, 148, 156,
...........................183
25......................14
11 4 ....36, 112
10......................19
14......................188
12 9 132
10......................46
12-17......................75
16 145
18......................102
21......................115
13 2......................147
6......................176
7 49
13......................118
14......................77
17......................123
19 ......51, 69, 123, 131,
...........................156
20......................73
21............137, 167
14 7 104
10............93, 103
21......................49
23......................51
26......................114
15 13......................41, 51
16......................26
17......................51
20......................49
23......................51
27......................51
30............51, 115
32......................51
16 14......................97
15......................42
17......................40
17 4 ....42, 158
6......................51
25-41......................138
26............57, 137
28......................185
29......................42

2 KINGS

17	36	182
18	4	103, 138
	9	50
	10	51
	13	79
	17	44
	19	63
	20	63
	21	156
	22	154
	23	49
	26	81
	31	105
	31-32	81
	32	94, 131
	33	124
	36	103
	37	56
19	3	57
	4	9, 43, 79, 93
	11	183
	15	55
	16	43
	22	7, 103
	25	107
	27	128
	29	81
	32	144
20	3	110, 116
	4	44, 169
	9	68, 184
	12	18
	13	44
	14	76
21	4	104
	6	120
	12	157
	22	21
22	1	47, 50
	7	176
	17	159
	18	135, 181
	19	158
	20	20, 21
23	3	29
	4	104
	9	74, 174
	10	104
	12	103
24	4	44
	12	51
	14	18, 19
25	1	19, 51
	5	22
	8	50, 51
	9	44
	16	44, 47
	17	50
	18	47
	22	98
	27	50
	28	17

ISAIAH

1	1	149
	2	81, 103, 173, 179
	3	19
	4	32, 33, 62, 188
	5	29, 53, 184
	7	31, 134, 137, 180, 181
	8	17, 103
	9	155
	11	35, 63, 109, 113
	14	128
	15	61, 63, 113, 154
	16	120
	17	123
	18	28, 82, 86
	18-20	154
	19	46, 63, 120
	21	185
	22	30
	23	53, 75
	24	82
	27-28	172
	28	35
	30	33, 134, 159
2	2	90, 138
	2-4	89
	3	107
	4	147, 148
	6	63, 159
	7	118
	8	23, 118
	9	102, 110
	11	6, 23, 68, 93, 102, 172
	12	150
	17	6, 30
	20	4, 6, 23, 32, 33
	22	133
3	1	17, 91
	3	33, 134
	5	14, 78
	6	143
	7	110, 114, 137
	8	159
	9	13, 188
	11	188
	12	181
	13	129
	16	3, 63, 102, 125, 158
	16-17	87
	24	41
4	1	176
	3	182
	4	67, 77, 102, 153
5	1	18, 82
	2	144
	3	140
	4	129, 132
	5	91, 94, 123, 127, 140, 179
	6	114, 132
	7	53, 159, 172
	8	88, 134, 137, 142

ISAIAH

5	9	43, 187
	11	34
	11-12	75
	12	42, 173
	13	22, 68
	14	68, 93
	15	68, 102
	18	31, 134
	19	83, 107, 159
	20	135
	23	23, 31, 137
	24	131
	25	5, 58, 102, 146, 150
	26	145
	27	136
	28	53, 137
6	1	97, 98, 114, 168
	2	14, 42, 51, 137, 149
	3	5, 42, 91
	4	74, 113, 118, 148
	5	33, 52, 188
	6	11, 168
	7	88
	8	7, 59, 81, 116, 150
	9	81, 125
	10	13, 30, 93, 160
	11	67, 77, 118, 158
	13	120, 156
7	2	24
	5	158
	7	3
	9	52, 141, 154, 155
	13	45, 128
	14	2, 13, 27, 59, 137
	15	123
	16	72
	17	128
	20	18
	22	130
	23	19
	24	13, 42
	25	14
8	4	13, 72
	5	62
	6	135, 158
	7	43
	9	105, 156
	12	10
	12-13	182
	17	135
	18	135
	23	10
9	1	29, 34, 68, 135, 181
	1-6	68
	2	34, 63
	3	33
	4	88, 181
	5	32, 68, 102, 179
	6	31
	8	22, 42
	9	118
	11	5

ISAIAH

9 12 134
17 75
18 ....118, 179
10 2 131
3.....................10, 185
4............................176
6 31
7............................41
10 46
11............................34
13 105
14 .... 28, 129, 130
15 .....19, 129, 130, 142
16 77
20.........................134
22....................154, 187
25........................58, 87
26............................88
27............................90
32............................131
33............................91
11 1-9 90
2 31
3............................77
4.............................173
5............................29
6 ....77, 90, 168
8.............................68
9 ..68, 118, 128, 138, 174
11............................51
12 4 136
5............................185
6 18
7............................105
13 2 81
3....................4, 33, 175
4................179, 188
5............................138
7............................20
7-9 93
8.............33, 42, 147
9....................68, 131
10............................68
12 78
14..............28, 42, 168
16 78
17 .... 59, 74, 91
18 74
19 129
22 21
14 1-3 90
2 138
3....................43, 90
5............................62
6 115
8 ....75, 135, 157, 175
9 17
10............................175
11............................144
15 176
17 137
19 ....34, 134

ISAIAH

14 23 123
24..........3, 62, 68, 187
26............................5
29............................42
31..............42, 127
32............................13
15 3 42
4............................22
7............................11
16 4 22
7............................42
8............................23
9............................113
10............................13
12 ....67, 153
13 157
14............................87
15 118
17 2 ....136, 168
5............................129
6 .... 21, 48, 118
18 2 135
3............................133
5............................88
6 78
19 4 43
8............................ 134
9 134
10............................33
11.........39, 44, 53, 142
12 ....106, 185
13 22
14 31
16 23
18 115
20............................135
22............................125
20 1 129
4 ....77, 114
6 .... 2, 185
21 1 131
5............................123, 127
7 ....44, 115, 156
11............................14
12 120
16............................87
22 1 185
2....................31, 33, 134
3............................ 134
5............................33
11............................19
13 ....123, 127
14 ....103, 187
16 .... 24, 28
17 ....91, 125
22 ....136, 172
24............................44
23 5............................33
8-9 62
12 .... 36, 44
13 6
16 120

ISAIAH

24 1 91
12 ....21, 118
13............................141
16 115
18 102
19............................125
21 77
23 45
25 9 ....44, 107
26 1 18
3............................138
10 ....17, 156
27 1 43
2............91, 182
4............4, 107
6 ....73, 90
7............................115
28 1 .... 35, 134
2............................68
4............13, 33, 35, 44
5............................90
6 134
7............................28
9 ....34, 112
13............................93
15 ....114, 155
16 .... 35, 44, 135
18 ....41, 155
19 ....128, 158
21 44
22 17
24............................13
25 154
26............................103
28............................124, 125
29 1 12
2............................118
4............................91
5........................28, 91
7............................91
8............................94, 136
11 .... 5, 94, 156
12 ....94, 156
13............................158
14 ....91, 125
15 ....95, 120
16 ....183, 188
17 87
19 32
21 ....134, 137
24............................33
30 2 ....21, 137
5............................10
7............................145
10 17
12 ..... 102, 130, 131, 158
12-13 87
14 76
15 123
16 ....45, 141
17 158
18 34

ISAIAH		
30	19	124
	20	21, 41
	22	4, 23, 33
	23	4
	26	51, 131
31	1	137
	4	161
	5	94, 125, 126
	6	10, 62
	7	33
	8	142
32	2	31, 33
	4	17
	8	17
	11	18
	12	13
	13	141
	15	93
33	1	121
	9	24, 63
	22	55
	24	134
34	3	28
	8	33
	10	46
	13	23
	16	14
35	1	78, 104
	2	68, 104, 125
	3	43
	6	68
36	5	39
	6	94
	8	91
	9	35, 46
	18	160
	20	7
37	3	33, 35
	16	2, 55
	22	29, 32, 36
	26	114
	28	128
	29	87, 158
	30	127
38	9	30
	10	83, 118
	15	149
	18	31, 134
	20	131
	21	96
	22	96
39	1	96, 101
	3	40, 185
40		3
	1-11	179
	3	179
	6	13, 53, 91
	7	52, 53, 141, 179
	7-8	62
	8	31
	9	32, 180
	11	180

ISAIAH		
40	12	7, 172
	14	20
	15	59
	17	46, 118
	18	7, 8
	20	10, 34, 76
	21	62, 184
	22	135
	23	135
	24	101, 175
	25	7, 106
	27	93
	28	52
	30	104
41	2	11, 28
	4	3
	5-7	75
	7	116
	10	38, 175
	11	59
	14	2, 32
	16	78
	20	93, 159
	23	82
	24	11, 46
	25	11
	26	106, 175
	28	106, 156
42	1	61
	2	110
	3	18
	4	172
	5	19
	6	104
	7	43
	9	17, 59, 172
	15	78
	16	11, 78
	17	115
	18	27
	19	39
	21	121
	22	127
	23	7
	24	123
43	1	14
	2	154
	3	61
	4	131, 159
	6	17, 170
	9	7, 69
	10	3
	11	1
	12	2
	13	3, 44, 175
	14	68, 93, 102
	17	18, 75, 179
	18	17
	19	59, 91
	24	176
	25	1
	28	32, 105

ISAIAH		
44	1	62
	8	57
	12	38, 174
	16	188
	21	4
	25	137
	26	137
	28	132
45	1	131
	4	97
	5	58
	9	148
	17	18, 115
	22	105
	23	187
46	4	3
	11	175
	13	68
47	1	120
	3	38
	7	3
	8	13, 28, 58
	9	48, 68
	10	134
	12	141
48	1	137
	4	53
	4-5	97
	5	73
	6	17
	8	111, 175
	12	3
	13	156
	20	102
	21	102
49	4	145, 148
	6	45, 63
	7	92
	14	62
	15	175
	20	58, 77
	21	7, 168, 185
	25	174
	26	13
50	1	59
	2	59, 124
	4	113, 116
	8	7, 8, 33, 134
	9	7, 11
	11	7, 59
51	1	11
	2	71, 105
	8	28
	9	2
	10	2, 29
	11	33
	12	1, 76, 97
52	5	91
	7	63
	14	161
	15	68, 161
53	2	106
	3	138

ISAIAH

53 4 .... 31, 114, 134, 141
5 .... 4, 31, 148
6 .... 28, 64, 101, 172
7 .... 28, 119
9 149
11 44
12 159
28 82
54 1 28
5 19
6 33
9 132
11 .... 28, 138
14 81
15 .... 8, 155
55 3 107
4 35
5 11
7 120
8 .... 31, 53
9 .... 63, 161
10 .... 113, 176
13 10
56 1 .... 105, 170
2 10
3 29
5 23
9 29
10 .... 34, 128
57 1 62
2 145
3 12
8 18
11 37
15 11
17 .... 105, 126
20 .... 44, 123
58 2 112
5 33
6 .... 123, 127
10 104
11 .... 17, 114
59 2 138
4 .... 123, 127
9 17
10 83
12 23
13 .... 123, 127
20 31
60 4 68
7 149
11 168
14 .... 34, 145
61 10 .... 73, 108, 150
62 1 76
5 161
63 3 105
5-6 105
7 44
8 .... 141, 176
10 .... 13, 103
11 134

ISAIAH

63 19 .... 69, 186
64 2 17
3 34
7 172
9 33
10 .... 23, 33, 35
65 1 .... 4, 11, 119
2 135
3 135
4 42
8 161
18 .... 81, 105, 114
23 145
24 72
66 5 138
7 73
8 170
10 .... 105, 115

JEREMIAH

1 1 31
6 120
12 120
16 117
2 2 .... 127, 138
5 8
6 .... 11, 175
8 11
11 .... 11, 168
12 52
14 184
16 145
17 138
18 8
19 172
21 42
23 185
24 16
25 44
28 145
31 27
33 175
37 168
3 1 .... 92, 127
5 .... 18, 110
7 44
9 103
10 44
12 127
13 176
14 48
15 126
19 .... 46, 79
20 161
4 3 81
5 172
10 103
11 35
12 175
13 63
14 .... 23, 185

JEREMIAH

4 19 .... 83, 188
21 83
22 138
29 68
31 188
5 4 176
6 63
9 14
14 158
15 11
16 53
21-22 75
22 156
24 13
6 10 83
13 45
14 149
15 .... 124, 174
16 44
19 97
20 44
23 75
25 172
28 46
29 125
7 3 63
4 30
9 .... 94, 127
10 94
13 .... 87, 126, 158
17 183
18 127
19 13
26 110
8 3 .... 67, 119
4 13
5 115
6 .... 42, 101
7 62
9 7
10 42
13 .... 11, 125
14 20
15 127
16 .... 34, 45, 102
17 91
18 149
22 57
23 .... 106, 186
9 1 .... 106, 186
11 184
12 131
14 134
21 .... 62, 136, 168
22 .... 105, 140
23 .... 116, 123
10 3 .... 23, 53
5 123
13 .... 101, 102
20 58
11 7 126
19 150

JEREMIAH

11 22 59
12 1 43
   3 33
   4 23
   6 182
   7 62
   8 110
   12 35
   17 126
13 10 137
   12 124
   16 93
   18 120
   19 ....24, 42
   20 10
   23 128
   27 ....181, 182
14 2-6 62
   5 126
   8 10
   9 11
   10 141
   12 57
   16 138
   17 ....36, 115, 118
   18 153
   19 127
   22 2
15 11 187
   13 37
   15 ....44, 45, 128
16 6 13
   7 31
   8 144
   12 ....120, 132
   13 116
   14 174
   16 44
17 2 44
   5-8 ....89, 94
   7 11
   10 132
   18 ....2, 82
   23 132
   24 132
   27 132
18 2 ....144, 145
   3 ....4, 59
   4 156
   8 156
   15 138
   16 110
   18 82
   21 134
19 1 14
   12 132
   13 127
20 7 ....42, 62
   8 158
   9 ....44, 94, 156
   10 ....106, 141
   14 82

JEREMIAH

20 17 ....33, 62, 101, 158
21 1 129
   8 31
   9 95
22 5 ....61, 187
   10 ....93, 125
   12 12
   14 127
   17 44
   18 188
   19 ....115, 126
   24 ....155, 187
   26 44
23 9 11
   14 94
   15 134
   17 ....125, 128
   18 107
   22 153
   28 145
   29 ....11, 76
   30 134
   33 154
   36 43
   38 158
   39 ....88, 124
24 2 ....32, 42, 44
25 3 50
   5 105
   9 95
   15 94
   29 183
   30 115
   34 133
26 5 126
   15 ....154, 187
   18 138
   19 124
   20 138
27 3 ....44, 135, 144
   7 2
   12 105
   16 145
   18 143
   21 143
28 7 176
   9 ....9, 110
   16 28
29 19 126
   25 18
30 6 ....18, 134
   11 ....77, 176
   12 44
   13 57
   14 115
   16 77
   21 68
31 1 42
   5 ....13, 68
   6 68
   8 56
   9 24

JEREMIAH

31 18 11
   21 6
   25 10
   33 93
32 1 51
   4 124
   10 27
   14 ....44, 94
   15 58
   17 45
   20 37
   27 45
   33 126
   44 ....126, 127
33 1 137
   11 56
   22 34
34 3 124
35 14 ....118, 126
   15 126
36 2 12
   10 143
   18 74
   22 117
   23 ....48, 127
   30 138
   32 ....21, 51, 118
37 9 13
   10 153
   14 188
   20 107
38 9 97
   14 44
   16 135
   23 14
   24 107
39 11 96
   14 130
40 2 118
   7 18
   15 93
41 4 133
   6 125
42 1 36
   6 ....39, 159
   16 91
   17 91
   19 61
44 3 ....9, 11
   18 157
   19 132
   25 21
   26 186
   28 14
46 5 125
   9 36
   16 ....44, 82, 175
   18 12
48 1 188
   9 125
   15 24
   32 26

JEREMIAH

48 36.....................12, 22
    37.........................170
    38..........................42
49 9...........................153
    36...........................27
50 10..........................144
    21.....................181, 182
    27..........................188
    28...........................31
    46...........................21
51 8............................141
    24..........................144
    25..........................144
    31..........................164
    46..........................160
    49..........................132
    56..........................181
52 7............................74
    15...........................18
    16...........................18

EZEKIEL

1   1.............................50
    6.............................51
    8.............................48
    23...........................14
2   1.............................32
    3............................135
    4.............................63
    8.............................42
    9.............................43
3   21...........................42
4   1-8...........................89
    13............................44
    14...........................138
5   5..............................5
    8.............................38
    9............................149
    11............................38
    16............................82
6   9.............................13
    11...........................188
7   2.............................48
    24............................44
8   6............................130
9   2...............44, 133, 135
    3............................133
    7............................104
    9.............................45
10 3.............................42
    9.............................44
    22...........................117
11 1.............................49
    13...........................115
    15............................42
    16...........................142
    17............................90
    24...........................144
13 2.............................34
    6.............................88
    12...........................156

EZEKIEL

13 22.....................41, 132
    3............................124
    5.............................42
    7............................104
    9............................155
    13...........................155
    15...........................155
    22...............117, 135, 156
15 4............................156
16 4............................125
    11...........................109
    27............................41
17 10...........................129
    21...........................117
    22............................90
18 5............................155
    6.............................41
    18...........................155
    19............................68
    23...........................124
    24...........................181
19 9............................160
20 16...........................117
    22...........................103
    31...........................183
    38............................24
    40............................42
    43............................13
21 31...........................127
22 18............................41
    24...........................138
23 16...........................144
    30...........................127
24 2.............................13
    6............................188
25 3............................188
    12...........................115
26 2............................188
    6............................119
    17............................29
27 15............................3
    30...........................144
    36............................42
28 7.............................44
29 7.............................94
    16............................20
    26...........................110
30 2............................188
    16............................34
    18...........................181
31 2.............................63
    16............................35
    18............................63
32 7............................181
33 2............................155
    4.............................13
    6............................155
    9............................155
    13...........................182
34 4.............................18
    12............................44
35 10...........................117

EZEKIEL

36 3............................116
    7.............................61
    31............................13
    38............................32
38 11............................34
    16...........................131
    17............................14
39 27............................44
40 2............................168
    10............................51
    28............................44
    31............................44
41 9............................142
    22...........................144
42 2.............................49
    14............................42
44 3............................117
    7.............................42
    15...........................182
45 3.............................48
    12............................49
    23.............................3
46 17...........................176
48 14............................82

HOSEA

1   2..................12, 144, 161
    4.............................87
    6....................120, 138
2   1.............................12
    4............................107
    5...........28, 93, 128, 150
    7...............18, 36, 134
    8..........................2, 3
    9...................45, 150
    11..............18, 92, 120
    12............................14
    14............................10
    15...................116, 157
    16...........................137
    17...........................128
    21............................36
    23............................90
    24............................36
3   1............128, 129, 137
    4............................144
    5............................147
4   2............................127
    4.............................81
    6...........22, 38, 68, 175
    7............................161
    8.....................23, 75
    11............................21
    12............................31
    13............................75
    14..................13, 76
    17...........................134
5   1.............................27
    5.............................68
    8............................164
    9.............................17

HOSEA

5 10 134
   1 121
   14 137
   15 93
6 2 48
   4 ....28, 168
   6 ....46, 148
   8 134
   9 141
7 1 170
   1-2 75
   2 13
   4 121
   5 144
   6 144
   7 93
   8 138
   9 38
   10 5
   14-16 75
8 1 188
   4 159
   6 141
   7 145
   12 156
   13 101
9 2 21
   4 23
   6 ....22, 156
   7 43
   9 ....120, 121
   12 141
   13 132
   14 21
   15 82
   16 154
   17 ....78, 138
10 1 118
   4 ....23, 123, 127
   5 22
   6 118
   7 68
   10 133
   12 80
   13 145
11 1 ....96, 157
   4 134
   7 22
   10 11
12 1 19
   3 132
   5 143
   9 176
   15 145
13 6 97
   8 16
   10 ....10, 185
   13 ....138, 142
14 1 24
   2 149
   5 144
   10 160

JOEL

1 2 ....27, 184
   13 22
   15 188
   19 63
   20 23
2 1 170
   2 82
   14 80
3 4 35
4 14 42

AMOS

1 1 ....26, 31
   3 ....47, 129, 159
   3-15 48
   3-4 87
   5 22
   6 ....47, 159
   9 ....47, 131, 159
   11 ......23, 94, 131, 159
2 1-6 48
   2 24
   3 24
   6 ....28, 130
   7 ....159, 160
   9 2
   10 2
   11 ....183, 184
   13 133
   14 56
   15 34
   16 33
3 3 ....79, 154, 176
   4 ....154, 168
   5 ....124, 149, 168
   6 168
   7 ....74, 141, 176
   8 79
   10 ....17, 120, 128
   11 37
   12 ....28, 74
4 1 135
   2 ....59, 91
   4 ....81, 105, 120
   6 ....173, 175
   7 ....172, 175
   7-8 90
   8 48
   9 29
   10 37
   12 ....159, 179
   13 55
5 2 137
   3 135
   4 105
   6 ....93, 105, 137
   7-12 137
   8 ....101, 133
   9 133
   11 ....131, 158
   12 111

AMOS

5 13 135
   14 25
   15 ....25, 79
   16 ....25, 188
   18 133
   19 ....28, 94
   21 63
   22 154
   27 ....11, 88
6 1 ....12, 46
   2 ....44, 184
   3 ....101, 118, 138
   4 135
   6 46
   7 95
   8 13
   10 ....132, 184, 188
   11 ....111, 114
   12 13
   13 142
7 1 ....136, 137
   2 ....8, 120, 154
   3 5
   4 ....103, 137
   5 8
   6 3
   7 ....137, 168
   12 150
   13 29
   17 118
8 3 6
   4 132
   5 ....106, 185
   8 27
   9 ....6, 118
   10 31
   11 ....91, 137
   11-14 90
   13 90
   14 ....34, 137, 186
9 1 100
   2 153
   2-4 ....87, 154
   5 ....101, 137
   6 55
   8 ....124, 176
   9 111
   15 101

OBADIAH

1 5 153
   9 119
   10 32

JONAH

1 3 18
   4 18
   6 ....8, 179
   10 115
   11 106
   14 ....82, 105

JONAH

2	11	111
3	3	46
	4	144
	5	45
	9	80
4	2	120
	4	63
	9	63
	10	12
	11	49, 183

MICAH

1	2	28
	5	8
	6	114
	9	23, 24
	10	124
2	1	94
	3	145
	4	13
	7	44
	8	134
	10	10
	11	155
	12	26, 42
	13	102
3	2	128, 135
	3	135
	5	135, 137, 156
	8	63, 174
	9	17, 137
	11	75
	12	27, 118
4	2	77
	6	18, 135
	9	115, 125
	11	21, 23
	12	28
	13	114
5	2	13, 67
	4	42, 48
	7	153
6	8	8, 129, 148, 176
	13	126
	16	160
7	1	188
	2	57, 144
	3	101
	4	45
	6	52
	10	185
	16	29
	17	147, 148
	19	120

NAHUM

1	3	53, 55
	4	101
	12	161
2	5-6	75

NAHUM

2	6	144
	9	3
3	11	73, 175
	17	185

HABAKKUK

1	6	11
	13	45
	14	138
2	1	172
	12	95
	14	11
	15	127
	16	46, 128
	17	32
	18	68
	19	34
	20	188
3	1	35
	3	71
	8	41
	9	125
	17	23
	19	97

ZEPHANIAH

1	2	125
	7	188
	9	133
	14	52, 144
2	2	130
	12	28
	13	104
	14	37
3	4	17, 33
	5	138
	7	121
	8	118
	9	144
	11	33
	17	10, 76
	19	18, 172

HAGGAI

1	4	2, 44
	6	127
	9	127
2	3	7
	7	22
	12	184
	13	184
	15	133
	17	29, 117

ZECHARIAH

1	2	115
	6	176
	13	41
	14	115

ZECHARIAH

1	15	115
2	2	54
	5	168
	6	185
	17	188
3	1	27
	3	138
	4	127
	8	27
4	7	44
	10	41
5	11	24
6	5	47
	7	18, 21, 24
	10	127
	12	11
	14	21
7	1	50
	2	96
	3	126, 185
	5	4, 124, 127
	7	51, 117
	9	115
	10	14
8	2	115
	10	105
	13	42
	15	121
	17	14
	23	111
9	5	73
	9	20, 37
10	7	73
11	2	44, 158
	4	33
	5	23
12	4	28
	10	127
13	9	130
14	4	44
	10	44
	12	23

MALACHI

1	4	120
	6	153
	7	138
	10	186
2	6	21
	7	26
	11	24
	16	12
	17	177
3	2	7
	9	27
	11	45
	14	8
	15	174
	19	161
	24	144

PSALMS

1 1.........27, 32, 62, 188
   2.................62, 174
   3.................149
   3-6...............74
   4.................9, 174
   4-6...............28
   6.................173
2 1.................62, 164
   2.................29
   3.................82
   6.............4, 33, 173
   7...53, 61, 64, 147, 179
   8.................29
   9.................32, 78
   10................91
   12................34, 93
3 2.........61, 63, 134
   3.................145, 150
   6.................102
   8.................69, 145
   9.................185
4 2.................69
   7.................151, 186
   8.................12
5 4.................144
   5.................79
   6.................63
   7.................33, 35
   11................180
6 4.................185
   6.................179
   7.................63, 179
   9.................68
   10................68
   11................144
7 2.................63
   5.................134
   7.................69
   10................43
   11................29
   17................172
8 2.................19
   3.................31
   5.........8, 79, 97, 160
   6.................113, 173
9 16................11
   19................164
   21................111
10 75
   3.................62
   5.................42, 182
   6.................37
   11................111
   13..........62, 68, 111
   14................62
   16................69
   17................69
11 1.................63, 79
   3.................68
   6.................73
   7.................52
12 3.................42, 115

PSALMS

12 6.................11, 78
   7.................51
13 2.................79
   3.................79
   4.................115
   5.................164
   6.................63
14 2-2...............62
   5.................115
   7.................186
15 2-3...............137
   24................142
16 1.................63
   5.................52
   6.................17, 38
   8.................143
   9.........63, 102, 175
   10................75, 150
   11................17, 20
17 5.................127
   6.................69
   8.................5
   10-11.............63
   11................145
   14................5
18 ....71, 116
   1.................12
   4.................133
   5.................5
   9.................151
   14-15.............100
   16................24
   18................44
   26................172
   27................173
   28................43
   31................182
   33..........134, 135, 137
   35................23
   38................105
   40................134
   42................164
   43................105
   44................11
   49................175
19 1.................30
   3.................170
   4.................179
   5.................170
   6.................150
   8.................31, 134
   8-10..............53
   8-11..............179
   9.................134
   9-11..............179
   10................42, 135
   11................133, 135
   12................179
20 4.................83
   7.................68
   8.................6
   9.................68, 102

PSALMS

22 3.................75
   8.................75, 110
   9.................132
   10................173
   13................63, 172
   18-19.............75
   22................147
   30................68, 102
   32................133, 137
23 1.................52
   2.................33
   4.................109, 154
24 4.................33
   6.................5
   8.................8
25 1.................75
   2.................63, 82
   7.................31
   8.................52
   9.........73, 104, 170
   10................42
   11................69, 88
   14................131
   16................52
26 1.................76
   4-4...............63
   5.................170
   6.........75, 104, 170
27 1.........7, 52, 148
   2.................36
   9.................107
   10................173
28 1.................75
29 5.................164
   6.................24
   8-9...............75
30 1.................27
   10................8
   13................160
31 2.................63
   6.................69
   7.................63
   20................44
32 2.................11
   7.................134
   8.................104
   10................44
33 8.................82
   10................62
   17................28
34 8.................101
35 8.................168, 182
   11-12.............75
   17................185
   19................41
   21................188
   23................20
36 6.................146
   7.................46, 164
37 14................62
   24................154
   27................105

PSALMS

37	30	74, 170
	31	23
	38	68
	40	102
38	9	103
	14	11
	15	138
	20	41
39	6	29
	8	68, 91
	12	156
40	5	62, 63
	6	132
	9	63
	11	151
	16	188
41	7	154
42	1	35
	2	11
	3	185
	4	130
	5	4, 74, 83
	6	58, 101, 149
	7	149
	11	130
43	1	142, 148
44	5	2
	10-15	71
	21	154
45	8	17, 144
	9	36, 42
	12	107
	13	45
	14	142
46	2	142
	3	130
	4	156
	5	20, 45
	7	62
47	9	63
48	6	161
	9	161
	11	161
49	7	135
	8	124
	8-10	106
	13	11
	15	102, 131
50	4	129
	5	149
	10	29
	12	154
	16	8, 102
	18	154
	19-20	75
	21	111
51	2	129
	3	32, 179
	4	120
	6	160
	9-11	179
	13	140

PSALMS

51	14	5, 113
	18	106
	19	179
	20	179
52	5	46
	7	78
	9	101
53	6	134
55	3	83
	4-6	75
	7	107, 186
	8	120
	13	106, 134
	15	74
	18	83, 97
	19	147
	20	97
	22	42
56	1	129
	3	145
	4	12
	4-7	75
	9	69
	10	12
	14	164
57	5	83
58	2	145
	5	73
59	6	25
	16	97
	17	12
60	5	41
	6	69
	10	31
61	3	75
	6	69
	8	107
62	4	44, 135
	10	46
	11	155
	12	48
63	6	115
	7	20
64	2	81, 179
	6	111
	7	35
	8	144
	8-10	102
	9	78
65	5	11, 45, 164
	10	62
	12	62, 74
	14	113, 175
66	6	83
	10	129
67	3	133
	5	182
	6	69
	7	69
	8	69
68		67
	5	150

PSALMS

68	8-15	71
	9	6
	10	37
	15	71, 119
	16	46
	19	66, 67
	21	151
	22	35
	23	78
	34	59
69	5	41
	6	118
	14-15	82
	15	107
	36	104
70	4	188
71	7	41
	9	5
72	1	31
	5	148
	13	73
	17	29
	19	118
73	2	23
	5-9	75
	10	44
	12	5
	13	145
	15	155
	16	3
	17	83
	18	118
	27	134
	28	44, 129
74	1	63
	2	7, 114
	3-8	71
	4-8	180
	10	185
	11	37
	12	52
	12-15	71
	12-17	180
	13	19
	15	44
	23	134
	26	71
	52	71
75	3	145, 154
	8	6
76	7	37
	8	133
	10	129
	11	141
77	2	75
	4	83
	7	83
	12	141
78		67, 180
	6	77, 104
	9	36
	12	180

PSALMS

78   13 .... 66, 180
      14 71
      15 180
      24 67
      25 67
      26 100
      30 180
      35 110
      40 185
      49 44
      54...................... 7
      68......................173
79   10......................135
80   5.................. 25, 68
      8...................... 25
      9-13 71
      11.................. 46, 118
      15 .... 7, 25
      20...................... 25
81   6 12
      9 .... 107, 186
      11..................107, 134
      14..................155, 186
82   2 185
83   3-6......................75
      10 150
      12......................42
      15 11
84   4 .... 38, 62
      6 10
      7......................34
      11......................179
      12 151
85   2-4 69
      5......................11
      9......................37
      10......................5
      11......................68
      12......................68
      13 170
88   6 ....31, 134
      8 144
      9......................20
      11......................121
      16......................83
      17-19......................63
89   7 .... 7, 164
      10......................133
      28......................130
      36......................187
      48...................... 8
      51 44
90   2 157
      3......................73, 95
      3-6......................75
      5-9......................62
      6 94
      6-9 179
      10......................179
      13 179
      14......................107
      15 12

PSALMS

91   4 104
      6 144
      7 170
      15 150
92   6 ....63, 164
      8 102
      9 42
      12 44
      13-15......................75
93   1 ....64, 113, 175
      2...................... 157
94   17 155
      22-23......................102
95   1 83
      6 .... 83, 105
      7 186
      8 150
      9 157
      10 100
      11......................161
96   4 133
      5.................. 53, 172
      10 64
      11 .... 105, 170
      11-12......................82
97   1 82
      6-9 62
98   7-8......................82
100   3 179
      4 ....109, 134, 144
      5......................37
101   1 5
      2......................185
      3......................128
102   3 63
      3..................12, 75
      6-8 63
      7......................63
      9..................63, 134
      9-10......................63
      12......................75
      14......................121
      19 ....133, 137
      27......................172
      28......................3
103   5 ....23, 107
      7......................30
      8..................52, 55
      9..................110, 170
      10-13......................62
      11......................174
      13 74
      14......................138
      15 172
      15-16......................74, 75
      17......................172
104   1 .... 61, 63
      4 63
      6-9 71
      8.................. 7, 12
      10-13......................75
      11......................29

PSALMS

104   13......................114
      14......................131
      15......................131
      18...................... 44
      20.................. 29, 104
      21......................132
      22......................156
      24......................63
      27-30 156
      30......................104, 170
      32 ....101, 104, 170
      33 ....4, 58
105 67
106 67
      13......................121
      14......................115
      23 .... 130, 155
      26......................130
      27......................130
      6......................66
      8......................173
107   ....67, 71
      2......................66
      4......................66
      5......................175
      16......................172
      20..................5, 105
      21-22......................105
      27......................105
      29......................71
      30......................31
      42 ....69, 104
109   2 ....44, 115
      2-3......................63
      4 42
      7......................56
      11......................105
      12......................105
      15......................105
      19 ....11, 108
      25......................156
      28...................... 69
      29......................113
110   1 158
      2...................... 81
      3...................... 42
      4 24
111   4-5 62
      7 42
      8...................... 44
113   4 146
      5...................... 7
      5-6 120
      5-7 135
114   8......................114, 164
115   8......................135
116   3-4......................71
      14 145
      15......................36, 145
      18......................145
118   2......................19
      8......................45

PSALMS

118	8-9	128
	9	45
	19	107
	20	36
	22	11
	27	97
119	5	186
	11	160
	17	107
	21	69, 135
	22	140
	33-39	81
	40	63
	62	144
	67	73
	72	44
	75	145
	78	145
	80	160
	86	41, 53, 145
	92	72, 155
	103	22
	105	52
	113	172
	129	52
	136	159
	137	1, 44, 52
	151	53
	155	44
120	5	188
	6	150
	7	42
121	1	185
	3	82
	5	52
	7	164
122	1	63
	2	138
	3	12
	4	12
123	2	161
124	3	114
	4	145
	8	12
125	1	11
	2	181
	3	145
126	6	125
127	1	140, 143, 153
	2	144
128	5	105
129	4	69
	8	61
130	1	61, 69, 75
	2	43
	3	7
	5	63
	7	148
	56	69
	57-61	69
	59	69
132	1	128

PSALMS

132	3	187
	4	187
	5	20
	12	7
	15	113
	16	112
	18	112
133	1	8
136	3	19
	4-7	134
	14	104
	15	104
	19	118
	20	118
	21	104
137	3	14, 112
	5	87
	7	150
	8	12, 133
	9	12
138	3	12, 97
	7	75, 170
	8-11	101
139	1-6	63
	4	108
	8	58, 83, 154, 156
	9	156
	11	156
	12	45, 150
	14	145, 159
	18	4, 156
	19	186
	22	115
	24	31
140	8	69
141	1	75
	10	23
142	2-8	75
	4	129
143	2	14
	4	149
	7	107
144	2	11
	3	97
	4	63
	6	115
	13	22
145	7	44
	20	173
146	2	4
	4	156
147	1	44
	4	172
	14-16	137
148		81
	13	29
149	2	19

PROVERBS

1	3	123
	7	32, 62

PROVERBS

1	9	33
	18	13
	20-21	74
	22	185
	26	38
	27	129
	31	114
2	1	148
	5	140, 155
	18	32
	19	32, 134
	21	109, 170
3	3	179
	4	35
	7	179
	10	113
	13	62, 170
	16	179
	17	42, 170
	18	23, 53, 172, 179
	19-20	179
	21	179
	24	156, 179
	27-31	179
	31	180
4	14	172
	16	94
	18	126
5	6	168
	8	170
	19	33
	20	104
	22	42
6	8	75
	9	185
	11	88
	13	110
	16-19	48
	17	43
	18	43
	22	156
	23	53, 172
7	7	83
	10	145
	14	149
	19	27
	23	158
	26	44
8	1	170
	6	17
	19	170
	25	157
	27	130
	30	42
9	5	151
	10	53, 172
	11	13, 104
	13	8
	14	88
	16	181
10		172
	1	52, 170, 172, 173

PROVERBS

10	1-3	74
	3	172
	4	74, 115, 172
	5	52
	12	172
	15	179
	20	179
	22	180
	23	128
	25	157
11	2	148, 156, 171
	4	182
	6	31
	16	161
	24	57
	26	181
	31	175
12	2	74
	4	172
	5	52, 179
	16	181
	18	57
	21	63
	22	172
	26	73
13	3	181
	5	74
	7	57
	19	128
	21	116
	23	57
	24	144
14	2	54, 134
	9	23
	12	57
	13	174
	19	62, 170
	21	181
	24	5, 52
	35	23
15	1	74
	8	53
	11	175
	12	123
	19	53
	20	32
	22	127
	25	104
16	2	53
	6	128
	7	175
	12	128
	15	171
	16	128
	20	181
	21	171
17	1	44
	3	161
	7	175
	12	127
	13	157
	20	34

PROVERBS

17	25	170
	28	56
18	7	170
	10	94
	11	52
	13	157
	17	94
	19	171
	22	156
19	5	170
	6	171
	7	175
	8	131
	9	170
	25	14
20	6	7
	7	158
	9	63
	10	42
	11	39
	23	44, 53
21	2	53
	3	45
	6	35
	9	45, 128
	14	146
	16	123
	22	101
22	6	175
	19	2
	21	41
	23	112
23	2	33
	15	2
	15-16	104
	22	7
24	11	186
	22	7
	23	123
	31	118
	32	2
25	3	161
	4	97, 123, 127, 157
	5	123, 127, 157
	8	129
	17	113
	20	161
	24	33, 128
	25	161
	26	161, 172
	27	123
	28	161
26	1	161
	2	131
	7	161
	8	161
	9	161
	12	14, 156
	14	161
	17	11
	18	135, 161
	19	161

PROVERBS

26	20	74
	21	161
	26	156
27	14	56, 157
	16	23
	23	5
	24	184
28	1	23, 168
	11	52
	21	123
29	21	157
30	2	141
	3	19
	15-16	48, 62
	17	104
	18-19	48
	20	62
	21	48
	25	97, 142
	28	14
	30	171
31	5	104
	9	145
	10	7, 33
	13	62
	29	44

JOB

1	1	11, 65
	1-5	100
	2	47
	3	49
	4	48
	5	73, 141
	6	27, 28
	7	76, 185
	10	148
	11	187
	12	13
	13	28
	14	3, 22, 138
	15	3, 24
	16	6
	16-18	168
	20	62
	21	56
2	1	28
	3	97, 137
	5	174
	6	58, 176
	10	46, 183
3	3	12, 71
	4	42
	10	3, 100
	13	105, 155
	15	11
	17-18	62
	19	53
	20	33
	25	156
	25-26	63

JOB

4 5................ 3, 101, 179
6 .... 53, 179
7 11
9 119
11-12 62
12-16 71
13 148
15 18
17 79
20 110

5 2 118
7 161
8 174
10 135
15 102
16 102
19-22..........................48
20..........................68
21 151
22 81
23 68
24..........................42

6 2 ....13, 124, 186
3..........................79
4 4
6 79
7 120
8 186
9 120
11..................... 79, 160
12 183
17 12
19-21.....................62
21 101
22 141
25..........................123
27..........................110
28..........................183

7 2 .... 11, 74, 76, 109
3..........................13
4 ....153, 185
5..........................113
6 63
7 110
8 134
9 .... 62, 101
10..........................185
12 ....79, 160, 184
13 154
14..........................119
15 46
16.............61, 63, 79
17 79
17-18..........................101
20..........................156

8 3..........................184
4 154
6 155
8 110
9..........................42
11..........................142
11-19 75

JOB

8 19 22

9 2..........................8
4 .... 33, 101, 110
11..........................5
11-12..........................59
12 7
13 179
14 175
15 .... 79, 154
16 .... 79, 101, 154
17 18
18 123
20 79
21 179
22 3
25..........................171
25-26 63
26.......... 76, 148, 171
32..........106, 107
33..........106, 107
35 107

10 1 149
7 149
14 153
15 188
16 ....120, 156
22 96

11 2..................... 33, 184
5..................... 174, 186
6 118
7 79
13 153
15 ....149, 155
16 .... 11, 155
17 46

12 2..........................141
3..........................138
4 102
7 23
9 68
11..........................161
17 114
18 101
22-25.....................101

13 3.................123, 174
4 174
5.......... 106, 124, 186
9 130
13 .... 8, 107
14 184
19 ....7, 11, 156
23 185
24..........................114
27..........................104
28 11

14 1.................31, 134
2..........................101
3.............. 38, 175
4 186
7..........................57
10..........................101
11..........................161

JOB

14 12 161
13..........................186
18 174
18-22..........................75
19 23

15 7 71
8..........................71
10..........................34
16 ....133, 175
17 7

16 3..........................177
4 155
6 .... 83, 154
9 110
10 110
12 104
16 23
19 91
20 106
21 106

17 1 20
2..........................73
15..........................185

18 5-20 75
7 33
9 73

19 3................ 6, 51, 120
4 156
11..........................114
18 .... 83, 156
19 7
21 27
23 .... 27, 118, 185, 186
25.............56, 111
28-29 87

20 4 ....130, 133
6 172
11..........................23
14 153
17 36
23 104
26.............21, 73
28..........................73

21 4 184
6 153
7 145
12 74
16 69
17 185
21 .... 23, 158
27..........................11
34 145

22 3.........................184
8..........................181
13..........................8
18 69
30..........................142

23 3..........................186
3-5 106
4 5
10 156
13..........................156

Job

23 17 13
24 2 101
   5 .... 34, 56
   10 .... 56, 62, 114
   19 11
25 2 123
   5 .... 59, 63
   6 175
26 4 7
   7 8
   14 8
27 2 186
   8 73
   12 .... 115, 125, 184
   19 56
   21-23 104
   22 104
28 2 114
   3-11 62
29 2 186
   10 23
   12 138
30 1 34
   2 151
   6 132
   16-22 75
31 153
   1 8
   5 154
   9 154
   11 3
   12 10
   15 134
   18 4
   21 154
   24 154
   31 186
   33 154
   35 186
   39 19
32 3 101
   13 160
   22 120
33 14 .... 48, 51
   27 44
34 8 132
   22 129
   29 37
   32 .... 11, 154
35 14 111
   18 19
36 7 102
   8-9 97
   14 73
37 4 73
   5 .... 73, 145
   7 130
38 12 148
   19 181
   20 5
   21 23
   24 73

Job

38 26 11
   35 59
39 13 183
   15 110
   21 104
   25 188
40 2 127
   4 63
   5 .... 48, 51
   8 .... 73, 184
   9 .... 73, 134
   10 109
   15 19
   18 52
   24 5
   29 150
41 3 106
42 5 .... 64, 101
   12 49

Song

1 1 46
   6 .... 15, 36
   7 12
   8 149
   11 26
2 2 148
   7 61
   9 148
   14 112
3 1 12
   3 183
   7 42
   8 138
   10 144
5 3 108
   8 33
6 8 3
   9 18
7 1 30
   2 63
   8 .... 6, 63
   10 44
   13 147
8 1 .... 35, 156
   5 11
   6 .... 46, 170
   8 12

Ruth

1 2-4 55
   4 .... 12, 150
   6 2
   8 3
   9 .... 3, 106
   11 .... 88, 92
   12 .... 45, 63, 153
   14 58
   16 29
   17 188

Ruth

1 19 5
   21 .... 56, 168
   22 .... 3, 29
   29 29
   36 29
2 2 10
   3 36
   7 .... 94, 157
   8 140
   10 .... 129, 131
   12 9
   17 41
   18 151
   21 .... 36, 67
3 2 58
   4 18
   8 143
   9 88
   12 .... 57, 141
   14 143
   15 50
   18 .... 176, 185
4 1 14
   3 .... 29, 61
   11 106

Lamentations

1 1 .... 24, 33
   2 57
   5 145
   8 115
   9 145
   10 .... 36, 120
   11 107
   14 11
   17 110
   19 107
   21 69
2 1 185
   13 .... 8, 26, 106
   15 12
   17 179
   20 183
   22 103
3 1 11
   15 .... 113, 114
   22 141
   26 37
   27 56
   43-66 180
   44 36
   45 123
   48 113
   50 83
   55 69
4 1 185
   12 110
   14 120
   15 111
5 10 24

Ecclesiastes

1	2	46
	7	12
	8	53
	9	8, 12, 62
	11	182
	13	44, 103
	16	2, 148, 181
2	1	2, 13
	7	23
	9	103
	11	2
	13	103, 172
	14	181
	15	2, 72, 103, 140
	16	148
	17	53
	21	57
3	2	133
	14	132
	15	131, 180
4	1	127
	2	127
	3	117
	8	57
	13-16	179
	16	141
5	4	56
	5	184
	13	103
6	1	57
	10	110
7	1	170
	3	52
	4	172
	7	141
	12	19
	15	57
	20	141
	24	42
	26	28
	29	110
8	10	44
9	1	110, 132
	11	127
10	8	181
11	2	48
	9	80
12	3	12
	9	58

Esther

1	1	50
	8	42
	22	42
2	11	42
	15	138
3	4	110
4	2	132
	11	110
	14	7, 80
	16	21

Esther

6	2	56, 110
7	4	133
8	6	120
	8	127, 132
9	1	127
	4	126
	6	127
	12	127
	16	127
	17	127
	23	103
10	2	184

Daniel

1	4	35
	5	3, 47
	8	110
	12	47
	15	47, 56
	16	138
	17	48
	20	51
	21	51
2	1	51
	13	111
5	19	138
7	13	32
	18	19
8	9	3
	12	71, 105
	13	41
9	5	127
	9	20
	13	117
	25	120
	26	135
10	3	124
	7	141
	9	138
	12	62
11	4	104
	10	104, 124
	11	42
	13	124
	14	36
	16-19	104
	27	42
12	2	6
	11	132

Ezra

1	5	12
2	64	49
3	6	50
	10	103
	12	6, 42
5	12	3
	13	51
6	22	103
7	6	6

Ezra

7	8	51
	9	128
	21	2
8	15	47
	16	118
	21	40
	24	118
	25	29
	30	103
	36	103
9	1	40, 42
	4	74
	13	158
	15	56, 132
10	3	3
	12	115
	13	42, 120, 141
	14	29, 42
	17	29

Nehemiah

1	1	51
	4	138
	9	3
2	1	51
	3	158
	9	96
	10	115
	11	47
	12	22, 41
	13	138
	15	138
4	4	19
	6	51
	12	133
	17	3
5	11	51
	14	21, 51
	19	62
6	1	119
	2	20
	6	138
	10	14
	12	141
8	6	111
	10	12
	13	132
	14	110
	15	110
9	3	138
	5	138
	6	2, 55
	19	117
	28	4, 44
	32	117
	34	117
	35	44
10	29	121
13	10	23
	17	96
	20	51, 103

Nehemiah

13	21	29
	24	42

1 Chronicles

2	22	49
3	20	48
4	9	111
5	1	132
	9	40
	20	127
	26	42, 118
6	17	138
	34	132
7	5	20
	24	97
9	22	3, 42
	25	131
	27	37
10	13	132
11	7	13
	8	74
	9	126
12	8	131
	28	49
	34	42
	39	47
13	1	118
14	11	13
15	2	132
	12	11, 12
	19	41
16	37	118
18	2	23
	5	23
	13	23
	14	138
19	12	24
	15	23
	16	23
	18	23
	19	23
20	3	74
	6	42
	8	19
21	12	41
	17	2
	18	111
	24	132
22	7	182
	14	47
	18	103
23	1	103
	22	3
	26	132
	31	128
24	12-18	50
	16	51
25	5	47
	18-31	50
	19	51
26	13	42

1 Chronicles

26	26	6
	28	29
27	2-13	50
	15	51
	27	12
	29	22
28	5	44
	14	42
	16	42
	18	41
29	3	12
	7	49
	8	29
	14	111
	17	29
	29	184

2 Chronicles

1	4	11, 12, 29
	10	6
2	2	61, 96
	7	32
	12	118
	13	28
	14	28
3	12	47
4	2	75
	7	3
	8	47
	10	44
	11	3
	13	41
5	2	72
	11	132
7	17	132
	18	110
	21	118
8	10	36
	11	36
	13	132
	14	42
9	5	42
	15	75
	21	73
	28	14
10	11	42
11	12	42
13	21	48
15	1	182
16	9	11, 12, 21
	11	184
17	12	126
18	15	185
19	5	42
	7	128
20	6	2, 132
	17	132
	22	12
	35	120
21	10	72
	17	45

2 Chronicles

22	6	75
	9	132
23	1	118
	6	182
24	18	6
	21	145
25	9	50
	16	13, 184
26	13	19
27	7	184
28	19	127
29	17	50
	27	12
30	10	138
	19	12
32	32	184
36	16	138

INDEX OF SUBJECTS

(References are to §§)

———— • ————

Abstract nouns, 18*a*, 20*b*, 33*b*

Accusative, does not exist in Hebr: 27, 88 R.1, 117

Action, expressed by YIQTOL; simple action by short YIQTOL 61; not always punctual 62; extended action (iterative, frequentative, customary, distributive, etc.) by long YIQTOL 63*l*

Adjective, classifying function 41; concord of 42, 42 R.1-4; comparison 43, superlative 44; used adverbially 117

Adjectival, uses of construct state 35

Adnominal, modifying or qualifying a noun or its equivalent 8 R.2, 35 R.5, 49*e*, 114, 116*b*, *d*, 117, 119, 144

Adverb, adverbial, cognate object has almost adv. force 93*a*; infin. absol. used adverbially 102; independent adverbs 115; function 116; modifying verb or whole clause 116; negative and affirmative 116*b*, *c*; adnominal uses 116*d*; list of 116 R.1; order of 116 R.2; nouns and adjectives as 117; prepos. phrases 118; adverbial clauses 119ff.; interrogative adverbs 153 R.3

Affirmation, by infin absol. 101; by clausal adverbs 116*c*; oath of affirmation 156*b*

Agent, in constr. state 33*b*; with passive verbs 95*c*

Agreement, see Concord

Answers, 49 R.2, 63 R.3, 153 R.1

Antithesis, 1*b*, 85, 116*c*; antith. sentences 142; expressed by exclusive conjunctions 144*c*, *d*, *e*

Appellatives, 29 R.1

Apposition, nominal 39; clausal 146, 147; common in poetry 147*d*; to be distinguished from asyndeton 148

Arabic, 27, 49 R.1, 88 R.1

Aramaic, 1 R.2, 39 R.3, 84*d*, 90 R.2, 104 R.1

Article, no indefinite art. 28; some nouns not requiring 29; determination expressed by 30; sometimes used where Engl. uses indefinite art. 30*e*; generic art. (class nouns) 31; in comparisons 31*e*; often lacking in poetry 31 R.2; sometimes in prose 31 R.2, 46 R.2 (numerals); as relative 31 R.3

Aspect, expressed by Hebr. verb 55

Asyndeton, 58 R.1, 97*c*, 146, 148

Beth essentiae, pretii, 118 R.2

Case, not a category in Hebr. 27; survivals, without function 27 R.1

Casus pendens, see Extraposition

Causal clauses and infin. phrases, 125

Causative verb with object, 89*b*, 91*b*, *c*, 92*b*

Chiastic sentences, 138, 140

Circumstantial clauses (sentences), word order in 1, 23, 41, 49*c*; indicating pause in sequence 58*b*, 64*a*; off-line 72 R.4; in narrative prose 80; non-sequential 84; with participle 113*f*; expressing causality 125; beginning narrative or episode 136*a*; accompanying time statement 136*b*; expressing closure 136*c*; describing concomitant action 137; problems concerning 137 R.1

Clause, independent or dependent (subordinate) 131; relative 9ff.; subject 51; object 90; adverbial 119ff.; circumstantial 135ff.; coordinated clauses in compound sentences 138ff., 143ff.

Class nouns, 31

Cohortative, 68; pseudo use 68 R.3; with simple *Vav* 87

Collective noun, 18*b*, 21, 21 R.2, 47 R.1; concord of 25

Comparative, expressed by adjective with prepos. 43; by prepos. 118 R.2; by clause or infin. phrase 130

Complement, subject 50; with verb *to be* 50; in other verbal clauses 50; object 92, 93; infin. absol. as 101

Concord, of subject with verb 22ff.; of simple subject 23; of composite subject 24; of collectives 25; of certain plurals 26, 26 R.2, 3; of names of nations 26 R.4; of adjective 41, 42; of numerals 45ff.

Conditional sentence (clause), 120ff.; protasis and apodosis 120; real 121*a*, *b*; protasis may have own section 121*c*; examples 121 R.1; legal uses 121 R.3; unreal (irreal) 122; condition expressed by coordination 123

Conjunctions 119; adverbial (subordinating) 120ff.; coordinating 138ff., 143ff. See also *Vav*

Conjunctive sentence, 138, 139

Consecutive, see *Vav* Consecutive

Consequence, see Result

Construct state, two nouns (A, B) brought into close relation 32; subjective uses 33; exceptions 35 R.1; objective uses 34; adjectival uses 35; these common after certain nouns 35 R.3; B replaced by relative clause 36*d*; relation not normally split 36*b*, *c*; use of periphrasis instead of 36*c*, 36 R.3; exceptional uses 36 R.1, 4

Context, importance of 3 R. 3, 44 R. 3, 89 R. 4, 106 R. 1, 107, 118*b*, 132, 137; especially in indicating "tense" 49, 52, 54, 55, 57 R. 2, 58, 59, 62, 63, 64, 69 R. 1, 72, 74, 75, 79, 82; or mood 60, 60 R. 1, 64, 68 R. 3, 71*a*, 76, 127 R. 2

Contingency, 56, 61, 64*d*

Contrastive sentences, 141

Coordination, nominal 37; inclusive 38*a;* exclusive 38*b;* disjunctive 38*c;* verbal (clausal) 84ff., 131, 135ff., 138ff.; inclusive 143; exclusive 144; disjunctive 145

Copula, personal pronoun equivalent to 1*b;* verb *to be* not used as 49

Dates, dating, 36 R. 3, 48*c*

Dativus ethicus, 118 R. 2

Definiteness, see Article; 94 R. 3

Demonstrative pronoun 4ff; adding emphasis to question etc. 6 R. 3; as relative in poetry 6 R. 4

Direct speech, 90. See also Discourse

Discontinuous elements, 134 R. 1

Discourse, in effect what is not narrative (including most poetry, direct speech, predictive, precative, etc.) 57, 58*a,c*, 59, 63, 64*a, b*, 72 R. 4, 73, 103*b*, 137, 138, 140*a*, 146, 148

Disjunction, nominal 38*c;* clausal 145

Distributive, expressed by numerals 48 R. 2; by long YIQTOL 63 R. 1

Divine name, 1 R. 1, 20*c*, 20 R. 5, 35 R. 6, 49 R. 3, 57 R. 3; superlative expressed by 44 R. 5

Double-duty, suffix 3 R. 3; other clausal elements 132. See also Ellipsis

Dual, 21 R. 1, 42, 48 R. 3

Ellipsis, of suffix 3 R. 3; of object 89 R. 4; in incomplete sentences 132; especially in poetry (gapping) 132; in conjunctive sentences 139; in antithetical sentences 142; in inclusive sentences 143; in exclusive sentences 147; in disjunctive questions 153; in oaths 156*b*

Emphasis, force, focus, prominence, 1*b, c, d*, 1 R. 1, 4, 4 R. 3, 6 R. 3, 7*a*, 37, 38*a*, 54, 54 R. 2, 64 R. 2, 65, 66 R. 1, 72, 80 R. 1, 83 R. 1, 94, 94 R. 6, 7, 101, 133, 139, 143 R. 1, 149

Enclitic *Mem*, 27 R. 2

English, usage often to be distinguished from Hebr., 27, 28, 30*e*, 32, 33*b*, 37, 38*a*, 49, 53, 54, 55 R. 2, 57*d*, 57 R. 3, 58*b, d*, 62*a*, 64*a, c*, 69, 69 R. 1, 70, 73, 78 R. 1, 80 R. 1, 81*a, b*, 82*b*, 88, 89*a*, 89 R. 3, 4, 90*b*, 91, 92, 96, 99, 114, 118*b, c*, 120, 121*b*, 133, 137, 141, 142

Epicene, 16

Epistolary "perfect", 57*b*

Ergative, 94 R. 6

Ēt, particle, uses of 88, 94

Exclamations, 157; interr. pronouns as 7; *hinnēh* as 54

Exclusion, nominal 38*b;* exclusive sentences 144

Extraposition (*casus pendens*), sentences with 149; to facilitate syntax 151*a;* macrosyntactic uses 151*b;* in legal texts 151*c*

Feminine, see Gender

Final (purpose, telic) clauses and infin. phrases 126

Focus, see Emphasis

Force, see Emphasis

Fractions, 48 R. 4

Frequentative, expressed by long YIQTOL 63; in past 63*a;* in present 63*b*

Gapping, 132

Gender, of animate beings 16; epicene nouns 16*c;* inanimate things as fem. 17; other uses of fem. 18; priority of mas. 18 R. 2; gender concord 22ff., 41ff.; attraction of gender 25 R. 1

Gerund, infin. absol. equivalent to 99, 100; infin. constr. equivalent to 104, 105, 118 R. 2

Gerundive, infin. constr. equivalent to 108*c*, 118 R. 2; Niph ptcp. as equivalent to 110 R. 1

Greek, 27, 134 R. 2

Hāyāh, verb *to be*; not used as copula in nominal sentence 49; takes subject complement 50; *Vav* consecutive forms of used in macrosyntactic role 72, 80; both forms impersonal 72; to be distinguished from normal verbal use 72 R. 2; with partic. 113 R. 2

Hē of direction (*locale*), 27; enfeebled 117 R. 1

Imperative, 65ff.; cannot be used with negative 66; long imperative 66 R. 1; rhetorical uses 66 R. 2; with simple *Vav*, 86

Imperfect(ive), not a suitable term for YIQTOL, 55 R. 1

Impersonal construction, 95 R. 2

Inclusion, nominal 38*a;* inclusive sentences 143

Incomplete sentences, see Ellipsis

Indefinite, pronoun 7; other ways of expressing 15; no indefinite art. 28; indefinite construct 3 R. 1, 29 R. 2, 39*d*

Indirect, question 8; speech 90; object 91

Infinitive absolute, 99ff.; not inflected 100; as noun or gerund 100; as complement 101; adverbial use 102; instead of inflected form 103

Infinitive construct, 104ff.; as noun or gerund 105; with subject or object 106; may be used either nominally 106*a*, 106 R. 2; or verbally 106*b;* subject omitted 106 R. 1; suffixes with 106 R. 3; as clause substitute 107; use of *lᵉ* with 108; negative infin. 109; with *Vav* 109 R. 2

Infinitive phrases, function adverbially 118; kinds of 119ff.

Interrogative, pronoun 7; used indirectly 8; interr. adverbs 152; in disjunctive questions 153; list of 153 R. 3; rhetorical uses 7, 153 R. 2, 3

Jussive, 66; as negative imperative 66; rhetorical uses 67 R. 4; with simple *Vav* 87

Ketib, *Qere*, 3 R. 2, 26 R. 3, 29 R. 4, 46 R. 1, 47 R. 1, 67 R. 1
Kuntillet Ajrud inscription, 35 R. 6, 49 R. 3

Late Hebrew, 1 R. 4, 6 R. 1, 12 R. 4, 13 R. 2, 31 R. 3, 46 R. 3, 68 R. 3, 84*d*, 109*b*, 113 R. 2, 5
Latin, 110 R. 1, 118*b*, 128*b*, 149
Le, non-prepositional uses, 94; with infin. constr. 105*a*
Liturgical syntax, 49 R. 3
Locative, see *Hē locale*

Macrosyntactic role, of *vehāyāh* in discourse 72; of other devices 72 R. 4; of *vehāyāh* in narrative 80; of *vayhī* in narrative 80; of other devices 80; of circumstantial clauses (subject-verb order) 136; of extraposition 151*b*
Marked, unmarked, 133
Masculine, see Gender; priority of 1 R. 4, 18 R. 2
Moabite stone, 1 R. 2, 6 R. 2
Mood, modal, 55; imperative 65-66; jussive 67; cohortative 68; long YIQTOL 64; QATAL not modal except in context 60, 71*a*; modal usages after simple *Vav* 86ff.; in adverbial clauses 119ff.
Multiplicatives, 48 R. 3

Names, definite in themselves 29; personal names do not take suffix 35 R. 6; place names 35 R. 6; naming 12 R. 2
Narrative, QATAL in prose narrative 58*b*; in poetic 58*c*, *d*; short YIQTOL in 62*a*; long YIQTOL in 63*a*; *Vav* consec. forms in 72, 80; simple *Vav* in 84*d*
Negative, implied 7, 8 R. 3; neg. exclusion 38*b*; neg. disjunction 38*c*; in nominal clause 49 R. 4; not sequential 58*b*, 64*a*; with moods 65, 66, 67, 87 R. 4; no reversion to another conjugation following 69; with infin. constr. 109; with participle 113*d*, 113 R. 3; neg. clausal adverbs 116*b*; compounds formed with 116*d*; in conditional clause 120, 122; neg. purpose 126*b*, *c*, 128; gapping of 132; antithesis by or after 142*b*, *c*, *d*; exclusion following 144*d*; neg. question 152*c*; in oaths 156*b*
Neuter, feminine as 1 R. 3, 4 R. 1
Nominal, coordination with *Vav* or other conjunction 38; nom. apposition 30; nom. clauses 49
Noun, see Gender, Number, Article, Construct
Number, 19ff.; nouns used only in plural 20; collectives 21; dual 21 R. 1; plural expressing uncertainty or choice 21 R. 4; plural of compound expressions 21 R. 6; concord of 22ff.

Numerals, number *one* 45; cardinals of units 46; cardinals above units 47; ordinals 48; numerical sayings 46 R. 4

Oaths, 156
Object, direct 89; obj. clauses 90; indirect 92; cognate 93; *'et* not exclusively mark of 94; with infin. constr. 106*b*
Objective, uses of construct state 34

Participle, active and passive 110; construction of 111; as noun, adjective or complement 112; in apposition, equivalent to relative clause 112; does not contain subject 113*a*; as predicate 49*d*, 113*b*; order of 110 R. 1, 113*b*; used in any time setting 113*c*, 113 R. 1; negative 113*d*; followed by *Vav* consecutive 113*e*; striking effect of 113*f*; with verb *to be* 113 R. 2
Passive, 95
Perfect(ive), not a suitable term for QATAL 55 R. 1
Personal pronoun, order of in nominal clause 1*a*; resumption by 1*b*; not expressed in verb unless subject is composite or for emphasis 1*c*; independent form used following noun, other pronoun, or suffix 1*d*; suffixed form 2; usually subjective but sometimes objective in function 2
Periphrasis , 36*c*, 36 R. 3
Perspective of speaker, with prepositions 118 R. 4
Phrasal verbs, 89*e*, 118*c*
Phrase, group of words at lower lever than clause, construct phr. 32; prepositional phr. 118; infinitive phr. 107, 119
Plural, see Number
Poetry, double-duty suffix in 3 R. 3; omission of relative in 11, 12 R. 3; plural in 21 R. 3; enclitic *Mēm* in 27 R. 2; article often lacking in 28, 31 R. 2; QATAL in 57*c*, *d*, 57 R. 4, 58*a*, *c*, *d*, 59; short YIQTOL in 62; long YIQTOL in 63, 64; rhetorical uses of imperative in 66 R. 2; of jussive in 67 R. 4; *Vav* consecutive used less in 69; VAYYIQTOL following YIQTOL in 78, 81; *'et* less employed in 94; infin. constr. with *and* in 109 R. 2; omission of preposition after verb in 111 R. 1; in nominal phrases in 117 R. 2; rare uses of prepositions in 118 R. 4; ellipsis (gapping) in 132; certain kinds of sentence common in 138; apposition and asyndeton commoner in 147*d*, 148*b*
Precative "perfect", 60*c*
Pregnant construction, see Prepositions
Prepositions, form 118*a*; function 118*b*; list of 118 R. 1; monoconsonantal prepositions 118 R. 2; compound prepositions 118 R. 3; perspective of speaker 118 R. 4
Process, expressed by long YIQTOL, 61
Prominence, see Emphasis
Pronoun, see Demonstrative, Indefinite, Interrogative, Personal, Relative; other pronominal expressions 14, 15; quasi-pronominal

expressions 15 R.1
Prophetic "perfect", 59*b*
Punctual, see Action
Purpose, expressed by simple *Vav* and modal form 87. See also final clauses

Quasi-pronominal expressions 15 R.1; quasi-verbal nominal clauses 52
QATAL, indicates states or actions regarded as states 56; in discourse and poetry 57; in past contexts 58; not a true narrative form 58*b*; in narrative within discourse and poetry 58*c, d;* in future contexts 59; equivalent to Engl. future perfect 59*a;* representing a future action as state 59*b;* prophetic "perfect" 59*b;* not modal, but may attract modal nuances from context 60; precative "perfect" 60
Questions, 152; disjunctive questions 153. See also Interrogative

Reflexive pronoun, wanting, supplied in various ways 14
Relative pronoun, forming clause 9; indeclinable, resumed by personal pronoun or adverb of place 9; including antecedent (*he who,* etc.) 10; omission of relative 11, 12; antecedent put in constr. state 13; demonstrative pronoun as 13 R.2; the relative *še* 13 R.2
Result, expressed by simple *Vav* and modal verb 87; result clauses 129
Rhetorical uses, of interr. pronouns 7, 153 R.3; of moods 66 R.2, 67 R.4

Sentence, simple, complex, compound 131; incomplete 132; discontinuous elements 133 R.1; simple nominal sentences (clauses) 49; simple quasi-verbal nominal sentences (clauses) 52ff.; complex sentences with relative clause 9ff.; with subject and object clause 51, 90; with adverbial clauses 119ff.; circumstantial sentences (clauses) 135ff.; compound sentences with *Vav* 139ff.; with other conjunctions 143ff.; appositional sentences 146ff.; sentences with extra-position 149ff.
Septuagint, 29 R.1, 4, 42 R.2, 152 R.2, 156 R.3
Singular, see Number
State, stative, construct state 32; adjective expressing 41; QATAL expressing 57; so VᵉQATAL 69; stative verbs in narrow sense 57 R.1. See further QATAL
Subject, 131; concord of with verb 23ff.; order of in nominal clause 49; subject complement 50; subject clause 51; of infin. constr. 106*a;* subject-verb order 133, 134, 135, 137 R.1
Subjective, uses of constr. state 33
Subordinate clause, 119, 131
Suffix, pronominal, to nouns 2*a;* to verbs 2*b;* suffixed noun sometimes indefinite 3 R.1; with quasi-verbal expressions 3 R.2; ellipsis

of 3 R.3
Superlative, expressed by simple noun or adjective in constr. 44; by joining a noun with its own plural 44 R.3; by connection with divine name 44 R.5

Telic, see final
Temporal, expressions with pronoun 6 R.2; clauses and infin. phrases, 124
Tense, not a category in Hebr., expressed by context 55, 55 R.2. See also Context
Times (*once, twice,* etc.), 48 R.3
Transitivity, 88, 89 R.1
Two verb constructions, 96, 97

Ugaritic, 27, 101, 118 R.4
Unmarked, see Marked

Vav, ubiquity of 134; coordinating nouns 37; explanatory use with nouns 37; coordinating clauses, as *Vav* consecutive 69; as simple *Vav* 84ff.; as *Vav apodosi* (VeQATAL) 71; as explanatory or interpretative (VAY-YIQTOL) 78; in circumstantial clauses 135ff.; various sentence types with 138ff.; omission of (asyndeton) 148
Vav Consecutive, function sequential, sometimes logical 69; not conversive 69; less common in poetry 69. See further VAYYIQTOL, VeQATAL
VAYYIQTOL, related to short YIQTOL 77; denotes a sequential simple action 78; has explanatory or interpretative functions 78; sometime equivalent to pluperfect 78 R.1; beginning main clause following previous statement indicating ground or occasion 79; following such in narrative 80; or other VAYYIQTOL 80; use of *vayhī* 80, 80 R.1; sequence broken if other word or phrase initial 80; previous clause or statement may be of some length 80 R.2; following antecedent QATAL or short YIQTOL in same sequence 81; in past contexts 81; in present and future contexts 82; after prophetic "perfect" 82*c;* continuing infin. or participle 83
VeQATAL, form 70; with *Vav apodosi* in conditional sentences 71*a;* in temporal and causal clauses 71*b;* following infin. phrases 71*c;* following a variety of other expressions 71*d;* beginning new development 71*e;* in discourse and narrative 72; following initial statement 72; use of *wᵉhāyāh* 72, 72 R.4; continuing antecedent YIQTOL in same sequence 73; in sense of future indicative 74*a;* in modal senses 74*b;* as past customary 75; continuing verbal forms related to YIQTOL 76; moods 76*a;* infin. 76*b;* participle 76*c*
Verb, conjugations mark aspect, not tense 55; conjugations 55ff.; moods 65ff.; two verb constructions 96; passive 95; infinitive and participle 98ff.; order of in clause 133
Vocative, 30 R.1, 157

Wish, expressed by jussive or cohortative 67, 68; by more formal means 155

Word-order 133; of adjective 41; in nominal clause 1, 49a, b; in verbal clause 133; of object 91, 92; of negative 116b, c; of adverbs and prepositional phrases 116 R.2; overriding of normal word-order 49, 133, 134; of long YIQTOL, not usually initial 63; in infin. phrases 101; of participle 49d, 113b; 113 R.2; in circumstantial clause 135, 137d, 137 R.1; in compound sentences with Vav 138ff.

YIQTOL, expresses actions and processes 61; short YIQTOL expressing simple action, not necessarily punctual 62; in prose restricted to Vav consec., not in poetry 62a; in future time 62b; other conjunctions with YIQTOL 62 R.1; long YIQTOL expresses extended action (processes, frequentative, iterative, customary, etc.) 63; resists initial position 63; in past contexts 63a; or present 63b; distributive use 63 R.1; in questions 63 R.3; in future contexts 64; in indicative contexts 64a; in extended prose discourse 64a; in poetic discourse 64b; in modal contexts 64c, d